THE BODLEY HEAD

JACK LONDON

VOLUME TWO

THE BODLEY HEAD

JACK LONDON

VOLUME II

EDITED AND INTRODUCED BY
ARTHUR CALDER-MARSHALL

JOHN BARLEYCORN
THE CRUISE OF THE DAZZLER
THE ROAD

THE BODLEY HEAD
LONDON · SYDNEY
TORONTO

All rights reserved
Introduction © Arthur Calder-Marshall 1964
SBN 370 00573 2
Printed and bound in Great Britain for
THE BODLEY HEAD LTD
9 Bow Street, London WC2
by William Clowes & Sons Ltd, Beccles
Set in Linotype Plantin
First published 1964
Reprinted 1968

CONTENTS

INTRODUCTION

John Barleycorn, the longest work in this second volume of
The Bodley Head Jack London, is conceded by the few
modern critics who have read it, to be 'a classic of alcoholism'. But in my view it is a literary masterpiece, not merely
the greatest book which Jack London wrote, but, seen in
its true setting, one of the most poignant documents of our
century, a fortuitous work of inhibited and tortured genius.

Anyone picking it up is carried on by its immense dramatic power, London's compelling readability; and yet is
puzzled by the apparent contradictions. Why should a man
who has liberated himself from the dominance of this
jovial-seeming devil John Barleycorn need to have alcohol
banished by the women of the United States, while at the
same time protesting that he will continue to drink as long
as it is legal to do so? Supposing that it was possible to
abolish alcohol, would the social companionship of booze
which he acknowledged be established on coffee or soft
drinks? Is alcohol really the invention of savage man and
will civilization grow to a stage when it has to be abolished,
rather than not abused? Is society to impose controls which
should properly be exercised by the individual? Must a
temperance tyranny be imposed to keep Jack London
sober?

Today we know the tragic results of trying to impose
legal instead of moral restraint on the consumption of alcohol. *John Barleycorn*, first serialized by the *Saturday Evening Post* and later published by the Century Company,
New York (1913) and Mills & Boon, London (1914), gave
temperance lecturers ammunition far more exciting than
the old charts with livers and kidneys painted in alarming
colours. *John Barleycorn* was quoted from the platform
and the pulpit. A film was made of it which the distillers

7

desperately tried to suppress and in 1919, three years after London's death at the age of forty, the Volstead Act was passed to bring the coming generation the temperate bliss which London envisaged.

One of my correspondents, a university professor of English with an interest in spiritualism, tells me that in the nineteen-thirties, some twenty years after his death, Jack London, according to a medium he met on top of a tram, was still suffering agonies of thirst. If his spirit could have communicated, I would have expected rather a terrible sense of contrition at having been responsible for making it socially respectable for not merely young men but also young women to drink bad liquor in speak-easies. I would have expected delight at the repeal of the Volstead Act, but further agony at knowing that the organized forces of vice first mobilized to defeat Prohibition had moved into protection rackets and labour unions.

These things are not forgotten in the United States, a country more prone to the emotional promptings of idealism and less forgetful of their misguidance. Jack London, who was as popular in Nazi Germany, as the apostle of the Aryan National Socialist, as he still is in the U.S.S.R., as a Marxist proletarian, has not yet been forgiven in the U.S.A. for his part in the fiasco of temperance by law.

Though publicly he was all, privately he was none of these *personae*. The time has come to rescue him from the entanglements of his political and social projections. But the task had not been simplified by his biographers.

Charmian Kittredge London, his second wife and author of a momentously prattling two-volume definitive biography, erected a monument to her wifely devotion; and Irving Stone's *Sailor on Horseback*, though far more detached, made no claim to be a scholarly work, so that it is impossible to check any of his sources. Perhaps a man predetermines his biographers. Jack London, slapdash about facts and concerned less with truth than effects, has got the treatment he deserves.

But even from the published sources it is possible to add something to *John Barleycorn*.

The theme of suicide runs throughout the book, drink being at one moment the alternative to suicide and at another suicide being the alternative to drink. This theme began before Jack London was born, when his mother Flora Wellman tried to kill herself (or pretended to try to kill herself), finding that she had been deserted by her lover, the radical wandering astrologer 'Prof' W. H. Chaney, Jack London's father. It ended three years after *John Barleycorn* was written with London's suicide at the age of forty.

Suicide is a stated theme. A theme unstated is the knowledge that John London, a man whom throughout *John Barleycorn* he calls his father, was not his father, though he was far closer to him than his musical spiritualistic, money-mad mother or 'Prof' Chaney.

There are two things which are essential, even in non-religious families, to children's happiness. The first is love. The second is continuity. Jack London had neither. His Negress foster-mother, Mamma Jennie, gave him security for a short time and his step-sister, Eliza London, prolonged it. But Eliza found home such hell that she married young to get away and left Jack in the lurch. Equally unsettling were the shifts in the family's habitat. He never stayed long enough anywhere to make friends. But instead of moving up in the world, they moved from one disaster to another.

Jack London's mother, devoid alike of religious faith and common thrift, combined in her spiritualism a parody of God and Mammon. One of Jack's earliest recollections was lying on a table in a darkened room as the centre of a séance. His mother used spirits to advise her on the stockmarket. They were invariably wrong. Her husband developed project after project and her greed cheated them of the reward.

It is a blemish of *John Barleycorn* that there is no mention of this family background. But this 'materialistic

1*

monist' was still supporting his crazy mother and an adopted son on whom she lavished all the love she had failed to give Jack himself.

Or rather it would be a blemish, if in *John Barleycorn* one looked for a fully honest and self-conscious work of art. But it is not.

V. S. Pritchett has described the art of certain short stories as 'reality caught out of the tail of one's eye', an angled glance which by its very distortion reveals more than the steady gaze. Many novelists have used the same device deliberately by telling their stories through a narrator not fully conscious of the implications of what he is saying. The reader thus participates in the creative act as an interpreter.

Jack London knew very much more than he revealed in *John Barleycorn*. According to his biographer, Irving Stone,* he remarked, 'The only trouble about *John Barleycorn* is that I did not put in the whole truth. I did not dare put in the whole truth.' Though Stone gives no source for this remark it seems probable that London made such an observation. Even if he didn't, he must have thought it.

He had no qualms about precise truth. Strength of expression was more important than precision. Then again he exercised a conscious censorship. He prided himself on writing what was 'healthy'. Alcoholism was not a healthy subject and his choice of the demonic figure of John Barleycorn was probably prompted as much by the feeling that this was a healthier expression than alcohol as it was by the certainty that it would be more popular.

But the book came from a deeper level, straining its way past various inhibitions. Some of these inhibitions he accepted as absolutes which could not be challenged; others he did not even realize were inhibitions. It was a book which had to be written in the desperate hope of self-cure, but which could not be written openly.

So for psychological, rather than artistic, reasons it

* Irving Stone, *Sailor on Horseback*, Bodley Head, 1948, p. 280.

achieved the subtlety of a reality caught out of the tail of the eye. It was presented as a Prohibitionist tract and has been accepted and rejected as such. But its force, its fire and its brilliance come from London's need to confess, to tell not all but enough to cure himself from the morbid cravings which he feared with very good reason would destroy him. 'Be warned by my example,' he says. 'Here am I, not a dipsomaniac, not an alcoholic, a strong, successful man, aware that even with me John Barleycorn is an insidious demon. If I, Jack London, will admit this publicly, do thou likewise; and master this demon as I have done. To make this easier for you, I demand that alcohol should be publicly forbidden, even though this will be rather tiresome to people like me who have learnt to drink socially.'

Of course it wasn't true. It was the alcoholic's dream of a youth without drink and a middle age in which he had it in control. If he only wrote it powerfully enough, it might become true, he hoped. It was published in 1913. Three years later, Jack London committed suicide by an overdose of two mutually conflicting drugs, knowing that his body was being poisoned by uraemia due to the effects of alcoholic nephritis.

His wife, Charmian Kittredge London, succeeded in hushing up this fact, perhaps because she felt it was a reflection on her husband's greatness, but also perhaps because, as Stone suggests, his life insurance policies would not have been paid if it had been known that he took his life by his own hand.

One cannot blame her for this, because if he hadn't killed himself he would have died of uraemia anyway in a matter of days. But the concealment of the fact that Jack London's death was caused secondarily by the effects of alcoholism meant that *John Barleycorn* was still viewed as a Prohibitionist Tract. No critic pointed out the tragic fact that at a deeper level it was written so that the author could try to reassure himself that he was not an alcoholic.

Both these elements are abundantly plain to the modern

reader. But there are deeper levels, to appreciate which a knowledge of Jack London's life is necessary.

I have already mentioned his illegitimacy—or, as it appeared to him, the mystery of his birth. According to fragments of an unfinished autobiography quoted by Irving Stone, Jack London learned, while he was still a little boy, that the man he called 'Father', John London, was not his real father. He overheard this during a quarrel between John London and his mother.

During his childhood, this set up an odd conflict, because he felt more love for and sympathy with his step-father and his step-sister Eliza than he did with his neurotic, feckless mother—though, with a respect for the Mosaic law illogical in an atheist, he never breathed a word in her dishonour.

When he reached young manhood, he learnt the name of 'Prof' Chaney and wrote to him several times to ask what truth there was in the rumours that Chaney was his father. Chaney admitted having known his mother before her marriage to John London, but denied paternity. He had married and settled down and was frightened of being unsettled up by the appearance of an impoverished by-blow. Perhaps if Jack London had waited until he was rich and famous, the 'Prof' would have acknowledged paternity and joined the retinue of his son's parasites. As it was, Jack London was haunted throughout his life by the insecurity of being a bastard without any certain knowledge of who his father was.

The novel by Ouida with the last forty pages missing which Jack London mentions in Chapter Five of *John Barleycorn* was *Signa*, the romantic story of the bastard child of an Italian peasant girl and a vagabond artist who rose through poverty and suffering to be a great composer. This proved a significant prototype of Jack's own career.

'Far more formative than the two horrifying drinking episodes which, in Chapters Three and Four, London dramatizes with more regard for forcefulness than truth was his lack of childhood security. He had little family

love, no settled home, no constant neighbours, no prolonged friendships, not even the security of regular
meals.'*

In a lecture before which the chairman had introduced
him as a famous author, he repudiated this introduction.
By birth, he claimed, he was a proletarian who had become
an artist parasite. But this was imprecise. His mother, Flora
Wellman before her marriage, was the daughter of a well-
to-do engineer and inventor in Massillon, Ohio. A bout of
typhoid in youth had injured her eyesight, deprived her of
hair (she wore a man's wig) and so alienated her affections
that she ran away from home. She was not a proletarian,
but a *bourgeoise déclassée*, proud of her British stock and
lamenting the invasion of the United States by wops, japs
and dagoes. His father, Chaney, was an Irish vagabond, a
grass-roots radical and hokum-peddler, no horny-handed
member of the toiling masses. And his step-father, who
despite his bad health was a really hard worker, was by
nature a smallholder and market gardener, a sturdy independent relying on his green fingers and knowledge of the
heart of the soil, until he was reduced to wage-slavery by
the improvidence and bad judgment of his wife.

The claim to be a proletarian, despite the years in the
cannery, the jute-mill, the power-house and the laundry,
was false, an attempt to find a niche in a society into which
he could not fit because he had no certain place.

Jack London's life was in fact a hectic search for a place
in society; hectic because his point of departure was schizo-
phrenically unique and his points of arrival always unsatis-
factory.

Like many men who appear and act tough, he was abnor-
mally sensitive. He swung between poles of inferiority and
superiority. A boy without a childhood, he watched those
older than himself and then with enormous bravado
charged in and did, not necessarily better, but larger and
more recklessly.

* Irving Stone, *op. cit.*

In *John Barleycorn*, Jack London tackled the way he had tried to join the society of the oyster pirates. His violence afloat and ashore is honestly told. But he clearly never saw his companions as they really were. They were challenges to his inferiority. Like Ouida's hero, he achieved not equality but conspicuous distinction (or eminent conspicuousness). Fame was the spur to ambition but it was also the curb to friendship and love.

In the saloons, with the aid of alcohol, the relaxer of inhibitions, Jack London achieved an intimacy with his fellow creatures, hitherto and otherwise denied. But even so it was intimacy of a superficial sort, large talk of strange lands, high adventure, violence and danger, the sort of incidents which exteriorized conflicts which lay too deep within London's personality for him to analyse; and for the kid that he was, they provided a challenge, which he met by the extravagance of his behaviour on the smaller stage of San Francisco bay and waterfront. Nostalgically he may look back at his childhood passion for candy at this period, but the drive to achieve maturity found its satisfaction in the First and Last Chance Saloon and the adventures among small boats.

London was right to protest that he was no dipsomaniac, compelled by the chemistry of his blood to seek the destructive spirit (though his contemptuous dismissal of such unfortunates as 'weaklings' is unsympathetic). But his denunciation of society for making saloons available is typical of an unsophisticated socialism which sought the cure of spiritual and psychological problems in legislation and economic change. He showed no awareness that his drinking was merely a symptom of a disease springing from his birth and aggravated by the circumstances of his childhood. Some small part of the blame could be laid on the *laissez-faire* capitalism of the time, but the major part resided in the peculiar and unhappy environment of his family, produced by the hypertension of a neurotic and feckless mother and the weaknesses of his gentle but ineffectual step-father.

John Barleycorn, being 'Alcoholic Memoirs', avoided discussion of the dualism of Jack London's personality. He advances himself as the average, normal man, differing from others chiefly in having risen from lower depths to dizzier heights. I dislike the concept of average normality, firstly because it is an illusion and secondly because it causes needless suffering both to those who attempt to conform and those who are aware that they cannot. But if there does exist some broad band of human personality and behaviour which may be generalized as average or normal, Jack London's do not fall within that band. He was exceptional.

In his short novel *The Cruise of the Dazzler*, written primarily for boys but of great interest to anyone exploring London's life and personality, there are two boys, each displaying one aspect of London's boyhood psyche. There is Joe, the tough son of a well-to-do San Franciscan living on the Heights, who hates all he learns at school, except literature, and who wants to run away to sea. And there is 'Frisco Kid, an orphan living aboard the *Dazzler*, working for French Pete, a brutal and drunken pirate. 'Frisco Kid pines for the education and security which Joe despises.

Jack London in his life alternated between the extremes of Joe and 'Frisco Kid, always perhaps like them yearning for what at the time he was not. His later alternations were less acute than those of his youth. The swings were violent between cannery and oyster-piracy, jute-mill and sealing, passing coal in a power-house and bumming the railroads, studying at high school and university, working in a laundry and joining the Alaska Gold Rush. Consciously or unconsciously, he tried to order his life so that these two conflicting demands of his nature, to strike roots and to wander, could be satisfied without destroying one another.

What he called 'the books' helped him to do this, at least in his own opinion. These books were only a small section of what would have been found in any well-stocked library of his day, the works of nineteenth-century materialists, Darwin, Huxley, Herbert Spencer, Haeckel, Renan, Marx and the like. If their 'truths' were harsh, this was because life itself was harsh in a world that had evolved by the survival of the fittest and where the class struggle repeated in modern society the bloody conflicts of the primitive jungle.

This crude materialism gave him a philosophy to explain the harsh experiences of his childhood and he clung to it with all the vehemence of his nature. But it provided no clue to the resolution of his conflicts, because it ignored their psychological complexity.

Anna Strunsky, a young socialist whom he met in his political work, might through her combination of intellect and emotion have brought him to maturity if they had married. But though Jack London was attracted to her, he was scared by her independence. He wanted a woman more pliable, less challenging, a housekeeper who could bear him healthy children. Quixotically he proposed to Bessie Maddern, a schoolteacher with whom he had been exchanging lessons in literature and mathematics. She did not love him and he did not love her but she had a broad pelvis for childbearing, she could earn her own living by teaching and in the evenings could type his manuscripts. Materialistically it was an admirable match.

If Bessie had given birth to a son, it is possible that Jack London's life would have been very different. Materialistic monist though he was, he dreamed of giving to a son all the joys and advantages of a happy childhood which he had lacked.

But Bessie produced only two daughters and, as Jack became more and more successful, she made no effort to accommodate herself socially to their new position, wore clothes as dowdy as she had when they were poor and resented the crowds of men and increasingly smart young women who came to her house.

After the birth of the first daughter, Jack London's restlessness had reasserted itself. He jumped at the chance of going to South Africa to report the end of the Boer War and, when that assignment collapsed before he had sailed from England, he spent three months incognito in the East

End of London collecting material for *The People of the Abyss* and then went to Europe to write the book. The second daughter, Joan, was born in his absence.

Though he had an affection for both these children, the joy of them of which he speaks in *John Barleycorn* is untrue. After their father's divorce from Bessie, they lived with their mother and, though Jack made numerous efforts to win them over by lavish treats and presents, their loyalty was unshaken. They preferred Bessie's love to Jack London's generosity.

The failure of Jack London's first marriage became inevitable. All that remained doubtful was which of the women in his circle would secure possession of this valuable, and rapidly appreciating, literary property by evicting its first owner, Bessie. In *John Barleycorn* London refers to 'the silly superficial chatterings of women, who, underneath all their silliness and softness, were as primitive, direct, and deadly in their pursuit of biological destiny as the monkeys women were before they shed their furry coats and replaced them with the furs of other animals'.

To this generality, Jack London at the time of his desertion made an exception of Miss Charmian Kittredge, a young lady some years older than himself, who had read all the daring books of the day and at the same time delighted in riding, swimming and the open air life in a way that Bessie didn't. She appeared delightfully the New Woman for his New Man, a companion and a mate.

What Jack London calls in Nietzsche's words 'the long sickness' is rather vague in *John Barleycorn*. This occupied the two years which passed between Jack London's abandoning his wife and family at the instancy of Miss Kittredge and their precipitate marriage as soon as the divorce, on grounds of desertion, had gone through.

Miss Kittredge had proved herself the New Woman by becoming Jack's mistress prior to his abandoning his family. To achieve her purpose of becoming the new Mrs Jack London without a stain on her maidenly reputation, she was forced to play a very difficult game. She had to maintain Jack London's passion at a height sufficient to prevent him returning to his children, as he was tempted to do, to preserve her name from scandal even if that involved the good name of Anna Strunsky instead of her own, to grant her favours only in such small quantities as would inflame him to desire their full enjoyment in marriage and at the same time to preserve London's illusion that she was not being primitive, direct and deadly in her pursuit of biological destiny. It was not an easy matter and in Jack London it produced the psychosomatic disturbances which he calls 'the long sickness'. In the course of it, he drank more than he would have done otherwise, but, as in his social drinking, this was merely the symptom of a deeper psychological anxiety.

In his marriage to Charmian, Jack London anticipated not merely far more than he had from Bessie but more than most men expect from a wife. This is revealed in a letter, written to her some time during the long sickness, in which London spoke of 'a dream of my boyhood and manhood', 'a dead dream . . . of the great Man Comrade. I who have been comrades with many men, and a good comrade, I believe, *have never had a comrade at all, and in the deeper sense of it have never been able to be the comrade I was capable of being.* Always it was here this one failed, and there that one failed, until all failed. And then, one day, like Omar, "clear-eyed I looked, and laughed, and sought no more". It was plain that it was not possible. I could never hope to find that comradeship, that closeness, that sympathy and understanding, whereby the man and I might merge and become one in understanding and sympathy for love and life.

'How can I say what I mean? This man should be so much one with me that we could never misunderstand. He should love the flesh, as he should the spirit, honouring and loving each and giving each its due. There should be in him both fact and fancy. He should be practical in so far as the mechanics of life were concerned; and fanciful, imaginative, sentimental where the thrill of life was concerned. He should be delicate and tender, brave and game; sensitive as he pleased in the soul of him, and in the body of him unfearing and unwitting of pain. . . .'*

I think that the nearest that Jack London came to such a David and Jonathan friendship was aboard the *Reindeer* with Young Scratch Nelson. And how very far *that* was from the dream!

To George Sterling the poet, whom he once described as 'a friend, the dearest in the world', he wrote: 'You know that I do not know you—no more than you know me. We have really never touched the intimately personal note in all the time of our friendship. I suppose we never shall.'†

The sort of Man-Comradeship of which Jack London had dreamed would certainly be impossible outside the bonds of homosexual marriage, and most improbable within them. The wealthier and more successful London became, the more impossible even everyday friendships became. Friendships subsist between peers. As London became a Prince among writers, as he had previously become Prince of the Oyster Bay, he turned his friends, actual and potential, into parasites. He gave them hospitality instead of love and received in return gratitude at best but often only envy. So he who had begun life in the loneliness of poverty achieved the isolation of riches.

Onto Charmian Kittredge Jack London pinned all his hope. 'I abandoned the dream of the great Man Comrade who was to live Youth with me, perpetual Youth with me, down to the grave. And then You came, after your trip abroad, into my life. Before that I had met you quite perfunctorily, a couple of times, and liked you. But after that we met in fellowship. . . . It was not long before I began to find in you the something all-around that I had failed to find in any man; began to grow aware of that kinship that was comradeship, and to wish you were a man. . . . And then, by the time I was convinced of the possibility of a

* *Jack London*, by Charmian London, Mills & Boon, Vol II, p. 100. My italics. A.C.-M.

† Op. cit., Vol I, pp. 397–8. Date: June 1903.

great comradeship between us, and of the futility of attempting to realize it, something else began to creep in—the woman in you twining around my heart. It was inevitable. But the wonder of it is that in a woman I should find, not only the comradeship and kinship I had sought in men alone, but the great woman-love as well; and this woman is YOU, YOU!'*

When Jack London sailed on the *Snark* without taking liquor aboard, he clearly hoped to allay his fears of alcoholic addiction; and how much better than John Barleycorn should be the person who combined the comradeship of a man with a woman's love. This was to be the beginning of a new life.

Charmian can scarcely be blamed for failing to fill so impossible a role. It is indeed remarkable that a woman who from her own writings appears so sentimental, imperceptive and downright silly, did clearly provide London with much of the comradeship for which he hankered as well as a chocolate casing for his soft centre.

It may seem astonishing that Charmian remained so oblivious of the extent and danger of London's drinking. But London did not approve of women drinking and his head was so good that when he returned from drinking with men, he probably seemed only pleasantly 'jingled'.

Though London ascribed his strange collapse in the Solomons to the effect of tropic light on white skin, he was probably suffering from pellagra, due to alcohol inhibiting the absorption of vitamin B. This was a condition not known at that time, but it seems surprising that London, who after all had visited Paris, was unaware of the toxic

* Op. cit., Vol. II, p. 101. Irving Stone, *Sailor on Horseback*, pp. 136–7, says that when her aunt Mrs Eames first introduced Jack London, Charmian sniffed at his shabby clothes. 'She showed emotion only when Mrs Eames told Jack that her niece was a typist in an office close by. Miss Kittredge promptly kicked her aunt in the shin for revealing that she had to work for a living.' Stone gives no authority for this anecdote. He interviewed the aunt, who no longer viewed her niece with quite such favour, but malice and memory can play tricks.

effect of wormwood in absinthe. One shudders at his remark that he had to drink such large quantities of it before
he noticed any effect.

I have stressed that drinking too much began as a symptom of a deeper unease. But at some stage alcohol became
the dominant. With any alcoholic, it is hard to say precisely
when drinking becomes an overriding necessity. In Jack
London's case, it is even harder, because he was as vague
about dates as Charmian was in her *Jack London*. The
drinking process undermines the banks of will power and
physical resistance by a sort of tidal erosion.

The abandonment of that seven-year world cruise in the
Snark after two most harrowing years, London is careful
to emphasize, was not a defeat by alcohol. This was true to
the extent that it was not a defeat by alcohol alone. One
can see the inevitability of defeat in that dream of the
'Comrade who was to live Youth with me, perpetual Youth
with me, down to the grave'.

London was a conspicuous victim of W. E. Henley's
hybristic fallacy, 'I am the master of my fate.' In *John
Barleycorn*, he does not mention that on the return voyage
from Australia, Mate became pregnant.

Immediately London's fantasies turned from years of
wandering to building a house in the Valley of the Moon
which should stand for a thousand years (the same number
that Hitler, a visionary in a different field, was to predict
for the Third Reich). This was to be the seat of the London dynasty, built from red rocks of the Valley and
timbered with planks and beams from the ten-thousand-
year-old redwoods.

Just as the *Snark* built to his own designs had cost five
times as much as a shipwright-built boat and had proved
half as efficient, so this Wolf House of his built for his son
was to end after conspicuous expense in even more conspicuous disaster.

Long before it was finished, Charmian gave birth. The
child was a daughter, who lived only for three days. Eliza
London Shepard, Jack's step-sister, whom he had put in

charge of his ranch, aware that he had not the time and Charmian not the competence to manage it, supervised the burial. Jack went out and got drunk in a waterfront pub. The proprietor had him beaten up before he escaped; and though the proprietor was arrested, he was acquitted by the judge. Jack London caught in a drunken brawl, with his wife in hospital and his baby just dead, splashed headlines all over the States.

A friend told London that the reason why the judge had acquitted the saloon-keeper was because the judge owned the premises. London wrote a letter to the judge, copies of which he sent to the press syndicates. It ended, 'Someday, somewhere, somehow, I am going to get you, and I shall get you to the full hilt of the law.' He inserted an advertisement in all the neighbourhood papers, asking for information about the judge's political, judicial or social misdemeanours. He may have considered that he was standing up for his socialist principles, but sophisticated heads shook, not entirely in sorrow. 'Jack London is slipping.'

London looked on life, as Hemingway did after him, as a game, a fight; and he was losing that fight. Charmian, to whom he was still devoted, had failed to produce even a girl-child. She was wonderful company—but could one be with her all the time? And she was not, as his dream Man-Comrade should be, 'practical in so far as the mechanics of life were concerned'. Eliza London Shepard was concerned with them. The sphere in which Charmian exercised her charm was shrinking and the temptations to suicide, that easeful death which his mother had not so very seriously sought when he was small in her womb, grew greater.

Of course he continued to work, like an overbusy beaver gathering everything to build his dam against the flood of disaster which his instinct told him was coming. That much of the material which he gathered to fend off the disaster was rotten is understandable. What is surprising is that so much was good. The monthly costs of his building, his farming and his retinue were always several coils higher up the mounting spiral than his income. Friends talked of Jack's monthly miracle. It was more like the Indian rope trick, performed by a magician who had continually to disappear to have a drink.

It was at this stage, with the Wolf House building for a millennium of little Londons as yet unborn and the Jack London ranch supervised by Eliza exploring principles of good farming—which were to be accepted a quarter of a century later by Roosevelt's Triple A scheme to combat erosion and restore heart to the plundered soil—that Jack London decided to write *John Barleycorn*.

In the book, it sounds as though one evening Jack London proposed to write it and next day he sat down and started it. But nothing in London's life at this stage happened as simply as that.

Having proposed the book, Jack went with Charmian to New York. They would sail in one of the old sailing ships round Cape Horn. It was something he had always wanted to do. She would love it. He would do a lot of work on *Barleycorn* and other things. Perhaps she would become pregnant again.

In New York City, before they sailed from Boston, he spent two months. Bearing in mind the extreme reticence of Charmian, her account of their stay is significant: 'Nine-tenths of the two months' time we made our headquarters in Morningside Park East, he was not his usual self. During the other tenth, cropping up in unexpected moments, the manifestation of his dearest self and his love were never warmer nor more illuminating.

'Coincidentally with our arrival, he warned that he was going to invite one last, thoroughgoing bout with alcohol, and that when he should sail on the Cape Horn voyage, it would be "Good-bye, forever, to John Barleycorn." To me, the promised end was worth the threatened means; and my comprehension and acceptance of his intention were appreciated. But I could not fail to regret that new friends should know and base their judgment of Jack London upon this unfortunate phenomenon of him.'*

The rather strange 'white logic' phase of *John Barleycorn* was reached during this supposedly renunciatory research into the effects of alcohol. This 'white logic' took him into depths of depression in which he recognized clearly the falsity of his philosophy and his human relations. He did not appear tight. But he drove home hard facts which he dodged in sobriety. Having no faith in God, he depended upon human beings; and during the 'white logic', he saw that Charmian was just like all the rest of them.

'I knew my man,' said Charmian, 'and, content or not, waited, remembering that I had never yet waited in vain to welcome back the sane and lovable boy. More and more deeply am I convinced that it is not the irks by the wayside that should count in one's valuing of event or individual. I knew my man. I could only wish that some others had had such vision for crises like these in Jack London's contact with his kind.'†

The faith in the People, which had sustained London during the long sickness, had abandoned him. He helped jail-birds, down-and-outs, political prisoners and their families, strikers. But the innate goodness of 'The People' had disappeared. He was too busy a man to help with kindness or advice. He wrote a cheque instead. When he went into a bar back home, he stood drinks all round. He never got with a man and sat at a table and talked about his problems, standing treat round by round. He was the Prince of Writers and while he despised the others for drinking his drinks, they despised him for giving them drinks instead of sympathy and the white logic drove him harder and harder to emphasize all those hurtful things which were the truth. And everybody was an enemy, especially newspaper men blazoning across the continent that he was a drunk.

Irving Stone says that when they sailed from Baltimore on the *S.S. Dirigo*, a 3,000-ton steel windjammer, bound

* Op. cit., Vol II, p. 241.
† Op. cit., Vol II, pp. 241–2.

for California round Cape Horn, Jack London loaded one thousand books and pamphlets he wanted to study and forty gallons of whisky. Without giving his source, he quotes London as saying, 'When we dock at Seattle either my thousand books will have been studied, or the forty gallons of whisky will be gone.' He left the ship, Stone adds, 'with the thousand volumes annotated, the whisky untouched'.

I distrust this journalistic neatness. London might have consumed, with the help of others, forty gallons of whisky in 148 days. But he would certainly have worked like a beaver all the same. His thousand words a day were sacred to him. And for that, he would have continued his reading.

London arrived in Seattle purged of alcohol, able to say that he had John Barleycorn in control. The newspapers were lying. His worst fears had been allayed. He could dive into a bender and then come out without any after-effects. And once again Charmian was pregnant. There would be an heir in the Wolf House.

Jack finished *John Barleycorn* which he had worked on during the voyage; but Charmian did not finish her pregnancy. A miscarriage dashed her hopes of this child or any future children.

This was the stage that had been reached when *John Barleycorn* was serialized by the *Saturday Evening Post* for a sum which Charmian considered did not compensate for loss of book sales.

But the tragedy which is contained in this oblique masterpiece needs an epilogue. The Wolf House, built to last a thousand years, was gutted by arson before it was ever occupied. Every effort that Jack London made to lure his daughters back to his home, even if it meant building a house for Bessie on the estate, was repulsed with frigid contempt. Charmian, his Mate-Woman with sterile womb and fading looks, held the ranch against any other woman who might take Jack London away from her as she had taken him away from Bessie Maddern, but reports of his infidelities in other places filtered back to the Valley of the Moon.

Saddled with debts and treacheries and law-suits, surprised that workers paid more than the union wage for the job perpetually shirked, because their employer was an absentee landlord, gypped right and left, the target of any cheap newspaperman who filed a story about cheques bounced or maidenheads taken by Jack London doubles, Jack London himself slogged on.

Astonishingly, he continued to write, every so often magnificently, as in *The Valley of the Moon*. When he wrote his worst, as in *The Little Lady of the Big House*, he was trying to resurrect the image of Charmian. What he succeeded in doing was to portray a silly, sentimental horror, from whom any normal man would have fled.

Perhaps this was his intention. But I doubt it. I think, with his very rigid views against free love, he clung to the one woman who had given him a sense of being loved in a motherly way, however sloppily. In the evening of the night he killed himself, he laid his head in her lap, like a little boy.

Though Charmian London claimed that shortly before his death Jack London was drinking very little, this was merely because his physique had already collapsed with nephritis. It seems fantastic that Charmian should have been unaware of the physical damage he was doing to himself. The only explanation I can imagine is that she was terrified that if she tried to stop him, another woman would do to her what she had done to the first Mrs Jack London.

I have chosen for the accompaniment of *John Barleycorn* two semi-autobiographical volumes which throw a different light on the early days described in *Barleycorn*. To *The Cruise of the Dazzler* I have alluded above. I have rearranged the stories from *The Road* so that they fall as nearly as possible into a chronological order. *Road-kids and Gay-cats* certainly and *Confession* probably belong to the period in the first paragraph of Chapter Thirteen of *John Barleycorn*, when London first learnt to ride the rods. The remainder cover the transcontinental bum described in Chapter Twenty-one. *The Road* appeared first in *Cosmopolitan* as a series of tramp articles. His publisher Brett of the Macmillan Company asked London if he would waive book publication, if he could prove that the book would damage London's reputation with his public. London answered, 'In *The Road*, as in all my work, I have been true. As my character has developed through my work there have been flurries of antagonism, attacks and condemnations. But I pulled through them all. I have always insisted that the cardinal literary virtue is sincerity. If I am wrong in that belief, if the world downs me on it, I'll say, "Good-bye, proud world," retire to the ranch and plant potatoes and raise chickens to keep my stomach full. It was my refusal to take cautious advice that made me.'

To season that high sincerity, let me quote from one of *The Road* stories, *Confession*. 'The beggar must "size up" his victim. . . . In order to get the food whereby I lived, I was compelled to tell tales that rang true. At the back door, out of inexorable necessity, is developed that convincingness and sincerity laid down by all authorities on the art of the short-story.'

A. CALDER-MARSHALL

JOHN
BARLEYCORN
OR
ALCOHOLIC MEMOIRS

IT ALL came to me one election day. It was on a warm California afternoon, and I had ridden down into the Valley of the Moon from the ranch to the little village to vote Yes and No to a host of proposed amendments to the Constitution of the State of California. Because of the warmth of the day I had had several drinks before casting my ballot, and divers drinks after casting it. Then I had ridden up through the vine-clad hills and rolling pastures of the ranch, and arrived at the farm-house in time for another drink and supper.

'How did you vote on the suffrage amendment?' Charmian asked.

'I voted for it.'

She uttered an exclamation of surprise. For, be it known, in my younger days, despite my ardent democracy, I had been opposed to woman suffrage. In my later and more tolerant years I had been unenthusiastic in my acceptance of it as an inevitable social phenomenon.

'Now just why did you vote for it?' Charmian asked.

I answered. I answered at length. I answered indignantly. The more I answered, the more indignant I became. (No; I was not drunk. The horse I had ridden was well named 'The Outlaw'. I'd like to see any drunken man ride her.)

And yet—how shall I say?—I was lighted up, I was feeling 'good', I was pleasantly jingled.

'When the women get the ballot, they will vote for prohibition,' I said. 'It is the wives, and sisters, and mothers, and they only, who will drive the nails into the coffin of John Barleycorn——'

'But I thought you were a friend to John Barleycorn,' Charmian interpolated.

'I am. I was. I am not. I never am. I am never less his friend than when he is with me and when I seem most his friend. He is the king of liars. He is the frankest truthsayer. He is the august companion with whom one walks with the gods. He is also in league with the Noseless One. His way leads to truth naked, and to death. He gives clear vision, and muddy dreams. He is the enemy of life, and the teacher of wisdom beyond life's wisdom. He is a red-handed killer, and he slays youth.'

And Charmian looked at me, and I knew she wondered where I had got it.

I continued to talk. As I say, I was lighted up. In my brain every thought was at home. Every thought, in its little cell, crouched ready-dressed at the door, like prisoners at midnight waiting a jail-break. And every thought was a vision, bright-imaged, sharp-cut, unmistakable. My brain was illuminated by the clear, white light of alcohol. John Barleycorn was on a truth-telling rampage, giving away the choicest secrets on himself. And I was his spokesman. There moved the multitudes of memories of my past life, all orderly arranged like soldiers in some vast review. It was mine to pick and choose. I was a lord of thought, the master of my vocabulary and of the totality of my experience, unerringly capable of selecting my data and building my exposition. For so John Barleycorn tricks and lures, setting the maggots of intelligence gnawing, whispering his fatal intuitions of truth, flinging purple passages into the monotony of one's days.

I outlined my life to Charmian, and expounded the make-up of my constitution. I was no hereditary alcoholic. I had been born with no organic, chemical predisposition toward alcohol. In this matter I was normal in my generation. Alcohol was an acquired taste. It had been painfully acquired. Alcohol had been a dreadfully repugnant thing —more nauseous than any physic. Even now I did not like the taste of it. I drank it only for its 'kick'. And from the age of five to that of twenty-five I had not learned to care for its kick. Twenty years of unwilling apprenticeship had been required to make my system rebelliously tolerant of alcohol, to make me, in the heart and deeps of me, desirous of alcohol.

I sketched my first contacts with alcohol, told of my first intoxications and revulsions, and pointed out always the one thing that in the end had won me over—namely, the accessibility of alcohol. Not only had it always been accessible, but every interest of my developing life had drawn me to it. A newsboy on the streets, a sailor, a miner, a wanderer in far lands, always where men came together to exchange ideas, to laugh and boast and dare, to relax, to forget the dull toil of tiresome nights and days, always they came together over alcohol. The saloon was the place of congregation. Men gathered to it as primitive men gathered about the fire of the squatting place or the fire at the mouth of the cave.

I reminded Charmian of the canoe houses from which she had been barred in the South Pacific, where the kinky-haired cannibals escaped from their womenkind and feasted and drank by themselves, the sacred precincts taboo to women under pain of death. As a youth, by way of the saloon I had escaped from the narrowness of woman's influence into the wide free world of men. All ways led to the saloon. The thousand roads of romance and adventure drew together in the saloon, and thence led out and on over the world.

'The point is,' I concluded my sermon, 'that it is the accessibility of alcohol that has given me my taste for alcohol. I did not care for it. I used to laugh at it. Yet here I am, at the last, possessed with the drinker's desire. It took twenty years to implant that desire; and for ten years more that desire has grown. And the effect of satisfying that desire is anything but good. Temperamentally I am wholesome-hearted and merry. Yet when I walk with John Barleycorn I suffer all the damnation of intellectual pessimism.

'But,' I hastened to add (I always hasten to add), 'John Barleycorn must have his due. He does tell the truth. That is the curse of it. The so-called truths of life are not true. They are the vital lies by which life lives, and John Barleycorn gives them the lie.'

'Which does not make toward life,' Charmian said.

'Very true,' I answered. 'And that is the perfectest hell of it. John Barleycorn makes toward death. That is why I voted for the amendment today. I read back in my life and saw how the accessibility of alcohol had given me the taste for it. You see, comparatively few alcoholics are born in a generation. And by alcoholic I mean a man whose chemistry craves alcohol and drives him resistlessly to it. The great majority of habitual drinkers are born not only without desire for alcohol, but with actual repugnance toward it. Not the first, nor the twentieth, nor the hundredth drink, succeeded in giving them the liking. But they learned, just as men learn to smoke; though it is far easier to learn to smoke than to learn to drink. They learned because alcohol was so accessible. The women know the game. They pay for it—the wives and sisters and mothers. And when they come to vote, they will vote for prohibition. And the best of it is that there will be no hardship worked on the coming generation. Not having access to alcohol, not being predisposed toward alcohol, it will never miss alcohol. It will mean life more abundant for the manhood of the young boys born and growing up —ay, and life more abundant for the young girls born and growing up to share the lives of the young men.'

'Why not write all this up for the sake of the young men and women coming?' Charmian asked. 'Why not write it so as to help the wives and sisters and mothers to the way they should vote?'

'The "Memoirs of an Alcoholic",' I sneered— or, rather, John Barleycorn sneered; for he sat with me there at table in my pleasant, philanthropic jingle, and it is a trick of John Barleycorn to turn the smile to a sneer without an instant's warning.

'No,' said Charmian, ignoring John Barleycorn's roughness, as so many women have learned to do. 'You have shown yourself no alcoholic, no dipsomaniac, but merely an habitual drinker, one who has made John Barleycorn's acquaintance through long years of rubbing shoulders with him. Write it up and call it "Alcoholic Memoirs".'

2

AND, ere I begin, I must ask the reader to walk with me in all sympathy; and, since sympathy is merely understanding, begin by me and whom and what I write about. In the first place, I am a seasoned drinker. I have no constitutional predisposition for alcohol. I am not stupid. I am not a swine. I know the drinking game from A to Z, and I have used my judgment in drinking. I never have to be put to bed. Nor do I stagger. In short, I am a normal, average man; and I drink in the normal, average way, as drinking goes. And this is the very point: I am writing of the effects of alcohol on the normal, average man. I have no word to say for or about the microscopically unimportant excessivist, the dipsomaniac.

There are, broadly speaking, two types of drinkers. There is the man whom we all know, stupid, unimaginative, whose brain is bitten numbly by numb maggots; who walks generously with wide-spread, tentative legs, falls frequently in the gutter, and who sees, in the extremity of his ecstasy, blue mice and pink elephants. He is the type that gives rise to the jokes in the funny papers.

The other type of drinker has imagination, vision. Even when most pleasantly jingled, he walks straight and naturally, never staggers nor falls, and knows just where he is and what he is doing. It is not his body but his brain that is drunken. He may bubble with wit, or expand with good fellowship. Or he may see intellectual spectres and phantoms that are cosmic and logical and that take the forms of syllogisms. It is when in this condition that he strips away the husks of life's healthiest illusions and gravely considers the iron collar of necessity welded about the neck of his soul. This is the hour of John Barleycorn's subtlest power. It is easy for any man to roll in the gutter. But it is a terrible ordeal for a man to stand upright on his two legs unswaying, and decide that in all the universe he finds for himself but one freedom—namely, the anticipating of the day of his death. With this man this is the hour of the white logic (of which more anon), when he knows that he may know only the laws of things —the meaning of things never. This is his danger hour. His feet are taking hold of the pathway that leads down into the grave.

All is clear to him. All these baffling head-reaches after immortality are but the panics of souls frightened by the fear of death, and cursed with the thrice-cursed gift of imagination. They have not the instinct for death, they lack the will to die when the time to die is at hand. They trick themselves into believing they will outwit the game and win to a future, leaving the other animals to the darkness of the grave or the annihilating heats of the crematory. But he, this man in the hour of his white logic, knows that they trick and outwit themselves. The one event happeneth to all alike. There is no new thing under the sun, not even that yearned-for bauble of feeble souls —immortality. But he knows, *he* knows, standing upright on his two legs unswaying. He is compounded of meat and wine and sparkle, of sun-mote and world-dust, a frail mechanism made to run for a span, to be tinkered at by doctors of divinity and doctors of physic, and to be flung into the scrap-heap at the end.

Of course, all this is soul-sickness, life-sickness. It is the penalty the imaginative man must pay for his friendship with John Barleycorn. The penalty paid by the stupid man is simpler, easier. He drinks himself into sottish unconsciousness. He sleeps a drugged sleep, and, if he dream, his dreams are dim and inarticulate. But to the imaginative man, John Barleycorn sends the pitiless, spectral syllogisms of the white logic. He looks upon life and all its affairs with the jaundiced eye of a pessimistic German philosopher. He sees through all illusions. He transvalues all values. Good is bad, truth is a cheat, and life is a joke. From his calm-mad heights, with the certitude of a god, he beholds all life as evil. Wife, children, friends—in the clear, white light of his logic they are exposed as frauds and shams. He sees through them, and all that he sees is their frailty, their meagreness, their sordidness, their pitifulness. No longer do they fool him. They are miserable little egotisms, like all the other little humans, fluttering their Mayfly life-dance of an hour. They are without freedom. They are puppets of chance. So is he. He realizes that. But there is one difference. He sees; he knows. And he knows his one freedom: he may anticipate the day of his death. All of which is not good for a man who is made to live and love and be loved. Yet suicide, quick or slow, a sudden spill or a gradual oozing away through the years, is the price John Barleycorn exacts. No friend of his ever escapes making the just, due payment.

3

I WAS five years old the first time I got drunk. It was on a hot day, and my father was ploughing in the field. I was sent from the house, half a mile away, to carry to him a pail of beer. 'And be sure you don't spill it,' was the parting injunction.

It was, as I remember it, a lard pail, very wide across the top, and without a cover. As I toddled along, the beer slopped over the rim upon my legs. And as I toddled, I pondered. Beer was a very precious thing. Come to think of it, it must be wonderfully good. Else why was I never permitted to drink of it in the house? Other things kept from me by the grown-ups I had found good. Then this, too, was good. Trust the grown-ups. They knew. And, anyway, the pail was too full. I was slopping it against my legs and spilling it on the ground. Why waste it? And no one would know whether I had drunk or spilled it.

I was so small that, in order to negotiate the pail, I sat down and gathered it into my lap. First I sipped the foam. I was disappointed. The preciousness evaded me. Evidently it did not reside in the foam. Besides, the taste was not good. Then I remembered seeing the grown-ups blow the foam away before they drank. I buried my face in the foam and lapped the solid liquid beneath. It wasn't good at all. But still I drank. The grown-ups knew what they were about. Considering my diminutiveness, the size of the pail in my lap, and my drinking out of it with my breath held and my face buried to the ears in foam, it was rather difficult to estimate how much I drank. Also, I was gulping it down like medicine, in nauseous haste to get the ordeal over.

I shuddered when I started on, and decided that the good taste would come afterwards. I tried several times more in the course of that long half-mile. Then, astounded by the quantity of beer that was lacking, and remembering having seen stale beer made to foam afresh, I took a stick and stirred what was left till it foamed to the brim.

And my father never noticed. He emptied the pail with the wide thirst of the sweating ploughman, returned it to me, and started up the plough. I endeavoured to walk beside the horses. I remember tottering and falling against their heels in front of the shining share, and that my father hauled back on the lines so violently that the horses nearly sat down on me. He told me afterwards that it was by only a matter of inches that I escaped disembowelling. Vaguely, too, I remember, my father carried me in his arms to the trees on the edge of the field, while all the world reeled and swung about me, and I was aware of deadly nausea mingled with an appalling conviction of sin.

I slept the afternoon away under the trees, and when my father roused me at sundown it was a very sick little boy that got up and dragged wearily homeward. I was exhausted, oppressed by the weight of my limbs, and in my stomach was a harp-like vibrating that extended to my throat and brain. My condition was like that of one who had gone through a battle with poison. In truth, I had been poisoned.

In the weeks and months that followed I had no more interest in beer than in the kitchen stove after it had burned me. The grown-ups were right. Beer was not for children. The grown-ups didn't mind it; but neither did they mind taking pills and castor oil. As for me, I could manage to get along quite well without beer. Yes, and to the day of my death I could have managed to get along quite well without it. But circumstances decreed otherwise. At every turn in the world in which I lived, John Barleycorn beckoned. There was no escaping him. All paths led to him. And it took twenty years of contact, of exchanging greetings and passing on with my tongue in my cheek, to develop in me a sneaking liking for the rascal.

4

MY NEXT bout with John Barleycorn occurred when I was seven. This time my imagination was at fault, and I was frightened into the encounter. Still farming, my family had moved to a ranch on the bleak sad coast of San Mateo County, south of San Francisco. It was a wild, primitive countryside in those days; and often I heard my mother pride herself that we were old American stock and not immigrant Irish and Italians like our neighbours. In all our section there was only one other old American family.

One Sunday morning found me, how or why I cannot now remember, at the Morrisey ranch. A number of young people had gathered there from the nearer ranches. Besides, the oldsters had been there, drinking since early dawn, and, some of them, since the night before. The Morriseys were a huge breed, and there were many strapping great sons and uncles, heavy-booted, big-fisted, rough-voiced.

Suddenly there were screams from the girls and cries of 'Fight!' There was a rush. Men hurled themselves out of the kitchen. Two giants, flushed-faced, with greying hair, were locked in each other's arms. One was Black Matt, who, everybody said, had killed two men in his time. The women screamed softly, crossed themselves, or prayed brokenly, hiding their eyes and peeping through their fingers. But not I. It is a fair presumption that I was the most interested spectator. Maybe I would see that wonderful thing, a man killed. Anyway, I would see a manfight. Great was my disappointment. Black Matt and Tom Morrisey merely held on to each other and lifted their clumsy-booted feet in what seemed a grotesque, elephantine dance. They were too drunk to fight. Then the peacemakers got hold of them and led them back to cement the new friendship in the kitchen.

Soon they were all talking at once, rumbling and roaring as big-chested open-air men will, when whisky has whipped their taciturnity. And I, a little shaver of seven, my heart in my mouth, my trembling body strung tense as a deer's on the verge of flight, peered wonderingly in at the open door and learned more of the strangeness of men. And I marvelled at Black Matt and Tom Morrisey, sprawled over the table, arms about each other's neck, weeping lovingly.

The kitchen-drinking continued, and the girls outside grew timorous. They knew the drink game, and all were certain that something terrible was going to happen. They protested that they did not wish to be there when it happened, and some one suggested going to a big Italian rancho four miles away, where they could get up a dance.

Immediately they paired off, lad and lassie, and started down the sandy road. And each lad walked with his sweetheart—trust a child of seven to listen and to know the love-affairs of his countryside. And behold, I too, was a lad with a lassie. A little Irish girl of my own age had been paired off with me. We were the only children in this spontaneous affair. Perhaps the oldest couple might have been twenty. There were chits of girls, quite grown up, of fourteen and sixteen, walking with their fellows. But we were uniquely young, this little Irish girl and I, and we walked hand in hand, and, sometimes, under the tutelage of our elders, with my arm around her waist. Only that wasn't comfortable. And I was very proud, on that bright Sunday morning, going down the long bleak road among the sandhills. I, too, had my girl, and was a little man.

The Italian rancho was a bachelor establishment. Our visit was hailed with delight. The red wine was poured in tumblers for all, and the long dining-room was partly cleared for dancing. And the young fellows drank and danced with the girls to the strains of an accordion. To me that music was divine. I had never heard anything so glorious. The young Italian who furnished it would even get up and dance, his arms around his girl, playing the accordion behind her back. All of which was very wonderful for me, who did not dance, but who sat at a table and gazed wide-eyed at the amazingness of life. I was only a little lad, and there was so much of life for me to learn. As the time passed, the Irish lads began helping themselves to the wine, and jollity and high spirits reigned. I noted that some of them staggered and fell down in the dances, and that one had gone to sleep in a corner. Also, some of the girls were complaining, and wanting to leave, and others of the girls were titteringly complacent, willing for anything to happen.

When our Italian hosts had offered me wine in a general sort of way, I had declined. My beer experience

2*

had been enough for me, and I had no inclination to traffic further in the stuff, or in anything related to it. Unfortunately, one young Italian, Peter, an impish soul, seeing me sitting solitary, stirred by a whim of the moment, half-filled a tumbler with wine and passed it to me. He was sitting across the table from me. I declined. His face grew stern, and he insistently proffered the wine. And then terror descended upon me—a terror which I must explain.

My mother had theories. First, she steadfastly maintained that brunettes and all the tribe of dark-eyed humans were deceitful. Needless to say, my mother was a blonde. Next, she was convinced that the dark-eyed Latin races were profoundly sensitive, profoundly treacherous, and profoundly murderous. Again and again, drinking in the strangeness and the fearsomeness of the world from her lips, I had heard her state that if one offended an Italian, no matter how slightly and unintentionally, he was certain to retaliate by stabbing one in the back. That was her particular phrase—'stab you in the back'.

Now, although I had been eager to see Black Matt kill Tom Morrisey that morning, I did not care to furnish to the dancers the spectacle of a knife sticking in *my* back. I had not yet learned to distinguish between facts and theories. My faith was implicit in my mother's exposition of the Italian character. Besides, I had some glimmering inkling of the sacredness of hospitality. Here was a treacherous, sensitive, murderous Italian, offering me hospitality. I had been taught to believe that if I offended him he would strike at me with a knife precisely as a horse kicked out when one got too close to its heels and worried it. Then, too, this Italian, Peter, had those terrible black eyes I had heard my mother talk about. They were eyes different from the eyes I knew, from the blues and greys and hazels of my own family, from the pale and genial blues of the Irish. Perhaps Peter had had a few drinks. At any rate, his eyes were brilliantly black and sparkling with devilry. They were the mysterious, the unknown, and who was I, a seven-year-old, to analyse them and know their prankishness? In them I visioned sudden death, and I declined the wine half-heartedly. The expression in his eyes changed. They grew stern and imperious as he shoved the tumbler of wine closer.

What could I do? I have faced real death since in my life, but never have I known the fear of death as I knew it then. I put the glass to my lips, and Peter's eyes relented. I knew he would not kill me just then. That was a relief. But the wine was not. It was cheap, new wine, bitter and sour, made of the leavings and scrapings of the vineyards and the vats, and it tasted far worse than beer. There is only one way to take medicine, and that is to take it. And that is the way I took that wine. I threw my head back and gulped it down. I had to gulp again and hold the poison down, for poison it was to my child's tissues and membranes.

Looking back now, I can realize that Peter was astounded, he half-filled a second tumbler and shoved it across the table. Frozen with fear, in despair at the fate which had befallen me, I gulped the second glass down like the first. This was too much for Peter. He must share the infant prodigy he had discovered. He called Dominick, a young moustached Italian to see the sight. This time it was a full tumbler that was given me. One will do anything to live. I gripped myself, mastered the qualms that rose in my thoat, and downed the stuff.

Dominick had never seen an infant of such heroic calibre. Twice again he refilled the tumbler, each time to the brim, and watched it disappear down my throat. By this time my exploits were attracting attention. Middle-aged Italian labourers, old-country peasants who did not talk English, and who could not dance with the Irish girls, surrounded me. They were swarthy and wild-looking; they wore belts and red shirts; and I knew they carried knives; and they ringed me around like a pirate chorus. And Peter and Dominick made me show off for them.

Had I lacked imagination, had I been stupid, had I been stubbornly mulish in having my own way, I should never have got in this pickle. And the lads and lassies were dancing, and there was no one to save me from my fate. How much I drank I do not know. My memory of it is of an age-long suffering of fear in the midst of a murderous crew, and of an infinite number of glasses of red wine passing across the bare boards of a wine-drenched table and going down my burning throat. Bad as the wine was, a knife in the back was worse, and I must survive at any cost.

Looking back with the drinker's knowledge, I know now why I did not collapse stupefied upon the table. As I have said, I was frozen, I was paralysed, with fear. The only movement I made was to convey that never-ending procession of glasses to my lips. I was a poised and motionless receptacle for all that quantity of wine. It lay inert in my fear-inert stomach. I was too frightened, even, for my stomach to turn. So all that Italian crew looked on and marvelled at the infant phenomenon that downed wine with the *sang-froid* of an automaton. It is not in the spirit of braggadocio that I dare to assert they had never seen anything like it.

The time came to go. The tipsy antics of the lads had led a majority of the soberer-minded lassies to compel a departure. I found myself, at the door, beside my little maiden. She had not had my experience, so she was sober. She was fascinated by the titubations of the lads who strove to walk beside their girls, and began to mimic them. I thought this a great game, and I, too, began to stagger tipsily. But she had no wine to stir up, while my movements quickly set the fumes rising to my head. Even at the start, I was more realistic than she. In several minutes I was astonishingly myself. I saw one lad, after reeling half a dozen steps, pause at the side of the road, gravely peer into the ditch, and gravely, and after apparent deep thought, fall into it. To me this was excruciatingly

funny. I staggered to the edge of the ditch, fully intending
to stop on the edge. I came to myself, in the ditch, in
process of being hauled out by several anxious-faced girls.

I didn't care to play at being drunk any more. There was
no more fun in me. My eyes were beginning to swim,
and with wide-open mouth I panted for air. A girl led me
by the hand on either side, but my legs were leaden. The
alcohol I had drunk was striking my heart and brain like
a club. Had I been a weakling of a child, I am confident
that it would have killed me. As it was, I know I was
nearer death than any of the scared girls dreamed. I could
hear them bickering among themselves as to whose fault
it was; some were weeping—for themselves, for me,
and for the disgraceful way their lads had behaved. But
I was not interested. I was suffocating, and I wanted air.
To move was agony. It made me pant harder. Yet those
girls persisted in making me walk, and it was four miles
home. Four miles! I remember my swimming eyes saw
a small bridge across the road an infinite distance away.
In fact, it was not a hundred feet distant. When I reached
it, I sank down and lay on my back panting. The girls
tried to lift me, but I was helpless and suffocating. Their
cries of alarm brought Larry, a drunken youth of seventeen, who preceeded to resuscitate me by jumping on my
chest. Dimly I remember this, and the squalling of the
girls as they struggled with him and dragged him away.
And then I knew nothing, though I learned afterwards that
Larry wound up under the bridge and spent the night
there.

When I came to, it was dark. I had been carried unconscious for four miles and been put to bed. I was a
sick child, and, despite the terrible strain on my heart
and tissues, I continually relapsed into the madness of
delirium. All the contents of the terrible and horrible in
my child's mind spilled out. The most frightful visions
were realities to me. I saw murders committed, and I
was pursued by murderers. I screamed and raved and

fought. My sufferings were prodigious. Emerging from such delirium, I would hear my mother's voice: 'But the child's brain. He will lose his reason.' And sinking back into delirium, I would take the idea with me and be immured in madhouses, and be beaten by keepers, and surrounded by screeching lunatics.

One thing that had strongly impressed my young mind was the talk of my elders about the dens of iniquity in San Francisco's Chinatown. In my delirium I wandered deep beneath the ground through a thousand of these dens, and behind locked doors of iron I suffered and died a thousand deaths. And when I would come upon my father, seated at tables in these subterranean crypts, gambling with Chinese for great stakes of gold, all my outrage gave vent in the vilest cursing. I would rise in bed, struggling against the detaining hands, and curse my father till the rafters rang. All the inconceivable filth a child running at large in a primitive countryside may hear men utter was mine; and though I had never dared utter such oaths, they now poured from me, at the top of my lungs, as I cursed my father sitting there underground and gambling with long-haired, long-nailed Chinamen.

It is a wonder that I did not burst my heart or brain that night. A seven-year-old child's arteries and nerve-centres are scarcely fitted to endure the terrific paroxysms that convulsed me. No one slept in the thin, frame farm-house that night when John Barleycorn had his will of me. And Larry, under the bridge, had no delirium like mine. I am confident that his sleep was stupefied and dreamless, and that he awoke next day merely to heaviness and moroseness, and that if he lives today he does not remember that night, so passing was it as an incident. But my brain was seared for ever by that experience. Writing now, thirty years afterwards, every vision is as distinct, as sharp-cut, every pain as vital and terrible, as on that night.

I was sick for days afterward, and I needed none of my mother's injunctions to avoid John Barleycorn in the future. My mother had been dreadfully shocked. She held

that I had done wrong, very wrong, and that I had gone
contrary to all her teaching, And how was I, who was
never allowed to talk back, who lacked the very words with
which to express my psychology—how was I to tell my
mother that it was her teaching that was directly responsible for my drunkenness? Had it not been for her theories
about dark eyes and Italian character, I should never have
wet my lips with the sour, bitter wine. And not until man-
grown did I tell her the true inwardness of that disgraceful affair.

In those after days of sickness, I was confused on some
points, and very clear on others. I felt guilty of sin, yet
smarted with a sense of injustice. It had not been my
fault, yet I had done wrong. But very clear was my resolution never to touch liquor again. No mad dog was ever
more afraid of water than was I of alcohol.

Yet the point I am making is that this experience,
terrible as it was, could not in the end deter me from
forming John Barleycorn's cheek-by-jowl acquaintance. All
about me, even then, were the forces moving me toward
him. In the first place, barring my mother, ever extreme
in her views, it seemed to me all the grown-ups looked
upon the affair with tolerant eyes. It was a joke, something
funny that had happened. There was no shame attached.
Even the lads and lassies giggled and snickered over their
part in the affair, narrating with gusto how Larry had
jumped on my chest and slept under the bridge, how
So-and-So had slept out in the sandhills that night, and
what had happened to the other lad who fell in the ditch.
As I say, so far as I could see, there was no shame anywhere. It had been something ticklishly, devilishly fine—
a bright and gorgeous episode in the monotony of life
and labour on that bleak, fog-girt coast.

The Irish ranchers twitted me good-naturedly on my
exploit, and patted me on the back until I felt that I had
done something heroic. Peter and Dominick and the other
Italians were proud of my drinking prowess. The face of
morality was not set against drinking. Besides, everybody

drank. There was not a teetotaller in the community. Even
the teacher of our little country school, a greying man of
fifty, gave us vacations on the occasions when he wrestled
with John Barleycorn and was thrown. Thus there was
no spiritual deterrence. My loathing for alcohol was purely
physiological. I didn't like the damned stuff.

5

THIS PHYSICAL loathing for alcohol I have never got
over. But I have conquered it. To this day I conquer it
every time I take a drink. The palate never ceases to rebel,
and the palate can be trusted to know what is good for the
body. But men do not drink for the effect alcohol pro-
duces on the body. What they drink for is the brain-effect;
and if it must come through the body, so much the worse
for the body.

And yet, despite my physical loathing for alcohol, the
brightest spots in my child life were the saloons. Sitting on
the heavy potato wagons, wrapped in fog, feet stinging
from inactivity, the horses plodding slowly along the deep
road through the sandhills, one bright vision made the
way never too long. The bright vision was the saloon
at Colma, where my father, or whoever drove, always
got out to get a drink. And I got out to warm by the great
stove and get a soda cracker. Just one soda cracker, but a
fabulous luxury. Saloons were good for something. Back
behind the plodding horses, I would take an hour in consuming that one cracker. I took the smallest nibbles, never
losing a crumb, and chewed the nibble till it became the
thinnest and most delectable of paste. I never voluntarily
swallowed this paste. I just tasted it, and went on tasting
it, turning it over with my tongue, spreading it on the inside of the other cheek, until, at the end, it eluded me and
in tiny drops and oozelets, slipped and dribbled down my

throat. Horace Fletcher had nothing on me when it came to soda crackers.

I liked saloons. Especially I liked the San Francisco saloons. They had the most delicious dainties for the taking—strange breads and crackers, cheeses, sausages, sardines—wonderful foods that I never saw on our meagre home-table. And once, I remember, a barkeeper mixed me a sweet temperance drink of syrup and soda-water. My father did not pay for it. It was the barkeeper's treat, and he became my ideal of a good, kind man. I dreamed day-dreams of him for years. Although I was seven years old at the time, I can see him now with un-diminished clearness, though I never laid eyes on him but that one time. The saloon was south of Market Street in San Francisco. It stood on the west side of the street. As you entered, the bar was on the left. On the right, against the wall, was the free lunch counter. It was a long, narrow room, and at the rear, beyond the beer kegs on tap, were small, round tables and chairs. The barkeeper was blue-eyed, and had fair, silky hair peeping out from under a black silk skull-cap. I remember he wore a brown Cardigan jacket, and I know precisely the spot, in the midst of the array of bottles, from which he took the bottle of red-coloured syrup. He and my father talked long, and I sipped my sweet drink and worshipped him. And for years afterwards I worshipped the memory of him.

Despite my two disastrous experiences, here was John Barleycorn, prevalent and accessible everywhere in the community, luring and drawing me. Here were connotations of the saloon making deep indentations in a child's mind. Here was a child, forming its first judgments of the world, finding the saloon a delightful and desirable place. Stores, nor public buildings, nor all the dwellings of men ever opened their doors to me and let me warm by their fires or permitted me to eat the food of the gods from narrow shelves against the wall. Their doors were ever closed to me; the saloon's doors were ever open. And always and everywhere I found saloons, on highway and byway, up narrow alleys and on busy thoroughfares, bright-lighted and cheerful, warm in winter, and in summer dark and cool. Yes, the saloon was a mighty fine place, and it was more than that.

By the time I was ten years old, my family had abandoned ranching and gone to live in the city. And here, at ten, I began on the streets as a newsboy. One of the reasons for this was that we needed the money. Another reason was that I needed the exercise. I had found my way to the free public library, and was reading myself into nervous prostration. On the poor ranches on which I had lived there had been no books. In ways truly miraculous, I had been lent four books, marvellous books, and them I had devoured. One was the life of Garfield; the second, Paul du Chaillu's African travels; the third, a novel by Ouida with the last forty pages missing; and the fourth, Irving's 'Alhambra'. This last had been lent me by a schoolteacher. I was not a forward child. Unlike Oliver Twist, I was incapable of asking for more. When I returned the 'Alhambra' to the teacher I hoped she would lend me another book. And because she did not—most likely she deemed me unappreciative—I cried all the way home on the three-mile tramp from the school to the ranch. I waited and yearned for her to lend me another book. Scores of times I nerved myself almost to the point of asking her, but never quite reached the necessary pitch of effrontery.

And then came the city of Oakland, and on the shelves of that free library I discovered all the great world beyond the skyline. Here were thousands of books as good as my four wonder-books, and some were even better. Libraries were not concerned with children in those days, and I had strange adventures. I remember, in the catalogue, being impressed by the title, *The Adventures of Peregrine Pickle*. I filled an application blank and the librarian handed me the collected and entirely unexpurgated works of Smollett in one huge volume. I read everything, but principally history and adventure, and all the old travels and voyages. I read mornings, afternoons, and nights. I read in bed, I read at table, I read as I walked to and from school, and I read at recess while the other boys were playing. I began to get the 'jerks'. To everybody I replied: 'Go away. You make me nervous.'

And so, at ten, I was out on the streets, a newsboy. I had no time to read. I was busy getting exercise and learning how to fight, busy learning forwardness, and brass and bluff. I had an imagination and a curiosity about all things that made me plastic. Not least among the things I was curious about was the saloon. And I was in and out of many a one. I remember, in those days, on the east side of Broadway, between Sixth and Seventh, from corner to corner, there was a solid block of saloons.

In the saloons life was different. Men talked with great voices, laughed great laughs, and there was an atmosphere of greatness. Here was something more than common every-day where nothing happened. Here life was always very live, and, sometimes, even lurid, when blows were struck, and blood was shed, and big policemen came shouldering in. Great moments, these, for me, my head filled with all the wild and valiant fighting of the gallant adventurers on sea and land. There were no big moments when I trudged along the street throwing my papers in at doors. But in the saloons, even the sots, stupefied, sprawling across the tables or in the sawdust, were objects of mystery and wonder.

And more, the saloons were right. The city fathers sanctioned them and licensed them. They were not the terrible places I heard boys deem them who lacked my opportunities to know. Terrible they might be, but then that only meant they were terribly wonderful, and it is the terribly wonderful that a boy desires to know. In the same way pirates, and shipwrecks, and battles were terrible; and what healthy boy wouldn't give his immortal soul to participate in such affairs?

Besides, in saloons I saw reporters, editors, lawyers, judges, whose names and faces I knew. They put the seal of social approval on the saloon. They verified my own feeling of fascination in the saloon. They, too, must have found there that something different, that something beyond, which I sensed and groped after. What it was, I did not know; yet there it must be, for there men focused like buzzing flies about a honey pot. I had no sorrows, and the world was very bright, so I could not guess that what these men sought was forgetfulness of jaded toil and stale grief.

Not that I drank at that time. From ten to fifteen I rarely tasted liquor, but I was intimately in contact with drinkers and drinking places. The only reason I did not drink was because I didn't like the stuff. As the time passed, I worked as a boy-helper on an ice-wagon, set up pins in a bowling alley with a saloon attached, and swept out saloons at Sunday picnic grounds.

Big jovial Josie Harper ran a road house at Telegraph Avenue and Thirty-ninth Street. Here for a year I delivered an evening paper, until my route was changed to the water-front and tenderloin of Oakland. The first month, when I collected Josie Harper's bill, she poured me a glass of wine. I was ashamed to refuse, so I drank it. But after that I watched the chance when she wasn't around so as to collect from her barkeeper.

The first day I worked in the bowling alley, the barkeeper, according to custom, called us boys up to have a drink after we had been setting up pins for several hours. The others asked for beer. I said I'd take ginger ale. The boys snickered, and I noticed the barkeeper favoured me with a strange, searching scrutiny. Nevertheless, he opened a bottle of ginger ale. Afterwards, back in the alleys, in the pauses between games, the boys enlightened me. I had offended the bar keeper. A bottle of ginger ale cost the saloon ever so much more than a glass of steam beer; and it was up to me, if I wanted to hold my job, to drink beer. Besides, beer was food. I could work better on it. There was no food in ginger ale. After that, when I couldn't sneak out of it, I drank beer and wondered what men found in it that was so good. I was always aware that I was missing something.

What I really liked in those days was candy. For five cents I could buy five 'cannon-balls'—big lumps of the most delicious lastingness. I could chew and worry a single one for an hour. Then there was a Mexican who sold big slabs of brown chewing taffy for five cents each. It required a quarter of a day properly to absorb one of them. And many a day I made my entire lunch off one of those slabs. In truth, I found food there, but not in beer.

6

BUT THE time was rapidly drawing near when I was to begin my second series of bouts with John Barleycorn. When I was fourteen, my head filled with the tales of the old voyagers, my vision with tropic isles and far sea-rims, I was sailing a small centreboard skiff around San Francisco Bay and on the Oakland Estuary. I wanted to go to sea. I wanted to get away from monotony and the commonplace. I was in the flower of my adolescence, a-thrill with romance and adventure, dreaming of wild life in the wild man-world. Little I guessed how all the warp and woof of that man-world was entangled with alcohol.

So, one day, as I hoisted sail on my skiff, I met Scotty. He was a husky youngster of seventeen, a runaway apprentice, he told me, from an English ship in Australia. He had just worked his way on another ship to San Francisco; and now he wanted to see about getting a berth on a whaler. Across the estuary, near where the whalers lay, was lying the sloop-yacht *Idler*. The caretaker was a harpooner who intended sailing next voyage on the whale ship *Bonanza*. Would I take him, Scotty, over in my skiff to call upon the harpooner?

Would I? Hadn't I heard the stories and rumours about the *Idler*?—the big sloop that had come up from the Sandwich Islands where it had been engaged in smuggling opium. And the harpooner who was caretaker! How often had I seen him and envied him his freedom. He never had to leave the water. He slept aboard the *Idler* each night, while I had to go home upon the land to go to bed. The harpooner was only nineteen years old (and I have never had anything but his word that he was a harpooner); but he had been too shining and glorious a personality for me ever to address as I paddled around the yacht at a wistful distance. Would I take Scotty, the runaway sailor, to visit the harpooner, on the opium-smuggler *Idler*? *Would I!*

The harpooner came on deck to answer our hail, and invited us aboard. I played the sailor and the man, fending off the skiff so that it would not mar the yacht's white paint, dropping the skiff astern on a long painter, and making the painter fast with two nonchalant half-hitches. We went below. It was the first sea-interior I had ever seen. The clothing on the wall smelled musty. But what of that? Was it not the sea-gear of men?—leather jackets lined with corduroy, blue coats of pilot cloth, sou'westers, sea-boots, oilskins. And everywhere was in evidence the economy of space—the narrow bunks, the swinging tables, the incredible lockers. There were the tell-tale compass, the sea-lamps in their gimbals, the blue-backed charts carelessly rolled and tucked away, the signal-flags in alphabetical order, and a mariner's dividers jammed into the woodwork to hold a calendar. At last I was living. Here I sat, inside my first ship, a smuggler, accepted as a comrade by a harpooner and a runaway English sailor who said his name was Scotty.

The first thing that the harpooner, aged nineteen, and the sailor, aged seventeen, did to show that they were men was to behave like men. The harpooner suggested the eminent desirableness of a drink, and Scotty searched his pockets for dimes and nickels. Then the harpooner carried away a pink flask to be filled in some blind pig, for there were no licensed saloons in that locality. We drank the cheap rotgut out of tumblers. Was I any the less strong, any the less valiant, than the harpooner and the sailor?

They were men. They proved it by the way they drank. Drink was the badge of manhood. So I drank with them, drink by drink, raw and straight, though the damned stuff couldn't compare with a stick of chewing taffy or a delectable 'cannon-ball'. I shuddered and swallowed my gorge with every drink, though I manfully hid all such symptoms.

Divers times we filled the flask that afternoon. All I had was twenty cents, but I put it up like a man, though with secret regret at the enormous store of candy it could have bought. The liquor mounted in the heads of all of us, and the talk of Scotty and the harpooner was upon running the Easting down, gales off the Horn and pamperos off the Plate, lower topsail breezes, southerly busters, North Pacific gales, and of smashed whaleboats in the Arctic ice.

'You can't swim in that ice water,' said the harpooner confidentially to me. 'You double up in a minute and go down. When a whale smashes your boat, the thing to do is to get your belly across an oar, so that when the cold doubles you you'll float.'

'Sure,' I said, with a grateful nod and an air of certitude that I, too, would hunt whales and be in smashed boats in the Arctic Ocean. And truly, I registered his advice as singularly valuable information, and filed it away in my brain, where it persists to this day.

But I couldn't talk—at first. Heavens! I was only fourteen, and had never been on the ocean in my life. I could only listen to the two sea-dogs, and show my manhood by drinking with them, fairly and squarely, drink and drink.

The liquor worked its will with me; the talk of Scotty and the harpooner poured through the pent space of the *Idler*'s cabin and through my brain like great gusts of wide, free wind; and in imagination I lived my years to come and rocked over the wild, mad, glorious world on multitudinous adventures.

We unbent. Our inhibitions and taciturnities vanished. We were as if we had known each other for years and years, and we pledged ourselves to years of future voyag-

ings together. The harpooner told of misadventures and
secret shames. Scotty wept over his poor old mother in
Edinburgh—a lady, he insisted, gently born—who was in
reduced circumstances, who had pinched herself to pay the
lump sum to the shipowners for his apprenticeship, whose
sacrificing dream had been to see him a merchantman
officer and a gentleman, and who was heartbroken because
he had deserted his ship in Australia and joined another as
a common sailor before the mast. And Scotty proved it. He
drew her last sad letter from his pocket and wept over it
as he read it aloud. The harpooner and I wept with him,
and swore that all three of us would ship on the whaleship
Bonanza, win a big pay-day, and, still together, make a
pilgrimage to Edinburgh and lay our store of money in the
dear lady's lap.

And, as John Barleycorn heated his way into my brain,
thawing my reticence, melting my modesty, talking through
me and with me and as me, my adopted twin brother and
alter ego, I, too, raised my voice to show myself a man and
an adventurer, and bragged in detail and at length of how
I had crossed San Francisco Bay in my open skiff in a roaring southwester when even the schooner sailors doubted
my exploit. Further, I—or John Barleycorn, for it was the
same thing—told Scotty that he might be a deep-sea sailor
and know the last rope on the great deep-sea ships, but
that when it came to small-boat sailing I could beat him
hands down and sail circles around him.

The best of it was that my assertion and brag were true.
With reticence and modesty present, I could never have
dared tell Scotty my small-boat estimate of him. But it is
ever the way of John Barleycorn to loosen the tongue and
babble the secret thought.

Scotty, or John Barleycorn, or the pair, was very naturally offended by my remarks. Nor was I loath. I could
whip any runaway sailor seventeen years old. Scotty and I
flared and raged like young cockerels, until the harpooner
poured another round of drinks to enable us to forgive and
make up. Which we did, arms around each other's necks,

protesting vows of eternal friendship—just like Black Matt and Tom Morrisey, I remembered, in the ranch kitchen in San Mateo. And, remembering, I knew that I was at last a man—despite my meagre fourteen years—a man as big and manly as those two strapping giants who had quarrelled and made up on that memorable Sunday morning of long ago.

By this time the singing stage was reached, and I joined Scotty and the harpooner in snatches of sea songs and chanties. It was here, in the cabin of the *Idler*, that I first heard 'Blow the Man Down', 'Flying Cloud', and 'Whisky, Johnny, Whisky'. Oh, it was brave. I was beginning to grasp the meaning of life. Here was no commonplace, no Oakland Estuary, no weary round of throwing newspapers at front doors, delivering ice, and setting up ninepins. All the world was mine, all its paths were under my feet, and John Barleycorn, tricking my fancy, enabled me to anticipate the life of adventure for which I yearned.

We were not ordinary. We were three tipsy young gods, incredibly wise, gloriously genial, and without limit to our powers. Ah!—and I say it now, after the years—could John Barleycorn keep one at such a height, I should never draw a sober breath again. But this is not a world of free freights. One pays according to an iron schedule—for every strength the balanced weakness; for every high a corresponding low; for every fictitious god-like moment an equivalent time in reptilian slime. For every feat of telescoping long days and weeks of life into mad magnificent instants, one must pay with shortened life, and, oft-times, with savage usury added.

Intenseness and duration are as ancient enemies as fire and water. They are mutually destructive. They cannot coexist. And John Barleycorn, mighty necromancer though he be, is as much a slave to organic chemistry as we mortals are. We pay for every nerve marathon we run, nor can John Barleycorn intercede and fend off the just payment. He can lead us to the heights, but he cannot keep us there, else would we all be devotees. And there is no devotee but pays for the mad dances John Barleycorn pipes.

Yet the foregoing is all in after wisdom spoken. It was no part of the knowledge of the lad, fourteen years old, who sat in the *Idler*'s cabin between the harpooner and the sailor, the air rich in his nostrils with the musty smell of men's sea-gear, roaring in chorus: 'Yankee ship come down de ribber—pull, my bully boys, pull!'

We grew maudlin, and all talked and shouted at once. I had a splendid constitution, a stomach that would digest scrap-iron, and I was still running my marathon in full vigour when Scotty began to fail and fade. His talk grew incoherent. He groped for words and could not find them, while the ones he found his lips were unable to form. His poisoned consciousness was leaving him. The brightness went out of his eyes, and he looked as stupid as were his efforts to talk. His face and body sagged as his consciousness sagged. (A man cannot sit upright save by an act of will.) Scotty's reeling brain could not control his muscles. All his correlations were breaking down. He strove to take another drink, and feebly dropped the tumbler on the floor. Then, to my amazement, weeping bitterly, he rolled into a bunk on his back and immediately snored off to sleep.

The harpooner and I drank on, grinning in a superior way to each other over Scotty's plight. The last flask was opened, and we drank it between us, to the accompaniment of Scotty's stertorous breathing. Then the harpooner faded away into his bunk, and I was left alone, unthrown, on the field of battle.

I was very proud, and John Barleycorn was proud with me. I could carry my drink. I was a man. I had drunk two men, drink for drink, into unconsciousness. And I was still on my two feet, upright, making my way on deck to get air into my scorching lungs. It was in this bout on the *Idler* that I discovered what a good stomach and a strong head I had for drink—a bit of knowledge that was to be a source of pride in succeeding years, and that ultimately I was to come to consider a great affliction. The fortunate man is the one who cannot take more than a couple of drinks without becoming intoxicated. The unfortunate wight is the one who can take many glasses without betraying a sign; who *must* take numerous glasses in order to get the 'kick'.

The sun was setting when I came on the *Idler*'s deck. There were plenty of bunks below. I did not need to go home. But I wanted to demonstrate to myself how much I was a man. There lay my skiff astern. The last of a strong ebb was running out in channel in the teeth of an ocean breeze of forty miles an hour. I could see the stiff white-caps, and the suck and run of the current was plainly visible in the face and trough of each one.

I set sail, cast off, took my place at the tiller, the sheet in my hand, and headed across channel. The skiff heeled over and plunged into it madly. The spray began to fly. I was at the pinnacle of exaltation. I sang 'Blow the Man Down' as I sailed. I was no boy of fourteen, living the mediocre ways of the sleepy town called Oakland. I was a man, a god, and the very elements rendered me allegiance as I bitted them to my will.

The tide was out. A full hundred yards of soft mud intervened between the boat-wharf and the water. I pulled up my centreboard, ran full tilt into the mud, took in sail, and, standing in the stern, as I had often done at low tide, I began to shove the skiff with an oar. It was then that my correlations began to break down. I lost my balance and pitched head-foremost into the ooze. Then, and for the first time, as I floundered to my feet covered with slime, the blood running down my arms from a scrape against a barnacled stake, I knew that I was drunk. But what of it? Across the channel two strong sailormen lay unconscious in their bunks where I had drunk them. I *was* a man. I was still on my legs, if they were knee-deep in mud. I disdained to get back into the skiff. I waded through the mud, shoving the skiff before me and yammering the chant of my manhood to the world.

I paid for it. I was sick for a couple of days, meanly sick, and my arms were painfully poisoned from the barnacle scratches. For a week I could not use them, and it was a torture to put on and take off my clothes.

I swore, 'Never again!' The game wasn't worth it. The price was too stiff. I had no moral qualms. My revulsion was purely physical. No exalted moments were worth such hours of misery and wretchedness. When I got back to my skiff, I shunned the *Idler*. I would cross the opposite side of the channel to go around her. Scotty had disappeared. The harpooner was still about, but him I avoided. Once, when he landed on the boat-wharf, I hid in a shed so as to escape seeing him. I was afraid he would propose some more drinking, maybe have a flask full of whisky in his pocket.

And yet—and here enters the necromancy of John Barleycorn—that afternoon's drunk on the *Idler* had been a purple passage flung into the monotony of my days. It was memorable. My mind dwelt on it continually. I went over the details, over and over again. Among other things, I had got into the cogs and springs of men's actions. I had seen Scotty weep about his own worthlessness and the sad case of his Edinburgh mother who was a lady. The harpooner had told me terribly wonderful things of himself. I had caught a myriad enticing and inflammatory hints of a world beyond my world, and for which I was certainly as fitted as the two lads who had drunk with me. I had got behind men's souls. I had got behind my own soul and found unguessed potencies and greatnesses.

Yes, that day stood out above all my other days. To this day it so stands out. The memory of it is branded in my brain. But the price exacted was too high. I refused to play and pay, and returned to my cannon-balls and taffy-slabs. The point is that all the chemistry of my healthy, normal body drove me away from alcohol. The stuff didn't agree with me. It was abominable. But despite this, circumstance was to continue to drive me towards John Barleycorn, to drive me again and again, until, after long years, the time should come when I would look up John Barleycorn in every haunt of men—look him up and hail him gladly as benefactor and friend. And detest and hate him all the time. Yes, he is a strange friend, John Barleycorn.

7

I WAS barely turned fifteen, and working long hours in a cannery. Month in and month out, the shortest day I ever worked was ten hours. When to ten hours of actual work at a machine is added the noon hour; the walking to work and walking home from work; the getting up in the morning, dressing, and eating; the eating at night, undressing, and going to bed, there remains no more than the nine hours out of the twenty-four required by a healthy youngster for sleep. Out of those nine hours, after I was in bed and ere my eyes drowsed shut, I managed to steal a little time for reading.

But many a night I did not knock off until midnight. On occasion I worked eighteen and twenty hours on a stretch. Once I worked at my machine for thirty-six consecutive hours. And there were weeks on end when I never knocked off work earlier than eleven o'clock, got home and in bed at half after midnight, and was called at half-past five to dress, eat, walk to work, and be at my machine at seven o'clock whistle blow.

No moments here to be stolen for my beloved books. And what had John Barleycorn to do with such strenuous, Stoic toil of a lad just turned fifteen? He had everything to do with it. Let me show you. I asked myself if this were the meaning of life—to be a work-beast? I knew of no horse in the city of Oakland that worked the hours I worked. If this were living, I was entirely unenamoured of it. I remembered my skiff, lying idle and accumulating barnacles at the boat-wharf; I remembered the wind that blew every day on the bay, the sunrises and sunsets I never saw; the

bite of the salt air in my nostrils, the bite of the salt water
on my flesh when I plunged overside; I remembered all the
beauty and the wonder and the sense-delights of the world
denied me. There was only one way to escape my deaden-
ing toil. I must get out and away on the water. I must earn
my bread on the water. And the way of the water led in-
evitably to John Barleycorn. I did not know this. And when
I did learn it, I was courageous enough not to retreat back
to my bestial life at the machine.

I wanted to be where the winds of adventure blew. And
the winds of adventure blew the oyster pirate sloops up
and down San Francisco Bay, from raided oyster-beds and
fights at night on shoal and flat, to markets in the morning
against city wharves, where peddlers and saloon-keepers
came down to buy. Every raid on an oyster-bed was a
felony. The penalty was State imprisonment, the stripes
and the lockstep. And what of that? The men in stripes
worked a shorter day than I at my machine. And there
was vastly more romance in being an oyster pirate or a
convict than in being a machine slave. And behind it all,
behind all of me with youth abubble, whispered Romance,
Adventure.

So I interviewed my Mammy Jennie, my old nurse at
whose black breast I had suckled. She was more prosperous
than my folks. She was nursing sick people at a good
weekly wage. Would she lend her 'white child' the money?
Would she? What she had was mine.

Then I sought out French Frank, the oyster pirate, who
wanted to sell, I had heard, his sloop, the *Razzle Dazzle*.
I found him lying at anchor on the Alameda side of the
estuary near the Webster Street bridge, with visitors
aboard, whom he was entertaining with afternoon wine.
He came on deck to talk business. He was willing to sell.
But it was Sunday. Besides, he had guests. On the morrow
he would make out the bill of sale and I could enter into
possession. And in the meantime I must come below and
meet his friends. They were two sisters, Mamie and Tess;
a Mrs Hadley, who chaperoned them; 'Whisky' Bob, a

youthful oyster pirate of sixteen; and 'Spider' Healey, a black-whiskered wharf-rat of twenty. Mamie, who was Spider's niece, was called the Queen of the Oyster Pirates, and, on occasion, presided at their revels. French Frank was in love with her, though I did not know it at the time; and she steadfastly refused to marry him.

French Frank poured a tumbler of red wine from a big demijohn to drink to our transaction. I remembered the red wine of the Italian rancho, and shuddered inwardly. Whisky and beer were not quite so repulsive. But the Queen of the Oyster Pirates was looking at me, a part-emptied glass in her own hand. I had my pride. If I was only fifteen, at least I could not show myself any less a man than she. Besides, there were her sister, and Mrs Hadley, and the young oyster-pirate, and the whiskered wharf-rat, all with glasses in their hands. Was I a milk-and-water sop? No; a thousand times no, and a thousand glasses no. I downed the tumblerful like a man.

French Frank was elated by the sale, which I had bound with a twenty-dollar goldpiece. He poured more wine. I had learned my strong head and stomach, and I was certain I could drink with them in a temperate way and not poison myself for a week to come. I could stand as much as they; and besides, they had already been drinking for some time.

We got to singing. Spider sang 'The Boston Burglar' and 'Black Lulu'. The Queen sang 'Then I Wisht I Were a Little Bird'. And her sister Tess sang 'Oh, Treat My Daughter Kindly'. The fun grew fast and furious. I found myself able to miss drinks without being noticed or called to account. Also, standing in the companionway, head and shoulders out and glass in hand, I could fling the wine overboard.

I reasoned something like this: It is a queerness of these people that they like this vile-tasting wine. Well, let them. I cannot quarrel with their tastes. My manhood, according to their queer notions, must compel me to appear to like this wine. Very well. I shall so appear. But I shall drink no more than is unavoidable.

And the Queen began to make love to me, the latest recruit to the oyster pirate fleet, and no mere hand, but a master and owner. She went upon deck to take the air, and took me with her. She knew, of course, but I never dreamed, how French Frank was raging down below. Then Tess joined us, sitting on the cabin; and Spider, and Bob; and at the last, Mrs Hadley and French Frank. And we sat there, glasses in hand, and sang, while the big demijohn went around; and I was the only strictly sober one.

And I enjoyed it as no one of them was able to enjoy it. Here, in this atmosphere of bohemianism, I could not but contrast the scene with my scene of the day before, sitting at my machine, in the stifling, shut-in air, repeating, endlessly repeating, at top speed, my series of mechanical motions. And here I sat now, glass in hand, in warm-glowing camaraderie, with the oyster pirates, adventurers who refused to be slaves to petty routine, who flouted restrictions and the law, who carried their lives and their liberty in their hands. And it was through John Barleycorn that I came to join this glorious company of free souls, unashamed and unafraid.

And the afternoon seabreeze blew its tang into my lungs, and curled the waves in mid-channel. Before it came the scow schooners, wing-and-wing, blowing their horns for the drawbridges to open. Red-stacked tugs tore by, rocking the *Razzle Dazzle* in the waves of their wake. A sugar barque towed from the 'boneyard' to sea. The sun-wash was on the crisping water, and life was big. And Spider sang:

> 'Oh, it's Lulu, black Lulu, my darling,
> Oh, it's where have you been so long?
> Been layin' in jail,
> A-waitin' for bail,
> Till my bully comes rollin' along.'

There it was, the smack and slap of the spirit of revolt, of adventure, of romance, of the things forbidden and done defiantly and grandly. And I knew that on the morrow I would not go back to my machine at the cannery. To-morrow I would be an oyster pirate, as free as a freebooter as the century and the waters of San Francisco Bay would permit. Spider had already agreed to sail with me as my crew of one, and, also, as cook while I did the deck work. We would outfit our grub and water in the morning, hoist the big mainsail (which was a bigger piece of canvas than any I had ever sailed under), and beat our way out of the estuary on the first of the seabreeze and the last of the ebb. Then we would slack sheets, and on the first of the flood run down the bay to the Asparagus Islands, where we would anchor miles off shore. And at last my dream would be realized: I would sleep upon the water. And next morning I would wake upon the water; and thereafter all my days and nights would be on the water.

And the Queen asked me to row her ashore in my skiff, when at sunset French Frank prepared to take his guests ashore. Nor did I catch the significance of his abrupt change of plan when he turned the task of rowing his skiff over to Whisky Bob, himself remaining on board the sloop. Nor did I understand Spider's grinning side-remark to me: 'Gee! There's nothin' slow about *you*.' How could it possibly enter my boy's head that a grizzled man of fifty should be jealous of me?

8

WE MET by appointment, early Monday morning, to complete the deal, in Johnny Heinhold's 'Last Chance'—a saloon, of course, for the transactions of men. I paid the money over, received the bill of sale, and French Frank treated. This struck me as an evident custom, and a logical one—the seller, who receives the money, to wet a piece of it in the establishment where the trade was consummated. But, to my surprise, French Frank treated the house. He and I drank, which seemed just; but why should Johnny Heinhold, who owned the saloon and waited behind the bar, be invited to drink? I figured it immediately that he made a profit on the very drink he drank. I could, in a way, considering that they were friends and shipmates, understand Spider and Whisky Bob being asked to drink; but why should the longshoremen, Bill Kelley and Soup Kennedy, be asked?

Then there was Pat, the Queen's brother, making a total of eight of us. It was early morning, and all ordered whisky. What could I do, here in this company of big men, all drinking whisky? 'Whisky,' I said, with the careless air of one who had said it a thousand times. And such whisky! I tossed it down. A-r-r-r-gh! I can taste it yet.

And I was appalled at the price French Frank had paid —eighty cents. *Eighty cents*! It was an outrage to my thrifty soul. Eighty cents—the equivalent of eight long hours of my toil at the machine, gone down our throats, and gone like that, in a twinkling, leaving only a bad taste in the mouth. There was no discussion that French Frank was a waster.

I was anxious to be gone, out into the sunshine, out over the water to my glorious boat. But all hands lingered. Even Spider, my crew, lingered. No hint broke through my obtuseness of why they lingered. I have often thought since of how they must have regarded me, the newcomer being welcomed into their company standing at bar with them, and not standing for a single round of drinks.

French Frank, who, unknown to me, had swallowed his chagrin since the day before, now that the money for the *Razzle Dazzle* was in his pocket, began to behave curiously towards me. I sensed the change in his attitude, saw the forbidding glitter in his eyes, and wondered. The more I saw of men, the queerer they became. Johnny Heinhold leaned across the bar and whispered in my ear: 'He's got it in for you. Watch out.'

I nodded comprehension of his statement, and acquiescence in it, as a man should nod who knows all about men. But secretly I was perplexed. Heavens! How was I, who had worked hard and read books of adventure, and who was only fifteen years old, who had not dreamed of giving the Queen of the Oyster Pirates a second thought, and who did not know that French Frank was madly in love with her—how was I to guess that I had done him shame? And how was I to guess that the story of how the Queen had thrown him down on his own boat, the moment I hove in sight, was already the gleeful gossip of the water-front? And by the same token, how was I to guess that her brother Pat's offishness with me was anything else than temperamental gloominess of spirit?

Whisky Bob got me aside a moment. 'Keep your eyes open,' he muttered. 'Take my tip. French Frank's ugly. I'm going up river with him to get a schooner for oystering. When he gets down on the beds, watch out. He says he'll run you down. After dark, any time he's around, change your anchorage and douse your riding light. Savve?'

Oh, certainly, I savve'd. I nodded my head, and, as one man to another, thanked him for his tip; and drifted back to the group at the bar. No; I did not treat. I never dreamed that I was expected to treat. I left with Spider, and my ears burn now as I try to surmise the things they must have said about me.

I asked Spider, in an off-hand way, what was eating French Frank. 'He's crazy jealous of you,' was the answer. 'Do you think so?' I said, and dismissed the matter as not worth thinking about.

But I leave it to anyone—the swell of my fifteen-years-old manhood at learning that French Frank, the adventurer of fifty, the sailor of all the seas of all the world, was jealous of me—and jealous over a girl most romantically named the Queen of the Oyster Pirates. I had read of such things in books, and regarded them as personal probabilities of a distant maturity. Oh, I felt a rare young devil, as we hoisted the big mainsail that morning, broke our anchor, and filled away close-hauled on the three-mile beat to windward out into the bay.

Such was my escape from the killing machine toil, and my introduction to the oyster pirates. True, the introduction had begun with drink, and the life promised to continue with drink. But was I to stay away from it for such reason? Wherever life ran free and great, there men drank. Romance and Adventure seemed always to go down the street locked arm in arm with John Barleycorn. To know the two, I must know the third. Or else I must go back to my free library books and read of the deeds of other men and do no deeds of my own save slave for ten cents an hour at a machine in a cannery.

No; I was not to be deterred from this brave life on the water by the fact that the water-dwellers had queer and expensive desires for beer and wine and whisky. What if their notions of happiness included the strange one of seeing me drink? When they persisted in buying the stuff and thrusting it upon me, why, I would drink it. It was the price I would pay for their comradeship. And I didn't have to get drunk. I had not got drunk the Sunday afternoon I arranged to buy the *Razzle Dazzle*, despite the fact that not one of the rest was sober. Well, I could go on into the future that way, drinking the stuff when it gave them pleasure that I should drink it, but carefully avoiding overdrinking.

9

GRADUAL AS was my development as a heavy drinker among the oyster pirates, the real heavy drinking came suddenly, and was the result, not of desire for alcohol, but of an intellectual conviction.

The more I saw of the life, the more I was enamoured of it. I can never forget my thrills the first night I took part in a concerted raid, when we assembled on board the *Annie*—rough men, big and unafraid, and weazened wharf-rats, some of them ex-convicts, all of them enemies of the law and meriting jail, in sea-boots and sea-gear, talking in gruff low voices, and 'Big' George with revolvers strapped about his waist to show that he meant business.

Oh, I know, looking back, that the whole thing was sordid and silly. But I was not looking back in those days when I was rubbing shoulders with John Barleycorn and beginning to accept him. The life was brave and wild, and I was living the adventure I had read so much about.

Nelson, 'Young Scratch' they called him, to distinguish him from 'Old Scratch', his father, sailed in the sloop *Reindeer*, partners with one 'Clam'. Clam was a dare-devil, but Nelson was a reckless maniac. He was twenty years old, with the body of a Hercules. When he was shot in Benicia, a couple of years later, the coroner said he was the greatest-shouldered man he had ever seen laid on a slab.

Nelson could not read or write. He had been 'dragged' up by his father on San Francisco Bay, and boats were second nature with him. His strength was prodigious, and his reputation along the water-front for violence was anything but savoury. He had Berserker rages and did mad, terrible things. I made his acquaintance the first cruise of the *Razzle Dazzle*, and saw him sail the *Reindeer* in a blow and dredge oysters all around the rest of us as we lay at two anchors, troubled with fear of going ashore.

He was some man, this Nelson; and when, passing by the Last Chance saloon, he spoke to me, I felt very proud. But try to imagine my pride when he promptly asked me in to have a drink. I stood at the bar and drank a glass of beer with him, and talked manfully of oysters, and boats, and of the mystery of who had put the load of buckshot through the *Annie*'s mainsail.

We talked and lingered at the bar. It seemed to me

strange that we lingered. We had had our beer. But who was I to lead the way outside when great Nelson chose to lean against the bar? After a few minutes, to my surprise, he asked me to have another drink, which I did. And still we talked, and Nelson evinced no intention of leaving the bar.

Bear with me while I explain the way of my reasoning and of my innocence. First of all, I was very proud to be in the company of Nelson, who was the most heroic figure among the oyster pirates and bay adventurers. Unfortunately for my stomach and mucous membranes, Nelson had a strange quirk of nature that made him find happiness in treating me to beer. I had no moral disinclination for beer, and just because I didn't like the taste of it and the weight of it was no reason I should forgo the honour of his company. It was his whim to drink beer, and to have me drink beer with him. Very well, I would put up with the passing discomfort.

So we continued to talk at the bar, and to drink beer ordered and paid for by Nelson. I think, now, when I look back upon it, that Nelson was curious. He wanted to find out just what kind of a gink I was. He wanted to see how many times I'd let him treat without offering to treat in return.

After I had drunk half a dozen glasses, my policy of temperateness in mind, I decided that I had had enough for that time. So I mentioned that I was going aboard the *Razzle Dazzle*, then lying at the city wharf, a hundred yards away.

I said good-bye to Nelson, and went on down the wharf. But John Barleycorn, to the extent of six glasses, went with me. My brain tingled and was very much alive. I was uplifted by my sense of manhood. I, a truly-true oyster pirate, was going aboard my own boat after hobnobbing in the Last Chance with Nelson, the greatest oyster pirate of us all. Strong in my brain was the vision of leaning against the bar and drinking beer. And curious it was, I decided, this whim of nature that made men happy in spending good money for beer for a fellow like me who didn't want it.

As I pondered this, I recollected that several times other men, in couples, had entered the Last Chance, and first one, then the other, had treated to drinks. I remembered, on the drunk on the *Idler*, how Scotty and the harpooner and myself had raked and scraped dimes and nickels with which to buy the whisky. Then came my boy code: when on a day a fellow gave another a 'cannon-ball' or a chunk of taffy, on some other day he would expect to receive back a cannon-ball or a chunk of taffy.

That was why Nelson had lingered at the bar. Having bought a drink, he had waited for me to buy one. *I had let him buy six drinks and never once offered to treat.* And he was the great Nelson! I could feel myself blushing with shame. I sat down on the stringer-piece of the wharf and buried my face in my hands. And the heat of my shame burned up my neck and into my cheeks and forehead. I have blushed many times in my life, but never have I experienced so terrible a blush as that one.

And sitting there on the stringer-piece in my shame, I did a great deal of thinking and transvaluing of values. I had been born poor. Poor I had lived. I had gone hungry on occasion. I had never had toys nor playthings like other children. My first memories of life were pinched by poverty. The pinch of poverty had been chronic. I was eight years old when I wore my first little undershirt actually sold in a store across the counter. And then it had been only one little undershirt. When it was soiled I had to return to the awful home-made things until it was washed. I had been so proud of it that I insisted on wearing it without any outer garment. For the first time I mutinied against my mother—mutinied myself into hysteria, until she let me wear the store undershirt so all the world could see.

Only a man who has undergone famine can properly value food; only sailors and desert-dwellers know the meaning of fresh water. And only a child, with a child's imagination, can come to know the meaning of things it has been long denied. I early discovered that the only things I could have were those I got for myself. My meagre childhood developed meagreness. The first things I had been able to get for myself had been cigarette pictures, cigarette posters, and cigarette albums. I had not had the spending of the money I earned, so I traded 'extra' newspapers for these treasures. I traded duplicates with the other boys, and circulating, as I did, all about town, I had greater opportunities for trading and acquiring.

It was not long before I had complete every series issued by every cigarette manufacturer—such as the Great Race Horses, Parisian Beauties, Women of All Nations, Flags of All Nations, Noted Actors, Champion Prize Fighters, etc. And each series I had three different ways: in the card from the cigarette package, in the poster, and in the album.

Then I began to accumulate duplicate sets, duplicate albums. I traded for other things that boys valued and which they usually bought with money given them by their parents. Naturally, they did not have the keen sense of values that I had, who was never given money to buy anything. I traded for postage-stamps, for minerals, for curios, for birds' eggs, for marbles (I had a more magnificent collection of agates than I have ever seen any boy possess—and the nucleus of the collection was a handful worth at least three dollars, which I had kept as security for twenty cents I loaned to a messenger-boy who was sent to reform school before he could redeem them).

I'd trade anything and everything for anything else, and turn it over in a dozen more trades until it was transmuted into something that was worth something. I was famous as a trader. I was notorious as a miser. I could even make a junkman weep when I had dealings with him. Other boys called me in to sell for them their collections of bottles, rags, iron, grain, and gunny-sacks, and five-gallon oil-cans—aye, and gave me a commission for doing it.

And this was the thrifty, close-fisted boy, accustomed to slave at a machine for ten cents an hour, who sat on the stringer-piece and considered the matter of beer at five cents a glass and gone in a moment with nothing to show for it. I was now with men I admired. I was proud to be with them. Had all my pinching and saving brought me the equivalent of one of the many thrills which had been mine since I came among the oyster pirates? Then what was worth while—money or thrills? These men had no horror of squandering a nickel, or many nickels. They were magnificently careless of money, calling up eight men to drink whisky at ten cents a glass, as French Frank had done. Why, Nelson had just spent sixty cents on beer for the two of us.

Which was it to be? I was aware that I was making a grave decision. I was deciding between money and men, between niggardliness and romance. Either I must throw overboard all my old values of money and look upon it as something to be flung about wastefully, or I must throw overboard my comradeship with these men whose peculiar quirks made them like strong drink.

I retracted my steps up the wharf to the Last Chance, where Nelson still stood outside. 'Come on and have a beer,' I invited. Again we stood at the bar and drank and talked, but this time it was I who paid ten cents! a whole hour of my labour at a machine for a drink of something I didn't want and which tasted rotten. But it wasn't difficult. I had achieved a concept. Money no longer counted. It was comradeship that counted. 'Have another?' I said. And we had another, and I paid for it. Nelson, with the wisdom of the skilled drinker, said to the barkeeper, 'Make mine a small one, Johnny.' Johnny nodded and gave him a glass that contained only a third as much as the glasses we had been drinking. Yet the charge was the same—five cents.

By this time I was getting nicely jingled, so such extravagance didn't hurt me much. Besides, I was learning. There was more in this buying of drinks than mere quantity. I got my finger on it. There was a stage when the beer

3*

didn't count at all, but just the spirit of comradeship of drinking together. And, ha!—another thing! I, too, could call for small beers and minimize by two-thirds the detestable freightage with which comradeship burdened one.

'I had to go aboard to get some money,' I remarked casually, as we drank, in the hope Nelson would take it as an explanation of why I had let him treat six consecutive times.

'Oh, well, you didn't have to do that,' he answered. 'Johnny'll trust a fellow like you—won't you, Johnny?'

'Sure,' Johnny agreed, with a smile.

'How much you got down against me?' Nelson queried.

Johnny pulled out the book he kept behind the bar, found Nelson's page, and added up the account of several dollars. At once I became possessed with a desire to have a page in that book. Almost it seemed the final badge of manhood.

After a couple more drinks, for which I insisted on paying, Nelson decided to go. We parted true comradely, and I wandered down the wharf to the *Razzle Dazzle*. Spider was just building the fire for supper.

'Where'd you get it?' he grinned up at me through the open companion.

'Oh, I've been with Nelson,' I said carelessly trying to hide my pride.

Then an idea came to me. Here was another one of them. Now that I had achieved my concept, I might as well practise it thoroughly. 'Come on,' I said, 'up to Johnny's and have a drink.'

Going up the wharf, we met Clam coming down. Clam was Nelson's partner, and he was a fine, brave, handsome, moustached man of thirty—everything, in short, that his nickname did not connote. 'Come on,' I said, 'and have a drink.' He came. As we turned into the Last Chance, there was Pat, the Queen's brother, coming out.

'What's your hurry?' I greeted him. 'We're having a drink. Come on along.' 'I've just had one,' he demurred. 'What of it?—we're having one now,' I retorted. And Pat consented to join us, and I melted my way into his good graces with a couple of glasses of beer. Oh! I was learning things that afternoon about John Barleycorn. There was more in him than the bad taste when you swallowed him. Here, at the absurd cost of ten cents, a gloomy, grouchy individual, who threatened to become an enemy, was made into a good friend. He became even genial, his looks were kindly, and our voices mellowed together as we talked water-front and oyster-bed gossip.

'Small beer for me, Johnny,' I said, when the others had ordered schooners. Yes, and I said it like the accustomed drinker, carelessly, casually, as a sort of spontaneous thought that had just occurred to me. Looking back, I am confident that the only one there who guessed I was a tyro at bar-drinking was Johnny Heinhold.

'Where'd he get it?' I overheard Spider confidentially ask Johnny.

'Oh, he's been sousin' here with Nelson all afternoon,' was Johnny's answer.

I never let on that I'd heard, but *proud*? Aye, even the barkeeper was giving me a recommendation as a man. '*He's been sousin' here with Nelson all afternoon.*' Magic words! The accolade delivered by a barkeeper with a beer glass!

I remembered that French Frank had treated Johnny the day I bought the *Razzle Dazzle*. The glasses were filled and we were ready to drink. 'Have something yourself, Johnny,' I said, with an air of having intended to say it all the time, but of having been a trifle remiss because of the interesting conversation I had been holding with Clam and Pat.

Johnny looked at me with quick sharpness, divining, I am positive, the strides I was making in my education, and poured himself whisky from his private bottle. This hit me for a moment on my thrifty side. He had taken a ten-cent drink when the rest of us were drinking five-cent drinks! But the hurt was only for a moment. I dismissed it as ignoble, remembered my concept, and did not give myself away.

'You'd better put me down in the book for this,' I said, when we had finished the drink. And I had the satisfaction of seeing a fresh page devoted to my name and a charge pencilled for a round of drinks amounting to thirty cents. And I glimpsed, as through a golden haze, a future wherein that page would be much charged, and crossed off, and charged again.

I treated a second time around, and then, to my amazement, Johnny redeemed himself in that matter of the ten-cent drink. He treated us around from behind the bar, and I decided that he had arithmetically evened things up handsomely.

'Let's go around to the St Louis House,' Spider suggested when we got outside. Pat, who had been shovelling coal all day, had gone home, and Clam had gone upon the *Reindeer* to cook supper.

So around Spider and I went to the St Louis House— my first visit—a huge bar-room, where perhaps fifty men, mostly longshoremen, were congregated. And there I met Soup Kennedy for the second time, and Billy Kelley. And Smith, of the *Annie*, drifted in—he, of the belt-buckled revolvers. And Nelson showed up. And I met others, including the Vigy brothers, who ran the place, and, chiefest of all, Joe Goose, with the wicked eyes, the twisted nose, and the flowered vest, who played the harmonica like a roystering angel and went on the most atrocious tears that even the Oakland water-front could conceive of and admire.

As I bought drinks—others treated as well—the thought flickered across my mind that Mammy Jennie wasn't going to be repaid much on her loan out of that week's earnings of the *Razzle Dazzle*. 'But what of it?' I thought, or rather, John Barleycorn thought it for me. 'You're a man and you're getting acquainted with men. Mammy Jennie doesn't need the money as promptly as all that. She isn't starving. You know that. She's got other money in the bank. Let her wait, and pay her back gradually.'

And thus it was I learned another trait of John Barleycorn. He inhibits morality. Wrong conduct that it is impossible for one to do sober, is done quite easily when one is not sober. In fact, it is the only thing one can do, for John Barleycorn's inhibition rises like a wall between one's immediate desires and long-learned morality.

I dismissed my thought of debt to Mammy Jennie and proceeded to get acquainted at the trifling expense of some trifling money and a jingle that was growing unpleasant. Who took me on board and put me to bed that night I do not know, but I imagine it must have been Spider.

10

AND SO I won my manhood's spurs. My status on the water-front and with the oyster pirates became immediately excellent. I was looked upon as a good fellow, as well as no coward. And somehow, from the day I achieved that concept sitting on the stringer-piece of the Oakland City Wharf, I have never cared much for money. No one has ever considered me a miser since, while my carelessness of money is a source of anxiety and worry to some that knew me.

So completely did I break with my parsimonious past that I sent word home to my mother to call in the boys of the neighbourhood and give to them all my collections. I never even cared to learn what boys got what collections. I was a man now, and I made a clean sweep of everything that bound me to my boyhood.

My reputation grew. When the story went around the water-front of how French Frank had tried to run me down with his schooner, and of how I had stood on the deck of the *Razzle Dazzle*, a cocked double-barrelled shot-

gun in my hands, steering with my feet and holding her to
her course, and compelled him to put up his wheel and
keep away, the water-front decided that there was something in me despite my youth. And I continued to show
what was in me. There were the times I brought the
Razzle Dazzle in with a bigger load of oysters than any
other two-man craft; there was the time when we raided
far down in Lower Bay, and mine was the only craft back
at daylight to the anchorage off Asparagus Island; there
was the Thursday night we raced for market and I brought
the *Razzle Dazzle* in without a rudder, first of the fleet,
and skimmed the cream of the Friday morning trade; and
there was the time I brought her in from the Upper Bay
under a jib, when Scotty burned my mainsail. (Yes; it was
Scotty of the *Idler* adventure. Irish had followed Spider
on board the *Razzle Dazzle*, and Scotty, turning up, had
taken Irish's place.)

But the things I did on the water only partly counted.
What completed everything, and won for me the title of
'Prince of the Oyster Beds', was that I was a good fellow
ashore with my money, buying drinks like a man. I little
dreamed that the time would come when the Oakland
water-front, which had shocked me at first would be
shocked and annoyed by the devilry of the things I did.

But always the life was tied up with drinking. The
saloons are poor men's clubs. Saloons are congregating
places. We engaged to meet one another in saloons. We
celebrated our good fortune or wept our grief in saloons.
We got acquainted in saloons.

Can I ever forget the afternoon I met 'Old Scratch',
Nelson's father? It was in the Last Chance. Johnny
Heinhold introduced us. That Old Scratch was Nelson's
father was noteworthy enough. But there was more in it
than that. He was owner and master of the scow-schooner
Annie Mine, and some day I might ship as a sailor with
him. Still more, he was romance. He was a blue-eyed,
yellow-haired, raw-boned Viking, big-bodied and strong-

muscled despite his age. And he had sailed the seas in ships of all nations in the old savage sailing days.

I had heard many weird tales about him, and worshipped him from a distance. It took the saloon to bring us together. Even so, our acquaintance might have been no more than a hand-grip and a word—he was a laconic old fellow—had it not been for the drinking.

'Have a drink,' I said, with promptitude, after the pause which I had learned good form in drinking dictates. Of course, while we drank our beer, which I had paid for, it was incumbent on him to listen to me and to talk to me. And Johnny, like a true host, made the tactful remarks that enabled us to find mutual topics of conversation. And of course, having drunk my beer, Captain Nelson must now buy beer in turn. This led to more talking, and Johnny drifted out of the conversation to wait on other customers.

The more beer Captain Nelson and I drank, the better we got acquainted. In me he found an appreciative listener, who, by virtue of book-reading, knew much about the sea-life he had lived. So he drifted back to his wild young days, and spun many a rare yarn for me, while we downed beer, treat by treat, all through a blessed summer afternoon. And it was only John Barleycorn that made possible that long afternoon with the old sea-dog.

It was Johnny Heinhold who secretly warned me across the bar that I was getting pickled and advised me to take small beers. But as long as Captain Nelson drank large beers, my pride forbade anything else than large beers. And not until the skipper ordered his first small beer did I order one for myself. Oh, when we came to a lingering fond farewell, I was drunk. But I had the satisfaction of seeing Old Scratch as drunk as I. My youthful modesty scarcely let me dare believe that the hardened old buccaneer was even more drunk.

And afterwards, from Spider, and Pat, and Clam, and Johnny Heinhold, and others, came the tips that Old Scratch liked me and had nothing but good words for the fine lad I was. Which was the more remarkable, because he was known as a savage, cantankerous old cuss who never liked anybody. (His very nickname, 'Scratch', arose from a Berserker trick of his, in fighting, of tearing off his opponent's face.) And that I had won his friendship, all thanks were due to John Barleycorn. I have given the incident merely as an example of the multitudinous lures and draws and services by which John Barleycorn wins his followers.

II

AND STILL there arose in me no desire for alcohol, no chemical demand. In years and years of heavy drinking, drinking did not beget the desire. Drinking was the way of the life I led, the way of the men with whom I lived. While away on my cruises on the bay, I took no drink along; and while out on the bay the thought of the desirableness of a drink never crossed my mind. It was not until I tied the *Razzle Dazzle* up to the wharf and got ashore in the congregating places of men, where drink flowed, that the buying of drinks for other men, and the accepting of drinks from other men, developed upon me as a social duty and a manhood rite.

Then, too, there were the times, lying at the city wharf or across the estuary on the sandspit, when the Queen, and her sister, and her brother Pat, and Mrs. Hadley came aboard. It was my boat, I was host, and I could only dispense hospitality in the terms of their understanding of it. So I would rush Spider, or Irish, or Scotty, or whoever was my crew, with the can for beer and the demijohn for red wine. And again, lying at the wharf disposing of my oysters, there were dusky twilights when big policemen and plain-clothes men stole on board. And because we lived in the shadow of the police, we opened oysters and fed them to them with squirts of pepper sauce, and rushed the growler or got stronger stuff in bottles.

Drink as I would, I couldn't come to like John Barleycorn. I valued him extremely well for his associations, but not for the taste of him. All the time I was striving to be a man amongst men, and all the time I nursed secret and shameful desires for candy. But I would have died before I'd let anybody guess it. I used to indulge in lonely debauches, on nights when I knew my crew was going to sleep ashore. I would go up to the Free Library, exchange my books, buy a quarter's worth of all sorts of candy that chewed and lasted, sneak aboard the *Razzle Dazzle*, lock myself in the cabin, go to bed, and lie there long hours of bliss, reading and chewing candy. And those were the only times I felt that I got my real money's worth. Dollars and dollars, across the bar, couldn't buy the satisfaction that twenty-five cents did in a candy store.

As my drinking grew heavier, I began to note more and more that it was in the drinking bouts the purple passages occurred. Drunks were always memorable. At such times things happened. Men like Joe Goose dated existence from drunk to drunk. The longshoremen all looked forward to their Saturday night drunk. We of the oyster boats waited until we had disposed of our cargoes before we got really started, though a scattering of drinks and a meeting of a chance friend sometimes precipitated an accidental drunk.

In ways, the accidental drunks were the best. Stranger and more exciting things happened at such times. As, for instance, the Sunday when Nelson and French Frank and Captain Spink stole the stolen salmon boat from Whisky Bob and Nicky the Greek. Changes had taken place in the personnel of the oyster boats. Nelson had got into a fight with Bill Kelley on the *Annie* and was carrying a bullet-hole through his left hand. Also, having quarrelled with Clam and broken partnership, Nelson had sailed the *Reindeer*, his arm in a sling, with a crew of two deepwater sailors, and he had sailed so madly as to frighten them ashore. Such was the tale of his recklessness they spread, that no one on the water-front would go out with Nelson. So the *Reindeer*, crewless, lay across the estuary at the sandspit. Beside her lay the *Razzle Dazzle* with a burned mainsail and Scotty and me on board. Whisky Bob had fallen out with French Frank and gone on a raid 'up river' with Nicky the Greek.

The result of this raid was a brand-new Columbia River salmon boat, stolen from an Italian fisherman. We oyster pirates were all visited by the searching Italian, and we were convinced, from what we knew of their movements, that Whisky Bob and Nicky the Greek were the guilty parties. But where was the salmon boat? Hundreds of Greek and Italian fishermen, up river and down bay, had searched every slough and tule patch for it. When the owner despairingly offered a reward of fifty dollars, our interest increased and the mystery deepened.

One Sunday morning old Captain Spink paid me a visit. The conversation was confidential. He had just been fishing in his skiff in the old Alameda ferry slip. As the tide went down, he had noticed a rope tied to a pile under water and leading downward. In vain he had tried to heave up what was fast on the other end. Farther along, to another pile, was a similar rope, leading downward and unheavable. Without doubt, it was the missing salmon boat. If we restored it to its rightful owner there was fifty dollars in it for us. But I had queer ethical notions about honour amongst thieves, and declined to have anything to do with the affair.

But French Frank had quarrelled with Whisky Bob, and Nelson was also an enemy. (Poor Whisky Bob!—without viciousness, goodnatured, generous, born weak, raised poorly, with an irresistible chemical demand for alcohol, still prosecuting his vocation of bay pirate, his body was picked up, not long afterward, beside a dock where it had sunk full of gunshot wounds.) Within an hour after I had rejected Captain Spink's proposal, I saw him sail down the estuary on board the *Reindeer* with Nelson. Also, French Frank went by on his schooner.

It was not long ere they sailed back up the estuary, curiously side by side. As they headed in for the sandspit, the submerged salmon boat could be seen, gunwales awash and held up from sinking by ropes fast to the schooner and the sloop. The tide was half out, and they sailed squarely in on the sand, grounding in a row, with the salmon boat in the middle.

Immediately Hans, one of French Frank's sailors, was into a skiff and pulling rapidly for the north shore. The big demijohn in the sternsheets told his errand. They couldn't wait a moment to celebrate the fifty dollars they had so easily earned. It is the way of the devotees of John Barleycorn. When good fortune comes they drink. When they have no fortune, they drink to the hope of good fortune. If fortune be ill, they drink to forget it. If they meet a friend, they drink. If they quarrel with a friend and lose him, they drink. If their love-making be crowned with success, they are so happy they needs must drink. If they be jilted, they drink for the contrary reason. And if they haven't anything to do at all, why, they take a drink, secure in the knowledge that when they have taken a sufficient number of drinks the maggots will start crawling in their brains and they will have their hands full with things to do. When they are sober they want to drink; and when they have drunk they want to drink more.

Of course, as fellow comrades, Scotty and I were called in for the drinking. We helped to make a hole in that fifty dollars not yet received. The afternoon, from just an ordinary common summer Sunday afternoon, became a gorgeous, purple afternoon. We all talked and sang and ranted and bragged, and ever French Frank and Nelson sent more drinks around. We lay in full sight of the Oakland water-front, and the noise of our revels attracted friends. Skiff after skiff crossed the estuary and hauled up on the sandspit, while Hans' work was cut out for him— ever to row back and forth for more supplies of booze.

Then Whisky Bob and Nicky the Greek arrived, sober, indignant, outraged in that their fellow pirates had raised their plant. French Frank, aided by John Barleycorn, orated hypocritically about virtue and honesty, and, despite his fifty years, got Whisky Bob out on the sand and proceeded to lick him. When Nicky the Greek jumped in with a short-handled shovel to Whisky Bob's assistance, short work was made of him by Hans. And of course, when the bleeding remnants of Bob and Nicky were sent packing in their skiff, the event must needs be celebrated in further carousal.

By this time, our visitors being numerous, we were a large crowd compounded of many nationalities and diverse temperaments, all aroused by John Barleycorn, all restraints cast off. Old quarrels revived, ancient hates flared up. Fight was in the air. And whenever a longshoreman remembered something against a scow-schooner sailor, or vice versa, or an oyster pirate remembered or was remembered, a fist shot out and another fight was on. And every fight was made up in more rounds of drinks, wherein the combatants, aided and abetted by the rest of us, embraced each other and pledged undying friendship.

And, of all times, Soup Kennedy selected this time to come to retrieve an old shirt of his, left aboard the *Reindeer* from the trip he sailed with Clam. He had espoused Clam's side of the quarrel with Nelson. Also, he had been drinking in the St. Louis House, so that it was John Barleycorn who led him to the sandspit in quest of his old shirt. Few words started the fray. He locked with Nelson in the cockpit of the *Reindeer*, and in the mix-up barely escaped being brained by an iron bar wielded by irate French Frank—irate because a two-handed man had attacked a one-handed man. (If the *Reindeer* still floats, the dent of the iron bar remains in the hard-wood rail of her cockpit.)

But Nelson pulled his bandaged hand, bullet-perforated, out of its sling, and, held by us, wept and roared his Berserker belief that he would lick Soup Kennedy onehanded. And we let them loose on the sand. Once, when it looked as if Nelson were getting the worst of it, French

Frank and John Barleycorn sprang unfairly into the fight. Scotty protested and reached for French Frank, who whirled upon him and fell on top of him in a pummelling clinch after a sprawl of twenty feet across the sand. In the course of separating these two, half a dozen fights started amongst the rest of us. These fights were finished, one way or the other, or we separated them with drinks, while all the time Nelson and Soup Kennedy fought on. Occasionally we returned to them and gave advice, such as, when they lay exhausted in the sand, unable to strike a blow, 'Throw sand in his eyes.' And they threw sand in each other's eyes, recuperated, and fought on to successive exhaustions.

And now, of all this that is squalid, and ridiculous, and bestial, try to think what it meant to me, a youth not yet sixteen, burning with the spirit of adventure, fancy-filled with tales of buccaneers and sea-rovers, sacks of cities and conflicts of armed men, and imagination-maddened by the stuff I had drunk. It was life raw and naked, wild and free—the only life of that sort which my birth in time and space permitted me to attain. And more than that. It carried a promise. It was the beginning. From the sandspit the way led out through the Golden Gate to the vastness of adventure of all the world, where battles would be fought, not for old shirts and over stolen salmon boats, but for high purposes and romantic ends.

And because I told Scotty what I thought of his letting an old man like French Frank get away with him, we too, brawled and added to the festivity of the sandspit. And Scotty threw up his job as crew, and departed in the night with a pair of blankets belonging to me. During the night, while the oyster pirates lay stupefied in their bunks, the schooner and the *Reindeer* floated on the high water and swung about to their anchors. The salmon boat, still filled with rocks and water, rested on the bottom.

In the morning, early, I heard wild cries from the *Reindeer*, and tumbled out in the chill grey to see a spectacle that made the water-front laugh for days. The beautiful

salmon boat lay on the hard sand, squashed flat as a pan-
cake, while on it were perched French Frank's schooner
and the *Reindeer*. Unfortunately two of the *Reindeer*'s
planks had been crushed in by the stout oak stem of the
salmon boat. The rising tide had flowed through the hole,
and just awakened Nelson by getting into his bunk with
him. I lent a hand, and we pumped the *Reindeer* out and
repaired the damage.

Then Nelson cooked breakfast, and while we ate we
considered the situation. He was broke. So was I. The
fifty dollars reward would never be paid for that pitiful
mess of splinters on the sand beneath us. He had a
wounded hand and no crew. I had a burned mainsail and
no crew. 'What d'ye say, you and me?' Nelson queried.
'I'll go you,' was my answer. And thus I became partners
with 'Young Scratch' Nelson, the wildest, maddest of them
all. We borrowed the money for an outfit of grub from
Johnny Heinhold, filled our water-barrels, and sailed away
that day for the oyster-beds.

12

NOR HAVE I ever regretted those months of mad devilry I
put in with Nelson. He *could* sail, even if he did frighten
every man that sailed with him. To steer to miss destruction by an inch or an instant was his joy. To do what
everybody else did not dare attempt to do was his pride.
Never to reef down was his mania, and in all the time
I spent with him, blow high or low, the *Reindeer* was
never reefed. Nor was she ever dry. We strained her open
and sailed her open and sailed her open continually. And
we abandoned the Oakland water-front and went wider
afield for our adventures.

And all this glorious passage in my life was made possible for me by John Barleycorn. And this is my com-

plaint against John Barleycorn. Here I was, thirsting for the wild life of adventure, and the only way for me to win to it was through John Barleycorn's mediation. It was the way of the men who lived the life. Did I wish to live the life, I must live it the way they did. It was by virtue of drinking that I gained that partnership and comradeship with Nelson. Had I drunk only the beer he paid for, or had I declined to drink at all, I should never have been selected by him as a partner. He wanted a partner who would meet him on the social side, as well as the work side of life.

I abandoned myself to the life, and developed the misconception that the secret of John Barleycorn lay in going on mad drunks, rising through the successive stages that only an iron constitution could endure to final stupefaction and swinish unconsciousness. I did not like the taste, so I drank for the sole purpose of getting drunk, of getting hopelessly, helplessly drunk. And I, who had saved and scraped, traded like a Shylock and made junkmen weep; I, who had stood aghast when French Frank, at a single stroke, spent eighty cents for whisky for eight men; I turned myself loose with a more lavish disregard for money than any of them.

I remember going ashore one night with Nelson. In my pocket were one hundred and eighty dollars. It was my intention, first, to buy me some clothes, after that, some drinks. I needed the clothes. All I possessed were on me, and they were as follows: a pair of sea-boots that providentially leaked the water out as fast as it ran in, a pair of fifty-cent overalls, a forty-cent cotton shirt, and a sou'wester. I had no hat, so I had to wear the sou'wester, and it will be noted that I have listed neither underclothes nor socks. I didn't own any.

To reach the stores where clothes could be bought, we had to pass a dozen saloons. So I bought me the drinks first. I never got to the clothing stores. In the morning, broke, poisoned, but contented, I came back on board, and we set sail. I possessed only the clothes I had gone ashore in, and not a cent remained of the one hundred and eighty dollars. It might well be deemed impossible, by those who have never tried it, that in twelve hours a lad can spend all of one hundred and eighty dollars for drinks, I know otherwise.

And I had no regrets. I was proud. I had shown them I could spend with the best of them. Amongst strong men I had proved myself strong. I had clinched again, as I had often clinched, my right to the title of 'Prince'. Also, my attitude may be considered, in part, as a reaction from my childhood's meagreness and my childhood's excessive toil. Possibly my inchoate thought was: Better to reign among booze-fighters a prince than to toil twelve hours a day at a machine for ten cents an hour. There are no purple passages in machine toil. But if the spending of one hundred and eighty dollars in twelve hours isn't a purple passage, then I'd like to know what is.

Oh, I skip much of the details of my trafficking with John Barleycorn during this period, and shall only mention events that will throw light on John Barleycorn's ways. There were three things that enabled me to pursue this heavy drinking: first, a magnificent constitution far better than the average; second, the healthy open-air life on the water; and third, the fact that I drank irregularly. While out on the water, we never carried any drink along.

The world was opening up to me. Already I knew several hundred miles of the water-ways of it, and of the towns and cities and fishing hamlets on the shores. Came the whisper to range farther. I had not found it yet. There was more behind. But even this much of the world was too wide for Nelson. He wearied for his beloved Oakland water-front, and when he elected to return to it we separated in all friendliness.

I now made the old town of Benicia, on the Carquinez Straits, my headquarters. In a cluster of fishermen's arks, moored in the tules on the water-front, dwelt a congenial crowd of drinkers and vagabonds, and I joined them. I had longer spells ashore, between fooling with salmon fishing and making raids up and down bay and rivers as a deputy fish patrolman, and I drank more and learned more about drinking. I held my own with any one, drink for drink; and often drank more than my share to show the strength of my manhood. When, on a morning, my unconscious carcass was disentangled from the nets on the drying-frames, whither I had stupidly, blindly crawled the night before; and when the waterfront talked it over many a giggle and laugh and another drink; I was proud indeed. It was an exploit.

And when I never drew a sober breath, on one stretch, for three solid weeks, I was certain I had reached the top. Surely, in that direction, one could go no farther. It was time for me to move on. For always, drunk or sober, at the back of my consciousness something whispered that this carousing and bay-adventuring was not all of life. This whisper was my good fortune. I happened to be so made that I could hear it calling, always calling, out and away over the world. It was not canniness on my part. It was curiosity, desire to know, an unrest and a seeking for things wonderful that I seemed somehow to have glimpsed or guessed. What was this life for, I demanded, if this were all? No; there was something more, away and beyond. (And, in relation to my much later development as a drinker, this whisper, this promise of the things at the back of life, must be noted, for it was destined to play a dire part in my more recent wrestlings with John Barleycorn.)

But what gave immediacy to my decision to move on was a trick John Barleycorn played me—a monstrous, incredible trick that showed abysses of intoxication hitherto undreamed. At one o'clock in the morning, after a prodigious drunk, I was tottering aboard a sloop at the end of the wharf, intending to go to sleep. The tides sweep through Carquinez Straits as in a mill-race, and the full ebb was on when I stumbled overboard. There was nobody on the wharf, nobody on the sloop. I was borne away by the current. I was not startled. I thought the misadventure delightful. I was a good swimmer, and in my inflamed condition the contact of the water with my skin soothed me like cool linen.

And then John Barleycorn played me his maniacal trick. Some maundering fancy of going out with the tide suddenly obsessed me. I had never been morbid. Thoughts of suicide had never entered my head. And now that they entered, I thought it fine, a splendid culminating, a perfect rounding off of my short but exciting career. I, who had never known girl's love, nor woman's love, nor the love of children; who had never played in the wide joy-fields of art, nor climbed the star-cool heights of philosophy, nor seen with my eyes more than a pinpoint's surface of the gorgeous world; I decided that this was all, that I had seen all, lived all, been all, that was worth while, and that now was the time to cease. This was the trick of John Barleycorn, laying me by the heels of my imagination and in a drug-dream dragging me to death.

Oh, he was convincing. I had really experienced all of life, and it didn't amount to much. The swinish drunkenness in which I had lived for months (this was accompanied by the sense of degradation and the old feeling of conviction of sin) was the last and best, and I could see for myself what it was worth. There were all the broken-down old bums and loafers I had bought drinks for. That was what remained of life. Did I want to become like them? A thousand times no; and I wept tears of sweet sadness over my glorious youth going out with the tide. (And who has not seen the weeping drunk, the melancholic drunk? They are to be found in all the bar-rooms, if they can find no other listener, telling their sorrows to the bar-keeper, who is paid to listen.)

The water was delicious. It was a man's way to die. John Barleycorn changed the tune he played in my drink-maddened brain. Away with tears and regret. It was a hero's death, and by the hero's own hand and will. So I struck up my death-chant and was singing it lustily, when the gurgle and splash of the current-riffles in my ears reminded me of my more immediate situation.

Below the town of Benicia, where the *Solano* wharf projects, the Straits widen out into what bay-farers call the 'Bight of Turner's Shipyard'. I was in the shore-tide that swept under the *Solano* wharf and on into the bight. I knew of old the power of the suck which developed when the tide swung around the end of Dead Man's Island and drove straight for the wharf. I didn't want to go through those piles. It wouldn't be nice, and I might lose an hour in the bight on my way out with the tide.

I undressed in the water and struck out with a strong, single-overhand stroke, crossing the current at right-angles. Nor did I cease until, by the wharf lights, I knew I was safe to sweep by the end. Then I turned over and rested. The stroke had been a telling one, and I was a little time in recovering my breath.

I was elated, for I had succeeded in avoiding the suck. I started to raise my death-chant again—a purely extemporized farrago of a drug-crazed youth. 'Don't sing—yet,' whispered John Barleycorn. 'The *Solano* runs all night. There are railroad men on the wharf. They will hear you, and come out in a boat and rescue you, and you don't want to be rescued.' I certainly didn't. What? Be robbed of my hero's death? Never. And I lay on my back in the starlight, watching the familiar wharf-lights go by, red and green and white, and bidding sad sentimental farewell to them, each and all.

When I was well clear, in mid-channel, I sang again. Sometimes I swam a few strokes, but in the main I contented myself with floating and dreaming long drunken dreams. Before daylight, the chill of the water and the passage of the hours had sobered me sufficiently to make me wonder what portion of the Straits I was in, and also to wonder if the turn of the tide wouldn't catch me and take me back ere I had drifted out into San Pablo Bay.

Next I discovered that I was very weary and very cold, and quite sober, and that I didn't in the least want to be drowned. I could make out the Selby Smelter on the

Contra Costa shore and the Mare Island lighthouse. I
started to swim for the Solano shore, but was too weak and
chilled, and made so little headway, and at the cost of such
painful effort, that I gave it up and contented myself with
floating, now and then giving a stroke to keep my balance
in the tide-rips which were increasing their commotion
on the surface of the water. And I knew fear. I was sober
now, and I didn't want to die. I discovered scores of
reasons for living. And the more reasons I discovered, the
more liable it seemed that I was going to drown anyway.

Daylight, after I had been four hours in the water,
found me in a parlous condition in the tide-rips off Mare
Island light, where the swift ebbs from Vallejo Straits and
Carquinez Straits were fighting with each other, and
where, at that particular moment, they were fighting the
flood tide setting up against them from San Pablo Bay.
A stiff breeze had sprung up, and the crisp little waves
were persistently lapping into my mouth, and I was beginning to swallow salt water. With my swimmer's knowledge, I knew the end was near. And then the boat came
—a Greek fisherman running in for Vallejo; and again
I had been saved from John Barleycorn by my constitution
and physical vigour.

And, in passing, let me note that this maniacal trick
John Barleycorn played me is nothing uncommon. An
absolute statistic of the percentage of suicides due to John
Barleycorn would be appalling. In my case, healthy, normal, young, full of the joy of life, the suggestion to kill
myself was unusual; but it must be taken into account
that it came on the heels of a long carouse, when my nerves
and brain were fearfully poisoned, and that the dramatic,
romantic side of my imagination, drink-maddened to
lunacy, was delighted with the suggestion. And yet, the
older, more morbid drinkers, more jaded with life and
more disillusioned, who kill themselves, do so usually after
a long debauch, when their nerves and brains are
thoroughly poison-soaked.

13

So I left Benicia, where John Barleycorn had nearly got me, and ranged wider afield in pursuit of the whisper from the back of life to come and find. And wherever I ranged, the way lay along alcohol-drenched roads. Men still congregated in saloons. They were the poor man's clubs, and they were the only clubs to which I had access. I could get acquainted in saloons. I could go into a saloon and talk with any man. In the strange towns and cities I wandered through, the only place for me to go was the saloons. I was no longer a stranger in any town the moment I had entered a saloon.

And right here let me break in with experiences no later than last year. I harnessed four horses to a light trap, took Charmian along, and drove for three months and a half over the wildest mountain parts of California and Oregon. Each morning I did my regular day's work of writing fiction. That completed, I drove on through the middle of the day and the afternoon to the next stop. But the irregularity of occurrence of stopping-places, coupled with widely varying road conditions, made it necessary to plan, the day before, each day's drive and my work. I must know when I was to start driving in order to start writing in time to finish my day's output. Thus, on occasion, when the drive was to be long, I would be up and at my writing by five in the morning. On easier driving days I might not start writing till nine o'clock.

But how to plan? As soon as I arrived in a town, and put the horses up, on the way from the stables to the hotel I dropped into the saloons. First thing, a drink—oh, I wanted the drink, but also it must not be forgotten that, because of wanting to know things, it was in this very way I had learned to want a drink. Well, the first thing, a drink. 'Have something yourself,' to the barkeeper. And then, as we drink, my opening query about roads and stopping-places on ahead.

'Let me see,' the barkeeper will say, 'there's the road across Tarwater Divide. That used to be good. I was over it three years ago. But it was blocked this spring. Say, I'll tell you what. I'll ask Jerry ——' And the barkeeper turns and addresses some man sitting at a table or leaning against the bar farther along, and who may be Jerry, or Tom, or Bill. 'Say, Jerry, how about the Tarwater road? You was down to Wilkins last week.'

And while Bill or Jerry or Tom is beginning to unlimber his thinking and speaking apparatus, I suggest that he join us in the drink. Then discussions arise about the advisability of this road or that, what the best stopping-places may be, what running time I may expect to make, where the best trout streams are, and so forth, in which other men join, and which are punctuated with more drinks.

Two or three more saloons, and I accumulate a warm jingle and come pretty close to knowing everybody in town, all about the town, and a fair deal about the surrounding country. I know the lawyers, editors, business men, local politicians, and the visiting ranchers, hunters, and miners, so that by evening, when Charmian and I stroll down the main street and back, she is astounded by the number of my acquaintances in that totally strange town.

And thus is demonstrated a service John Barleycorn renders, a service by which he increases his power over men. And over the world, wherever I have gone, during all the years, it has been the same. It may be a cabaret in the Latin Quarter, a café in some obscure Italian village, a boozing ken in sailor-town, and it may be up at the club over Scotch and soda; but always it will be where John Barleycorn makes fellowship that I get immediately in touch, and meet, and know. And in the good days coming, when John Barleycorn will have been banished out of existence along with the other barbarisms, some other institution than the saloon will have to obtain, some other congregating place of men where strange men and stranger men may get in touch, and meet, and know.

But to return to my narrative. When I turned my back on Benicia, my way led through saloons. I had developed no moral theories against drinking, and I disliked as much as ever the taste of the stuff. But I had grown respectfully suspicious of John Barleycorn. I could not forget that trick he had played on me—on *me* who did not want to die. So I continued to drink, and to keep a sharp eye on John Barleycorn, resolved to resist all future suggestions of self-destruction.

In strange towns I made immediate acquaintances in the saloons. When I hoboed, and hadn't the price of a bed, a saloon was the only place that would receive me and give me a chair by the fire. I could go into a saloon and wash up, brush my clothes, and comb my hair. And saloons were always so damnably convenient. They were everywhere in my western country.

I couldn't go into the dwellings of strangers that way. Their doors were not open to me; no seats were there for me by their fires. Also, churches and preachers I had never known. And from what I didn't know I was not attracted toward them. Besides, there was no glamour about them, no haze of romance, no promise of adventure. They were the sort with whom things never happened. They lived and remained always in the one place, creatures of order and system, narrow, limited, restrained. They were without greatness, without imagination, without camaraderie. It was the good fellows, easy and genial, daring, and, on occasion, mad, that I wanted to know—the fellows, generous-hearted and -handed, and not rabbit-hearted.

And here is another complaint I bring against John Barleycorn. It is these good fellows that he gets—the fellows with the fire and the go in them, who have bigness, and warmness, and the best of the human weaknesses. And John Barleycorn puts out the fire, and soddens the agility, and, when he does not more immediately kill them or make maniacs of them, he coarsens and grossens them, twists

and malforms them out of the original goodness and fine-
ness of their natures.

Oh!—and I speak out of later knowledge—Heaven fore-
fend me from the most of the average run of male humans
who are not good fellows, the ones cold of heart and cold
of head who don't smoke, drink, or swear, or do much of
anything else that is brave, and resentful, and stinging,
because in their feeble fibres there has never been the
stir and prod of life to well over its boundaries and be
devilish and daring. One doesn't meet these in saloons,
nor rallying to lost causes, nor flaming on the adventure-
paths, nor loving as God's own mad lovers. They are too
busy keeping their feet dry, conserving their heartbeats,
and making unlovely life-successes of their spirit-medioc-
rity.

And so I draw the indictment home to John Barleycorn.
It is just those, the good fellows, the worth while, the
fellows with the weakness of too much strength, too much
spirit, too much fire and flame of fine devilishness, that he
solicits and ruins. Of course, he ruins weaklings; but with
them, the worst we breed, I am not here concerned. My
concern is that it is so much of the best we breed whom
John Barleycorn destroys. And the reason why these best
are destroyed is because John Barleycorn stands on every
highway and byway, accessible, law-protected, saluted by
the policeman on the beat, speaking to them, leading them
by the hand to the places where the good fellows and daring ones forgather and drink deep. With John Barleycorn
out of the way, these daring ones would still be born,
and they would do things instead of perishing.

Always I encountered the camaraderie of drink. I might
be walking down the track to the watertank to lie in wait
for a passing freight-train, when I would chance upon a
bunch of 'alki-stiffs'. An alki-stiff is a tramp who drinks
druggist's alcohol. Immediately, with greeting and saluta-
tion, I am taken into the fellowship. The alcohol, shrewdly
blended with water, is handed to me, and soon I am caught
up in the revelry, with maggots crawling in my brain and

John Barleycorn whispering to me that life is big, and that we are all brave and fine—free spirits sprawling like careless gods upon the turf and telling the two-by-four, cut-and-dried, conventional world to go hang.

14

BACK IN Oakland from my wanderings, I retured to the water-front and renewed my comradeship with Nelson, who was now on shore all the time and living more madly than before. I, too, spent my time on shore with him, only occasionally going for cruises of several days on the bay to help out on short-handed scow-schooners.

The result was that I was no longer reinvigorated by periods of open-air abstinence and healthy toil. I drank every day, and whenever opportunity offered I drank to excess; for I still laboured under the misconception that the secret of John Barleycorn lay in drinking to bestiality and unconsciousness. I became pretty thoroughly alcohol-soaked during this period. I practically lived in saloons; became a bar-room loafer, and worse.

And right here was John Barleycorn getting me in a more insidious though no less deadly way than when he nearly sent me out with the tide. I had a few months still to run before I was seventeen; I scorned the thought of a steady job at anything; I felt myself a pretty tough individual in a group of pretty tough men; and I drank because these men drank and because I had to make good with them. I never had a real boyhood, and in this, my precocious manhood, I was very hard and woefully wise. Though I had never known a girl's love even, I had crawled through such depths that I was convinced absolutely that I knew the last word about love and life. And it wasn't a pretty knowledge. Without being pessimistic, I was quite satisfied that life was a rather cheap and ordinary affair.

You see, John Barleycorn was blunting me. The odd
stings and prods of the spirit were no longer sharp. Curiosity was leaving me. What did it matter what lay on the
other side of the world? Men and women, without doubt,
very much like the men and women I knew; marrying and
giving in marriage and all the petty run of petty human
concerns; and drinks, too. But the other side of the world
was a long way to go for a drink. I had but to step to the
corner and get all I wanted at Joe Vigy's. Johnny Heinhold
still ran the Last Chance. And there were saloons on all the
corners and between the corners.

The whispers from the back of life were growing dim as
my mind and body soddened. The old unrest was drowsy.
I might as well rot and die here in Oakland as anywhere
else. And I should have so rotted and died, and not in very
long order either, at the pace John Barleycorn was leading
me, had the matter depended wholly on him. I was learning what it was to have no appetite. I was learning what it
was to get up shaky in the morning, with a stomach that
quivered, with fingers touched with palsy, and to know the
drinker's need for a stiff glass of whisky neat in order to
brace up. (Oh! John Barleycorn is a wizard dopester. Brain
and body, scorched and jangled and poisoned, return to be
tuned up by the very poison that caused the damage.)

There is no end to John Barleycorn's tricks. He had tried
to inveigle me into killing myself. At this period he was doing his best to kill me at a fairly rapid pace. But, not satisfied with that, he tried another dodge. He very nearly got
me, too, and right there I learned a lesson about him—
became a wiser, a more skilful drinker. I learned there were
limits to my gorgeous constitution, and that there were no
limits to John Barleycorn. I learned that in a short hour or
two he could master my strong head, my broad shoulders
and deep chest, put me on my back, and with a devil's grip
on my throat proceed to choke the life out of me.

Nelson and I were sitting in the Overland House. It was
early in the evening, and the only reason we were there was
because we were broke and it was election time. You see,

in election time local politicians, aspirants for office, have a way of making the rounds of the saloons to get votes. One is sitting at a table, in a dry condition, wondering who is going to turn up and buy him a drink, or if his credit is good at some other saloon and if it's worth while to walk that far to find out, when suddenly the saloon doors swing wide, and enters a bevy of well-dressed men, themselves usually wide and exhaling an atmosphere of prosperity and fellowship.

They have smiles and greetings for everybody—for you, without the price of a glass of beer in your pocket, for the timid hobo who lurks in the corner and who certainly hasn't a vote, but who may establish a lodging-house registration. And do you know, when these politicians swing wide the doors and come in, with their broad shoulders, their deep chests, and their generous stomachs which cannot help making them optimists and masters of life, why, you perk right up. It's going to be a warm evening after all, and you know you'll get a souse started at the very least. And—who knows?—the gods may be kind, other drinks may come, and the night culminate in glorious greatness. And the next thing you know, you are lined up at the bar, pouring drinks down your throat and learning the gentlemen's names and the offices which they hope to fill.

It was during this period, when the politicians went their saloon rounds, that I was getting bitter bits of education and having illusions punctured—I, who had pored and thrilled over *The Rail-Splitter,* and *From Canal Boy to President.* Yes, I was learning how noble politics and politicians are.

Well, on this night, broke, thirsty, but with the drinker's faith in the unexpected drink, Nelson and I sat in the Overland House waiting for something to turn up, especially politicians. And there entered Joe Goose—he of the unquenchable thirst, the wicked eyes, the crooked nose, the flowered vest.

'Come on, fellows—free booze—all you want of it. I didn't want you to miss it.'

'Where?' we wanted to know.

'Come on. I'll tell you as we go along. We haven't a minute to lose.' And as we hurried up town, Joe Goose explained: 'It's the Hancock Fire Brigade. All you have to do is wear a red shirt and a helmet, and carry a torch. They're going down on a special train to Haywards to parade.'

(I think the place was Haywards. It may have been San Leandro or Niles. And, to save me, I can't remember whether the Hancock Fire Brigade was a republican or a democratic organization. But anyway, the politicians who ran it were short of torch-bearers, and anybody who would parade could get drunk if he wanted to.)

'The town'll be wide open,' Joe Goose went on. 'Booze? It'll run like water. The politicians have bought the stocks of the saloons. There'll be no charge. All you got to do is walk right up and call for it. We'll raise hell.'

At the hall, on Eighth Street near Broadway, we got into the firemen's shirts and helmets, were equipped with torches, and, growling because we weren't given at least one drink before we started, were herded aboard the train. Oh, those politicians had handled our kind before. At Haywards there were no drinks either. Parade first, and earn your booze, was the order of the night.

We paraded. Then the saloons were opened. Extra barkeepers had been engaged, and the drinkers jammed six deep before every drink-drenched and unwiped bar. There was no time to wipe the bar, nor wash glasses, nor do anything save fill glasses. The Oakland water-front can be real thirsty on occasion.

This method of jamming and struggling in front of the bar was too slow for us. The drink was ours. The politicians had bought it for us. We'd paraded and earned it, hadn't we? So we made a flank attack around the end of the bar, shoved the protesting barkeepers aside, and helped ourselves to bottles.

Outside, we knocked the necks of the bottles off against the concrete kerbs, and drank. Now Joe Goose and Nelson had learned discretion with straight whisky, drunk in quantity. I hadn't. I still laboured under the misconception that one was to drink all he could get—especially when it didn't cost anything. We shared our bottles with others, and drank a good portion ourselves, while I drank most of all. And I didn't like the stuff. I drank it as I had drunk beer at five, wine at seven. I mastered my qualms and downed it like so much medicine. And when we wanted more bottles, we went into other saloons where the free drink was flowing, and helped ourselves.

I haven't the slightest idea of how much I drank— whether it was two quarts or five. I do know that I began the orgy with half-pint draughts and with no water afterwards to wash the taste away or to dilute the whisky.

Now the politicians were too wise to leave the town filled with drunks from the water-front of Oakland. When train time came, there was a round-up of the saloons. Already I was feeling the impact of the whisky. Nelson and I were hustled out of a saloon, and found ourselves in the very last rank of a disorderly parade. I struggled along heroically, my correlations breaking down, my legs tottering under me, my head swimming, my heart pounding, my lungs panting for air.

My helplessness was coming on so rapidly that my reeling brain told me I would go down and out and never reach the train if I remained at the rear of the procession. I left the ranks and ran down a pathway beside the road under broad-spreading trees. Nelson pursued me, laughing. Certain things stand out, as in memories of nightmare. I remember those trees especially, and my desperate running along under them, and how, every time I fell, roars of laughter went up from the other drunks. They thought I was merely antic drunk. They did not dream that John Barleycorn had me by the throat in a death-clutch. But I knew it. And I remember the fleeting bitterness that was mine as I realized that I was in a struggle with death, and that these others did not know. It was as if I were drowning before a crowd of spectators who thought I was cutting up tricks for their entertainment.

And running there under the trees, I fell and lost consciousness. What happened afterwards, with one glimmering exception, I had to be told. Nelson, with his enormous strength, picked me up and dragged me on and aboard the train. When he had got me into a seat, I fought and panted so terribly for air that even with his obtuseness he knew I was in a bad way. And right there, at any moment, I know now, I might have died. I often think it is the nearest to death I have ever been. I have only Nelson's description of my behaviour to go by.

I was scorching up, burning alive internally, in an agony of fire and suffocation, and I wanted air. I madly wanted air. My efforts to raise a window were vain, for all the windows in the car were screwed down. Nelson had seen drink-crazed men, and thought I wanted to throw myself out. He tried to restrain me, but I fought on. I seized some man's torch and smashed the glass.

Now there were pro-Nelson and anti-Nelson factions on the Oakland water-front, and men of both factions, with more drink in them than was good, filled the car. My smashing of the window was the signal for the antis. One of them reached for me, and dropped me, and started the fight, of which I have no knowledge save what was told me afterwards, and a sore jaw next day from the blow that put me out. The man who struck me went down across my body, Nelson followed him, and they say there were few unbroken windows in the wreckage of the car that followed as the free-for-all fight had its course.

This being knocked cold and motionless was perhaps the best thing that could have happened to me. My violent struggles had only accelerated my already dangerously accelerated heart, and increased the need for oxygen in my suffocating lungs.

After the fight was over and I came to, I did not come to myself. I was no more myself than a drowning man is who continues to struggle after he has lost consciousness. I have no memory of my actions, but I cried 'Air! Air!' so insistently, that it dawned on Nelson that I did not contemplate self-destruction. So he cleared the jagged glass from the window-ledge and let me stick my head and shoulders out. He realized, partially, the seriousness of my condition, and held me by the waist to prevent me from crawling farther out. And for the rest of the run in to Oakland I kept my head and shoulders out, fighting like a maniac whenever he tried to draw me inside.

And here my one glimmering streak of true consciousness came. My sole recollection, from the time I fell under the trees until I awoke the following evening, is of my head out of the window, facing the wind caused by the train, cinders striking and burning and blinding me, while I breathed with will. All my will was concentrated on breathing—on breathing the air in the hugest lung-full gulps I could, pumping the greatest amount of air into my lungs in the shortest possible time. It was that or death, and I was a swimmer and diver, and I knew it; and in the most intolerable agony of prolonged suffocation, during those moments I was conscious, I faced the wind and the cinders and breathed for life.

All the rest is a blank. I came to the following evening, in a water-front lodging house. I was alone. No doctor had been called in. And I might well have died there, for Nelson and the others, deeming me merely 'sleeping off my drunk', had let me lie there in a comatose condition for seventeen hours. Many a man, as every doctor knows, has died of the sudden impact of a quart or more of whisky. Usually one reads of them so dying, strong drinkers, on account of a wager. But I didn't know—then. And so I learned; and by no virtue nor prowess, but simply through good fortune and constitution. Again my constitution had triumphed over John Barleycorn. I had escaped from another death-pit, dragged myself through another morass, and perilously acquired the discretion that would enable me to drink wisely for many another year to come.

Heavens! That was twenty years ago, and I am still very

much and wisely alive; and I have seen much, done much, lived much, in that intervening score of years; and I shudder when I think how close a shave I ran, how near I was to missing that splendid fifth of a century that has been mine. And, oh, it wasn't John Barleycorn's fault that he didn't get me that night of the Hancock Fire Brigade.

15

IT WAS during the early winter of 1892 that I resolved to go to sea. My Hancock Fire Brigade experience was very little responsible for this. I still drank and frequented saloons—practically lived in saloons. Whisky was dangerous, in my opinion, but not wrong. Whisky was dangerous like other dangerous things in the natural world. Men died of whisky; but then, too, fishermen were capsized and drowned, hoboes fell under trains and were cut to pieces. To cope with winds and waves, railroad trains, and barrooms, one must use judgment. To get drunk after the manner of men was all right, but one must do it with discretion. No more quarts of whisky for me.

What really decided me to go to sea was that I had caught my first vision of the death-road which John Barleycorn maintains for his devotees. It was not a clear vision, however, and there were two phases of it, somewhat jumbled at the time. It struck me, from watching those with whom I associated, that the life we were living was more destructive than that lived by the average man.

John Barleycorn, by inhibiting morality, incited to crime. Everywhere I saw men doing, drunk, what they would never dream of doing sober. And this wasn't the worst of it. It was the penalty that must be paid. Crime was destructive. Saloon-mates I drank with, who were good fellows and harmless, sober, did most violent and lunatic things when they were drunk. And then the police gathered them in and they vanished from our ken. Sometimes I visited them behind the bars and said good-bye ere they journeyed across the bay to put on the felon's stripes. And time and again I heard the one explanation: *'If I hadn't been drunk I wouldn't a-done it.'* And sometimes, under the spell of John Barleycorn, the most frightful things were done—things that shocked even my case-hardened soul.

The other phase of the death-road was that of the habitual drunkards, who had a way of turning up their toes without apparent provocation. When they took sick, even with trifling afflictions that any ordinary man could pull through, they just pegged out. Sometimes they were found unattended and dead in their beds; on occasion their bodies were dragged out of the water; and sometimes it was just plain accident, as when Bill Kelley, unloading cargo while drunk, had a finger jerked off, which, under the circumstances, might just as easily have been his head.

So I considered my situation and knew that I was getting into a bad way of living. It made towards death too quickly to suit my youth and vitality. And there was only one way out of this hazardous manner of living, and that was to get out. The sealing fleet was wintering in San Francisco Bay, and in the saloons I met skippers, mates, hunters, boat-steerers and boat-pullers. I met the seal-hunter, Pete Holt, and agreed to be his boat-puller and to sign on any schooner he signed on. And I had to have half a dozen drinks with Pete Holt there and then to seal our agreement.

And at once awoke all my old unrest that John Barleycorn had put to sleep. I found myself actually bored with the saloon life of the Oakland water-front, and wondered what I had ever found fascinating in it. Also, with this death-road concept in my brain, I began to grow afraid that something would happen to me before sailing day, which was set for some time in January. I lived more circumspectly, drank less deeply, and went home more frequently. When drinking grew too wild, I got out. When

4*

Nelson was in his maniacal cups, I managed to get separated from him.

On the 12th of January, 1893, I was seventeen, and the
20th of January I signed before the shipping commissioner
the articles of the *Sophie Sutherland*, a three-topmast sealing schooner bound on a voyage to the coast of Japan. And
of course we had to drink on it. Joe Vigy cashed my advance note, and Pete Holt treated, and other hunters
treated. Well, it was the way of men, and who was I, just
turned seventeen, that I should decline the way of life of
these fine, chesty, man-grown men?

16

THERE WAS nothing to drink on the *Sophie Sutherland*,
and we had fifty-one days of glorious sailing, taking the
southern passage in the north-east trades to Bonin Islands.
This isolated group, belonging to Japan, had been selected
as the rendezvous of the Canadian and American sealing
fleets. Here they filled their water-barrels and made repairs
before starting on the hundred days' harrying of the seal-
herd along the northern coasts of Japan to Behring Sea.

Those fifty-one days of fine sailing and intense sobriety
had put me in splendid fettle. The alcohol had been
worked out of my system, and from the moment the voyage
began I had not known the desire for a drink. I doubt if I
even thought once about a drink. Often, of course, the talk
in the forecastle turned on drink, and the men told of their
more exciting or humorous drunks, remembering such passages more keenly, with greater delight, than all the other
passages of their adventurous lives.

In the forecastle, the oldest man, fat and fifty, was Louis.
He was a broken skipper. John Barleycorn had thrown him,
and he was winding up his career where he had begun it,
in the forecastle. His case made quite an impression on me.

John Barleycorn did other things besides kill a man. He hadn't killed Louis. He had done much worse. He had robbed him of power and place and comfort, crucified his pride, and condemned him to the hardship of the common sailor that would last as long as his healthy breath lasted, which promised to be for a long time.

We completed our run across the Pacific, lifted the volcanic peaks, jungle-clad, of the Bonin Islands, sailed in among the reefs to the land-locked harbour, and let our anchor rumble down where lay a score or more of sea-gypsies like ourselves. The scents of strange vegetation blew off the tropic land. Aborigines, in queer outrigger canoes, and Japanese, in queerer sampans, paddled about the bay and came aboard. It was my first foreign land; I had won to the other side of the world, and I would see all I had read in the books come true. I was wild to get ashore.

Victor and Axel, a Swede and a Norwegian, and I planned to keep together. (And so well did we, that for the rest of the cruise we were known as the 'Three Sports'.) Victor pointed out a pathway that disappeared up a wild canyon, emerged on a steep bare lava slope, and thereafter appeared and disappeared, ever climbing, among the palms and flowers. We would go over that path, he said, and we agreed, and we would see beautiful scenery, and strange native villages, and find, Heaven alone knew, what adventure at the end. And Axel was keen to go fishing. The three of us agreed to that, too. We would get a sampan, and a couple of Japanese fishermen who knew the fishing grounds, and we would have great sport. As for me, I was keen for anything.

And then, our plans made, we rowed ashore over the banks of living coral and pulled our boat up the white beach of coral sand. We walked across the fringe of beach under the coconut-palms and into the little town, and found several hundred riotous seamen from all the world, drinking prodigiously, singing prodigiously, dancing prodigiously—and all on the main street to the scandal of a helpless handful of Japanese police.

Victor and Axel said that we'd have a drink before we started on our long walk. Could I decline to drink with these two chesty shipmates? Drinking together, glass in hand, put the seal on comradeship. It was the way of life. Our teetotaller owner-captain was laughed at, and sneered at, by all of us because of his teetotalism. I didn't in the least want a drink, but I did want to be a good fellow and a good comrade. Nor did Louis' case deter me, as I poured the biting, scorching stuff down my throat. John Barleycorn had thrown Louis to a nasty fall, but I was young. My blood ran full and red; I had a constitution of iron; and—well, youth ever grins scornfully at the wreckage of age.

Queer, fierce, alcoholic stuff it was that we drank. There was no telling where or how it had been manufactured—some native concoction most likely. But it was hot as fire, pale as water, and quick as death with its kick. It had been filled into empty 'square-face' bottles which had once contained Holland gin, and which still bore the fitting legend 'Anchor Brand'. It certainly anchored us. We never got out of the town. We never went fishing in the sampan. And though we were there ten days, we never trod that wild path along the lava cliffs and among the flowers.

We met old acquaintances from other schooners, fellows we had met in the saloons of San Francisco before we sailed. And each meeting meant a drink; and there was much to talk about; and more drinks; and songs to be sung; and pranks and antics to be performed, until the maggots of imagination began to crawl, and it all seemed great and wonderful to me, these lusty hard-bitten sea-rovers, of whom I made one, gathered in wassail on a coral strand. Old lines about knights at table in the great banquet halls, and of those above the salt and below the salt, and of Vikings feasting fresh from sea and ripe for battle, came to me; and I knew that the old times were not dead and that we belonged to that selfsame ancient breed.

By mid-afternoon Victor went mad with drink, and wanted to fight everybody and everything. I have since seen lunatics in the violent wards of asylums that seemed to behave in no wise different from Victor's way, save that perhaps he was more violent. Axel and I interfered as peacemakers, were roughed and jostled in the mix-ups, and finally, with infinite precaution and intoxicated cunning, succeeded in inveigling our chum down to the boat and in rowing him aboard our schooner.

But no sooner did Victor's feet touch the deck than he began to clean up the ship. He had the strength of several men, and he ran amuck with it. I remember especially one man whom he got into the chain-boxes but failed to damage through inability to hit him. The man dodged and ducked, and Victor broke all the knuckles of both his fists against the huge links of the anchor chain. By the time we dragged him out of that, his madness had shifted to the belief that he was a great swimmer, and the next moment he was overboard and demonstrating his ability by floundering like a sick porpoise and swallowing much salt water.

We rescued him, and by the time we got him below, undressed, and into his bunk, we were wrecks ourselves. But Axel and I wanted to see more of shore, and away we went, leaving Victor snoring. It was curious, the judgment passed on Victor by his shipmates, drinkers themselves. They shook their heads disapprovingly and muttered: 'A man like that oughtn't to drink.' Now Victor was the smartest sailor and best-tempered shipmate in the forecastle. He was an all-round splendid type of seaman; his mates recognized his worth, and respected and liked him. Yet John Barleycorn metamorphosed him into a violent lunatic. And that was the very point these drinkers made. They knew that drink—and drink with a sailor is always excessive—made them mad, but only mildly mad. Violent madness was objectionable because it spoiled the fun of others and often culminated in tragedy. From their standpoint, mild madness was all right. But from the standpoint of the whole human race, is not all madness objectionable? And is there a greater maker of madness of all sorts than John Barleycorn?

But to return. Ashore, snugly ensconced in a Japanese

house of entertainment, Axel and I compared bruises, and over a comfortable drink talked of the afternoon's happenings. We liked the quietness of that drink and took another. A shipmate dropped in, several shipmates dropped in, and we had more quiet drinks. Finally, just as we had engaged a Japanese orchestra, and as the first strains of the *samisens* and *taikos* were rising, through the paper-walls came a wild howl from the street. We recognized it. Still howling, disdaining doorways, with blood-shot eyes and wildly waving muscular arms, Victor burst upon us through the fragile walls. The old amuck rage was on him, and he wanted blood, anybody's blood. The orchestra fled; so did we. We went through doorways, and we went through paper-walls—anything to get away.

And after the place was half wrecked, and we had agreed to pay the damage, leaving Victor partly subdued and showing symptoms of lapsing into a comatose state, Axel and I wandered away in quest of a quieter drinking-place. The main street was a madness. Hundreds of sailors rollicked up and down. Because the chief of police with his small force was helpless, the governor of the colony had issued orders to the captains to have all their men on board by sunset.

What! To be treated in such fashion! As the news spread among the schooners, they were emptied. Everybody came ashore. Men who had had no intention of coming ashore climbed into the boats. The unfortunate governor's ukase had precipitated a general debauch for all hands. It was hours after sunset, and the men wanted to see anybody try to put them on board. They went around inviting the authorities to try to put them on board. In front of the governor's house they were gathered thickest, bawling sea-songs, circulating square faces, and dancing uproarious Virginia reels and old-country dances. The police, including the reserves, stood in little forlorn groups, waiting for the command the governor was too wise to issue. And I thought this saturnalia was great. It was like the old days of the Spanish Main come back.

It was licence; it was adventure. And I was part of it, a chesty sea-rover along with all these other chesty sea-rovers among the paper houses of Japan.

The governor never issued the order to clear the streets, and Axel and I wandered on from drink to drink. After a time, in some of the antics, getting hazy myself, I lost him. I drifted along, making new acquaintances, downing more drinks, getting hazier and hazier. I remember, somewhere, sitting in a circle with Japanese fishermen, Kanaka boat-steerers from our own vessels, and a young Danish sailor fresh from cowboying in the Argentine and with a penchant for native customs and ceremonials. And with due and proper and most intricate Japanese ceremonial we of the circle drank *saki*, pale, mild and luke-warm, from tiny porcelain bowls.

And, later, I remember the runaway apprentices—boys of eighteen and twenty, of middle-class English families, who had jumped their ships and apprenticeships in various ports of the world and drifted into the forecastles of the sealing schooners. They were healthy, smooth-skinned, clear-eyed, and they were young—youths like me, learning the way of their feet in the world of men. And they *were* men. No mild *saki* for them, but square faces illicitly re-filled with corrosive fire that flamed through their veins and burst into conflagrations in their heads. I remember a melting song they sang, the refrain of which was:

> ' 'Tis but a little golden ring,
>   I give it to thee with pride,
>   Wear it for your mother's sake
>   When you are on the tide.'

They wept over it as they sang it, the graceless young scamps who had broken their mothers' prides, and I sang with them, and wept with them, and luxuriated in the pathos and the tragedy of it, and struggled to make glimmering inebriated generalizations on life and romance. And one last picture I have, standing out very clear and bright in the midst of vagueness before and blackness afterwards. We—the apprentices and I—are swaying and clinging to one another under the stars. We are singing a rollicking sea song, all save one who sits on the ground and weeps; and we are marking the rhythm with waving square faces. From up and down the street come far choruses of sea-voices similarly singing, and life is great, and beautiful and romantic, and magnificently mad.

And next, after the blackness, I open my eyes in the early dawn to see a Japanese woman, solicitously anxious, bending over me. She is the port pilot's wife and I am lying in her doorway. I am chilled and shivering, sick with the after-sickness of debauch. And I feel lightly clad. Those rascals of runaway apprentices! They have acquired the habit of running away. They have run away with my possessions. My watch is gone. My few dollars are gone. My coat is gone. So is my belt. And yes, my shoes.

And the foregoing is a sample of the ten days I spent in the Bonin Islands. Victor got over his lunacy, rejoined Axel and me, and after that we caroused somewhat more discreetly. And we never climbed that lava path among the flowers. The town and the square faces were all we saw.

One who has been burned by fire must preach about the fire. I might have seen and healthily enjoyed a whole lot more of the Bonin Islands, if I had done what I ought to have done. But, as I see it, it is not a matter of what one ought to do, or ought not to do. It is what one *does* do. That is the everlasting, irrefragable fact. I did just what I did. I did what all those men did in the Bonin Islands. I did what millions of men over the world were doing at that particular point in time. I did it because the way led to it, because I was only a human boy, a creature of my environment, and neither an anæmic nor a god. I was just human, and I was taking the path in the world that men took—men whom I admired, if you please; full-blooded men, lusty, breedy, chesty men, free spirits and anything but niggards in the way they foamed life away.

And the way was open. It was like an uncovered well in a yard where children play. It is small use to tell the brave boys toddling their way along into knowledge of life that they mustn't play near the uncovered well. They *will* play near it. Any parent knows that. And we know that a certain percentage of them, the livest and most daring, will fall into the well. The thing to do—we all know it—is to cover up the well. The case is the same with John Barleycorn. All the no-saying and no-preaching in the world will fail to keep men, and youths growing into manhood, away from John Barleycorn when John Barleycorn is everywhere accessible, and where John Barleycorn is everywhere the connotation of manliness, and daring, and great-spiritedness.

The only rational thing for the twentieth-century folk to do is to cover up the well; to make the twentieth century in truth the twentieth century, and to relegate to the nineteenth century and all the preceding centuries the things of those centuries, the witch-burnings, the intolerances, the fetiches, and, not least among such barbarisms, John Barleycorn.

17

NORTH WE raced from the Bonin Islands to pick up the seal-herd, and north we hunted it for a hundred days into frosty, mitten weather and into and through vast fogs which hid the sun from us for a week at a time. It was wild and heavy work, without a drink or thought of drink. Then we sailed south to Yokohama, with a big catch of skins in our salt and a heavy pay-day coming.

I was eager to be ashore and see Japan, but the first day was devoted to ship's work, and not until evening did we sailors land. And here, by the very system of things, by the way life was organized and men transacted affairs, John Barleycorn reached out and tucked my arm in his. The captain had given money for us to the hunters, and the hunters were waiting in a certain Japanese public house for us to come and get it. We rode to the place in rickshaws. Our own crowd had taken possession of it. Drink was flowing. Everybody had money, and everybody was treating. After the hundred days of hard toil and absolute abstinence, in the pink of physical condition, bulging with health, over-spilling with spirits that had long been pent by discipline and circumstance, of course we would have a drink or two. And after that we would see the town.

It was the old story. There were so many drinks to be drunk, and as the warm magic poured through our veins and mellowed our voices and affections we knew it was no time to make invidious distinctions—to drink with this shipmate and to decline to drink with that shipmate. We were all shipmates who had been through stress and storm together, who had pulled and hauled on the same sheets and tackles, relieved one another's wheels, laid out side by side on the same jib-boom when she was plunging into it and looked to see who was missing when she cleared and lifted. So we drank with all, and all treated, and our voices rose, and we remembered a myriad kindly acts of comradeship, and forgot our fights and wordy squabbles, and knew one another for the best fellows in the world.

Well, the night was young when we arrived in that public house, and for all of that first night that public house was what I saw of Japan—a drinking-place which was very like a drinking-place at home or anywhere else over the world.

We lay in Yokohama harbour for two weeks, and about all we saw of Japan was its drinking-places where sailors congregated. Occasionally, some one of us varied the monotony with a more exciting drunk. In such fashion I managed a real exploit by swimming off to the schooner one dark midnight and going soundly to sleep while the water-police searched the harbour for my body and brought my clothes out for identification.

Perhaps it was for things like that, I imagined, that men got drunk. In our little round of living what I had done was a noteworthy event. All the harbour talked about it. I enjoyed several days of fame among the Japanese boat-men and ashore in the pubs. It was a red-letter event. It was an event to be remembered and narrated with pride. I remember it today, twenty years afterward, with a secret glow of pride. It was a purple passage, just as Victor's wrecking of the tea-house in the Bonin Islands and my being looted by the runaway apprentices were purple passages.

The point is that the charm of John Barleycorn was still a mystery to me. I was so organically a non-alcoholic that alcohol itself made no appeal; the chemical reactions it produced in me were not satisfying because I possessed no need for such chemical satisfaction. I drank because the men I was with drank, and because my nature was such that I could not permit myself to be less of a man than other men at their favourite pastime. And I still had a sweet tooth, and on privy occasions when there was no man to see, bought candy and blissfully devoured it.

We hove up anchor to a jolly chanty, and sailed out of Yokohama harbour for San Francisco. We took the northern passage, and with the stout west wind at our back made the run across the Pacific in thirty-seven days of brave sailing. We still had a big pay-day coming to us, and for thirty-seven days, without a drink to addle our mental processes, we incessantly planned the spending of our money.

The first statement of each man—ever an ancient one in homeward-bound forecastles—was: 'No boarding-house sharks in mine.' Next, in parentheses, was regret at having spent so much money in Yokohama. And after that, each man proceeded to paint his favourite phantom. Victor, for instance, said that immediately he landed in San Francisco he would pass right through the water-front and the Barbary Coast, and put an advertisement in the papers. His advertisement would be for board and room in some simple working-class family. 'Then,' said Victor, 'I shall go to some dancing-school for a week or two, just to meet and get acquainted with the girls and fellows. Then I'll get the run of the different dancing crowds, and be invited to their homes, and to parties, and all that, and with the money I've got I can last out till next January, when I'll go sailing again.'

No; he wasn't going to drink. He knew the way of it, particularly his way of it, wine in, wit out, and his money would be gone in no time. He had his choice, based on bitter experience, between three days' debauch among the sharks and harpies of the Barbary Coast and a whole winter of wholesome enjoyment and sociability, and there wasn't any doubt of the way he was going to choose.

Said Axel Gunderson, who didn't care for dancing and social functions: 'I've got a good pay-day. Now I can go home. It is fifteen years since I've seen my mother and all the family. When I pay off, I shall send my money home to wait for me. Then I'll pick a good ship bound for Europe, and arrive there with another pay-day. Put them together, and I'll have more money than ever in my life before. I'll be a prince at home. You haven't any idea how cheap everything is in Norway. I can make presents to everybody and spend my money like what would seem to them a millionaire, and live a whole year there before I'd have to go back to sea.'

'The very thing I'm going to do,' declared Red John. 'It's three years since I've received a line from home and ten years since I was there. Things are just as cheap in Sweden, Axel, as in Norway, and my folks are real country folk and farmers. I'll send my pay-day home and ship on the same ship with you for around the Horn. We'll pick a good one.'

And as Axel Gunderson and Red John painted the pastoral delights and festive customs of their respective countries, each fell in love with the other's home place, and they solemnly pledged to make the journey together, and to spend, together, six months in the one's Swedish home and six months in the other's Norwegian home. And for the rest of the voyage they could hardly be pried apart, so infatuated did they become with discussing their plans.

Long John was not a home-body. But he was tired of the forecastle. No boarding-house sharks in his. He, too, would get a room in a quiet family, and he would go to a navigation school and study to be a captain. And so it went. Each man swore that for once he would be sensible and not squander his money. No boarding-house sharks, no sailor-town, no drink, was the slogan of our forecastle.

The men became stingy. Never was there such economy. They refused to buy anything more from the slopchest. Old rags had to last, and they sewed patch upon patch, turning out what are called 'homeward-bound patches' of the most amazing proportions. They saved on matches, even, waiting till two or three were ready to light their pipes from the same match.

As we sailed up the San Francisco water-front, the moment the port doctors passed us, the boarding-house runners were alongside in whitehall boats. They swarmed on board, each drumming for his own boarding-house, and each with a bottle of free whisky inside his shirt. But we waved them grandly and blasphemously away. We wanted none of their boarding-houses and none of their whisky. We were sober, thrifty sailormen, with better use for our money.

Came the paying off before the shipping commissioner. We emerged upon the sidewalk, each with a pocketful of money. About us, like buzzards, clustered the sharks and harpies. And we looked at each other. We had been seven months together, and our paths were separating. One last farewell rite of comradeship remained. (Oh, it was the way, the custom.) 'Come on, boys,' said our sailing master. There stood the inevitable adjacent saloon. There were a dozen saloons all around. And when we had followed the sailing master into the one of his choice, the sharks were thick on the sidewalk outside. Some of them even ventured inside, but we would have nothing to do with them.

There we stood at the long bar—the sailing master,

the mate, the six hunters, the six boat-steerers, and the five boat-pullers. There were only five of the last, for one of our number had been dropped overboard, with a sack of coal at his feet, between two snow squalls in a driving gale off Cape Jerimo. There were nineteen of us, and it was to be our last drink together. With seven months of men's work in the world, blow high, blow low, behind us, we were looking on each other for the last time. We knew it, for sailors' ways go wide. And the nineteen of us drank the sailing master's treat. Then the mate looked at us with eloquent eyes and called another round. We liked the mate just as well as the sailing master, and we liked them both. Could we drink with one, and not the other?

And Pete Holt, my own hunter (lost next year in the *Mary Thomas* with all hands), called a round. The time passed, the drinks continued to come on the bar, our voices rose, and the maggots began to crawl. There were six hunters, and each insisted, in the sacred name of comradeship, that all hands drink with him just once. There were six boat-steerers and five boat-pullers and the same logic held with them. There was money in all our pockets, and our money was as good as any man's, and our hearts were as free and generous.

Nineteen rounds of drinks. What more would John Barleycorn ask in order to have his will with men? They were ripe to forget their dearly cherished plans. They rolled out of the saloon and into the arms of the sharks and harpies. They didn't last long. From two days to a week saw the end of their money and saw them being carted by the boarding-house masters on board outward-bound ships. Victor was a fine body of a man, and through a lucky friendship managed to get into the life-saving service. He never saw the dancing-school nor placed his advertisement for a room in a working-class family. Nor did Long John win to navigation school. By the end of the week he was a transient lumper on a river steamboat. Red John and Axel did not send their pay-days home to the old country. Instead, and along with the rest, they were scattered on board sailing ships bound for the four quarters of the globe, where they had been placed by the boarding-house masters, and where they were working out advance money which they had neither seen nor spent.

What saved me was that I had a home and people to go to. I crossed the bay to Oakland, and, among other things, took a look at the death-road. Nelson was gone—shot to death while drunk and resisting the officers. His partner in that affair was lying in prison. Whisky Bob was gone. Old Cole, Old Smoudge, and Bob Smith were gone. Another Smith, he of the belted guns and the *Annie*, was drowned. French Frank, they said, was lurking up river, afraid to come down because of something he had done. Others were wearing the stripes in San Quentin or Folsom. Big Alec, the King of the Greeks, whom I had known well in the old Benicia days, and with whom I had drunk whole nights through, had killed two men and fled to foreign parts. Fitzsimmons, with whom I had sailed on the Fish Patrol, had been stabbed in the lung through the back and had died a lingering death complicated with tuberculosis. And so it went, a very lively and well-patronized road, and, from what I knew of all of them, John Barleycorn was responsible, with the sole exception of Smith of the *Annie*.

18

MY INFATUATION for the Oakland water-front was quite dead. I didn't like the looks of it, nor the life. I didn't care for the drinking, nor the vagrancy of it, and I wandered back to the Oakland Free Library and read the books with greater understanding. Then, too, my mother said I had sown my wild oats and it was time I settled down to a regular job. Also, the family needed the money. So I got a job at the jute mills—a ten-hour day at ten cents an hour. Despite my increase in strength and general efficiency, I was receiving no more than when I worked in the cannery several years before. But, then, there was a promise of a rise to a dollar and a quarter a day after a few months.

And here, so far as John Barleycorn is concerned, began a period of innocence. I did not know what it was to take a drink from month end to month end. Not yet eighteen years old, healthy and with labour-hardened but unhurt muscles, like any young animal I needed diversion, excitement, something beyond the books and the mechanical toil.

I strayed into Young Men's Christian Associations. The life there was healthful and athletic, but too juvenile. For me it was too late. I was not boy, nor youth, despite my paucity of years. I had bucked big with men. I knew mysterious and violent things. I was from the other side of life so far as concerned the young men I encountered in the Y.M.C.A. I spoke another language, possessed a sadder and more terrible wisdom. (When I come to think it over, I realize now that I have never had a boyhood.) At any rate, the Y.M.C.A. young men were too juvenile for me, too unsophisticated. This I would not have minded, could they have met and helped me mentally. But I had got more out of the books than they. Their meagre physical experiences, plus their meagre intellectual experiences, made a negative sum so vast that it overbalanced their wholesome morality and healthful sports.

In short, I couldn't play with the pupils of a lower grade. All the clean splendid young life that was theirs was denied me—thanks to my earlier tutelage under John Barleycorn. I knew too much too young. And yet, in the good time coming, when alcohol is eliminated from the needs and the institutions of men, it will be the Y.M.C.A., and similar unthinkably better and wiser and more virile congregating-places, that will receive the men who now go to saloons to find themselves and one another. In the meantime, we live today, here and now, and we discuss today, here and now.

I was working ten hours a day in the jute mills. It was hum-drum machine toil. I wanted life. I wanted to realize myself in other ways than at a machine for ten cents an hour. And yet I had had my fill of saloons. I wanted something new. I was growing up. I was developing unguessed and troubling potencies and proclivities. And at this very stage, fortunately, I met Louis Shattuck and we became chums.

Louis Shattuck, without one vicious trait, was a real innocently devilish young fellow, who was quite convinced that he was a sophisticated town boy. And I wasn't a town boy at all. Louis was handsome, and graceful, and filled with love for the girls. With him it was an exciting and all-absorbing pursuit. I didn't know anything about girls. I had been too busy being a man. This was an entirely new phase of existence which had escaped me. And when I saw Louis say good-bye to me, raise his hat to a girl of his acquaintance, and walk on with her side by side down the sidewalk, I was made excited and envious. I, too, wanted to play this game.

'Well, there's only one thing to do,' said Louis, 'and that is, you must get a girl.'

Which is more difficult than it sounds. Let me show you, at the expense of a slight going aside. Louis did not know girls in their home life. He had the entrée to no girl's home. And of course, I, a stranger in this new world, was similarly circumstanced. But, further, Louis and I were unable to go to dancing-schools, or to public dances, which were very good places for getting acquainted. We didn't have the money. He was a blacksmith's apprentice, and was earning but slightly more than I. We both lived at home and paid our way. When we had done this, and bought our cigarettes, and the inevitable clothes and shoes, there remained to each of us, for personal spending, a sum that varied between seventy cents and a dollar for the week. We whacked this up, shared it, and sometimes loaned all of what was left of it when one of us needed it for some more gorgeous girl-adventure, such as a car-fare out to Blair's Park and back—twenty cents, bang, just like that; and ice-cream for two—thirty cents; or tamales in a tamale-parlour, which came cheaper and which for two cost only twenty cents.

I did not mind this money meagreness. The disdain I had learned for money from the oyster pirates had never left me. I didn't care overweeningly for it for personal gratification; and in my philosophy I completed the circle, finding myself as equable with the lack of a ten-cent piece as I was with the squandering of scores of dollars in call-ing all men and hangers-on up to the bar to drink with me.

But how to get a girl? There was no girl's home to which Louis could take me and where I might be intro-duced to girls. I knew none. And Louis' several girls he wanted for himself; and anyway, in the very human nature of boys' and girls' ways, he couldn't turn any of them over to me. He did persuade them to bring girl-friends for me; but I found them weak sisters, pale and ineffectual alongside the choice specimens he had.

'You'll have to do like I did,' he said finally. 'I got these by getting them. You'll have to get one the same way.'

And he initiated me. It must be remembered that Louis and I were hard situated. We really had to struggle to pay our board and maintain a decent appearance. We met each other in the evening, after the day's work, on the street corner, or in a little candy store on a side street, our sole frequenting-place. Here we bought our cigarettes, and occasionally, a nickel's worth of 'red-hots'. (Oh, yes; Louis and I unblushingly ate candy—all we would get. Neither of us drank. Neither of us ever went into a saloon.)

But the girl. In quite primitive fashion, as Louis advised me, I was to select her and make myself acquainted with her. We strolled the streets in the early evenings. The girls, like us, strolled in pairs. And strolling girls *will* look at strolling boys who look. (And to this day, in

any town, city or village, in which I, in my middle age,
find myself, I look on with the eye trained of old experience, and watch the sweet innocent game played by the
strolling boys and girls who just *must* stroll when the
spring and summer evenings call.)

The trouble was that in this Arcadian phase of my history, I, who had come through, case-hardened, from the
other side of life, was timid and bashful. Again and again
Louis nerved me up. But I didn't know girls. They were
strange and wonderful to me after my precocious man's
life. I failed of the bold front and the necessary forwardness when the crucial moment came.

Then Louis would show me how—a certain, eloquent
glance of eye, a smile, a daring, a lifted hat, a spoken
word, hesitancies, giggles, coy nervousnesses—and, behold, Louis acquainted and nodding me up to be introduced. But when we paired off to stroll along boy and
girl together, I noted that Louis had invariably picked the
good-looker and left to me the little lame sister.

I improved, of course, after experiences too numerous to
enter upon, so that there were divers girls to whom I
could lift my hat and who would walk beside me in the
early evenings. But girl's love did not immediately come
to me. I was excited, interested, and I pursued the quest.
And the thought of drink never entered my mind. Some of
Louis' and my adventures have since given me serious
pause when casting sociological generalizations. But it was
all good and innocently youthful, and I learned one
generalization, biological rather than sociological, namely,
that the 'Colonel's lady and Judy O'Grady are sisters
under their skins'.

And before long I learned girl's love, all the dear fond
deliciousness of it, all the glory and the wonder. I shall
call her Haydee. She was between fifteen and sixteen. Her
little skirt reached her shoe-tops. We sat side by side in a
Salvation Army meeting. She was not a convert, nor was
her aunt who sat on the other side of her, and who, visiting
from the country where at that time the Salvation Army

was not, had dropped in to the meeting for half an hour
out of curiosity. And Louis sat beside me and observed—
I do believe he did no more than observe, because Haydee
was not his style of girl.

We did not speak, but in that great half-hour we
glanced shyly at each other, and shyly avoided or as shyly
returned and met each other's glances more than several
times. She had a slender oval face. Her brown eyes were
beautiful. Her nose was a dream, as was her sweet-lipped,
petulant-hinting mouth. She wore a tam-o'-shanter, and I
thought her brown hair the prettiest shade of brown I
had ever seen. And from that single experience of half
an hour I have ever since been convinced of the reality of
love at first sight.

All too soon the aunt and Haydee departed. (This is
permissible at any stage of a Salvation Army meeting.) I
was no longer interested in the meeting, and, after an
appropriate interval of a couple of minutes or less, started
to leave with Louis. As we passed out, at the back of the
hall a woman recognized me with her eyes, arose, and
followed me. I shall not describe her. She was of my own
kind and friendship of the old time on the water-front.
When Nelson was shot, he had died in her arms, and she
knew me as his one comrade. And she must tell me how
Nelson had died, and I did want to know; so I went with
her across the width of life from dawning boy's love for a
brown-haired girl in a tam-o'-shanter back to the old sad
savagery I had known.

And when I had heard the tale, I hurried away to find
Louis, fearing that I had lost my first love with the first
glimpse of her. But Louis was dependable. Her name was
—Haydee. He knew where she lived. Each day she passed
the blacksmith's shop where he worked, going to or from
the Lafayette School. Further, he had seen her on occasion
with Ruth, another schoolgirl, and, still further, Nita, who
sold us red-hots at the candy store, was a friend of Ruth.
The thing to do was to go around to the candy store and
see if we could get Nita to give a note to Ruth to give to

Haydee. If this could be arranged, all I had to do was write the note.

And it so happened, And in stolen half-hours of meeting I came to know all the sweet madness of boy's love and girl's love. So far as it goes it is not the biggest love in the world, but I do dare to assert that it is the sweetest. Oh, as I look back on it! Never did girl have more innocent boy-lover than I who had been so wicked-wise and violent beyond my years. I didn't know the first thing about girls. I, who had been hailed Prince of the Oyster Pirates, who could go anywhere in the world as a man amongst men; who could sail boats, lay aloft in black and storm, or go into the toughest hang-outs in sailor town and play my part in any rough-house that started or call all hands to the bar—I didn't know the first thing I might say or do with this slender little chit of a girl-woman whose scant skirt just reached her shoe-tops and who was as abysmally ignorant of life as I was, or thought I was, profoundly wise.

I remember we sat on a bench in the starlight. There was fully a foot of space between us. We slightly faced each other, our near elbows on the back of the bench; and once or twice our elbows just touched. And all the time, deliriously happy, talking in the gentlest and most delicate terms that might not offend her sensitive ears, I was cudgelling my brains in an effort to divine what I was expected to do. What did girls expect of boys, sitting on a bench and tentatively striving to find out what love was? What did she expect me to do? Was I expected to kiss her? Did she expect me to try? And if she did expect me, and I didn't, what would she think of me?

Ah, she was wiser than I—I know it now—the little innocent girl-woman in her shoe-top skirt. She had known boys all her life. She encouraged me in the ways a girl may. Her gloves were off and in one hand, and I remember, lightly and daringly, in mock reproof for something I had said, how she tapped my lips with a tiny flirt of those gloves. I was like to swoon with delight. It was the most wonderful thing that had ever happened to me. And I remember yet the faint scent that clung to those gloves and that I breathed in the moment they touched my lips.

Then came the agony of apprehension and doubt. Should I imprison in my hand that little hand with the dangling, scented gloves which had just tapped my lips? Should I dare to kiss her there and then, or slip my arm around her waist? Or dared I even sit closer?

Well, I didn't dare. I did nothing. I merely continued to sit there and love with all my soul. And when we parted that evening I had not kissed her. I do remember the first time I kissed her, on another evening, at parting —a mighty moment, when I took all my heart of courage and dared. We never succeeded in managing more than a dozen stolen meetings, and we kissed perhaps a dozen times—as boys and girls kiss, briefly and innocently, and wonderingly. We never went anywhere—not even to a matinée. We once shared together five cents worth of red-hots. But I have always fondly believed that she loved me. I know I loved her; and I dreamed day-dreams of her for a year and more, and the memory of her is very dear.

19

WHEN I was with people who did not drink, I never thought of drinking. Louis did not drink. Neither he nor I could afford it; but, more significant than that, we had no desire to drink. We were healthy, normal, non-alcoholic. Had we been alcoholic, we would have drunk whether or not we could have afforded it.

Each night, after the day's work, washed up, clothes changed, and supper eaten, we met on the street corner or in the little candy store. But the warm fall weather passed, and on bitter nights of frost or damp nights of drizzle, the street corner was not a comfortable meeting-place. And the candy store was unheated. Nita, or who-ever waited at the counter, between waitings lurked in a back living-room that was heated. We were not admitted to this room, and in the store it was cold as out-of-doors.

Louis and I debated the situation. There was only one solution: the saloon, the congregating-place of men, the place where men hobnobbed with John Barleycorn. Well do I remember the damp and draughty evening, shivering without overcoats because we could not afford them, that Louis and I started out to select our saloon. Saloons are always warm and comfortable. Now Louis and I did not go into this saloon because we wanted a drink. Yet we knew that saloons were not charitable institutions. A man could not make a lounging-place of a saloon without occasionally buying something over the bar.

Our dimes and nickels were few. We could ill spare any of them when they were so potent in paying car-fare for oneself and a girl. (We never paid car-fare when by ourselves, being content to walk.) So, in this saloon, we desired to make the most of our expenditure. We called for a deck of cards and sat down at a table and played euchre for an hour, in which time Louis treated once, and I treated once, to beer—the cheapest drink, ten cents for two. Prodigal! How we grudged it!

We studied the men who came into the place. They seemed all middle-aged and elderly workmen, most of them Germans, who flocked by themselves in old-acquaintance groups, and with whom we could have only the slightest contacts. We voted against that saloon, and went out cast-down with the knowledge that we had lost an evening and wasted twenty cents for beer that we didn't want.

We made several more tries on suceeding nights, and last found our way into the National, a saloon on Tenth and Franklin. Here was a more congenial crowd. Here Louis met a fellow or two he knew, and here I met fellows I had gone to school with when a little lad in knee pants. We talked of old days, and of what had become of this fellow, and what that fellow was doing now, and of course we talked it over drinks. They treated, and we drank. Then, according to the code of drinking, we had to treat. It hurt, for it meant forty to fifty cents a clatter.

We felt quite enlivened when the short evening was over; but at the same time we were bankrupt. Our week's spending money was gone. We decided that that was the saloon for us, and we agreed to be more circumspect thereafter in our drink-buying. Also, we had to economize for the rest of the week. We didn't even have car-fare. We were compelled to break an engagement with two girls from West Oakland with whom we were attempting to be in love. They were to meet us up town the next evening, and we hadn't the car-fare necessary to take them home. Like many others financially embarrassed, we had to disappear for a time from the gay whirl—at least until Saturday night pay-day. So Louis and I rendezvoused in a livery stable, and with coats buttoned and chattering teeth played euchre and casino until the time of our exile was over.

Then we returned to the National Saloon and spent no more than we could decently avoid spending for the comfort and warmth. Sometimes we had mishaps, as when one got stuck twice in succession in a five-handed game of Sancho Pedro for the drinks. Such a disaster meant anywhere between twenty-five to eighty cents, just according to how many of the players ordered ten-cent drinks. But we could temporarily escape the evil effects of such disaster, by virtue of an account we ran behind the bar. Of course, this only set back the day of reckoning and seduced us into spending more than we would have spent on a cash basis. (When I left Oakland suddenly for the adventure-path the following spring, I well remember I owed that saloon-keeper one dollar and seventy cents. Long after, when I returned, he was gone. I still owe him that dollar and seventy cents, and if he should chance to read these lines I want him to know that I'll pay on demand.)

The foregoing incident of the National Saloon I have given in order again to show the lure, or draw, or compulsion, towards John Barleycorn in society as at present organized with saloons on all the corners. Louis and I were two healthy youths. We didn't want to drink. We couldn't afford to drink. And yet we were driven by the circumstances of cold and rainy weather to seek refuge in a saloon, where we had to spend part of our pitiful dole for drink. It will be urged by some critics that we might have gone to the Y.M.C.A., to night school, and to the social circles and homes of young people. The only reply is that we didn't. That is the irrefragable fact. We didn't. And today, at this moment, there are hundreds of thousands of boys like Louis and me doing just what Louis and I did with John Barleycorn, warm and comfortable, beckoning and welcoming, tucking their arms in his and beginning to teach them his mellow ways.

20

THE JUTE MILLS failed of its agreement to increase my pay to a dollar and a quarter a day, and I, a free-born American boy whose direct ancestors had fought in all the wars from the old pre-Revolutionary Indian wars down, exercised my sovereign right of free contract by quitting the job.

I was still resolved to settle down, and I looked about me. One thing was clear. Unskilled labour didn't pay. I must learn a trade, and I decided on electricity. The need for electricians was constantly growing. But how to become an electrician? I hadn't the money to go to a technical school or university; besides, I didn't think much of schools. I was a practical man in a practical world. Also, I still believed in the old myths which were the heritage of the American boy when I was a boy.

A canal boy could become a President. Any boy who took employment with any firm could, by thrift, energy and sobriety, learn the business and rise from position to position until he was taken in as a junior partner. After that the senior partnership was only a matter of time. Very often—so ran the myth—the boy, by reason of his steadiness and application, married his employer's daughter. By this time I had been encouraged to such faith in myself in the matter of girls that I was quite certain I would marry my employer's daughter. There wasn't a doubt of it. All the little boys in the myths did it as soon as they were old enough.

So I bade farewell for ever to the adventure-path, and went out to the power plant of one of our Oakland street railways. I saw the superintendent himself, in a private office so fine that it almost stunned me. But I talked straight up. I told him I wanted to become a practical electrician, that I was unafraid of work, that I was used to hard work, and that all he had to do was look at me to see I was fit and strong. I told him that I wanted to begin right at the bottom and work up, that I wanted to devote my life to this one occupation and this one employment.

The superintendent beamed as he listened. He told me that I was the right stuff for success, and that he believed in encouraging American youth that wanted to rise. Why, employers were always on the lookout for young fellows like me, and also, they found them all too rarely. My ambition was fine and worthy, and he would see to it that I got my chance. (And as I listened with swelling heart, I wondered if it was his daughter I was to marry.)

'Before you can go out on the road and learn the more complicated higher details of the profession,' he said, 'you will, of course, have to work in the car-house with the men who install and repair the motors.' (By this time I was sure that it was his daughter, and I was wondering how much stock he might own in the company.)

'But,' he said, 'as you yourself so plainly see, you

couldn't expect to begin as a helper to the car-house electricians. That will come when you have worked up to it. You will really begin at the bottom. In the car-house your first employment will be sweeping up, washing the windows, keeping things clean. And after you have shown yourself satisfactory at that, then you may become a helper to the car-house electricians.'

I didn't see how sweeping and scrubbing a building was any preparation for the trade of electrician; but I did know that in the books all the boys started with the most menial task and by making good ultimately won to the ownership of the whole concern.

'When shall I come to work?' I asked, eager to launch on this dazzling career.

'But,' said the superintendent, 'as you and I have already agreed, you must begin at the bottom. Not immediately can you in any capacity enter the car-house. Before that you must pass through the engine-room as an oiler.'

My heart went down slightly and for the moment as I saw the road lengthen between his daughter and me; then it rose again. I would be a better electrician with knowledge of steam engines. As an oiler in the great engine-room I was confident that few things concerning steam would escape me. Heavens! My career shone more dazzling than ever.

'When shall I come to work?' I asked gratefully.

'But,' said the superintendent, 'you could not expect to enter immediately into the engine room. There must be preparation for that. And through the fire-room, of course. Come, you see the matter clearly, I know. And you will see that even the mere handling of coal is a scientific matter and not to be sneered at. Do you know that we weigh every pound of coal we burn? Thus, we learn the value of the coal we buy; we know to a tee the last penny of cost of every item of production, and we learn which firemen are the most wasteful, which firemen, out of stupidity or carelessness, get the least out of the coal they fire.' The Superintendent beamed again. 'You see how very important the little matter of coal is, and by as much as you learn of this little matter you will become that much better a workman—more valuable to us, more valuable to yourself. Now, are you prepared to begin?'

'Any time,' I said valiantly. 'The sooner the better.'

'Very well,' he answered. 'You will come tomorrow morning at seven o'clock.'

I was taken out and shown my duties. Also, I was told the terms of my employment—a ten-hour day, every day in the month including Sundays and holidays, with one day off each month, with a salary of thirty dollars a month. It wasn't exciting. Years before, at the cannery, I had earned a dollar a day for a ten-hour day. I consoled myself with the thought that the reason my earning capacity had not increased with my years and strength was because I had remained an unskilled labourer. But it was different now. I was beginning to work for skill, for a trade, for career and fortune, and the superintendent's daughter.

And I was beginning in the right way—right at the beginning. That was the thing. I was passing coal to the firemen, who shovelled it into the furnaces, where its energy was transformed into steam, which, in the engine-room, was transformed into the electricity with which the electricians worked. This passing coal was surely the very beginning—unless the superintendent should take it into his head to send me to work in the mines from which the coal came in order to get a complete understanding of the genesis of electricity for street railways.

Work! I, who had worked with men, found that I didn't know the first thing about real work. A ten-hour day! I had to pass coal for the day and night shifts, and, despite working through the noon-hour, I never finished my task before eight at night. I was working a twelve- to thirteen-hour day, and I wasn't being paid overtime as in the cannery.

I might as well give the secret away right here. I was doing the work of two men. Before me, one mature able-bodied labourer had done the day shift and another equally mature able-bodied labourer had done the night-shift. They had received forty dollars a month each. The superintendent, bent on an economical administration, had persuaded me to do the work of both men for thirty dollars a month. I thought he was making an electrician of me. In truth and fact, he was saving fifty dollars a month operating expenses to the company.

But I didn't know I was displacing two men. Nobody told me. On the contrary, the superintendent warned everybody not to tell me. How valiantly I went at it that first day. I worked at top speed, filling the iron wheelbarrow with coal, running it on the scales and weighing the load, then trundling it into the fire-room and dumping it on the plates before the fires.

Work! I did more than the two men whom I had displaced. They had merely wheeled in the coal and dumped it on the plates. But while I did this for the day coal, the night-coal I had to pile against the wall of the fire-room. Now the fire-room was small. It had been planned for a night coal-passer. So I had to pile the night coal higher and higher, buttressing up the heap with stout planks. Towards the top of the heap I had to handle the coal a second time, tossing it up with a shovel.

I dripped with sweat, but I never ceased from my stride, though I could feel exhaustion coming on. By ten o'clock in the morning, so much of my body's energy had I consumed, I felt hungry and snatched a thick double-slice of bread and butter from my dinner pail. This I devoured, standing, grimed with coal-dust, my knees trembling under me. By eleven o'clock, in this fashion I had consumed my whole lunch. But what of it? I realized that it would enable me to continue working through the noon hour. And I worked under the electric lights. The day fireman went off and the night fireman came on. I plugged away.

At half-past eight, famished, tottering, I washed up, changed my clothes, and dragged my weary body to the car. It was three miles to where I lived, and I had received a pass with the stipulation that I could sit down as long as there were no paying passengers in need of a seat. As I sank into a corner outside seat I prayed that no passenger might require my seat. But the car filled up, and, half-way in, a woman came on board, and there was no seat for her. I started to get up, and to my astonishment found that I could not. With the chill wind blowing on me, my spent body had stiffened into the seat. It took me the rest of the run in to unkink my complaining joints and muscles and get into a standing position on the lower step. And when the car stopped at my corner I nearly fell to the ground when I stepped off.

I hobbled two blocks to the house and limped into the kitchen. While my mother started to cook, I plunged into bread and butter; but before my appetite was appeased, or the steak fried, I was sound asleep. In vain my mother strove to shake me awake enough to eat the meat. Failing in this, with the assistance of my father she managed to get me to my room, where I collapsed dead asleep on the bed. They undressed me and covered me up. In the morning came the agony of being awakened. I was terribly sore, and, worst of all, my wrists were swelling. But I made up for my lost supper, eating an enormous breakfast, and when I hobbled to catch my car I carried a lunch twice as big as the one the day before.

Work! Let any youth just turned eighteen try to out-shovel two man-grown coal-shovellers. Work! Long before midday I had eaten the last scrap of my huge lunch. But I was resolved to show them what a husky young fellow determined to rise could do. The worst of it was that my wrists were swelling and going back on me. There are few who do not know the pain of walking on a sprained ankle. Then imagine the pain of shovelling coal and trundling a loaded wheelbarrow with two sprained wrists.

Work! More than once I sank down on the coal where no one could see me, and cried with rage, and mortification, and exhaustion, and despair. That second day was my hardest, and all that enabled me to survive it and get in the last of the night coal at the end of thirteen hours was the day fireman, who bound my wrists with broad leather straps. So tightly were they buckled that they were like slightly flexible plaster casts. They took the stresses and pressures which hitherto had been borne by my wrists, and they were so tight that there was no room for the inflammation to rise in the sprains.

And in this fashion I continued to learn to be an electrician. Night after night I limped home, fell asleep before I could eat my supper, and was helped into bed and undressed. Morning after morning, always with huger lunches in my dinner pail, I limped out of the house on my way to work.

I no longer read my library books. I made no dates with the girls. I was a proper work beast. I worked, and ate, and slept, while my mind slept all the time. The whole thing was a nightmare. I worked every day, including Sunday, and I looked far ahead to my one day off at the end of a month, resolved to lie abed all that day and just sleep and rest up.

The strangest part of this experience was that I never took a drink nor thought of taking a drink. Yet I knew that men under hard pressure almost invariably drank. I had seen them do it, and in the past had often done it myself. But so sheerly non-alcoholic was I that it never entered my mind that a drink might be good for me. I instance this to show how entirely lacking from my make-up was any predisposition towards alcohol. And the point of this instance is that later on, after more years had passed, contact with John Barleycorn at last did induce in me the alcoholic desire.

I had often noticed the day fireman staring at me in a curious way. At last, one day, he spoke. He began by swearing me to secrecy. He had been warned by the superintendent not to tell me, and in telling me he was risking his job. He told me of the day coal-passer and the night coal-passer, and of the wages they had received. I was doing for thirty dollars a month what they had received eighty dollars for doing. He would have told me sooner, the fireman said, had he not been so certain that I would break down under the work and quit. As it was, I was killing myself, and all to no good purpose. I was merely cheapening the price of labour, he argued, and keeping two men out of a job.

Being an American boy, and a proud American boy, I did not immediately quit. This was foolish of me, I know; but I resolved to continue the work long enough to prove to the superintendent that I could do it without breaking down. Then I would quit, and he would realize what a fine young fellow he had lost.

All of which I faithfully and foolishly did. I worked on until the time came when I got in the last of the night coal by six o'clock. Then I quit the job of learning electricity by doing more than two men's work for a boy's wages, went home, and proceeded to sleep the clock around.

Fortunately, I had not stayed by the job long enough to injure myself—though I was compelled to wear straps on my wrists for a year afterwards. But the effect of this work orgy in which I had indulged was to sicken me with work. I just wouldn't work. The thought of work was repulsive. I didn't care if I never settled down. Learning a trade could go hang. It was a whole lot better to royster and frolic over the world in the way I had previously done. So I headed out on the adventure-path again, starting to tramp East by beating my way on the railroads.

21

BUT BEHOLD! As soon as I went out on the adventure-path I met John Barleycorn again. I moved through a world of strangers, and the act of drinking together made one acquainted with men and opened the way to adventures. It might be in a saloon with jingled townsmen, or with a genial railroad man well lighted up and armed with pocket flasks, or with a bunch of alki-stiffs in a hang-out. Yes; and it might be in a prohibition state, such as Iowa was in 1894, when I wandered up the main street of Des Moines and was variously invited by strangers into various blind pigs—I remember drinking in barber-shops, plumbing establishments, and furniture stores.

Always it was John Barleycorn. Even a tramp, in those halcyon days, could get most frequently drunk. I remember, inside the prison at Buffalo, how some of us got magnificently jingled, and how, on the streets of Buffalo after our release, another jingle was financed with pennies begged on the main-drag.

I had no call for alcohol, but when I was with those who drank, I drank with them. I insisted on travelling or loafing with the livest, keenest men, and it was just these live, keen ones that did most of the drinking. They were the more comradely men, the more venturous, the more individual. Perhaps it was too much temperament that made them turn from the commonplace and humdrum to find relief in the lying and fantastic sureties of John Barleycorn. Be that as it may, the men I liked best, desired most to be with, were invariably to be found in John Barleycorn's company.

In the course of my tramping over the United States I achieved a new concept. As a tramp, I was behind the scenes of society—aye, and down in the cellar. I could watch the machinery work. I saw the wheels of the social machine go around, and I learned that the dignity of manual labour wasn't what I had been told it was by the teachers, preachers, and politicians. The men without trades were helpless cattle. If one learned a trade, he was compelled to belong to a union in order to work at his trade. And his union was compelled to bully and slug the employers' unions in order to hold up wages or hold down hours. The employers' unions likewise bullied and slugged. I couldn't see any dignity at all. And when a workman got old, or had an accident, he was thrown into the scrap-heap like any worn-out machine. I saw too many of this sort who were making anything but dignified ends of life.

5*

So my new concept was that manual labour was undignified, and that it didn't pay. No trade for me, was my decision, and no superintendent's daughters. And no criminality, I also decided. That would be almost as disastrous as to be a labourer. Brains paid, not brawn, and I resolved never again to offer my muscles for sale in the brawn market. Brain, and brain only, would I sell.

I returned to California with the firm intention of developing my brain. This meant school education. I had gone through the grammar school long ago, so I entered the Oakland High School. To pay my way I worked as a janitor. My sister helped me, too; and I was not above mowing anybody's lawn or taking up and beating carpets when I had half a day to spare. I was working to get away from work, and I buckled down to it with a grim realization of the paradox.

Boy and girl love was left behind, and, along with it, Haydee and Louis Shattuck, and the early evening strolls. I hadn't the time. I joined the Henry Clay Debating Society. I was received into the homes of some of the members, where I met nice girls whose skirts reached the ground. I dallied with little home clubs wherein we discussed poetry and art and the nuances of grammar. I joined the socialist local where we studied and orated political economy, philosophy, and politics. I kept half a dozen membership cards working in the free library and did an immense amount of collateral reading.

And for a year and a half on end I never took a drink, nor thought of taking a drink. I hadn't the time, and I certainly did not have the inclination. Between my janitor-work, my studies, and innocent amusements such as chess, I hadn't a moment to spare. I was discovering a new world, and such was the passion of my exploration that the old world of John Barleycorn held no inducements for me.

Come to think of it, I did enter a saloon. I went to see Johnny Heinhold in the Last Chance, and I went to borrow money. And right here is another phase of John Barleycorn. Saloon-keepers are notoriously good fellows. On an average they perform vastly greater generosities than do business men. When I simply had to have ten dollars, desperate, with no place to turn, I went to Johnny Heinhold. Several years had passed since I had been in his place or spent a cent across his bar. And when I went to borrow the ten dollars I didn't buy a drink, either. And Johnny Heinhold let me have the ten dollars without security or interest.

More than once, in the brief days of my struggle for an education, I went to Johnny Heinhold to borrow money. When I entered the university, I borrowed forty dollars from him, without interest, without security, without buying a drink. And yet—and here is the point, the custom, and the code—in the days of my prosperity, after the lapse of years, I have gone out of my way by many a long block to spend across Johnny Heinhold's bar deferred interest on the various loans. Not that Johnny Heinhold asked me to do it, or expected me to do it. I did it, as I have said, in obedience to the code I had learned along with all the other things connected with John Barleycorn. In distress, when a man has no other place to turn, when he hasn't the slightest bit of security which a savage-hearted pawnbroker would consider, he can go to some saloon-keeper he knows. Gratitude is inherently human. When the man so helped has money again, depend upon it that a portion will be spent across the bar of the saloon-keeper who befriended him.

Why, I recollect the early days of my writing career, when the small sums of money I earned from the magazines came with tragic irregularity, while at the same time I was staggering along with a growing family—a wife, children, a mother, a nephew, and my Mammy Jennie and her old husband fallen on evil days. There were two places at which I could borrow money: a barber shop and a saloon. The barber charged me five per cent. per month in advance. That is to say, when I borrowed one hundred dollars he handed me ninety-five. The other five dollars he retained as advance interest for the first month. And on the second month I paid him five dollars more, and continued so to do each month until I made a ten strike with the editors and lifted the loan.

The other place to which I came in trouble was the saloon. This saloon-keeper I had known by sight for a couple of years. I had never spent my money in his saloon, and even when I borrowed from him I didn't spend any money. Yet never did he refuse me any sum I asked of him. Unfortunately, before I became prosperous, he moved away to another city. And to this day I regret that he is gone. It is the code I have learned. The right thing to do, and the thing I'd do right now did I know where he is, would be to drop in on occasion and spend a few dollars across his bar for old sakes' sake and gratitude.

This is not to exalt saloon-keepers. I have written it to exalt the power of John Barleycorn and to illustrate one more of the myriad ways by which a man is brought in contact with John Barleycorn until in the end he finds he cannot get along without him.

But to return to the run of my narrative. Away from the adventure-path, up to my ears in study, every moment occupied, I lived oblivious to John Barleycorn's existence. Nobody about me drank. If any had drunk, and had they offered it to me, I surely would have drunk. As it was, when I had spare moments I spent them playing chess, or going with nice girls who were themselves students, or in riding a bicycle whenever I was fortunate enough to have it out of the pawnbroker's possession.

What I am insisting upon all the time is this: in me was not the slightest trace of alcoholic desire, and this despite the long and severe apprenticeship I had served under John Barleycorn. I had come back from the other side of life to be delighted with this Arcadian simplicity of student youth and student maidens. Also, I had found my way into the realm of the mind, and I was intellectually intoxicated. (Alas! as I was to learn at a later period, intellectual intoxication, too, has its katzenjammer.)

22

THREE YEARS was the time required to go through the high school. I grew impatient.

Also, my schooling was becoming financially impossible. At such rate I could not last out, and I did greatly want to go to the state university. When I had done a year of high school, I decided to attempt a short cut. I borrowed the money and paid to enter the senior class of a 'cramming joint' or academy. I was scheduled to graduate right into the university at the end of four months, thus saving two years.

And how I did cram! I had two years' new work to do in a third of a year. For five weeks I crammed, until simultaneous quadratic equations and chemical formulas fairly oozed from my ears. And then the master of the academy took me aside. He was very sorry, but he was compelled to give me back my tuition fee and to ask me to leave the school. It wasn't a matter of scholarship. I stood well in my classes, and did he graduate me into the university he was confident that in that institution I would continue to stand well. The trouble was that tongues were gossiping about my case. What! In four months accomplished two years' work! It would be a scandal, and the universities were becoming severer in their treatment of accredited prep schools. He couldn't afford such a scandal, therefore I must gracefully depart.

I did. And I paid back the borrowed money, and gritted my teeth, and started to cram by myself. There were three months yet before the university entrance examinations. Without laboratories, without coaching, sitting in my bedroom, I proceeded to compress that two years' work into three months and to keep reviewed on the previous year's work.

Nineteen hours a day I studied. For three months I kept

this pace, only breaking it on several occasions. My body grew weary, my mind grew weary, but I stayed with it. My eyes grew weary and began to twitch, but they did not break down. Perhaps, toward the last, I got a bit dotty, I know that at the time I was confident I had discovered the formula for squaring the circle; but I resolutely deferred the working of it out until after the examinations. Then I would show them.

Came the several days of the examinations, during which time I scarcely closed my eyes in sleep, devoting every moment to cramming and reviewing. And when I turned in my last examination paper I was in full possession of a splendid case of brain-fag. I didn't want to see a book. I didn't want to think or to lay eyes on anybody who was liable to think.

There was but one prescription for such a condition, and I gave it to myself—the adventure-path. I didn't wait to learn the result of my examinations. I stowed a roll of blankets and some cold food into a borrowed whitehall boat and set sail. Out of the Oakland Estuary I drifted on the last of an early morning ebb, caught the first of the flood up bay, and raced along with a spanking breeze. San Pablo Bay was smoking, and the Carquinez Straits off the Selby Smelter were smoking, as I picked up ahead and left astern the old landmarks I had first learned with Nelson in the unreefer *Reindeer*.

Benicia showed before me. I opened the bight of Turner's Shipyard, rounded the *Solano* wharf, and surged along abreast of the patch of tules and the clustering fishermen's arks where in the old days I had lived and drunk deep.

And right here something happened to me, the gravity of which I never dreamed for many a long year to come. I had had no intention of stopping at Benicia. The tide favoured, the wind was fair and howling—glorious sailing for a sailor. Bull Head and Army Points showed ahead, marking the entrance to Suisun Bay which I knew was smoking. And yet, when I laid eyes on those fishing arks lying in the water-front tules, without debate, on the instant, I put down my tiller, came in on the sheet, and headed for the shore. On the instant, out of the profound of my brain-fag, I knew what I wanted. I wanted to drink. I wanted to get drunk.

The call was imperative. There was no uncertainty about it. More than anything else in the world, my frayed and frazzled mind wanted surcease from weariness in the way it knew surcease would come. And right here is the point. For the first time in my life I consciously, deliberately, desired to get drunk. It was a new, a totally different manifestation of John Barleycorn's power. It was not a body need for alcohol. It was a mental desire. My over-worked and jaded mind wanted to forget.

And here the point is drawn to its sharpest. Granted my prodigious brain-fag, nevertheless, had I never drunk in the past, the thought would never have entered my mind to get drunk now. Beginning with physical intolerance for alcohol, for years drinking only for the sake of comradeship and because alcohol was everywhere on the adventure-path, I had now reached the stage where my brain cried out, not merely for a drink, but for a drunk. And had I not been so long used to alcohol, my brain would not have so cried out. I should have sailed on past Bull Head, and in the smoking white of Suisun Bay, and in the wine of wind that filled my sail and poured through me, I should have forgotten my weary brain and rested and refreshed it.

So I sailed in to shore, made all fast, and hurried up among the arks. Charley Le Grant fell on my neck. His wife, Lizzie, folded me to her capacious breast. Billy Murphy, and Joe Lloyd, and all the survivors of the old guard, got around me and their arms around me. Charley seized the can and started for Jorgensen's saloon across the railroad tracks. That meant beer. I wanted whisky, so I called after him to bring a flask.

Many times that flask journeyed across the railroad tracks and back. More old friends of the old free and easy times dropped in, fishermen, Greeks, and Russians, and

French. They took turns in treating, and treated all around in turn again. They came and went, but I stayed on and drank with all. I guzzled, I swilled. I ran the liquor down and joyed as the maggots mounted in my brain.

And Clam came in, Nelson's partner before me, handsome as ever, but more reckless, half insane, burning himself out with whisky. He had just had a quarrel with his partner on the sloop *Gazelle*, and knives had been drawn, and blows struck, and he was bent on maddening the fever of the memory with more whisky. And while we downed it, we remembered Nelson and that he had stretched out his great shoulders for the last long sleep in this very town of Benicia; and we wept over the memory of him, and remembered only the good things of him, and sent out the flask to be filled and drank again.

They wanted me to stay over, but through the open door I could see the brave wind on the water, and my ears were filled with the roar of it. And while I forgot that I had plunged into the books nineteen hours a day for three solid months, Charley Le Grant shifted my outfit into a big Columbia River salmon boat. He added charcoal and a fisherman's brazier, a coffee pot and frying pan, and the coffee and the meat, and a black bass fresh from the water that day.

They had to help me down the rickety wharf and into the salmon boat. Likewise they stretched my boom and sprit until the sail set like a board. Some feared to set the sprit; but I insisted, and Charley had no doubts. He knew me of old, and knew that I could sail as long as I could see. They cast off my painter. I put the tiller up, filled away before it, and with dizzy eyes checked and steadied the boat on her course and waved farewell.

The tide had turned, and the fierce ebb, running in the teeth of a fiercer wind, kicked up a stiff, upstanding sea. Suisun Bay was white with wrath and sea-lump. But a salmon boat can sail, and I knew how to sail a salmon boat. So I drove her into it, and through it, and across, and maundered aloud and chanted my disdain for all the books and schools. Cresting seas filled me a foot or so with water, but I laughed at it sloshing about my feet, and chanted my disdain of the wind and the water. I hailed myself a master of life, riding on the back of the unleashed elements, and John Barleycorn rode with me. Amid dissertations on mathematics and philosophy and spoutings and quotations, I sang all the old songs learned in the days when I went from the cannery to the oyster boats to be a pirate —such songs as: 'Black Lulu', 'Flying Cloud', 'Treat my Daughter Kind-i-ly', 'The Boston Burglar', 'Come all you Rambling, Gambling Men', 'I Wisht I was a Little Bird', 'Shenandoah', and 'Ranzo, Boys, Ranzo'.

Hours afterwards, in the fires of sunset, where the Sacramento and the San Joaquin tumble their muddy floods together, I took the New York Cut-Off, skimmed across the smooth land-locked water past Black Diamond, on into the San Joaquin, and on to Antioch, where, somewhat sobered and magnificently hungry, I laid alongside a big potato sloop that had a familiar rig. Here were old friends aboard, who fried my black bass in olive oil. Then, too, there was a meaty fisherman's stew, delicious with garlic, and crusty Italian bread without butter, and all washed down with pint mugs of thick and heady claret.

My salmon boat was a-soak, but in the snug cabin of the sloop dry blankets and a dry bunk were mine; and we lay and smoked and yarned of old days, while overhead the wind screamed through the rigging and taut halyards drummed against the mast.

23

MY CRUISE in the salmon boat lasted a week, and I returned ready to enter the university. During the week's cruise I did not drink again. To accomplish this I was compelled to avoid looking up old friends, for as ever the

adventure-path was beset with John Barleycorn. I had
wanted to drink that first day, and in the days that followed I did not want it. My tired brain had recuperated.
I had no moral scruples in the matter. I was not ashamed
nor sorry because of that first day's orgy at Benicia, and I
thought no more about it, returning gladly to my books
and studies.

Long years were to pass ere I looked back upon that
day and realized its significance. At the time, and for a
long time afterwards, I was to think of it only as a frolic.
But still later, in the slough of brain-fag and intellectual
weariness, I was to remember and know the craving for
the anodyne that resides in alcohol.

In the meantime, after this one relapse at Benicia, I went
on with my abstemiousness, primarily because I didn't
want to drink. And next, I was abstemious because my way
led among books and students where no drinking was. Had
I been out on the adventure-path, I should as a matter of
course have been drinking. For that is the pity of the
adventure-path, which is one of John Barleycorn's favourite stamping grounds.

I completed the first half of my freshman year, and in
January of 1897 took up my courses for the second half.
But the pressure from lack of money, plus a conviction
that the university was not giving me all that I wanted in
the time I could spare for it, forced me to leave. I was not
very disappointed. For two years I had studied, and in
those two years, what was far more valuable, I had done a
prodigious amount of reading. Then, too, my grammar
had improved. It is true, I had not yet learned that I must
say 'It is I'; but I no longer was guilty of a double negative in writing, though still prone to that error in excited
speech.

I decided immediately to embark on my career. I had
four preferences first, music; second, poetry; third, the
writing of philosophic, economic, and political essays; and,
fourth, and last, and least, fiction writing. I resolutely cut
out music as impossible, settled down in my bedroom, and

tackled my second, third, and fourth choices simultaneously. Heavens, how I wrote! Never was there a
creative fever such as mine from which the patient escaped
fatal results. The way I worked was enough to soften my
brain and send me to a mad-house. I wrote, I wrote everything—ponderous essays, scientific and sociological short
stories, humorous verse, verse of all sorts from triolets and
sonnets to blank verse tragedy and elephantine epics in
Spenserian stanzas. On occasion I composed steadily, day
after day, for fifteen hours a day. At times I forgot to eat,
or refused to tear myself away from my passionate out-
pouring in order to eat.

And then there was the matter of typewriting. My
brother-in-law owned a machine which he used in the day-
time. In the night I was free to use it. That machine was
a wonder. I could weep now as I recollect my wrestlings
with it. It must have been a first model in the year one of
the typewriter era. Its alphabet was all capitals. It was
informed with an evil spirit. It obeyed no known laws of
physics, and overthrew the hoary axiom that like things
performed to like things produce like results. I'll swear
that machine never did the same thing in the same way
twice. Again and again it demonstrated that unlike actions
produce like results.

How my back used to ache with it! Prior to that experience, my back had been good for every violent strain put
upon it in a none too gentle career. But that typewriter
proved to me that I had a pipe-stem for a back. Also, it
made me doubt my shoulders. They ached as with rheumatism after every bout. The keys of that machine had to be
hit so hard that to one outside the house it sounded like
distant thunder or someone breaking up the furniture. I
had to hit the keys so hard that I strained my first fingers
to the elbows, while the ends of my fingers were blisters
burst and blistered again. Had it been my machine I'd
have operated it with a carpenter's hammer.

The worst of it was that I was actually typing my manuscripts at the same time I was trying to master that

machine. It was a feat of physical endurance and a brain-storm combined to type a thousand words, and I was composing thousands of words every day which just had to be typed for the waiting editors.

Oh, between the writing and the typewriting I was well a-weary. I had brain and nerve fag, and body fag as well, and yet the thought of drink never suggested itself. I was living too high to stand in need of an anodyne. All my waking hours, except those with that infernal typewriter, were spent in a creative heaven. And along with this I had no desire for drink because I still believed in many things—in the love of all men and women in the matter of man and woman love; in fatherhood; in human justice; in art—in the whole host of fond illusions that keep the world turning around.

But the waiting editors elected to keep on waiting. My manuscripts made amazing round-trip records between the Pacific and the Atlantic. It might have been the weirdness of the typewriting that prevented the editors from accepting at least one little offering of mine. I don't know, and goodness knows the stuff I wrote was as weird as its typing. I sold my hard-bought school books for ridiculous sums to second-hand bookmen. I borrowed small sums of money wherever I could, and suffered my old father to feed me with the meagre returns of his failing strength.

It didn't last long, only a few weeks, when I had to surrender and go to work. Yet I was unaware of any need for the drink anodyne. I was not disappointed. My career was retarded, that was all. Perhaps I did need further preparation. I had learned enough from the books to realize that I had only touched the hem of knowledge's garment. I still lived on the heights. My waking hours, and most of the hours I should have used for sleep, were spent with the books.

24

OUT IN the country, at the Belmont Academy, I went to work in a small, perfectly appointed steam laundry. Another fellow and myself did all the work from sorting and washing to ironing the white shirts, collars, and cuffs, and the 'fancy starch' of the wives of the professors. We worked like tigers, especially as summer came on and the academy boys took to the wearing of duck trousers. It consumes a dreadful lot of time to iron one pair of duck trousers. And there were so many pairs of them. We sweated our way through long sizzling weeks at a task that was never done; and many a night, while the students snored in bed, my partner and I toiled on under the electric light at steam mangle or ironing board.

The hours were long, the work was arduous, despite the fact that we became past masters in the art of eliminating waste motion. And I was receiving thirty dollars a month and board—a slight increase over my coal-shovelling and cannery days, at least to the extent of board, which cost my employer little (we ate in the kitchen), but which was to me the equivalent of twenty dollars a month. My robuster strength of added years, my increased skill, and all I had learned from the books, were responsible for this increase of twenty dollars. Judging by my rate of development, I might hope before I died to be a night watchman for sixty dollars a month, or a policeman actually receiving a hundred dollars with pickings.

So relentlessly did my partner and I spring into our work throughout the week that by Saturday night we were frazzled wrecks. I found myself in the old familiar work-beast condition, toiling longer hours than the horses toiled, thinking scarcely more frequent thoughts than horses think. The books were closed to me. I had brought a trunkful to the laundry, but found myself unable to read them. I fell asleep the moment I tried to read; and if I did manage to keep my eyes open for several pages, I could not remember the contents of those pages. I gave over attempts on heavy study, such as jurisprudence, political economy, and biology, and tried lighter stuff, such as history. I fell asleep. I tried literature, and fell asleep. And finally, when I fell asleep over lively novels, I gave up. I never succeeded in reading one book in all the time I spent in the laundry.

And when Saturday night came, and the week's work was over until Monday morning, I knew only one desire besides the desire to sleep, and that was to get drunk. This was the second time in my life that I had heard the unmistakable call of John Barleycorn. The first time it had been because of brain-fag. But I had no overworked brain now. On the contrary, all I knew was the dull numbness of a brain that was not worked at all. That was the trouble. My brain had become so alert and eager, so quickened by the wonder of the new world the books had discovered to it, that it now suffered all the misery of stagnancy and inaction.

And I, the long-time intimate of John Barleycorn, knew just what he promised me—maggots of fancy, dreams of power, forgetfulness, anything and everything save whirling washers, revolving mangles, humming centrifugal wringers, and fancy starch and interminable processions of duck trousers moving in steam under my flying iron. And that's it. John Barleycorn makes his appeal to weakness and failure, to weariness and exhaustion. He is the easy way out. And he is lying all the time. He offers false strength to the body, false elevation to the spirit, making things seem what they are not and vastly fairer than what they are.

But it must not be forgotten that John Barleycorn is protean. As well as to weakness and exhaustion, does he appeal to too much strength, to superabundant vitality, to the ennui of idleness. He can tuck in his arm the arm of any man in any mood. He can throw the net of his lure over all men. He exchanges new lamps for old, the spangles of illusion for the drabs of reality, and in the end cheats all who traffic with him.

I didn't get drunk, however, for the simple reason that it was a mile and a half to the nearest saloon. And this, in turn, was because the call to get drunk was not very loud in my ears. Had it been loud, I would have travelled ten times the distance to win to the saloon. On the other hand, had the saloon been just around the corner, I should have got drunk. As it was, I would sprawl out in the shade on my one day of rest and dally with the Sunday papers. But I was too weary even for their froth. The comic supplement might bring a pallid smile to my face, and then I would fall asleep.

Although I did not yield to John Barleycorn while working in the laundry, a certain definite result was produced. I had heard the call, felt the gnaw of desire, yearned for the anodyne. I was being prepared for the stronger desire of later years.

And the point is that this development of desire was entirely in my brain. My body did not cry out for alcohol. As always, alcohol was repulsive to my body. When I was bodily weary from shovelling coal the thought of taking a drink had never flickered into my consciousness. When I was brain-wearied after taking the entrance examinations to the university, I promptly got drunk. At the laundry I was suffering physical exhaustion again, and physical exhaustion that was not nearly so profound as that of the coal-shovelling. But there was a difference. When I went coal-shovelling my mind had not yet awakened. Between that time and the laundry my mind had found the kingdom of the mind. While shovelling coal my mind was somnolent. While toiling in the laundry my mind, informed and eager to do and be, was crucified.

And whether I yielded to drink, as at Benicia, or whether I refrained, as at the laundry, in my brain the seeds of desire for alcohol were germinating.

25

AFTER THE laundry my sister and her husband grub-staked me into the Klondike.

It was the first gold rush into that region, the early fall rush of 1897. I was twenty-one years old, and in splendid physical condition. I remember, at the end of the twenty-eight-mile portage across Chilcoot from Dyea Beach to Lake Linderman, I was packing up with the Indians and out-packing many an Indian. The last pack into Linderman was three miles. I back-tripped it four times a day, and on each forward trip carried one hundred and fifty pounds. This means that over the worst trails I daily travelled twenty-four miles, twelve of which were under a burden of one hundred and fifty pounds.

Yes, I had let career go hang, and was on the adventure-path again in quest of fortune. And of course, on the adventure-path, I met John Barleycorn. Here were the chesty men again, rovers and adventurers, and while they didn't mind a grub famine, whisky they could not do without. Whisky went over the trail, while the flour lay cached and untouched by the trailside.

As good fortune would have it, the three men in my party were not drinkers. Therefore I didn't drink save on rare occasions and disgracefully when with other men. In my personal medicine chest was a quart of whisky. I never drew the cork till six months afterward, in a lonely camp, where, without anæsthetics, a doctor was compelled to operate on a man. The doctor and the patient emptied my bottle between them and then proceeded to the operation.

Back in California a year later, recovering from scurvy, I found that my father was dead and that I was the head and the sole bread-winner of a household. When I state that I had passed coal on a steamship from Behring Sea to British Columbia, and travelled in the steerage from there to San Francisco, it will be understood that I brought nothing back from the Klondike but my scurvy.

Times were hard. Work of any sort was difficult to get. And work of any sort was what I had to take, for I was still an unskilled labourer. I had no thought of career. That was over and done with. I had to find food for two mouths beside my own and keep a roof over our heads—yes, and buy a winter suit, my one suit being decidedly summery. I had to get some sort of work immediately. After that, when I had caught my breath, I might think about my future.

Unskilled labour is the first to feel the slackness of hard times, and I had no trades save those of sailor and laundryman. With my new responsibilities I didn't dare go to sea, and I failed to find a job at laundrying. I failed to find a job at anything. I had my name down in five employment bureaux. I advertised in three newspapers. I sought out the few friends I knew who might be able to get me work; but they were either uninterested or unable to find anything for me.

The situation was desperate. I pawned my watch, my bicycle, and a mackintosh of which my father had been very proud and which he had left to me. It was and is my sole legacy in this world. It had cost fifteen dollars, and the pawnbroker let me have two dollars on it. And—oh, yes—a water-front comrade of earlier years drifted along one day with a dress suit wrapped in newspapers. He could give no adequate explanation of how he had come to possess it, nor did I press for an explanation. I wanted the suit myself. No; not to wear. I traded him a lot of rubbish which, being unpawnable, was useless to me. He peddled the rubbish for several dollars, while I pledged the dress-suit with my pawnbroker for five dollars. And for all I know the pawnbroker still has the suit. I had never intended to redeem it.

But I couldn't get any work. Yet I was a bargain in the labour market. I was twenty-two years old, weighed one hundred and sixty-five pounds stripped, every pound of which was excellent for toil; and the last traces of my scurvy were vanishing before a treatment of potatoes chewed raw. I tackled every opening for employment. I tried to become a studio model, but there were too many fine-bodied young fellows out of jobs. I answered advertisements of elderly invalids in need of companions. And I almost became a sewing machine agent, on commission, without salary. But poor people don't buy sewing machines in hard times, so I was forced to forgo that employment.

Of course, it must be remembered that along with such frivolous occupations I was trying to get work as wop, lumper, and roustabout. But winter was coming on, and the surplus labour army was pouring into the cities. Also I, who had romped along carelessly through the countries of the world and the kingdom of the mind, was not a member of any union.

I sought odd jobs. I worked days, and half-days, at anything I could get. I mowed lawns, trimmed hedges, took up carpets, beat them, and laid them again. Further, I took the civil service examinations for mail carrier and passed first. But alas! there was no vacancy, and I must wait. And while I waited, and in between the odd jobs I managed to procure, I started to earn ten dollars by writing a newspaper account of a voyage I had made, in an open boat down the Yukon, of nineteen hundred miles in nineteen days. I didn't know the first thing about the newspaper game, but I was confident I'd get ten dollars for my article.

But I didn't. The first San Francisco newspaper to which I mailed it never acknowledged receipt of the manuscript, but held on to it. The longer it held on to it the more certain I was that the thing was accepted.

And here is the funny thing. Some are born to fortune, and some have fortune thrust upon them. But in my case I was clubbed into fortune, and bitter necessity wielded the club. I had long since abandoned all thought of writing as a career. My honest intention in writing that article was to earn ten dollars. And that was the limit of my intention. It would help to tide me along until I got steady employment. Had a vacancy occurred in the post office at that time, I should have jumped at it.

But the vacancy did not occur, nor did a steady job; and I employed the time between odd jobs with writing a twenty-one-thousand-word serial for the *Youth's Companion*. I turned it out and typed it in seven days. I fancy that was what was the matter with it, for it came back.

It took some time for it to go and come, and in the meantime I tried my hand at short stories. I sold one to the *Overland Monthly* for five dollars. The *Black Cat* gave me forty dollars for another. The *Overland Monthly* offered me seven dollars and a half, pay on publication, for all the stories I should deliver. I got my bicycle, my watch, and my father's mackintosh out of pawn and rented a typewriter. Also, I paid up the bills I owed to the several groceries that allowed me a small credit. I recall the Portuguese groceryman who never permitted my bill to go beyond four dollars. Hopkins, another grocer, could not be budged beyond five dollars.

And just then came the call from the post office to go to work. It placed me in a most trying predicament. The sixty-five dollars I could earn regularly every month was a terrible temptation. I couldn't decide what to do. And I'll never be able to forgive the postmaster of Oakland. I answered the call, and I talked to him like a man. I frankly told him the situation. It looked as if I might win out at writing. The chance was good, but not certain. Now, if he would pass me by and select the next man on the eligible list and give me a call at the next vacancy—

But he shut me off with: 'Then you don't want the position?'

'But I do,' I protested. 'Don't you see, if you will pass me over this time——'

'If you want it you will take it,' he said coldly.

Happily for me, the cursed brutality of the man made me angry.

'Very well,' I said. 'I won't take it.'

26

HAVING BURNED my ship, I plunged into writing. I am afraid I always was an extremist. Early and late I was at it —writing, typing, studying grammar, studying writing and all the forms of writing, and studying the writers who succeeded in order to find out how they succeeded. I managed on five hours' sleep in the twenty-four, and came pretty close to working the nineteen waking hours left to me. My light burned till two and three in the morning, which led a good neighbour woman into a bit of Sherlock-Holmes deduction. Never seeing me in the day-time, she concluded that I was a gambler, and that the light in my window was placed there by my mother to guide her erring son home.

The trouble with the beginner at the writing game is the long, dry spells, when there is never an editor's cheque and everything pawnable is pawned. I wore my summer suit pretty well through that winter, and the following summer experienced the longest, dryest spell of all, in the period when salaried men are gone on vacation and manuscripts lie in editorial offices until vacation is over.

My difficulty was that I had no one to advise me. I didn't know a soul who had written or who had ever tried to write. I didn't even know one reporter. Also, to succeed at the writing game, I found I had to unlearn everything the teachers and professors of literature of the high school and university had taught me. I was very indignant about this at the time; though now I can understand it. They did not know the trick of successful writing in the years 1895 and 1896. They knew all about *Snow Bound* and *Sartor Resartus*; but the American editors of 1899 did not want such truck. They wanted the 1899 truck, and offered to pay so well for it that the teachers and professors of literature would have quit their jobs could they have supplied it.

I struggled along, stood off the butcher and the grocer, pawned my watch and bicycle and my father's mackintosh, and I worked. I really did work, and went on short commons of sleep. Critics have complained about the swift education one of my characters, Martin Eden, achieved. In three years, from a sailor with a common school education, I made a successful writer of him. The critics say this is impossible. Yet I was Martin Eden. At the end of three working years, two of which were spent in high school and the university and one spent at writing, and all three in studying immensely and intensely, I was publishing stories in magazines such as the *Atlantic Monthly*, was correcting proofs of my first book (issued by Houghton, Mifflin Co.), was selling sociological articles to *Cosmopolitan* and *McClure's*, had declined an associate editorship proffered me by telegraph from New York City, and was getting ready to marry.

Now the foregoing means work, especially the last year of it, when I was learning my trade as a writer. And in that year, running short on sleep and tasking my brain to its limit, I neither drank nor cared to drink. So far as I was concerned, alcohol did not exist. I did suffer from brain-fag on occasion, but alcohol never suggested itself as an ameliorative. Heavens! Editorial acceptances and cheques were all the amelioratives I needed. A thin envelope from an editor in the morning's mail was more stimulating than half a dozen cocktails. And if a cheque of decent amount came out of the envelope, such incident in itself was a whole drunk.

Furthermore, at that time in my life I did not know what a cocktail was. I remember, when my first book was published, several Alaskans, who were members of the Bohemian Club, entertained me one evening at the club in San Francisco. We sat in most wonderful leather chairs, and drinks were ordered. Never had I heard such an ordering of liqueurs and of highballs of particular brands of Scotch. I didn't know what a liqueur or a highball was, and I didn't know that 'Scotch' meant whisky. I knew only poor

men's drinks, the drinks of the frontier and of sailor-town
—cheap beer and cheaper whisky that was just called
whisky and nothing else. I was embarrassed to make a
choice, and the steward nearly collapsed when I ordered
claret as an after-dinner drink.

27

As I succeeded with my writing, my standard of living
rose and my horizon broadened. I confined myself to writing and typing a thousand words a day, including Sundays
and holidays; and I still studied hard, but not so hard as
formerly. I allowed myself five and one-half hours of actual
sleep. I added this half-hour because I was compelled.
Financial success permitted me more time for exercise. I
rode my wheel more, chiefly because it was permanently
out of pawn; and I boxed and fenced, walked on my hands,
jumped high and broad, put the shot and tossed the caber,
and went swimming. And I learned that more sleep is required for physical exercise than for mental exercise. There
were tired nights, bodily, when I slept six hours; and on
occasion of very severe exercise I actually slept seven
hours. But such sleep orgies were not frequent. There was
so much to learn, so much to be done, that I felt wicked
when I slept seven hours. And I blessed the man who
invented alarm clocks.

And still no desire to drink. I possessed too many fine
faiths, was living at too keen a pitch. I was a socialist, intent
on saving the world, and alcohol could not give me the
fervours that were mine from my ideas and ideals. My
voice, on account of my successful writing, had added
weight, or so I thought. At any rate, my reputation as a
writer drew me audiences that my reputation as a speaker
never could have drawn. I was invited before clubs and
organizations of all sorts to deliver my message. I fought

the good fight, and went on studying and writing, and was very busy.

Up to this time I had had a very restricted circle of friends. But now I began to go about. I was invited out, especially to dinner; and I made many friends and acquaintances whose economic lives were easier than mine had been. And many of them drank. In their own houses they drank and offered me drink. They were not drunkards any of them. They just drank temperately, and I drank temperately with them as an act of comradeship and accepted hospitality. I did not care for it, neither wanted it nor did not want it, and so small was the impression made by it that I do not remember my first cocktail nor my first Scotch highball.

Well, I had a house. When one is asked into other houses, he naturally asks others into his house. Behold the rising standard of living. Having been given drink in other houses, I could expect nothing else of myself than to give drink in my own house. So I laid in a supply of beer and whisky and table claret. Never since that has my house not been well supplied.

And still, through all this period, I did not care in the slightest for John Barleycorn. I drank when others drank, and with them, as a social act. And I had so little choice in the matter that I drank whatever they drank. If they elected whisky, then whisky it was for me. If they drank root beer or sarsaparilla, I drank root beer or sarsaparilla with them. And when there were no friends in the house, why, I didn't drink anything. Whisky decanters were always in the room where I wrote, and for months and years I never knew what it was, when by myself, to take a drink.

When out at dinner I noticed the kindly, genial glow of the preliminary cocktail. It seemed a very fitting and gracious thing. Yet so little did I stand in need of it, with my own high intensity and vitality, that I never thought it worth while to have a cocktail before my own meal when I ate alone.

On the other hand, I well remember a very brilliant man,

somewhat older than I, who occasionally visited me. He liked whisky, and I recall sitting whole afternoons in my den, drinking steadily with him, drink for drink, until he was mildly lit up and I was slightly aware that I had drunk some whisky. Now why did I do this? I don't know, save that the old schooling held, the training of the old days and nights glass in hand with men, the drinking ways of drink and drinkers.

Besides, I no longer feared John Barleycorn. Mine was that most dangerous stage when a man believes himself John Barleycorn's master. I had proved it to my satisfaction in the long years of work and study. I could drink when I wanted, refrain when I wanted, drink without getting drunk, and to cap everything I was thoroughly conscious that I had no liking for the stuff. During this period I drank precisely for the same reason I had drunk with Scotty and the harpooner and with the oyster pirates—because it was an act that men performed with whom I wanted to behave as a man. These brilliant ones, these adventurers of the mind, drank. Very well. There was no reason I should not drink with them—I who knew so confidently that I had nothing to fear from John Barleycorn.

And the foregoing was my attitude of mind for years. Occasionally I got well jingled, but such occasions were rare. It interfered with my work, and I permitted nothing to interfere with my work. I remember, when spending several months in the East End of London, during which time I wrote a book* and adventured much amongst the worst of the slum classes, that I got drunk several times and was mightily wroth with myself because it interfered with my writing. Yet these very times were because I was out on the adventure-path where John Barleycorn is always to be found.

Then, too, with the certitude of long training and unholy intimacy, there were occasions when I engaged in drinking bouts with men. Of course, this was on the adventure-path in various parts of the world, and it was a matter of pride.

* *The People of The Abyss.*

It is a queer man-pride that leads one to drink with men in order to show as strong a head as they. But this queer man-pride is no theory. It is a fact.

For instance, a wild band of young revolutionists invited me as the guest of honour to a beer bust. It is the only technical beer bust I ever attended. I did not know the true inwardness of the affair when I accepted. I imagined that the talk would be wild and high, that some of them might drink more than they ought, and that I would drink discreetly. But it seemed these beer busts were a diversion of these high-spirited young fellows whereby they whiled away the tedium of existence by making fools of their betters. As I learned afterwards, they had got their previous guest of honour, a brilliant young radical, unskilled in drinking, quite pipped.

When I found myself with them, and the situation dawned on me, up rose my queer man-pride. I'd show them, the young rascals. I'd show them who was husky and chesty, who had the vitality and the constitution, the stomach and the head, who could make most of a swine of himself and show it least. These unlicked cubs who thought they could out-drink *me*!

You see, it was an endurance test, and no man likes to give another best. Faugh! it was steam beer. I had learned more expensive brews. Not for years had I drunk steam beer; but when I had, I had drunk with men, and I guessed I could show these youngsters some ability in beer-guzzling. And the drinking began, and I had to drink with the best of them. Some of them might lag, but the guest of honour was not permitted to lag.

And all my austere nights of midnight oil, all the books I had read, all the wisdom I had gathered, went glimmering before the ape and tiger in me that crawled up from the abysm of my heredity, atavistic, competitive and brutal, lustful with strength and desire to outswine the swine.

And when the session broke up I was still on my feet, and I walked, erect, unswaying—which was more than can be said of some of my hosts. I recall one of them in indignant tears on the street corner, weeping as he pointed out my sober condition. Little he dreamed the iron clutch, born of old training, with which I held to my consciousness in my swimming brain, kept control of my muscles and my qualms, kept my voice unbroken and easy and my thoughts consecutive and logical. Yes, and mixed up with it all I was privily a-grin. They hadn't made a fool of me in that drinking bout. And I was proud of myself for the achievement. Darn it, I am still proud, so strangely is a man compounded.

But I didn't write my thousand words next morning. I was sick, poisoned. It was a day of wretchedness. In the afternoon I had to give a public speech. I gave it, and I am confident it was as bad as I felt. Some of my hosts were there in the front rows to mark any signs on me of the night before. I don't know what signs they marked, but I marked signs on them and took consolation in the knowledge that they were just as sick as I.

Never again, I swore. And I have never been inveigled into another beer bust. For that matter, that was my last drinking bout of any sort. Oh, I have drunk ever since, but with more wisdom, more discretion, and never in a competitive spirit. It is thus that the seasoned drinker grows seasoned.

To show that at this period in my life drinking was wholly a matter of companionship, I remember crossing the Atlantic in the old *Teutonic*. It chanced, at the start, that I chummed with an English cable operator and a younger member of a Spanish shipping firm. Now the only thing they drank was 'horse's neck'—a long, soft, cool drink with an apple peel or an orange peel floating in it. And for that whole voyage I drank horse's necks with my two companions. On the other hand, had they drunk whisky, I should have drunk whisky with them. From this it must not be concluded that I was merely weak. I didn't care. I had no morality in the matter. I was strong with youth, and unafraid, and alcohol was an utterly negligible question so far as I was concerned.

28

NOT YET was I ready to tuck my arm in John Barley-corn's. The older I got, the greater my success, the more money I earned, the wider was the command of the world that became mine and the more prominently did John Barleycorn bulk in my life. And still I maintained no more than a nodding acquaintance with him. I drank for the sake of sociability, and when alone I did not drink. Sometimes I got jingled, but I considered such jingles the mild price I paid for sociability.

To show how unripe I was for John Barleycorn, when, at this time, I descended into my slough of despond, I never dreamed of turning to John Barleycorn for a helping hand. I had life troubles and heart troubles which are neither here nor there in this narrative. But, combined with them, were intellectual troubles which are indeed germane.

Mine was no uncommon experience. I had read too much positive science and lived too much positive life. In the eagerness of youth I had made the ancient mistake of pursuing Truth too relentlessly. I had torn her veils from her, and the sight was too terrible for me to stand. In brief, I lost my fine faith in pretty well everything except humanity, and the humanity I retained faith in was a very stark humanity indeed.

This long sickness of pessimism is too well known to most of us to be detailed here. Let it suffice to state that I had it very bad. I meditated suicide coolly, as a Greek philosopher might. My regret was that there were too many dependent directly upon me for food and shelter for me to quit living. But that was sheer morality. What really saved me was the one remaining illusion—the PEOPLE.

The things I had fought for and burned my midnight oil for had failed me. Success—I despised it. Recognition —it was dead ashes. Society, men and women above the ruck and the muck of the water-front and the forecastle—I was appalled by their unlovely mental mediocrity. Love of woman—it was like all the rest. Money—I could sleep in only one bed at a time, and of what worth was an income of a hundred porterhouses a day when I could eat only one? Art, culture—in the face of the iron facts of biology such things were ridiculous, the exponents of such things only the more ridiculous.

From the foregoing it can be seen how very sick I was. I was born a fighter. The things I had fought for had proved not worth the fight. Remained the PEOPLE. My fight was finished, yet something was left still to fight for—the PEOPLE.

But while I was discovering this one last tie to bind me to life, in my extremity, in the depths of despond, walking in the valley of the shadow, my ears were deaf to John Barleycorn. Never the remotest whisper arose in my consciousness that John Barleycorn was the anodyne, that he could lie me along to live. One way only was uppermost in my thought—my revolver, the crashing eternal darkness of a bullet. There was plenty of whisky in the house—for my guests. I never touched it. I grew afraid of my revolver —afraid during the period in which the radiant, flashing vision of the PEOPLE was forming in my mind and will. So obsessed was I with the desire to die that I feared I might commit the act in my sleep, and I was compelled to give my revolver away to others who were to lose it for me where my subconscious hand might not find it.

But the PEOPLE saved me. By the PEOPLE was I handcuffed to life. There was still one fight left in me, and here was the thing for which to fight. I threw all precaution to the winds, threw myself with fiercer zeal into the fight for socialism, laughed at the editors and publishers who warned me and who were the sources of my hundred porterhouses a day, and was brutally careless of whose feelings I hurt and of how savagely I hurt them. As the 'well-balanced radicals' charged at the time, my efforts were so strenuous, so unsafe and unsane, so ultra-revolutionary, that I retarded the socialist development in the

United States by five years. In passing, I wish to remark, at this late date, that it is my fond belief that I accelerated the socialist development in the United States by at least five minutes.

It was the PEOPLE, and no thanks to John Barleycorn, who pulled me through my long sickness. And when I was convalescent came the love of woman to complete the cure and lull my pessimism asleep for many a long day, until John Barleycorn again awoke it. But in the meantime, I pursued Truth less relentlessly, refraining from tearing her last veils aside even when I clutched them in my hand. I no longer cared to look up Truth naked. I refused to permit myself to see a second time what I had once seen. And the memory of what I had that time seen I resolutely blotted from my mind.

And I was very happy. Life went well with me, I took delight in little things. The big things I declined to take too seriously. I still read the books, but not with the old eagerness. I still read the books today, but never again shall I read them with that old glory of youthful passion that whispered me on to win to the mystery at the back of life and behind the stars.

The point of this chapter is that, in the long sickness that at some time comes to most of us, I came through without any appeal for aid to John Barleycorn. Love, socialism, the PEOPLE—healthful figments of man's mind —were the things that cured and saved me. If ever a man was not a born alcoholic, I believe that I am that man. And yet—well, let the succeeding chapters tell their tale, for in them will be shown how I paid for my previous quarter of a century of contact with ever-accessible John Barleycorn.

29

AFTER MY long sickness my drinking continued to be convivial. I drank when others drank and I was with them.

But, imperceptibly, my need for alcohol took form and began to grow. It was not a body need. I boxed, swam, sailed, rode horses, lived in the open an arrantly healthful life, and passed life insurance examinations with flying colours. In its inception, now that I look back upon it, this need for alcohol was a mental need, a nerve need, a good-spirits need. How can I explain?

It was something like this. Physiologically, from the standpoint of palate and stomach, alcohol was, as it had always been, repulsive. It tasted no better than beer did when I was five, than bitter claret did when I was seven. When I was alone, writing or studying, I had no need for it. But—I was growing old, or wise, or both, or senile as an alternative. When I was in company I was less pleased, less excited, with the things said and done. Erstwhile worth-while fun and stunts seemed no longer worth while; and it was a torment to listen to the insipidities and stupidities of women, to the pompous, arrogant sayings of the little half-baked men. It is the penalty one pays for reading the books too much, or for being oneself a fool. In my case it does not matter which was my trouble. The trouble itself was the fact. The condition of the fact was mine. For me the life, and light, and sparkle of human intercourse were dwindling.

I had climbed too high among the stars, or, maybe, I had slept too hard. Yet I was not hysterical nor in any way overwrought. My pulse was normal. My heart was an amazement of excellence to the insurance doctors. My lungs threw the said doctors into ecstasies. I wrote a thousand words every day. I was punctiliously exact in dealing with all the affairs of life that fell to my lot. I exercised in joy and gladness. I slept at night like a babe. But. . . .

Well, as soon as I got out in the company of others I was driven to melancholy and spiritual tears. I could neither laugh with nor at the solemn utterances of men I esteemed ponderous asses; nor could I laugh, nor engage in my old-time lightsome persiflage, with the silly superficial chatterings of women, who, underneath all their silliness and softness, were as primitive, direct, and deadly in their pursuit of biological destiny as the monkeys women were before they shed their furry coats and replaced them with the furs of other animals.

And I was not pessimistic. I swear I was not pessimistic. I was merely bored. I had seen the same show too often, listened too often to the same songs and the same jokes. I knew too much about the box office receipts. I knew the cogs of the machinery behind the scenes so well that the posing on the stage, and the laughter and the song, could not drown the creaking of the wheels behind.

It doesn't pay to go behind the scenes and see the angel-voiced tenor beat his wife. Well, I'd been behind, and I was paying for it. Or else I was a fool. It is immaterial which was my situation. The situation is what counts, and the situation was that social intercourse for me was getting painful and difficult. On the other hand, it must be stated that on rare occasions, on very rare occasions, I did meet rare souls, or fools like me, with whom I could spend magnificent hours among the stars, or in the paradise of fools. I was married to a rare soul, or a fool, who never bored me and who was always a source of new and unending surprise and delight. But I could not spend all my hours solely in her company. Nor would it have been fair, nor wise, to compel her to spend all her hours in my company. Besides, I had written a string of successful books, and society demands some portion of the recreative hours of a fellow that writes books. And any normal man, of himself and his needs, demands some hours of his fellow men.

And now we begin to come to it. How to face the social intercourse game with the glamour gone? John Barleycorn. The ever patient one had waited a quarter of a century and more for me to reach my hand out in need of him. His thousand tricks had failed, thanks to my constitution and good luck, but he had more tricks in his bag. A cocktail or two, or several, I found, cheered me up for the foolishness of foolish people. A cocktail, or several, before dinner, enabled me to laugh whole-heartedly at things which had long since ceased being laughable. The cocktail was a prod, a spur, a kick, to my jaded mind and bored spirits. It recrudesced the laughter and the song, and put a lilt into my own imagination so that I could laugh and sing and say foolish things with the liveliest of them, or platitudes with verve and intensity to the satisfaction of the pompous mediocre ones who knew no other way to talk.

A poor companion without a cocktail, I became a very good companion with one. I achieved a false exhilaration, drugged myself to merriment. And the thing began so imperceptibly that I, old intimate of John Barleycorn, never dreamed whither it was leading me. I was beginning to call for music and wine; soon I should be calling for madder music and more wine.

It was at this time I became aware of waiting with expectancy for the pre-dinner cocktail. I *wanted* it, and I was *conscious* that I wanted it. I remember, while war-corresponding in the Far East, being irresistibly attracted to a certain home. Besides accepting all invitations to dinner, I made a point of dropping in almost every afternoon. Now, the hostess was a charming woman, but it was not for her sake that I was under her roof so frequently. It happened that she made by far the finest cocktail procurable in that large city where drink-mixing on the part of the foreign population was indeed an art. Up at the club, down at the hotels, and in other private houses, no such cocktails were created. Her cocktails were subtle. They were masterpieces. They were the least repulsive to the palate and carried the most 'kick'. And yet, I desired her cocktails only for sociability's sake, to key myself to sociable moods. When I rode away from that city, across hundreds of miles of rice-fields and mountains, and through months of campaigning, and on with the victorious Japanese into Manchuria, I did not drink. Several bottles of whisky were always to be found on the backs of my pack-horses. Yet I never broached a bottle for myself, never took a drink by myself, and never knew a desire to take such a drink. Oh, if a white man came into my camp, I opened a bottle and we drank together according to the way of men, just as he would open a bottle and drink with me if I came into his camp. I carried that whisky for social purposes, and I so charged it up in my expense account to the newspaper for which I worked.

Only in retrospect can I mark the almost imperceptible growth of my desire. There were little hints then that I did not take, little straws in the wind that I did not see, little incidents the gravity of which I did not realize.

For instance, for some years it had been my practice each winter to cruise for six or eight weeks on San Francisco Bay. My stout sloop yacht, the *Spray*, had a comfortable cabin and a coal stove. A Korean boy did the cooking, and I usually took a friend or so along to share the joys of the cruise. Also, I took my machine along and did my thousand words a day. On the particular trip I have in mind, Cloudesley and Toddy came along. This was Toddy's first trip. On previous trips Cloudesley had elected to drink beer; so I had kept the yacht supplied with beer and had drunk beer with him.

But on this cruise the situation was different. Toddy was so nicknamed because of his diabolical cleverness in concocting toddies. So I brought whisky along—a couple of gallons. Alas! Many another gallon I bought, for Cloudesley and I got into the habit of drinking a certain hot toddy that actually tasted delicious going down and that carried the most exhilarating kick imaginable.

I *liked* those toddies. I grew to look forward to the making of them. We drank them regularly, one before breakfast, one before dinner, one before supper, and a final one when we went to bed. We never got drunk. But I will say that four times a day we were very genial. And when, in the middle of the cruise, Toddy was called back to San Francisco on business, Cloudesley and I saw to it that the Korean boy mixed toddies regularly for us according to formula.

6*

But that was only on the boat. Back on the land, in my house, I took no before breakfast eye-opener, no bed-going nightcap. And I haven't drunk hot toddies since, and that was many a year ago. But the point is, I *liked* those toddies. The geniality of which they were provocative was marvellous. They were eloquent proselytisers for John Barleycorn in their own small insidious way. They were tickles of the something destined to grow into daily and deadly desire. And I didn't know, never dreamed—I, who had lived with John Barleycorn for so many years and laughed at all his unavailing attempts to win me.

30

PART OF the process of recovering from my long sickness was to find delight in little things, in things unconnected with books and problems, in play, in games of tag in the swimming pool, in flying kites, in fooling with horses, in working out mechanical puzzles. As a result, I grew tired of the city. On the ranch, in the Valley of the Moon, I found my paradise. I gave up living in cities. All the cities held for me were music, the theatre, and Turkish baths.

And all went well with me. I worked hard, played hard, and was very happy. I read more fiction and less fact. I did not study a tithe as much as I had studied in the past. I still took an interest in the fundamental problems of existence, but it was a very cautious interest; for I had burned my fingers that time I clutched at the veils of Truth and wrested them from her. There was a bit of lie in this attitude of mine, a bit of hypocrisy; but the lie and the hypocrisy were those of a man desiring to live. I deliberately blinded myself to what I took to be the savage interpretation of biological fact. After all, I was merely forswearing a bad habit, forgoing a bad frame of mind.

And I repeat, I was very happy. And I add, that in all my days, measuring them with cold, considerative judgment, this was, far and away beyond all other periods, the happiest period of my life.

But the time was at hand, rhymeless and reasonless so far as I can see, when I was to begin to pay for my score of years of dallying with John Barleycorn. Occasionally guests journeyed to the ranch and remained a few days. Some did not drink. But to those who did drink, the absence of all alcohol on the ranch was a hardship. I could not violate my sense of hospitality by compelling them to endure this hardship. I ordered in a stock—for my guests.

I was never interested enough in cocktails to know how they were made. So I got a bar-keeper in Oakland to make them in bulk and ship them to me. When I had no guests I didn't drink. But I began to notice, when I finished my morning's work, that I was glad if there were a guest, for then I could drink a cocktail with him.

Now I was so clean of alcohol that even a single cocktail was provocative of pitch. A single cocktail would glow the mind and tickle a laugh for the few minutes prior to sitting down to table and starting the delightful process of eating. On the other hand, such was the strength of my stomach, of my alcoholic resistance, that the single cocktail was only the glimmer of a glow, the faintest tickle of a laugh. One day, a friend frankly and shamelessly suggested a second cocktail. I drank the second one with him. The glow was appreciably longer and warmer, the laughter deeper and more resonant. One does not forget such experiences. Sometimes I almost think that it was because I was so very happy that I started on my real drinking.

I remember one day Charmian and I took a long ride over the mountains on our horses. The servants had been dismissed for the day, and we returned late at night to a jolly chafing-dish supper. Oh, it was good to be alive that night while the supper was preparing, the two of us alone in the kitchen. I, personally, was at the top of life. Such things as the books and ultimate truth did not exist. My body was gloriously healthy, and healthily tired from the long ride. It had been a splendid day. The night was splendid. I was with the woman who was my mate, picnicking in gleeful abandon. I had no troubles. The bills were all paid, and a surplus of money was rolling in on me. The future ever-widened before me. And right there, in the kitchen, delicious things bubbled in the chafing-dish, our laughter bubbled, and my stomach was keen with a most delicious edge of appetite.

I felt so good, that somehow, somewhere, in me arose an insatiable greed to feel better. I was so happy that I wanted to pitch my happiness ever higher. And I knew the way. Ten thousand contacts with John Barleycorn had taught me. Several times I wandered out of the kitchen to the cocktail bottle, and each time I left it diminished by one man's-size cocktail. The result was splendid. I wasn't jingled, I wasn't lighted up; but I was warmed, I glowed, my happiness was pyramided. Munificent as life was to me, I added to that munificence. It was a great hour—one of my greatest. But I paid for it, long afterwards, as you will see. One does not forget such experiences, and, in human stupidity, cannot be brought to realize that there is no immutable law which decrees that same things shall produce same results. For they don't, else would the thousandth pipe of opium be provocative of similar delights to the first, else would one cocktail, instead of several, produce an equivalent glow after a year of cocktails.

One day, just before I ate midday dinner, after my morning's writing was done, when I had no guest, I took a cocktail by myself. Thereafter, when there were no guests, I took this daily pre-dinner cocktail. And right there John Barleycorn had me. I was beginning to drink regularly. I was beginning to drink alone. And I was beginning to drink, not for hospitality's sake, not for the sake of the taste, but for the effect of the drink.

I *wanted* that daily pre-dinner cocktail. And it never crossed my mind that there was any reason I should not have it. I paid for it. I could pay for a thousand cocktails each day if I wanted. And what was a cocktail—one cocktail—to me who on so many occasions for so many years had drunk inordinate quantities of stiffer stuff and been unharmed?

The programme of my ranch life was as follows: Each morning, at eight-thirty, having been reading or correcting proofs in bed since four or five, I went to my desk. Odds and ends of correspondence and notes occupied me till nine, and at nine sharp, invariably, I began my writing. By eleven, sometimes a few minutes earlier or later, my thousand words were finished. Another half-hour at cleaning up my desk, and my day's work was done, so that at eleven-thirty I got into a hammock under the trees with my mailbag and the morning newspaper. At twelve-thirty I ate dinner and in the afternoon I swam and rode.

One morning, at eleven-thirty, before I got into the hammock, I took a cocktail. I repeated this on subsequent mornings, of course, taking another cocktail just before I ate at twelve-thirty. Soon I found myself, seated at my desk in the midst of my thousand words, looking forward to that eleven-thirty cocktail.

At last, now, I was thoroughly conscious that I desired alcohol. But what of it? I wasn't afraid of John Barleycorn. I had associated with him too long. I was wise in the matter of drink. I was discreet. Never again would I drink to excess. I knew the dangers and the pitfalls of John Barleycorn, the various ways by which he had tried to kill me in the past. But all that was past, long past. Never again would I drink myself to stupefaction. Never again would I get drunk. All I wanted, and all I would take, was just enough to glow and warm me, to kick geniality alive in me and put laughter in my throat and stir the maggots of imagination slightly in my brain. Oh, I was thoroughly master of myself, and of John Barleycorn.

31

BUT THE same stimulus to the human organism will not continue to produce the same response. By and by I discovered there was no kick at all in one cocktail. One cocktail left me dead. There was no glow, no laughter tickle. Two or three cocktails were required to produce the original effect of one. And I wanted that effect. I drank my first cocktail at eleven-thirty when I took the morning's mail into the hammock, and I drank my second cocktail an hour later just before I ate. I got into the habit of crawling out of the hammock ten minutes earlier so as to find time and decency for two more cocktails ere I ate. This became schedule—three cocktails in the hour that intervened between my desk and dinner. And these are two of the deadliest drinking habits: regular drinking and solitary drinking.

I was always willing to drink when anyone was around. I drank by myself when no one was around. Then I made another step. When I had for guest a man of limited drinking calibre, I took two drinks to his one—one drink with him, the other drink without him and of which he did not know. I *stole* that other drink, and, worse than that, I began the habit of drinking alone when there was a guest, a man, a comrade, with whom I could have drunk. But John Barleycorn furnished the extenuation. It was a wrong thing to trip a guest up with excess of hospitality and get him drunk. If I persuaded him, with his limited calibre, into drinking up with me, I'd surely get him drunk. What could I do but steal that every second drink, or else deny myself the kick equivalent to what he got out of half the number?

Please remember, as I recite this development of my drinking, that I am no fool, no weakling. As the world measures such things, I am a success—I dare to say a success more conspicuous than the success of the average successful man, and a success that required a pretty fair amount of brains and will power. My body is a strong body. It has survived where weaklings died like flies. And yet these things which I am relating happened to my body and to me. I am a fact. My drinking is a fact. My drinking is a thing that has happened, and is no theory nor speculation; and, as I see it, it but lays the emphasis on the power of John Barleycorn—a savagery that we still permit to exist, a deadly institution that lingers from the mad old brutal days and that takes its heavy toll of youth and strength, and high spirit, and of very much of all of the best we breed.

To return. After a boisterous afternoon in the swimming pool, followed by a glorious ride on horseback over the mountains or up or down the Valley of the Moon, I found myself so keyed and splendid that I desired to be more highly keyed, to feel more splendid. I knew the way. A cocktail before supper was not the way. Two or three, at the very least, was what was needed. I took them. Why not? It was living. I had always dearly loved to live. This also became part of the daily schedule.

Then, too, I was perpetually finding excuses for extra cocktails. It might be the assembling of a particularly jolly crowd; a touch of anger against my architect or against a thieving stonemason working on my barn; the death of my favourite horse in a barbed wire fence; or news of good fortune in the morning mail from my dealings with editors and publishers. It was immaterial what the excuse might be, once the desire had germinated in me. The thing was: I *wanted* alcohol. At last, after a score and more of years of dallying and of not wanting, now I wanted it. And my strength was my weakness. I required two, three, or four drinks to get an effect commensurate with the effect the average man got out of one drink.

One rule I observed. I never took a drink until my day's work of writing a thousand words was done. And, when done, the cocktails reared a wall of inhibition in my brain between the day's work done and the rest of the day of fun to come. My work ceased from my consciousness. No thought of it flickered in my brain till next morning at nine o'clock when I sat at my desk and began my next thousand words. This was a desirable condition of mind to achieve. I conserved my energy by means of this alcoholic inhibition. John Barleycorn was not so black as he was painted. He did a fellow many a good turn, and this was one of them.

And I turned out work that was healthful, and wholesome, and sincere. It was never pessimistic. The way to life I had learned in my long sickness. I knew the illusions were right, and I exalted the illusions. Oh, I still turn out the same sort of work, stuff that is clean, alive, optimistic, and that makes toward life. And I am always assured by the critics of my superabundant and abounding vitality, and of how thoroughly I am deluded by these very illusions I exploit.

And while on this digression, let me repeat the question I have repeated to myself ten thousand times. *Why did I drink?* What need was there for it? I was happy. Was it because I was too happy? I was strong. Was it because I was too strong? Did I possess too much vitality? I don't know why I drank. I cannot answer, though I can voice the suspicion that ever grows in me. I had been in too-familiar contact with John Barleycorn through too many years. A left-handed man, by long practice, can become a right-handed man. Had I, a non-alcoholic, by long practice become an alcoholic?

I was so happy. I had won through my long sickness to the satisfying love of woman. I earned more money with less endeavour. I glowed with health. I slept like a babe. I continued to write successful books, and in sociological controversy I saw my opponents confuted with the facts of the times that daily reared new buttresses to my intellectual position. From day's end to day's end I never knew sorrow, disappointment, nor regret. I was happy all the time. Life was one unending song. I begrudged the very hours of blessed sleep because by that much was I robbed of the joy that would have been mine had I remained awake. And yet I drank. And John Barleycorn, all unguessed by me, was setting the stage for a sickness all his own.

The more I drank the more I was required to drink to get an equivalent effect. When I left the Valley of the Moon, and went to the city, and dined out, a cocktail served at table was a wan and worthless thing. There was no pre-dinner kick in it. On my way to dinner I was compelled to accumulate the kick—two cocktails, three, and, if I met some fellows, four or five, or six, it didn't matter within several. Once, I was in a rush. I had no time decently to accumulate the several drinks. A brilliant idea came to me. I told the barkeeper to mix me a double cocktail. Thereafter, whenever I was in a hurry, I ordered double cocktails. It saved time.

One result of this regular heavy drinking was to jade me. My mind grew so accustomed to spring and liven by artificial means that without artificial means it refused to spring and liven. Alcohol became more and more imperative in order to meet people, in order to become sociably fit. I had to get the kick and the hit of the stuff, the crawl of the maggots, the genial brain glow, the laughter tickle, the touch of devilishness and sting, the smile over the face of things, ere I could join my fellows and make one with them.

Another result was that John Barleycorn was beginning to trip me up. He was thrusting my long sickness back upon me, inveigling me into again pursuing Truth and snatching her veils away from her, tricking me into looking reality stark in the face. But this came on gradually. My thoughts were growing harsh again, though they grew harsh slowly.

Sometimes warning thoughts crossed my mind. Where was this steady drinking leading? But trust John Barleycorn to silence such questions. 'Come on and have a drink and I'll tell you all about it,' is his way. And it works. For instance, the following is a case in point, and one which John Barleycorn never wearied of reminding me:

I had suffered an accident which required a ticklish operation. One morning, a week after I had come off the table, I lay on my hospital bed, weak and weary. The sunburn of my face, what little of it could be seen through a scraggly growth of beard, had faded to a sickly yellow. My doctor stood at my bedside on the verge of departure. He glared disapprovingly at the cigarette I was smoking.

'That's what you ought to quit,' he lectured. 'It will get you in the end. Look at me.'

I looked. He was about my own age, broad-shouldered, deep-chested, eyes sparkling, and ruddy-cheeked with health. A finer specimen of manhood one would not ask.

' I used to smoke,' he went on. 'Cigars. But I gave even them up. And look at me.'

The man was arrogant, and rightly arrogant, with conscious well-being. And within a month he was dead. It was no accident. Half a dozen different bugs of long scientific names had attacked and destroyed him. The complications were astonishing and painful, and for days before he died the screams of agony of that splendid manhood could be heard for a block around. He died screaming.

'You see,' said John Barleycorn. 'He took care of himself. He even stopped smoking cigars. And that's what he got for it. Pretty rotten, eh? But the bugs will jump. There's no forefending them. Your magnificent doctor took every precaution, yet they got him. When the bug jumps you can't tell where it will land. It may be you. Look what he missed. Will you miss all I can give you, only to have a bug jump on you and drag you down? There is no equity in life. It's all a lottery. But I put the lying smile on the face of life and laugh at the facts. Smile with me and laugh. You'll get yours in the end, but in the meantime laugh. It's a pretty dark world. I illuminate it for you. It's a rotten world, when things can happen such as happened to your doctor. There's only one thing to do: take another drink and forget it.'

And, of course, I took another drink for the inhibition that accompanied it. I took another drink every time John Barleycorn reminded me of what had happened. Yet I drank rationally, intelligently. I saw to it that the quality of the stuff was of the best. I sought the kick and the inhibition, and avoided the penalties of poor quality and of drunkenness. It is to be remarked, in passing, that when a man begins to drink rationally and intelligently that he betrays a grave symptom of how far along the road he has travelled.

But I continued to observe my rule of never taking my first drink of the day until the last word of my thousand words was written. On occasion, however, I took a day's vacation from my writing. At such times, since it was no violation of my rule, I didn't mind how early in the day I took that first drink. And persons who have never been through the drinking game wonder how the drinking habit grows!

32

WHEN THE *Snark* sailed on her long cruise from San Francisco there was nothing to drink on board. Or, rather, we were all of us unaware that there was anything to drink, nor did we discover it for many a month. This sailing with a 'dry' boat was malice aforethought on my part. I had played John Barleycorn a trick. And it showed that I was listening ever so slightly to the faint warnings that were beginning to arise in my consciousness.

Of course, I veiled the situation to myself and excused myself to John Barleycorn. And I was very scientific about it. I said that I would drink only while in ports. During the dry sea-stretches my system would be cleansed of the alcohol that soaked it, so that when I reached a port I should be in shape to enjoy John Barleycorn more thoroughly. His bite would be sharper, his kick keener and more delicious.

We were twenty-seven days on the traverse between San Francisco and Honolulu. After the first day out, the thought of a drink never troubled me. This I take to show how intrinsically I am not an alcoholic. Sometimes, during the traverse, looking ahead and anticipating the delightful *lanai* luncheons and dinners of Hawaii (I had been there a couple of times before), I thought, naturally, of the drinks that would precede those meals. I did not think of those drinks with any yearning, with any irk at the length of the voyage. I merely thought they would be nice and jolly, part of the atmosphere of a proper meal.

Thus, once again I proved to my complete satisfaction that I was John Barleycorn's master. I could drink when I wanted, refrain when I wanted. Therefore I would continue to drink when I wanted.

Some five months were spent in the various islands of the Hawaiian group. Being ashore, I drank. I even drank a bit more than I had been accustomed to drink in California prior to the voyage. The people in Hawaii seemed to drink a bit more, on the average, than the people in more temperate latitudes. I do not intend the pun, and can awkwardly revise the statement to 'latitudes more remote from the equator'. Yet Hawaii is only sub-tropical. The deeper I got into the tropics, the deeper I found men drank, the deeper I drank myself.

From Hawaii we sailed for the Marquesas. The traverse occupied sixty days. For sixty days we never raised land, a sail, nor a steamer smoke. But early in those sixty days the cook, giving an overhauling to the galley, made a find. Down in the bottom of a deep locker he found a dozen bottles of angelica and muscatel. These had come down from the kitchen cellar of the ranch along with the home-preserved fruits and jellies. Six months in the galley heat had effected some sort of a change in the thick sweet wine —branded it, I imagine.

I took a taste. Delicious! And thereafter, once a day, at twelve o'clock, after our observations were worked up and the *Snark's* position charted, I drank half a tumbler of the stuff. It had a rare kick to it. It warmed the cockles of my geniality and put a fairer face on the truly fair face of the sea. Each morning, below, sweating out my thousand words, I found myself looking forward to that twelve o'clock event of the day.

The trouble was I had to share the stuff, and the length of the traverse was doubtful. I regretted that there were not more than a dozen bottles. And when they were gone I even regretted that I had shared any of it. I was thirsty for the alcohol, and eager to arrive in the Marquesas.

So it was that I reached the Marquesas the possessor of a real man's-size thirst. And in the Marquesas were several white men, a lot of sickly natives, much magnificent scenery, plenty of trade rum, an immense quantity of absinthe, but neither whisky nor gin. The trade rum scorched the skin off one's mouth. I know, because I tried it. But I had ever been plastic, and I accepted the absinthe. The trouble with the stuff was that I had to take such inordinate quantities in order to feel the slightest effect.

From the Marquesas I sailed with sufficient absinthe in ballast to last me to Tahiti, where I outfitted with Scotch and American whisky, and thereafter there were no dry stretches between ports. But please do not misunderstand. There was no drunkenness, as drunkenness is ordinarily understood—no staggering and rolling around, no be-fuddlement of the senses. The skilled and seasoned drinker, with a strong constitution, never descends to any-think like that. He drinks to feel good, to get a pleasant jingle, and no more than that. The things he carefully avoids are the nausea of over-drinking, the after-effect of over-drinking, the helplessness and loss of pride of over-drinking.

What the skilled and seasoned drinker achieves is a discreet and canny semi-intoxication. And he does it by the twelve-month around without any apparent penalty. There are hundreds of thousands of men of this sort in the United States today, in clubs, hotels and in their own homes—men who are never drunk, and who, though most of them will indignantly deny it, are rarely sober. And all of them fondly believe, as I fondly believed, that they are beating the game.

On the sea-stretches I was fairly abstemious; but ashore I drank more. I seemed to need more, anyway, in the tropics. This is a common experience, for the excessive consumption of alcohol in the tropics by white men is a notorious fact. The tropics is no place for white-skinned men. Their skin-pigment does not protect them against the excessive white light of the sun. The ultra-violet rays, from the upper end of the spectrum, rip and tear through their tissues, just as the X-ray ripped and tore through the tissues of so many experimenters before they learned the danger.

White men in the tropics undergo radical changes of nature. They become savage, merciless. They commit monstrous acts of cruelty that they would never dream of committing in their original temperate climate. They become nervous, irritable, and less moral. And they drink as they never drank before. Drinking is one form of the many forms of degeneration that set in when white men are exposed too long to too much white light. The increase of alcoholic consumption is automatic. The tropics is no place for a long sojourn. They seem doomed to die anyway, and the heavy drinking expedites the process. They don't reason about it. They just do it.

The sun sickness got me, despite the fact that I had been in the tropics only a couple of years. I drank heavily during this time, but right here I wish to forestall misunderstanding. The drinking was not the cause of the sickness, nor of the abandonment of the voyage. I was strong as a bull, and for many months I fought the sun sickness that was ripping and tearing my surface and nervous tissues to pieces. All through the New Hebrides and the Solomons and up among the atolls in the Line, during this period under a tropic sun, rotten with malaria, and suffering from a few minor afflictions such as Biblical leprosy with the silvery skin, I did the work of five men.

To navigate a vessel through the reefs and shoals and passages and unlighted coasts of the coral seas is a man's work in itself. I was the only navigator on board. There was no one to check me up on the working out of my observations, nor with whom I could advise in the ticklish darkness among uncharted reefs and shoals. And I stood all watches. There was no sea-man on board whom I could trust to stand a mate's watch. I was mate as well as captain. Twenty-four hours a day were the watches I stood at sea, catching cat-naps when I might. Third, I was doctor. And let me say right here that the doctor's job on the *Snark* at that time was a man's job. All on board suffered from malaria—the real, tropical malaria that can kill in three months. All on board suffered from perforating ulcers and from the maddening itch of *ngari-ngari*. A Japanese cook went insane from his too numerous afflictions. One of my Polynesian sailors lay at death's door with blackwater fever. Oh, yes, it was a full man's job, and I dosed and doctored, and pulled teeth, and dragged my patients through mild little things like ptomaine poisoning.

Fourth, I was a writer. I sweated out my thousand words a day, every day, except when the shock of fever smote me, or a couple of nasty squalls smote the *Snark*, in the morning. Fifth, I was a traveller and a writer, eager to see things and to gather material into my note-books. And, sixth, I was master and owner of the craft that was visiting strange places where visitors are rare and where visitors are made much of. So here I had to hold up the social end, entertain on board, be entertained ashore by planters, traders, governors, captains of war vessels, kinky-headed cannibal kings, and prime ministers sometimes fortunate enough to be clad in cotton shifts.

Of course I drank. I drank with my guests and hosts. Also, I drank by myself. Doing the work of five men, I thought, entitled me to drink. Alcohol was good for a man who overworked. I noted its effect on my small crew, when, breaking their backs and hearts at heaving up anchor in forty fathoms, they knocked off gasping and trembling at the end of half an hour and had new life put into them by stiff jolts of rum. They caught their breaths, wiped their mouths, and went to it again with a will. And when we careened the *Snark* and had to work in the water to our necks between shocks of fever, I noted how raw trade rum helped the work along.

And here again we come to another side of many-sided John Barleycorn. On the face of it, he gives something for nothing. Where no strength remains he finds new strength. The wearied one rises to greater effort. For the time being there is an actual accession of strength. I remember passing coal on an ocean steamer through eight days of hell, during which time we coal-passers were kept to the job by being fed with whisky. We toiled half drunk all the time. And without the whisky we could not have passed the coal.

This strength John Barleycorn gives is not fictitious strength. It is real strength. But it is manufactured out of the sources of strength, and it must ultimately be paid for, and with interest. But what weary human will look so far ahead? He takes this apparently miraculous accession of strength at its face value. And many an overworked business and professional man, as well as a harried common labourer, has travelled John Barleycorn's death road because of this mistake.

33

I WENT to Australia to go into hospital and get tinkered up, after which I planned to go on with the voyage. And during the long weeks I lay in hospital, from the first day I never missed alcohol. I never thought about it. I knew I should have it again when I was on my feet. But when I regained my feet I was not cured of my major afflictions. Naaman's silvery skin was still mine. The mysterious sun-sickness which the experts of Australia could not fathom, still ripped and tore my tissues. Malaria still festered in me and put me on my back in shivering delirium at the most unexpected moments, compelling me to cancel a double lecture tour which had been arranged.

So I abandoned the *Snark* voyage and sought a cooler climate. The day I came out of hospital I took up drinking again as a matter of course. I drank wine at meals. I drank cocktails before meals. I drank Scotch highballs when anybody I chanced to be with was drinking them. I was so thoroughly the master of John Barleycorn I could take up with him or let go of him whenever I pleased, just as I had done all my life.

After a time, for cooler climate, I went down to southernmost Tasmania in forty-three South. And I found myself in a place where there was nothing to drink. It didn't mean anything. I didn't drink. It was no hardship. I soaked in the cool air, rode horseback, and did my thousand words a day save when the fever shock came in the morning.

And for fear that the idea may still lurk in some minds that my preceding years of drinking were the cause of my disabilities, I here point out that my Japanese cabin boy, Nakata, still with me, was rotten with fever, as was Charmian, who in addition was in the slough of a tropical neurasthenia that required several years of temperate climates to cure, and that neither she nor Nakata drank or ever had drunk.

When I returned to Hobart Town, where drink was obtained, I drank as of old. The same when I arrived back in Australia. On the contrary, when I sailed from Australia on a tramp steamer commanded by an abstemious captain, I took no drink along, and had no drink for the forty-three days' passage. Arrived in Ecuador, squarely under the equatorial sun, where the humans were dying of yellow fever, smallpox and the plague, I promptly drank again—every drink of every sort that had a kick in it. I caught none of these diseases. Neither did Charmian nor Nakata who did not drink.

Enamoured of the tropics, despite the damage done me, I stopped in various places, and was a long while getting back to the splendid, temperate climate of California. I did my thousand words a day, travelling or stopping over, suffered my last faint fever shock, saw my silvery skin vanish and my sun-torn tissues healthily knit again, and drank as a broad-shouldered chesty man may drink.

34

BACK ON the ranch, in the Valley of the Moon, I resumed my steady drinking. My programme was no drink in the morning; first drink-time came with the completion of my thousand words. Then, between that and the midday meal, were drinks numerous enough to develop a pleasant jingle. Again, in the hour preceding the evening meal, I developed another pleasant jingle. Nobody ever saw me drunk, for the simple reason that I never was drunk. But I did get a jingle twice each day; and the amount of alcohol I consumed every day, if loosed in the system of one unaccustomed to drink, would have put such a one on his back and out.

It was the old proposition. The more I drank, the more I was compelled to drink in order to get an effect. The time came when cocktails were inadequate. I had neither the time in which to drink them nor the space to accommodate them. Whisky had a more powerful jolt. It gave quicker action with less quantity. Bourbon or rye, or cunningly aged blends, constituted the pre-midday drinking. In the late afternoon it was Scotch and soda.

My sleep, always excellent, now became not quite so excellent. I had been accustomed to read myself back asleep when I chanced to awake. But now this began to fail me. When I had read two or three of the small hours away and was as wide awake as ever, I found that a drink furnished the soporific effect. Sometimes two or three drinks were required.

So short a period of sleep then intervened before early morning rising that my system did not have time to work off the alcohol. As a result I awoke with mouth parched and dry, with a slight heaviness of head, and with a mild nervous palpitation in the stomach. In fact I did not feel good. I was suffering from the morning sickness of the steady, heavy drinker. What I needed was a pick-me-up, a bracer. Trust John Barleycorn, once he has broken down a man's defences! So it was a drink before breakfast to put me right for breakfast—the old poison of the snake that has bitten one! Another custom begun at this time was that of the pitcher of water by the bedside to furnish relief to my scorched and sizzling membranes.

I achieved a condition in which my body was never free from alcohol. Nor did I permit myself to be away from alcohol. If I travelled to out-of-the-way places, I declined to run the risk of finding them dry. I took a quart, or several quarts, along in my grip. In the past I had been amazed by other men guilty of this practice. Now I did it myself unblushingly. And when I got out with the fellows, I cast all rules by the board. I drank when they drank, what they drank, and in the same way they drank.

I was carrying a beautiful alcoholic conflagration around with me. The thing fed on its own heat and flamed the fiercer. There was no time, in all my waking time, that I didn't want a drink. I began to anticipate the completion of my daily thousand words by taking a drink when only five hundred words were written. It was not long until I prefaced the beginning of the thousand words with a drink.

The gravity of this I realized too well. I made new rules. Resolutely I would refrain from drinking until my work was done. But a new and most diabolical complication arose. The work refused to be done without drinking. It just couldn't be done. I had to drink in order to do it. I was beginning to fight now. I had the craving at last, and it was mastering me. I would sit at my desk and dally with pad and pen, but words refused to flow. My brain could not think the proper thoughts because continually it was obsessed with the one thought that across the room in the liquor cabinet stood John Barleycorn. When, in despair, I took my drink, at once my brain loosened up and began to roll off the thousand words.

In my town house, in Oakland, I finished the stock of liquor and wilfully refused to purchase more. It was no use, because, unfortunately, there remained in the bottom of the liquor cabinet a case of beer. In vain I tried to write. Now beer is a poor substitute for stronger waters; besides, I didn't like beer, yet all I could think of was that beer so singularly accessible in the bottom of the cabinet. Not until I had drunk a pint of it did the words begin to reel off, and the thousand were reeled off to the tune of numerous pints. The worst of it was that the beer caused me severe heart-burn; but despite the discomfort I soon finished off the case.

The liquor cabinet was now bare. I did not replenish it. By truly heroic perseverance I finally forced myself to write the daily thousand words without the spur of John Barleycorn. But all the time I wrote I was keenly aware of the craving for a drink. And as soon as the morning's work was done, I was out of the house and away downtown to get my first drink. Merciful goodness!—if John Barleycorn could get such sway over me, a non-alcoholic, what must be the sufferings of the true alcoholic, battling against the organic demands of his chemistry while those closest to him sympathize little, understand less, and despise and deride him!

35

BUT THE freight has to be paid. John Barleycorn began to collect, and he collected not so much from the body as from the mind. The old long sickness, which had been purely an intellectual sickness, recrudesced. The old ghosts, long laid, lifted their heads again. But they were different and more deadly ghosts. The old ghosts, intellectual in their inception, had been laid by a sane and normal logic. But now they were raised by the White Logic of John Barleycorn, and John Barleycorn never lays the ghosts of his raising. For this sickness of pessimism, caused by drink, one must drink further in quest of the anodyne that John Barleycorn promises but never delivers.

How to describe this White Logic to those who have never experienced it! It is perhaps better first to state how impossible such a description is. Take Hasheesh Land, for instance, the land of enormous extensions of time and space. In past years I have made two memorable journeys into that far land. My adventures there are seared in sharpest detail on my brain. Yet I have tried vainly, with endless words, to describe any tiny particular phase to persons who have not travelled there.

I use all the hyperbole of metaphor, and tell what centuries of time and profounds of unthinkable agony and horror can obtain in each interval of all the intervals between the notes of a quick jig played quickly on the piano. I talk for an hour, elaborating that one phase of Hasheesh Land, and at the end I have told them nothing. And when I cannot tell them this one thing of all the vastness of terrible and wonderful things, I know I have failed to give them the slightest concept of Hasheesh Land.

But let me talk with some other traveller in that weird region, and at once am I understood. A phrase, a word, conveys instantly to his mind what hours of words and phrases could convey to the mind of the non-traveller. So it is with John Barleycorn's realm where the White Logic reigns. To those untravelled there, the traveller's account must always seem unintelligible and fantastic. At the best, I may only beg of the untravelled ones to strive to take on faith the narrative I shall relate.

For there are fatal intuitions of truth that reside in

alcohol. Philip sober vouches for Philip drunk in this matter. There seem to be various orders of truth in this world. Some sorts of truth are truer than others. Some sorts of truth are lies, and these sorts are the very ones that have the greatest use-value to life that desires to realize and live. At once, O untravelled reader, you see how lunatic and blasphemous is the realm I am trying to describe to you in the language of John Barleycorn's tribe. It is not the language of your tribe, all of whose members resolutely shun the roads that lead to death and tread only the roads that lead to life. For there are roads and roads, and of truth there are orders and orders. But have patience. At least, through what seems no more than verbal yammerings, you may, perchance, glimpse faint far vistas of other lands and tribes.

Alcohol tells truth, but its truth is not normal. What is normal is healthful. What is healthful tends towards life. Normal truth is a different order, and a lesser order, of truth. Take a dray horse. Through all the vicissitudes of its life, from first to last, somehow, in unguessably dim ways, it must believe that life is good; that the drudgery in harness is good; that death, no matter how blind-instinctively apprehended, is a dread giant; that life is beneficent and worth while; that, in the end, with fading life, it will not be knocked about and beaten and urged beyond its sprained and spavined best; that old age, even, is decent, dignified, and valuable, though old age means a ribby scarecrow in a hawker's cart, stumbling a step to every blow, stumbling dizzily on through merciless servitude and slow disintegration to the end—the end, the apportionment of its parts (of its subtle flesh, its pink and springy bone, its juices and ferments, and all the sensateness that informed it) to the chicken farm, the hide-house, the glue-rendering works, and the bonemeal fertilizer factory. To the last stumble of its stumbling end this dray horse must abide by the mandates of the lesser truth that is the truth of life and that makes life possible to persist.

This dray horse, like all other horses, like all other animals, including man, is life-blinded and sense-struck. It will live, no matter what the price. The game of life is good, though all of life may be hurt, and though all lives lose the game in the end. This is the order of truth that obtains, not for the universe, but for the live things in it if they for a little space will endure ere they pass. This order of truth, no matter how erroneous it may be, is the same and normal order of truth, the rational order of truth that life must believe in order to live.

To man, alone among the animals, has been given the awful privilege of reason. Man, with his brain, can penetrate the intoxicating show of things and look upon the universe brazen with indifference towards him and his dreams. He can do this, but it is not well for him to do it. To live, and live abundantly, to sting with life, to be alive (which is to be what he is), it is good that man be life-blinded and sense-struck. What is good is true. And this is the order of truth, lesser though it be, that man must know and guide his actions by with unswerving certitude that it is absolute truth and that in the universe no other order of truth can obtain. It is good that man should accept at face value the cheats of sense and snares of flesh and through the fogs of sentiency pursue the lures and lies of passion. It is good that he shall see neither shadows nor futilities, nor be appalled by his lusts and rapacities.

And man does this. Countless men have glimpsed that other and truer order of truth and recoiled from it. Countless men have passed through the long sickness and lived to tell of it and deliberately to forget it to the end of their days. They lived. They realized life, for life is what they were. They did right.

And now comes John Barleycorn with the curse he lays upon the imaginative man who is lusty with life and desire to live. John Barleycorn sends his White Logic, the argent messenger of truth beyond truth, the antithesis of life, cruel and bleak as interstellar space, pulseless and frozen

as absolute zero, dazzling with the frost of irrefragable
logic and unforgettable fact. John Barleycorn will not let
the dreamer dream, the liver live. He destroys birth and
death, and dissipates to mist the paradox of being, until
his victim cries out, as in *The City of Dreadful Night*:
'Our life's a cheat, our death a black abyss.' And the feet
of the victim of such dreadful intimacy take hold of the
way of death.

36

BACK TO personal experiences and the effects in the past
of John Barleycorn's White Logic on me. On my lovely
ranch in the Valley of the Moon, brain-soaked with many
months of alcohol, I am oppressed by the cosmic sadness
that has always been the heritage of man. In vain do I
ask myself why I should be sad. My nights are warm. My
roof does not leak. I have food galore for all the caprices
of appetite. Every creature comfort is mine. In my body
are no aches nor pains. The good old flesh-machine is
running smoothly on. Neither brain nor muscle is overworked. I have land, money, power, recognition from the
world, a consciousness that I do my need of good in serving others, a mate whom I love, children that are of my
own fond flesh. I have done, and am doing, what a good
citizen of the world should do. I have built houses, many
houses, and tilled many a hundred acres. And as for trees,
have I not planted a hundred thousand? Everywhere, from
any window of my house, I can gaze forth upon these
trees of my planting, standing valiantly erect and aspiring
towards the sun.

My life has indeed fallen in pleasant places. Not a
hundred men in a million have been so lucky as I. Yet,
with all this vast good fortune, am I sad. And I am sad
because John Barleycorn is with me. And John Barleycorn
is with me because I was born in what future ages will

call the dark ages before the ages of rational civilisation. John Barleycorn is with me because in all the unwitting days of my youth John Barleycorn was accessible, calling to me and inviting me on every corner and on every street between the corners. The pseudo-civilisation into which I was born permitted everywhere licensed shops for the sale of soul-poison. The system of life was so organized that I (and millions like me) was lured and drawn and driven to the poison shops.

Wander with me through one mood of the myriad moods of sadness into which one is plunged by John Barleycorn. I ride out over my beautiful ranch. Between my legs is a beautiful horse. The air is wine. The grapes on a score of rolling hills are red with autumn flame. Across Sonoma Mountain wisps of sea fog are stealing. The afternoon sun smoulders in the drowsy sky. I have everything to make me glad I am alive. I am filled with dreams and mysteries. I am all sun and air and sparkle. I am vitalized, organic. I move, I have the power of movement, I command movement of the live thing I bestride. I am possessed with the pomps of being, and know proud passions and inspirations. I have ten thousand august connotations. I am a king in the kingdom of sense, and trample the face of the uncomplaining dust. . . .

And yet, with jaundiced eye I gaze upon all the beauty and wonder about me, and with jaundiced brain consider the pitiful figure I cut in this world that endured so long without me and that will again endure without me. I remember the men who broke their hearts and their backs over this stubborn soil that now belongs to me. As if anything imperishable could belong to the perishable! These men passed. I, too, shall pass. These men toiled, and cleared, and planted, gazed with aching eyes, while they rested their labour-stiffened bodies on these same sunrises and sunsets, at the autumn glory of the grape, and at the fog-wisps stealing across the mountain. And they are gone. And I know that I, too, shall some day, and soon, be gone.

Gone? I am going now. In my jaw are cunning artifices of the dentists which replace the parts of me already gone. Never again will I have the thumbs of my youth. Old fights and wrestlings have injured them irreparably. That punch on the head of a man whose very name is forgotten settled this thumb finally and for ever. A slip-grip at catch-as-catch-can did for the other. My lean runner's stomach has passed into the limbo of memory. The joints of the legs that bear me up are not so adequate as they once were, when, in wild nights and days of toil and frolic, I strained and snapped and ruptured them. Never again can I swing dizzily aloft and trust all the proud quick that is I to a single rope-clutch in the driving blackness of storm. Never again can I run with the sled-dogs along the endless miles of Arctic trail.

I am aware that within this disintegrating body which has been dying since I was born I carry a skeleton, that under the rind of flesh which is called my face is a bony, noseless death's head. All of which does not shudder me. To be afraid is to be healthy. Fear of death makes for life. But the curse of the White Logic is that it does not make one afraid. The world-sickness of the White Logic makes one grin jocosely into the face of the Noseless One and to sneer at all the phantasmagoria of living.

I look about me as I ride, and on every hand I see the merciless and infinite waste of natural selection. The White Logic insists upon opening the long-closed books, and by paragraph and chapter states the beauty and wonder I behold in terms of futility and dust. About me is murmur and hum, and I know it for the gnat-swarm of the living, piping for a little space its thin plaint of troubled air.

I return across the ranch. Twilight is on, and the hunting animals are out. I watch the piteous tragic play of life feeding on life. Here is no morality. Only in man is morality, and man created it—a code of action that makes toward living and that is of the lesser order of truth. Yet all this I knew before, in the weary days of my long sickness. These were the greater truths that I so successfully schooled myself to forget; the truths that were so serious that I refused to take them seriously, and played with gently, oh! so gently, as sleeping dogs at the back of consciousness which I did not care to waken. I did but stir them, and let them lie. I was too wise, too wicked wise, to wake them. But now White Logic willy-nilly wakes them for me, for White Logic, most valiant, is unafraid of all the monsters of the earthly dream.

'Let the doctors of all the schools condemn me,' White Logic whispers as I ride along. 'What of it? I am truth. You know it. You cannot combat me. They say I make for death. What of it? It is truth. Life lies in order to live. Life is a perpetual lie-telling process. Life is a mad dance in the domain of flux, wherein appearances in mighty tides ebb and flow, chained to the wheels of moons beyond our ken. Appearances are ghosts. Life is ghost land, where appearances change, transfuse, permeate each the other and all the others, that are, that are not, that always flicker, fade, and pass, only to come again as new appearances, as other appearances. You are such an appearance, composed of countless appearances out of the past. All an appearance can know is mirage. You know mirages of desire. These very mirages are the unthinkable and incalculable congeries of appearances that crowd in upon you and form you out of the past, and that sweep you on into dissemination into other unthinkable and incalculable congeries of appearances to people the ghost land of the future. Life is apparitional, and passes. You are an apparition. Through all the apparitions that preceded you and that compose the parts of you, you rose gibbering from the evolutionary mire, and gibbering you will pass on, interfusing, permeating the procession of apparitions that will succeed you.'

And of course it is all unanswerable, and as I ride along through the evening shadows I sneer at that Great Fetish which Comte called the world. And I remember what another pessimist of sentiency has uttered: 'Transient are all. They, being born, must die, and, being dead, are glad to be at rest.'

But here through the dusk comes one who is not glad to be at rest. He is a workman on the ranch, an old man, an immigrant Italian. He takes his hat off to me in all servility, because, forsooth, I am to him a lord of life. I am food to him, and shelter, and existence. He has toiled like a beast all his days, and lived less comfortably than my horses in their deep-strawed stalls. He is labour-crippled. He shambles as he walks. One shoulder is twisted higher than the other. His hands are gnarled claws, repulsive, horrible. As an apparition he is a pretty miserable specimen. His brain is as stupid as his body is ugly.

'His brain is so stupid that he does not know he is an apparition,' the White Logic chuckles to me. 'He is sense-drunk. He is the slave of the dream of life. His brain is filled with superrational sanctions and obsessions. He believes in a transcendent over-world. He has listened to the vagaries of the prophets, who have given to him the sumptuous bubble of Paradise. He feels inarticulate self-affinities, with self-conjured non-realities. He sees penumbral visions of himself titubating fantastically through days and nights of space and stars. Beyond the shadow of any doubt he is convinced that the universe was made for him, and that it is his destiny to live for ever in the immaterial and supersensuous realms he and his kind have builded of the stuff of semblance and deception.

'But you, who have opened the books and who share my awful confidence—you know him for what he is, brother to you and the dust, a cosmic joke, a sport of chemistry, a garmented beast that arose out of the ruck of screaming beastliness by virtue and accident of two opposable great toes. He is brother as well to the gorilla and the chimpanzee. He thumps his chest in anger, and roars and quivers with cataleptic ferocity. He knows monstrous, atavistic promptings, and he is composed of all manner of shreds of abysmal and forgotten instincts.'

'Yet he dreams he is immortal,' I argue feebly. 'It is vastly wonderful for so stupid a clod to bestride the shoulders of time and ride the eternities.'

'Pah!' is the retort. 'Would you then shut the books and exchange places with this thing that is only an appetite and a desire, a marionette of the belly and the loins?'

'To be stupid is to be happy,' I contend.

'Then your ideal of happiness is a jelly-like organism floating in a tideless, tepid twilight sea, eh?'

Oh, the victim cannot combat John Barleycorn!

'One step removed from the annihilating bliss of Buddha's Nirvana,' the White Logic adds. 'Oh, well, here's the house. Cheer up and take a drink. We know, we illuminated, you and I, all the folly and the farce.'

And in my book-walled den, the mausoleum of the thoughts of men, I take my drink, and other drinks, and roust out the sleeping dogs from the recesses of my brain and hallo them on over the walls of prejudice and law and through all the cunning labyrinths of superstition and belief.

'Drink,' says the White Logic. 'The Greeks believed that the gods gave them wine so that they might forget the miserableness of existence. And remember what Heine said.'

Well do I remember that flaming Jew's 'With the last breath all is done: joy, love, sorrow, macaroni, the theatre, lime-trees, raspberry drops, the power of human relations, gossip, the barking of dogs, champagne.'

'Your clear white light is sickness,' I tell the White Logic. 'You lie.'

'By telling too strong a truth,' he quips back.

'Alas, yes, so topsy-turvy is existence,' I acknowledge sadly.

'Ah, well, Liu Ling was wiser than you,' the White Logic girds. 'You remember him?'

I nod my head—Liu Ling, a hard drinker, one of the group of bibulous poets who called themselves the Seven Sages of the Bamboo Grove and who lived in China many an ancient century ago.

'It was Lue Ling', prompts the White Logic, 'who declared that to a drunken man the affairs of this world appear but as so much duckweed on a river. Very well. Have another Scotch, and let semblance and deception become duckweed on a river.'

And while I pour and sip my Scotch, I remember another Chinese philosopher, Chuang Tzŭ, who, four centuries before Christ, challenged this dreamland of the world, saying: 'How then do I know but that the dead repent of having previously clung to life? Those who dream of the banquet, wake to lamentation and sorrow. Those who dream of lamentation and sorrow, wake to join the hunt. While they dream, they do not know that they dream. Some will even interpret the very dream they are dreaming; and only when they awake do they know it was a dream.... Fools think they are awake now, and flatter themselves they know if they are really princes or peasants. Confucius and you are both dreams; and I who say you are dreams—I am but a dream myself.

'Once upon a time, I, Chuang Tzŭ, dreamt I was a butterfly, fluttering hither and thither, to all intents and purposes a butterfly. I was conscious only of following my fancies as a butterfly, and was unconscious of my individuality as a man. Suddenly, I awaked, and there I lay, myself again. Now I do not know whether I was then a man dreaming I was a butterfly, or whether I am now a butterfly dreaming I am a man.'

37

'COME,' says the White Logic, 'and forget these Asian dreamers of old time. Fill your glass and let us look at the parchments of the dreamers of yesterday who dreamed their dreams on your own warm hills.'

I pore over the abstract of title of the vineyard called Tokay on the rancho called Petaluma. It is a sad long list of the names of men, beginning with Manuel Micheltoreno, one time Mexican 'Governor, Commander-in-Chief and Inspector of the Department of the Californians', who deeded ten square leagues of stolen Indian land to Colonel Don Mariano Guadalupe Vallejo for services rendered his country and for moneys paid by him for ten years to his soldiers.

Immediately this musty record of man's land lust assumes the formidableness of a battle—the quick struggling with the dust. There are deeds of trust, mortgages, certificates of release, transfers, judgments, foreclosures, writs of attachment, orders of sale, tax liens, petitions for letters of administration, and decrees of distribution. It is like a monster ever unsubdued, this stubborn land that drowses in this Indian summer weather and that survives them all, the men who scratched its surface and passed.

Who was this James King of William, so curiously named? The oldest surviving settler in the Valley of the Moon knows him not. Yet only sixty years ago he loaned Mariano G. Vallejo eighteen thousand dollars on security of certain lands including the vineyard yet to be and to be called Tokay. Whence came Peter O'Connor, and whither vanished, after writing his little name of a day on the woodland that was to become a vineyard? Appears Louis Csomortanyi, a name to conjure with. He lasts through several pages of this record of the enduring soil.

Comes old American stock, thirsting across the Great American Desert, mule-backing across the Isthmus, wind-jamming around the Horn, to write brief and forgotten names where ten thousand generations of wild Indians are equally forgotten—names like Halleck, Hastings, Swett, Tait, Denman, Tracy, Grimwood, Carlton, Temple. There are no names like those today in the Valley of the Moon.

The names begin to appear fast and furiously, flashing from legal page to legal page and in a flash vanishing. But ever the persistent soil remains for others to scrawl themselves across. Come the names of men of whom I have vaguely heard but whom I have never known. Kohler and Frohling—who built the great stone winery on the vineyard called Tokay, but who built upon a hill up which other vineyardists refused to haul their grapes. So Kohler and Frohling lost the land; the earthquake of 1906 threw down the winery; and I now live in its ruins.

La Motte—he broke the soil, planted vines and orchards, instituted commercial fish culture, built a mansion renowned in its day, was defeated by the soil, and passed. And my name of a day appears. On the site of his orchards and vineyards, of his proud mansion, of his very fish ponds, I have scrawled myself with half a hundred thousand eucalyptus trees.

Cooper and Greenlaw—on what is called the Hill Ranch they left two of their dead, 'Little Lillie' and 'Little David', who rest today inside a tiny square of hand-hewn palings. Also, Cooper and Greenlaw in their time cleared the virgin forest from three fields of forty acres. Today I have those three fields sown with Canada peas, and in the spring they shall be ploughed under for green manure.

Haska—a dim legendary figure of a generation ago, who went back up the mountain and cleared six acres of brush in the tiny valley that took his name. He broke the soil, reared stone walls and a house, and planted apple trees. And already the site of the house is undiscoverable, the location of the stone walls may be deduced from the configuration of the landscape, and I am renewing the battle, putting in angora goats to browse away the brush that has overrun Haska's clearing and choked Haska's apple trees to death. So I, too, scratch the land with my brief endeavour and flash my name across a page of legal script ere I pass and the page grows musty.

'Dreamers and ghosts,' the White Logic chuckles.

'But surely the striving was not altogether vain,' I contend.

'It was based on illusion and is a lie.'

'A vital lie,' I retort.

'And pray what is a vital lie but a lie?' the White Logic challenges. 'Come. Fill your glass and let us examine these vital liars who crowd your bookshelves. Let us dabble in William James a bit.'

'A man of health,' I say. 'From him we may expect no philosopher's stone, but at least we will find a few robust tonic things to which to tie.'

'Rationality gelded to sentiment,' the White Logic grins. 'At the end of all his thinking he still clung to the sentiment of immortality. Facts transmuted in the alembic of hope into terms of faith. The ripest fruit of reason the stultification of reason. From the topmost peak of reason James teaches to cease reasoning and to have faith that all is well and will be well—the old, oh, ancient old, acrobatic flip of the metaphysicians whereby they reasoned reason quite away in order to escape the pessimism consequent upon the grim and honest exercise of reason.

'Is this flesh of yours you? Or is it an extraneous something possessed by you? Your body—what is it? A machine for converting stimuli into reactions. Stimuli and reactions are remembered. They constitute experience. Then you are in your consciousness these experiences. You are at any moment what you are thinking at that moment. Your I is both subject and object; it predicates things of itself and is the things predicated. The thinker is the thought, the knower is what is known, the possessor is the things possessed.

'After all, as you know well, man is a flux of state of consciousness, a flow of passing thoughts, each thought of self another self, a myriad thoughts, a myriad selves, a continual becoming but never being, a will-of-the-wisp flitting of ghosts in ghostland. But this, man will not accept of himself. He refuses to accept his own passing. He will not pass. He will live again if he has to die to do it.

'He shuffles atoms and jets of light, remotest nebulæ, drips of water, prick-points of sensation, slime-oozings and cosmic bulks, all mixed with pearls of faith, love of woman, imagined dignities, frightened surmises, and pompous arrogances, and of the stuff builds himself an immortality to startle the heavens and baffle the immensities. He squirms

7*

on his dunghill, and, like a child lost in the dark among goblins, calls to the gods that he is their younger brother, a prisoner of the quick that is destined to be as free as they —monuments of egotism reared by the epiphenomena; dreams and the dust of dreams, that vanish when the dreamer vanishes and are no more when he is not.

'It is nothing new, these vital lies men tell themselves, muttering and mumbling them like charms and incantations against the powers of Night. The voodoos and medicine men and the devil-devil doctors were the fathers of metaphysics. Night and the Noseless One were ogres that beset the way of light and life. And the metaphysicians would win by if they had to tell lies to do it. They were vexed by the brazen law of the Ecclesiast that men die like the beasts of the field and their end is the same. Their creeds were their schemes, their religions their nostrums, their philosophies their devices, by which they half-believed they would outwit the Noseless One and the Night.

'Bog-lights, vapours of mysticism, psychic overtones, soul orgies, wailings among the shadows, weird gnosticisms, veils and tissues of words, gibbering subjectivisms, gropings and maunderings, ontological fantasies, pan-psychic hallucinations—this is the stuff, the phantasms of hope, that fills your bookshelves. Look at them, all the sad wraiths of sad men and passionate rebels—your Schopenhauers, your Strindbergs, your Tolstois and Nietzsches.

'Come. Your glass is empty. Fill and forget.'

I obey, for my brain is now well a-crawl with the maggots of alcohol, and as I drink to the sad thinkers on my shelves I quote Richard Hovey:

> 'Abstain not! Life and Love like night and day
> Offer themselves to us on their own terms,
> Not ours. Accept their bounty while ye may,
> Before we be accepted by the worms.'

'I will cap you,' cries the White Logic.

'No,' I answer, while the maggots madden me. 'I know

you for what you are, and I am unafraid. Under your mask of hedonism you are yourself the Noseless One and your way leads to the Night. Hedonism has no meaning. It, too, is a lie, at best the coward's smug compromise——'

'Now will I cap you!' the White Logic breaks in.

'But if you would not this poor life fulfil,
  Lo, you are free to end it when you will,
  Without the fear of waking after death.'

And I laugh my defiance; for now, and for the moment, I know the White Logic to be the arch-impostor of them all, whispering his whispers of death. And he is guilty of his own unmasking, with his own genial chemistry turning the tables on himself, with his own maggots biting alive the old illusions, resurrecting and making to sound again the old voice from beyond of my youth, telling me again that still are mine the possibilities and powers which life and the books had taught me did not exist.

And the dinner gong sounds to the reversed bottom of my glass. Jeering at the White Logic, I go out to join my guests at table, and with assumed seriousness to discuss the current magazines and the silly doings of the world's day, whipping every trick and ruse of controversy through all the paces of paradox and persiflage. And, when the whim changes, it is most easy and delightfully disconcerting to play with the respectable and cowardly bourgeois fetishes and to laugh and epigram at the flitting god-ghosts and the debaucheries and follies of wisdom.

The clown's the thing! The clown! If one must be a philosopher, let him be Aristophanes. And no one at the table thinks I'm jingled. I am in fine fettle, that is all. I tire of the labour of thinking, and, when the table is finished, start practical jokes and set all playing at games, which we carry on with bucolic boisterousness.

And when the evening is over and good-night said, I go back through my book-walled den to my sleeping porch and to myself and to the White Logic which, undefeated, has never left me. And as I fall to fuddled sleep I hear youth crying, as Harry Kemp heard it:

> 'I heard Youth calling in the night:
> "Gone is my former world-delight;
> For there is naught my feet may stay;
> The morn suffuses into day,
> It dare not stand a moment still
> But must the world with light fulfil.
> More evanescent than the rose
> My sudden rainbow comes and goes,
> Plunging bright ends across the sky—
> Yea, I am Youth because I die!" '

38

THE FOREGOING is a sample roaming with the White Logic through the dusk of my soul. To the best of my power I have striven to give the reader a glimpse of a man's secret dwelling when it is shared with John Barleycorn. And the reader must remember that this mood, which he has read in a quarter of an hour, is but one mood of the myriad moods of John Barleycorn, and that the procession of such moods may well last the clock around through many a day and week and month.

My alcoholic reminiscences draw to a close. I can say, as any strong, chesty drinker can say, that all that leaves me alive today on the planet is my unmerited luck—the luck of chest, and shoulders, and constitution. I dare to say that a not large percentage of youths, in the formative stage of fifteen to seventeen, could have survived the stress of heavy drinking that I survived between my fifteenth and seventeenth years; that a not large percentage of men could have punished the alcohol I have punished in my manhood years and lived to tell the tale. I survived, through no personal virtue, but because I did not have the chemistry of a dipsomaniac and because I possessed an organism unusually resistant to the ravages of John Barleycorn. And, surviving, I have watched the others die, not so lucky, down all the long sad road.

It was my unmitigated and absolute good fortune, good luck, chance, call it what you will, that brought me through the fires of John Barleycorn. My life, my career, my joy in living, have not been destroyed. They have been scorched, it is true; like the survivors of forlorn hopes, they have by unthinkably miraculous ways come through the fight to marvel at the tally of the slain.

And like such a survivor of old red war who cries out, 'Let there be no more war!' so I cry out, 'Let there be no more poison-fighting by our youths!' The way to stop war is to stop it. The way to stop drinking is to stop it. The way China stopped the general use of opium was by stopping the cultivation and importation of opium. The philosophers, priests, and doctors of China could have preached themselves breathless against opium for a thousand years, and the use of opium, so long as opium was ever accessible and obtainable, would have continued unabated. We are so made, that is all.

We have with great success made a practice of not leaving arsenic and strychnine, and typhoid and tuberculosis germs lying around for our children to be destroyed by. Treat John Barleycorn the same way. Stop him. Don't let him lie around, licensed and legal, to pounce upon our youth. Not of alcoholics nor for alcoholics do I write, but for our youths, for those who possess no more than the adventure-stings and the genial predispositions, the social man-impulses, which are twisted all awry by our barbarian civilization which feeds them poison on all the corners. It is the healthy, normal boys, now born or being born, for whom I write.

It was for this reason, more than any other, and more ardently than any other, that I rode down into the Valley of the Moon, all a-jingle, and voted for equal suffrage. I voted that women might vote, because I knew that they,

the wives and mothers of the race, would vote John Barleycorn out of existence and back into the historical limbo of
our vanished customs of savagery. If I thus seem to cry
out as one hurt, please remember that I have been sorely
bruised and that I do dislike the thought that any son or
daughter of mine or yours should be similarly bruised.

The women are the true conservators of the race. The
men are the wastrels, the adventure-lovers and gamblers,
and in the end it is by their women that they are saved.
About man's first experiment in chemistry was the making
of alcohol, and down all the generations to this day man
has continued to manufacture and drink it. And there has
never been a day when the women have not resented man's
use of alcohol, though they have never had the power to
give weight to their resentment. The moment women get
the vote in any community, the first thing they proceed to
do is to close the saloons. In a thousand generations to
come men of themselves will not close the saloons. As well
expect the morphine victims to legislate the sale of morphine out of existence.

The women know. They have paid an incalculable price
of sweat and tears for man's use of alcohol. Ever jealous
for the race, they will legislate for the babes of boys yet
to be born; and for the babes of girls, too, for they must be
the mothers, wives, and sisters of these boys.

And it will be easy. The only ones that will be hurt will
be the topers and seasoned drinkers of a single generation.
I am one of these, and I make solemn assurance, based
upon long traffic with John Barleycorn, that it won't hurt
me very much to stop drinking when no one else drinks
and when no drink is obtainable. On the other hand, the
overwhelming proportion of young men are so normally
non-alcoholic, that, never having had access to alcohol,
they will never miss it. They will know of the saloon only
in the pages of history, and they will think of the saloon
as a quaint old custom similar to bull-baiting and the
burning of witches.

39

OF COURSE, no personal tale is complete without bringing the narrative of the person down to the last moment. But mine is no tale of a reformed drunkard. I was never a drunkard, and I have not reformed.

It chanced, some time ago, that I made a voyage of one hundred and forty-eight days in a windjammer around the Horn. I took no private supply of alcohol along, and, though there was no day of those one hundred and forty-eight days that I could not have got a drink from the captain, I did not take a drink. I did not take a drink because I did not desire a drink. No one else drank on board. The atmosphere for drinking was not present, and in my system there was no organic need for alcohol. My chemistry did not demand alcohol.

So there arose before me a problem, a clear and simple problem: *This is so easy, why not keep it up when you get back on land?* I weighed this problem carefully. I weighed it for five months, in a state of absolute non-contact with alcohol. And out of the data of past experience, I reached certain conclusions.

In the first place, I am convinced that not one man in ten thousand or in a hundred thousand is a genuine, chemical dipsomaniac. Drinking, as I deem it, is practically entirely a habit of mind. It is unlike tobacco, or cocaine, or morphine, or all the rest of the long list of drugs. The desire for alcohol is quite peculiarly mental in its origin. It is a matter of mental training and growth, and it is cultivated in social soil. Not one drinker in a million began drinking alone. All drinkers begin socially, and this drinking is accompanied by a thousand social connotations such as I have described out of my own experience in the first part of this narrative. These social connotations are the stuff of which the drink habit is largely composed. The part that alcohol itself plays is inconsiderable when compared with the part played by the social atmosphere in which it is drunk. The human is rarely born these days, who, without long training in the social associations of drinking, feels the irresistible chemical propulsion of his system towards alcohol. I do assume that such rare individuals are born, but I have never encountered one.

On this long, five-months' voyage, I found that among all my bodily needs not the slightest shred of a bodily need for alcohol existed. But this I did find: my need was mental and social. When I thought of alcohol, the connotation was fellowship. When I thought of fellowship, the connotation was alcohol. Fellowship and alcohol were Siamese twins. They always occurred linked together.

Thus, when reading in my deck chair or when talking with others, practically any mention of any part of the world I knew instantly aroused the connotation of drinking and good fellows. Big nights and days and moments, all purple passages and freedoms, thronged my memory. 'Venice' stares at me from the printed page, and I remember the café tables on the sidewalks. 'The Battle of Santiago', some one says, and I answer, 'Yes, I've been over the ground'. But I do not see the ground, nor Kettle Hill, nor the Peace Tree. What I see is the Café Venus, on the plaza of Santiago, where one hot night I drank and talked with a dying consumptive.

The East End of London, I read, or some one says; and first of all, under my eyelids, leap the visions of the shining pubs, and in my ears echo the calls for 'two of bitter' and 'three of Scotch'. The Latin Quarter—at once I am in the student cabarets, bright faces and keen spirits around me, sipping cool, well-dripped absinthe while our voices mount and soar in Latin fashion as we settle God and art and democracy and the rest of the simple problems of existence.

In a pampero off the River Plate we speculate, if we are disabled, of running into Buenos Ayres, the 'Paris of

America', and I have visions of bright congregating places of men, of the jollity of raised glasses, and of song and cheer and the hum of genial voices. When we have picked up the North-east Trades in the Pacific we try to persuade our dying captain to run for Honolulu, and while I persuade I see myself again drinking cocktails on the cool *lanais* and fizzes out at Waikiki where the surf rolls in. Some one mentions the way wild ducks are cooked in the restaurants of San Francisco, and at once I am transported to the light and clatter of many tables, where I gaze at old friends across the golden brims of long-stemmed Rhine-wine glasses.

And so I pondered my problem. I should not care to revisit all these fair places of the world except in the fashion I visited them before. *Glass in hand!* There is a magic in the phrase. It means more than all the words in the dictionary can be made to mean. It is a habit of mind to which I have been trained all my life. It is now part of the stuff that composes me. I like the bubbling play of wit, the chesty laughs, the resonant voices of men, when, glass in hand, they shut the grey world outside and prod their brains with the fun and folly of an accelerated pulse.

No, I decided; I shall take my drink on occasion. With all the books on my shelves, with all the thoughts of the thinkers shaded by my particular temperament, I decided coolly and deliberately that I should continue to do what I had been trained to want to do. I would drink—but oh, more skilfully, more discreetly, than ever before. Never again would I be a peripatetic conflagration. Never again would I invoke the White Logic. I had learned how not to invoke him.

The White Logic now lies decently buried alongside the Long Sickness. Neither will afflict me again. It is many a year since I laid the Long Sickness away; his sleep is sound. And just as sound is the sleep of the White Logic. And yet, in conclusion, I can well say that I wish my forefathers had banished John Barleycorn before my time. I regret that

John Barleycorn flourished everywhere in the system of society in which I was born, else I should not have made his acquaintance, and I was long trained in his acquaintance.

THE CRUISE
OF THE DAZZLER

CONTENTS

PART ONE

1. BROTHER AND SISTER

THEY RAN across the shining sand, the Pacific thundering
its long surge at their backs, and when they gained the
roadway leaped upon bicycles and dived at faster pace
into the green avenues of the park. There were three of
them, three boys, in as many bright-coloured sweaters, and
they 'scorched' along the cycle-path as dangerously near
the speed limit as is the custom of boys in bright-coloured
sweaters to go. They may have exceeded the speed-limit.
A mounted park policeman thought so, but was not sure,
and contented himself with cautioning them as they flashed
by. They acknowledged the warning promptly, and on the
next turn of the path as promptly forgot it, which is also
a custom of boys in bright-coloured sweaters.

Shooting out through the entrance to Golden Gate Park,
they turned into San Francisco, and took the long sweep
of the descending hills at a rate that caused pedestrians
to turn and watch them anxiously. Through the city streets
the bright sweaters flew, turning and twisting to escape
climbing the steeper hills, and, when the steep hills were
unavoidable, doing stunts to see which would first gain
the top.

The boy who more often hit up the pace, led the scorching, and instituted the stunts was called Joe by his companions. It was 'follow the leader', and he led, the merriest
and boldest in the bunch. But as they pedalled into the
Western Addition, among the large and comfortable residences, his laughter became less loud and frequent, and
he unconsciously lagged in the rear. At Laguna and Vallejo
Streets his companions turned off to the right.

'So long, Fred,' he called as he turned his wheel to the left. 'So long, Charley.'

'See you tonight!' they called back.

'No—I can't come,' he answered.

'Aw, come on,' they begged.

'No, I've got to dig.—So long!'

As he went on alone, his face grew grave and a vague worry came into his eyes. He began resolutely to whistle, but this dwindled away till it was a thin and very subdued little sound, which ceased altogether as he rode up the driveway to a large two-storied house.

'Oh, Joe!'

He hesitated before the door to the library. Bessie was there, he knew, studiously working up her lessons. She must be nearly through with them, too, for she was always done before dinner, and dinner could not be many minutes away. As for his lessons, they were as yet untouched. The thought made him angry. It was bad enough to have one's sister—and two years younger at that—in the same grade, but to have her continually head and shoulders above him in scholarship was a most intolerable thing. Not that he was dull. No one knew better than himself that he was not dull. But somehow—he did not quite know how—his mind was on other things, and he was usually unprepared.

'Joe—please come here.' There was the slightest possible plaintive note in her voice this time.

'Well?' he said, thrusting aside the portière with an impetuous movement.

He said it gruffly, but he was half sorry for it the next instant when he saw a slender little girl regarding him with wistful eyes across the big reading-table heaped with books. She was curled up, with pencil and pad, in an easy-chair of such generous dimensions that it made her seem more delicate and fragile than she really was.

'What is it, Sis?' he asked more gently, crossing over to her side.

She took his hand in hers and pressed it against her

cheek, and as he stood beside her came closer to him with a nestling movement.

'What is the matter, Joe, dear?' she asked softly. 'Won't you tell me?'

He remained silent. It struck him as ridiculous to confess his troubles to a little sister, even if her reports *were* higher than his. And the little sister struck him as ridiculous to demand his troubles of him. 'What a soft cheek she has!' he thought as she pressed her face gently against his hand. If he could but tear himself away—it was all so foolish! Only he might hurt her feelings, and, in his experience, girls' feelings were very easily hurt.

She opened her fingers and kissed the palm of his hand. It was like a rose leaf falling; it was also her way of asking her question all over again.

'Nothing's the matter,' he said decisively. And then, quite inconsistently, he blurted out, 'Father!'

His worry was now in her eyes. 'But father is so good and kind, Joe,' she began. 'Why don't you try to please him? He doesn't ask much of you, and it's all for your own good. It's not as though you were a fool, like some boys. If you would only study a little bit——'

'That's it! Lecturing!' he exploded, tearing his hand roughly away. 'Even you are beginning to lecture me now. I suppose the cook and the stable-boy will be at it next.'

He shoved his hands into his pockets and looked forward into a melancholy and desolate future filled with interminable lectures and lecturers innumerable.

'Was that what you wanted me for?' he demanded, turning to go.

She caught at his hand again. 'No, it wasn't; only you looked so worried that I thought—I——' Her voice broke, and she began again freshly. 'What I wanted to tell you was that we're planning a trip across the bay to Oakland, next Saturday, for a tramp in the hills.'

'Who's going?'

'Myrtle Hayes——'

'What! That little softy?' he interrupted.

'I don't think she is a softy,' Bessie answered with spirit. 'She's one of the sweetest girls I know.'

'Which isn't saying much, considering the girls you know. But go on. Who are the others?'

'Pearl Sayther, and her sister Alice, and Jessie Hilborn, and Sadie French, and Edna Crothers. That's all the girls.'

Joe sniffed disdainfully. 'Who are the fellows, then?'

'Maurice and Felix Clement, Dick Schofield, Burt Layton, and——'

'That's enough. Milk-and-water chaps, all of them.'

'I—I wanted to ask you and Fred and Charley,' she said in a quavering voice. 'That's what I called you in for—to ask you to come.'

'And what are you going to do?' he asked.

'Walk, gather wild flowers—the poppies are all out now —eat luncheon at some nice place, and—and——'

'Come home,' he finished for her.

Bessie nodded her head. Joe put his hands in his pockets again, and walked up and down.

'A sissy outfit, that's what it is,' he said abruptly; 'and a sissy programme. None of it in mine, please.'

She tightened her trembling lips and struggled on bravely. 'What would you rather do?' she asked.

'I'd sooner take Fred and Charley and go off somewhere and do something—well, anything.'

He paused and looked at her. She was waiting patiently for him to proceed. He was aware of his inability to express in words what he felt and wanted, and all his trouble and general dissatisfaction rose up and gripped hold of him.

'Oh, you can't understand!' he burst out. 'You can't understand. You're a girl. You like to be prim and neat, and to be good in deportment and ahead in your studies. You don't care for danger and adventure and such things, and you don't care for boys who are rough, and have life and go in them, and all that. You like good little boys in white collars, with clothes always clean and hair always combed, who like to stay in at recess and be petted by the teacher and told how they're always up in their studies;

nice little boys who never get into scrapes—who are too busy walking around and picking flowers and eating lunches with girls, to get into scrapes. Oh, I know the kind —afraid of their own shadows, and no more spunk in them than in so many sheep. That's what they are—sheep. Well, I'm not a sheep, and there's no more to be said. And I don't want to go on your picnic, and, what's more, I'm not going.'

The tears welled up in Bessie's brown eyes, and her lips were trembling. This angered him unreasonably. What were girls good for, anyway?—always blubbering, and interfering, and carrying on. There was no sense in them.

'A fellow can't say anything without making you cry,' he began, trying to appease her. 'Why, I didn't mean anything, Sis. I didn't, sure. I——'

He paused helplessly and looked down at her. She was sobbing, and at the same time shaking with the effort to control her sobs, while big tears were rolling down her cheeks.

'Oh, you—you girls!' he cried, and strode wrathfully out of the room.

2. 'THE DRACONIAN REFORMS'

A FEW minutes later, and still wrathful, Joe went in to dinner. He ate silently, though his father and mother and Bessie kept up a genial flow of conversation. There she was, he communed savagely with his plate, crying one minute, and the next all smiles and laughter. Now that wasn't his way. If *he* had anything sufficiently important to cry about, rest assured he wouldn't get over it for days. Girls were hypocrites, that was all there was to it. They didn't feel one-hundredth part of all that they said when they cried. It stood to reason that they didn't. It must be that they just carried on because they enjoyed it. It made them feel good to make other people miserable, especially boys. That was why they were always interfering.

Thus reflecting sagely, he kept his eyes on his plate, and did justice to the fare; for one cannot scorch from the Cliff House to the Western Addition *via* the park without being guilty of a healthy appetite.

Now and then his father directed a glance at him in a certain mildly anxious way. Joe did not see these glances, but Bessie saw them, every one. Mr Bronson was a middle-aged man, well developed and of heavy build, though not fat. His was a rugged face, square-jawed and stern-featured, though his eyes were kindly and there were lines about the mouth that betokened laughter rather than severity. A close examination was not required to discover the resemblance between him and Joe. The same broad forehead and strong jaw characterized them both, and the eyes, taking into consideration the difference of age, were as like as peas from one pod.

'How are you getting on, Joe?' Mr Bronson asked finally. Dinner was over, and they were about to leave the table.

'Oh, I don't know,' Joe answered carelessly, and then added: 'We have examinations tomorrow. I'll know then.'

'Whither bound?' his mother questioned, as he turned to leave the room. She was a slender, willowy woman, whose brown eyes Bessie's were, and likewise her tender ways.

'To my room,' Joe answered. 'To work,' he supplemented.

She rumpled his hair affectionately, and bent and kissed him. Mr Bronson smiled approval at him as he went out, and he hurried up the stairs, resolved to dig hard and pass the examinations of the coming day.

Entering his room, he locked the door and sat down at a desk most comfortably arranged for a boy's study. He ran his eye over his text-books. The history examination came the first thing in the morning, so he would begin on that. He opened the book where a page was turned down, and began to read:

'Shortly after the Draconian reforms, a war broke out between Athens and Megara respecting the Island of Salamis, to which both cities laid claim.'

That was easy; but what were the Draconian reforms? He must look them up. He felt quite studious as he ran over the back pages, till he chanced to raise his eyes above the top of the book and saw on a chair a baseball mask and a catcher's glove. They shouldn't have lost that game last Saturday, he thought, and they wouldn't have, either, if it hadn't been for Fred. He wished Fred wouldn't fumble so. He could hold a hundred difficult balls in succession, but when a critical point came, he'd let go of even a dewdrop. He'd have to send him out in the field and bring in Jones to first base. Only Jones was so excitable. He could hold any kind of a ball, no matter how critical the play was, but there was no telling what he would do with the ball after he got it.

Joe came to himself with a start. A pretty way of studying history! He buried his head in his book and began:

'Shortly after the Draconian reforms——'

He read the sentence through three times, and then recollected that he had not looked up the Draconian reforms.

A knock came at the door. He turned the pages over with a noisy flutter, but made no answer.

The knock was repeated, and Bessie's 'Joe, dear' came to his ears.

'What do you want?' he demanded. But before she could answer he hurried on: 'No admittance. I'm busy.'

'I came to see if I could help you,' she pleaded. 'I'm all done, and I thought——'

'Of course you're all done!' he shouted. 'You always are!'

He held his head in both his hands to keep his eyes on the book. But the baseball mask bothered him. The more he attempted to keep his mind on the history, the more in his mind's eye he saw the mask resting on the chair, and all the games in which it had played its part.

This would never do. He deliberately placed the book face downward on the desk and walked over to the chair. With a swift sweep he sent both mask and glove hurtling under the bed, and so violently that he heard the mask rebound from the wall.

'Shortly after the Draconian reforms, a war broke out between Athens and Megara——'

The mask had rolled back from the wall. He wondered if it had rolled back far enough for him to see it. No, he wouldn't look. What did it matter if it had rolled out? That wasn't history. He wondered——

He peered over the top of the book, and there was the mask peeping out at him from under the edge of the bed. This was not to be borne. There was no use attempting to study while that mask was around. He went over and fished it out, crossed the room to the closet, and tossed it inside, then locked the door. That was settled, thank goodness! Now he could do some work.

He sat down again.

'Shortly after the Draconian reforms, a war broke out between Athens and Megara respecting the Island of Salamis, to which both cities laid claim.'

Which was all very well, if he had only found out what the Draconian reforms were. A soft glow pervaded the room, and he suddenly became aware of it. What could cause it! He looked out of the window. The setting sun was slanting its long rays against low-hanging masses of summer clouds, turning them to warm scarlet and rosy red; and it was from them that the red light, mellow and glowing, was flung earthward.

His gaze dropped from the clouds to the bay beneath. The sea-breeze was dying down with the day, and off Fort Point a fishing-boat was creeping into port before the last light breeze. A little beyond, a tug was sending up a twisted pillar of smoke as it towed a three-masted schooner to sea. His eyes wandered over towards the Marin County shore. The line where land and water met was already in darkness, and long shadows were creeping up the hills toward Mount Tamalpais, which was sharply silhouetted against the western sky.

Oh, if he, Joe Bronson, were only on that fishing-boat and sailing in with a deep-sea catch! Or if he were on that schooner, heading out into the sunset, into the world! That was life, that was living, doing something and being something in the world. And, instead, here he was, pent up in a close room, racking his brains about people dead and gone thousands of years before he was born.

He jerked himself away from the window as though held there by some physical force, and resolutely carried his chair and history into the farthest corner of the room, where he sat down with his back to the window.

An instant later, so it seemed to him, he found himself again staring out of the window and dreaming. How he had got there he did not know. His last recollection was the finding of a sub-heading on a page on the right-hand side of the book which read: 'The Laws and Constitution of Draco.' And then, evidently like walking in one's sleep, he had come to the window. How long had he been there? he wondered. The fishing-boat which he had sten off Fort Point was now crawling into Meigg's Wharf. This denoted nearly an hour's lapse of time. The sun had long since set; a solemn greyness was brooding over the water, and the first faint stars were beginning to twinkle over the crest of Mount Tamalpais.

He turned, with a sigh, to go back into his corner, when a long whistle, shrill and piercing, came to his ears. That was Fred. He sighed again. The whistle repeated itself. Then another whistle joined it. That was Charley. They were waiting on the corner—lucky fellows!

Well, they wouldn't see him this night. Both whistles arose in duet. He writhed in his chair and groaned. No, they wouldn't see him this night, he reiterated, at the same time rising to his feet. It was certainly impossible for him to join them when he had not yet learned about the Draconian reforms. The same force which had held him to the window now seemed drawing him across the room to the desk. It made him put the history on top of his school-books, and he had the door unlocked and was half-way into the hall before he realized it. He started to return, but the thought came to him that he could go out for a little while and then come back and do his work.

A very little while, he promised himself, as he went downstairs. He went down faster and faster, till at the bottom he was going three steps at a time. He popped his cap on his head and went out of the side entrance in a rush; and ere he reached the corner, the reforms of Draco were as far away in the past as Draco himself, while the examinations on the morrow were equally far away in the future.

3. 'BRICK', 'SORREL-TOP', AND 'REDDY'

'What's up?' Joe asked, as he joined Fred and Charley.

'Kites,' Charley answered. 'Come on. We're tired out waiting for you.'

The three set off down the street to the brow of the hill, where they looked down upon Union Street, far below and almost under their feet. This they called the Pit, and it was well named. Themselves they called the Hill-dwellers, and a descent into the Pit by the Hill-dwellers was looked upon by them as a great adventure.

Scientific kite-flying was one of the keenest pleasures of these three particular Hill-dwellers, and six or eight kites strung out on a mile of twine and soaring into the clouds was an ordinary achievement for them. They were compelled to replenish their kite supply often; for when-ever an accident occurred, and the string broke, or a ducking kite dragged down the rest, or the wind suddenly died out, their kites fell into the Pit, from which place they were unrecoverable. The reason for this was the young people of the Pit were a piratical and robber race, with peculiar ideas of ownership and property rights.

On a day following an accident to a kite of one of the Hill-dwellers, the selfsame kite could be seen riding the air attached to a string which led down into the Pit to the lairs of the Pit People. So it came about that the Pit People, who were a poor folk and unable to afford scientific kite-flying, developed great proficiency in the art when their neighbours the Hill-dwellers took it up.

There was also an old sailorman who profited by this recreation of the Hill-dwellers; for he was learned in sails and air-currents, and being deft of hand and cunning, he fashioned the best-flying kites that could be obtained. He lived in a rattletrap shanty close to the water, where he could still watch with dim eyes the ebb and flow of the tide, and the ships pass out and in, and where he could revive old memories of the days when he, too, went down to the sea in ships.

To reach his shanty from the Hill one had to pass through the Pit, and thither the three boys were bound. They had often gone for kites in the daytime, but this was their first trip after dark, and they felt it to be, as it indeed was, a hazardous adventure.

In simple words, the Pit was merely the cramped and narrow quarters of the poor, where many nationalities crowded together in cosmopolitan confusion, and lived as best they could, amid much dirt and squalor. It was still early evening when the boys passed through on their way to the sailorman's shanty, and no mishap befell them, though some of the Pit boys stared at them savagely and hurled a taunting remark after them now and then.

The sailorman made kites which were not only splendid fliers but which folded up and were very convenient to carry. Each of the boys bought a few, and, with them wrapped in compact bundles and under their arms, started back on the return journey.

'Keep a sharp lookout for the b'ys,' the kite-maker cautioned them. 'They're like to be cruisin' round after dark.'

'We're not afraid,' Charley assured him; 'and we know how to take care of ourselves'.

Used to the broad and quiet streets of the Hill, the boys were shocked and stunned by the life that teemed in the close-packed quarter. It seemed some thick and monstrous growth of vegetation, and that they were wading through it. They shrank closely together in the tangle of narrow streets as though for protection, conscious of the strangeness of it all, and how unrelated they were to it.

Children and babies sprawled on the sidewalk and under their feet. Bareheaded and unkempt women gossiped in the doorways or passed back and forth with scant marketings in their arms. There was a general odour of decaying fruit and fish, a smell of staleness and putridity. Big hulking men slouched by, and ragged little girls walked gingerly through the confusion with foaming buckets of beer in their hands. There was a clatter and garble of foreign tongues and brogues, shrill cries, quarrels and wrangles, and the Pit pulsed with a great and steady murmur, like the hum of the human hive that it was.

'Phew! I'll be glad when we're out of it,' Fred said.

He spoke in a whisper, and Joe and Charley nodded grimly that they agreed with him. They were not inclined to speech, and they walked as rapidly as the crowd permitted, with much the same feelings as those of travellers in a dangerous and hostile jungle.

And danger and hostility stalked in the Pit. The inhabitants seemed to resent the presence of these strangers from the Hill. Dirty little urchins abused them as they passed, snarling with assumed bravery, and prepared to run away at the first sign of attack. And still other little urchins formed a noisy parade at the heels of the boys, and grew bolder with increasing numbers.

'Don't mind them,' Joe cautioned. 'Take no notice, but keep right on. We'll soon be out of it.'

'No; we're in for it,' said Fred, in an undertone. 'Look there!'

On the corner they were approaching, four or five boys of about their own age were standing. The light from a street lamp fell upon them and disclosed one with vivid red hair. It could be no other than 'Brick' Simpson, the redoubtable leader of a redoubtable gang. Twice within their memory he had led his gang up the Hill and spread panic and terror among the Hill-dwelling young folk, who fled wildly to their homes, while their fathers and mothers hurriedly telephoned for the police.

At sight of the group on the corner, the rabble at the heels of the three boys melted away on the instant with like manifestations of fear. This but increased the anxiety of the boys, though they held boldly on their way.

The red-haired boy detached himself from the group, and stepped before them, blocking their path. They essayed to go around him, but he stretched out his arm.

'Wot yer doin' here?' he snarled. 'Why don't yer stay where yer b'long?'

'We're just going home,' Fred said mildly.

Brick looked at Joe. 'Wot yer got under yer arm?' he demanded.

Joe contained himself and took no heed of him. 'Come on,' he said to Fred and Charley, at the same time starting to brush past the gang-leader.

But with a quick blow Brick Simpson struck him in the face, and with equal quickness snatched the bundle of kites from under his arm.

Joe uttered an inarticulate cry of rage, and, all caution flung to the winds, sprang at his assailant.

This was evidently a surprise to the gang-leader, who expected least of all to be attacked in his own territory. He retreated backward, still clutching the kites, and divided between desire to fight and desire to retain his capture.

The latter desire dominated him, and he turned and fled swiftly down the narrow side street into a labyrinth of streets and alleys. Joe knew that he was plunging into the wilderness of the enemy's country, but his sense of both property and pride had been offended, and he took up the pursuit hot-footed.

Fred and Charley followed after, though he outdistanced them, and behind came the three other members of the gang, emitting a whistling call while they ran, which was evidently intended for the assembling of the band. As the chase proceeded, these whistles were answered from many different directions, and soon a score of dark figures were tagging the heels of Fred and Charley, who in turn were straining every muscle to keep the swifter-footed Joe in sight.

Brick Simpson darted into a vacant lot, aiming for a 'slip', as such things are called, which are prearranged passages through fences and over sheds and houses and around dark holes and corners, where the unfamiliar pursuer must go more carefully and where the chances are many that he will soon lose the track.

But Joe caught Brick before he could attain his end, and together they rolled over and over in the dirt, locked in each other's arms. By the time Fred and Charley and the gang had come up, they were on their feet, facing each other.

'Wot d'ye want, eh?' the red-headed gang-leader was saying in a bullying tone. 'Wot d'ye want?' That's wot I wanter know.'

'I want my kites,' Joe answered.

Brick Simpson's eyes sparkled at the intelligence. Kites were something he stood in need of himself.

'Then you've got to fight fer 'em,' he announced.

'Why should I fight for them?' Joe demanded indignantly. 'They're mine.' Which went to show how ignorant he was of the ideas of ownership and property rights which obtained among the People of the Pit.

A chorus of jeers and catcalls went up from the gang, which clustered behind its leader like a pack of wolves.

'Why should I fight for them?' Joe reiterated.

"Cos I say so,' Simpson replied. 'An' wot I say goes. Understand?'

But Joe did not understand. He refused to understand that Brick Simpson's word was law in San Francisco, or any part of San Francisco. His love of honesty and right dealing was offended, and all his fighting blood was up.

'You give those kites to me, right here and now,' he threatened, reaching out his hand for them.

But Simpson jerked them away. 'D'ye know who I am?' he demanded. 'I'm Brick Simpson, an' I don't 'low no one to talk to me in that tone of voice.'

'Better leave him alone,' Charley whispered in Joe's ear. 'What are a few kites? Leave him alone and let's get out of this.'

'They're my kites,' Joe said slowly in a dogged manner. 'They're my kites, and I'm going to have them.'

'You can't fight the crowd,' Fred interfered; 'and if you do get the best of him they'll all pile on you.'

The gang observing this whispered colloquy, and mistaking it for hesitancy on the part of Joe, set up its wolf-like howling again.

'Afraid! afraid!' the young roughs jeered and taunted. 'He's too high-toned, he is! Mebbe he'll spoil his nice clean shirt, and then what'll mamma say?'

'Shut up!' their leader snapped authoritatively, and the noise obediently died away.

'Will you give me those kites?' Joe demanded, advancing determinedly.

'Will you fight for 'em?' was Simpson's counter-demand.

'Yes,' Joe answered.

'Fight! fight!' the gang began to howl again.

'And it's me that'll see fair play,' said a man's heavy voice.

All eyes were instantly turned upon the man who had approached unseen and made this announcement. By the electric light, shining brightly on them from the corner, they made him out to be a big, muscular fellow, clad in a working-man's garments. His feet were encased in heavy brogans, a narrow strap of black leather held his overalls about his waist, and a black and greasy cap was on his head. His face was grimed with coal-dust, and a coarse blue shirt, open at the neck, revealed a wide throat and massive chest.

'An' who're you?' Simpson snarled angry at the interruption.

'None of yer business,' the new-comer retorted tartly. 'But, if it'll do you any good, I'm a fireman on the China steamers, and, as I said, I'm goin' to see fair play. That's my business. Your business is to give fair play. So pitch in, and don't be all night about it.'

The three boys were as pleased by the appearance of the fireman as Simpson and his fellows were displeased. They conferred together for several minutes, when Simpson deposited the bundle of kites in the arms of one of his gang and stepped forward.

'Come on, then,' he said, at the same time pulling off his coat.

Joe handed his to Fred, and sprang towards Brick. They put up their fists and faced each other. Almost instantly Simpson drove in a fierce blow and ducked cleverly away and out of reach of the blow which Joe returned. Joe felt a sudden respect for the abilities of his antagonist, but the only effect upon him was to arouse all the doggedness of his nature and make him utterly determined to win.

Awed by the presence of the fireman, Simpson's followers confined themselves to cheering Brick and jeering Joe. The two boys circled round and round, attacking, feinting, and guarding, and now one and then the other getting in a telling blow. Their positions were in marked contrast. Joe stood erect, planted solidly on his feet, with legs wide apart and head up. On the other hand, Simpson crouched till his head was nearly lost between his shoulders, and all the while he was in constant motion, leaping and springing and manœuvring in the execution of a score or more of tricks quite new and strange to Joe.

At the end of a quarter of an hour, both were very tired, though Joe was much fresher. Tobacco, ill food, and unhealthy living were telling on the gang-leader, who was panting and sobbing for breath. Though at first (and because of superior skill) he had severely punished Joe, he was now weak, and his blows were without force. Growing desperate, he adopted what might be called not an unfair but a mean method of attack: he would manœuvre, leap in and strike swiftly, and then, ducking forward, fall to the ground at Joe's feet. Joe could not strike him while he was down, and so would step back until he could get on his feet again, when the thing would be repeated.

But Joe grew tired of this, and prepared for him. Timing his blows with Simpson's attack, he delivered it just as Simpson was ducking forward to fall. Simpson fell, but he fell over on one side, whither he had been driven by the impact of Joe's fist upon his head. He rolled over and got half-way to his feet, where he remained, crying and gasping. His followers called upon him to get up, and he tried once or twice, but was too exhausted and stunned.

'I give in,' he said. 'I'm licked.'

The gang had become silent and depressed at its leader's defeat.

Joe stepped forward.

'I'll trouble you for those kites,' he said to the boy who was holding them.

'Oh, I dunno,' said another member of the gang, shoving between Joe and his property. His hair was also a vivid red. 'You've got to lick me before you kin have 'em.'

'I don't see that,' Joe said bluntly. 'I've fought and I've won, and there's nothing more to it.'

'Oh yes, there is,' said the other. 'I'm "Sorrel-top" Simpson. Brick's my brother. See?'

And so, in this fashion, Joe learned another custom of the Pit People of which he had been ignorant.

'All right,' he said, his fighting blood more fully aroused than ever by the unjustness of the proceeding. 'Come on.'

Sorrel-top Simpson, a year younger than his brother, proved to be a most unfair fighter, and the good-natured fireman was compelled to interfere several times before the second of the Simpson clan lay on the ground and acknowledged defeat.

This time Joe reached for his kites without the slightest doubt that he was to get them. But still another lad stepped in between him and his property. The tell-tale hair, vividly red, sprouted likewise on this lad's head, and Joe knew him at once for what he was, another member of the Simpson clan. He was a younger edition of his brothers, somewhat less heavily built, with a face covered with a vast quantity of freckles, which showed plainly under the electric light.

'You don't git them there kites till you git me,' he challenged in a piping little voice. 'I'm "Reddy" Simpson, an' you ain't licked the fambly till you've licked me.'

The gang cheered admirably, and Reddy stripped a tattered jacket preparatory for the fray.

Joe's knuckles were torn, his nose was bleeding, his lip was cut and swollen, while his shirt had been ripped down from throat to waist. Further, he was tired, and breathing hard.

'How many more are there of you Simpsons?' he asked. 'I've got to get home, and if your family's much larger this thing is liable to keep on all night.'

'I'm the last an' the best,' Reddy replied. 'You gits me an' you gits the kites, Sure.'

'All right,' Joe sighed. 'Come on.'

While the youngest of the clan lacked the strength and skill of his elders, he made up for it by a wild-cat manner of fighting that taxed Joe severely. Time and again it seemed to him that he must give in to the little whirlwind; but each time he pulled himself together and went doggedly on. For he felt that he was fighting for principle, as his forefathers had fought for principle; also, it seemed to him that the honour of the Hill was at stake, and that he, as its representative, could do nothing less than his very best.

So he held on and managed to endure his opponent's swift and continuous rushes till that young and less experienced person at last wore himself out with his own exertions, and from the ground confessed that, for the first time in its history, the 'Simpson fambly was beat'.

4. THE BITER BITTEN

BUT LIFE in the Pit at best was a precarious affair, as the three Hill-dwellers were quickly to learn. Before Joe could even possess himself of his kites, his astonished eyes were greeted with the spectacle of all his enemies, the fireman included, taking to their heels in wild flight. As the little girls and urchins had melted away before the Simpson gang, so was melting away the Simpson gang before some new and correspondingly awe-inspiring group of predatory creatures.

Joe heard terrified cries of 'Fish gang!' 'Fish gang!' from those who fled, and he would have fled himself from this new danger, only he was breathless from his last encounter, and knew the impossibility of escaping whatever threatened. Fred and Charley felt mighty longings to run away from a danger great enough to frighten the redoubtable Simpson gang and the valorous fireman, but they could not desert their comrade.

Dark forms broke into the vacant lot, some surrounding the boys and others dashing after the fugitives. That the laggards were overtaken was evidence by the cries of distress that went up, and when later the pursuers returned, they brought with them the luckless and snarling Brick, still clinging fast to the bundle of kites.

Joe looked curiously at this latest band of marauders. They were young men of from seventeen and eighteen to twenty-three and four years of age, and bore the unmistakable stamp of the hoodlum class. There were vicious faces among them—faces so vicious as to make Joe's flesh creep as he looked at them. A couple grasped him tightly by the arms, and Fred and Charley were similarly held captive.

'Look here, you,' said one who spoke with the authority of leader, 'we've got to inquire into this. Wot's be'n goin' on here? Wot're you up to, Red-head? Wot you be'n doin'?'

'Ain't be'n doin' nothin',' Simpson whined.

'Looks like it.' The leader turned up Brick's face to the electric light. 'Who's been paintin' you up like that?' he demanded.

Brick pointed at Joe, who was forthwith dragged to the front.

'Wot was you scrappin' about?'

'Kites—my kites,' Joe spoke up boldly. 'That fellow tried to take them away from me. He's got them under his arm now.'

'Oh, he has, has he? Look here, you Brick, we don't put up with stealin' in this territory. See? You never rightly owned nothin'. Come, fork over the kites. Last call.'

The leader tightened his grasp threateningly, and Simpson, weeping tears of rage, surrendered the plunder.

'Wot yer got under yer arm?' the leader demanded abruptly of Fred, at the same time jerking out the bundle. 'More kites, eh? Reg'lar kite factory gone and got itself lost,' he remarked finally, when he had appropriated Charley's bundle. 'Now, wot I wants to know is wot we're goin' to do to you t'ree chaps?' he continued in a judicial tone.

'What for?' Joe demanded hotly. 'For being robbed of our kites?'

'Not at all, not at all,' the leader responded politely; 'but for luggin' kites round these quarters an' causin' all this unseemly disturbance. It's disgraceful; that's wot it is —disgraceful.'

At this juncture, when the Hill-dwellers were the centre of attraction. Brick suddenly wormed out of his jacket, squirmed away from his captors, and dashed across the lot to the slip for which he had been originally headed when overtaken by Joe. Two or three of the gang shot over the fence after him in noisy pursuit. There was much barking and howling of backyard dogs and clattering of shoes over sheds and boxes. Then there came a splashing of water, as though a barrel of it had been precipitated to the ground. Several minutes later the pursuers returned, very sheepish and very wet from the deluge presented them by the wily Brick, whose voice, high up in the air from some friendly housetop, could be heard defiantly jeering them.

This event apparently disconcerted the leader of the gang, and just as he turned to Joe and Fred and Charley, a long and peculiar whistle came to their ears from the street—the warning signal, evidently, of a scout posted to keep a lookout. The next moment the scout himself came flying back to the main body, which was already beginning to retreat.

'Cops!' he panted.

Joe looked, and he saw two helmeted policemen approaching, with bright stars shining on their breasts.

'Let's get out of this,' he whispered to Fred and Charley.

The gang had already taken to flight, and they blocked the boys' retreat in one quarter, and in another they saw the policemen advancing. So they took to their heels in the direction of Brick Simpson's slip, the policemen hot after them and yelling bravely for them to halt.

But young feet are nimble, and young feet when frightened become something more than nimble, and the boys were first over the fence and plunging wildly through a maze of backyards. They soon found that the policemen were discreet. Evidently they had had experiences in slips, and they were satisfied to give over the chase at the first fence.

8*

No street lamps shed their light here, and the boys blundered along through the blackness with their hearts in their mouths. In one yard, filled with mountains of crates and fruit-boxes, they were lost for a quarter of an hour. Feel and quest about as they would, they encounted nothing but endless heaps of boxes. From this wilderness they finally emerged by way of a shed roof, only to fall into another yard, cumbered with countless empty chicken-coops.

Farther on they came upon the contrivance which had soaked Brick Simpson's pursuers with water. It was a cunning arrangement. Where the slip led through a fence with a board missing, a long slat was so arranged that the ignorant wayfarer could not fail to strike against it. This slat was the spring of the trap. A light touch upon it was sufficient to disconnect a heavy stone from a barrel perched overhead and nicely balanced. The disconnecting of the stone permitted the barrel to turn over and spill its contents on the one beneath who touched the slat.

The boys examined the arrangement with keen appreciation. Luckily for them, the barrel was overturned, or they too would have received a ducking, for Joe, who was in advance, had blundered against the slat.

'I wonder if this is Simpson's backyard?' he queried softly.

'It must be,' Fred concluded; 'or else the backyard of some member of his gang.'

Charley put his hands warningly on both their arms.

'Hist! What's that?' he whispered.

They crouched down on the ground. Not far away was the sound of someone moving about. Then they heard a noise of falling water, as from a faucet into a bucket. This was followed by steps boldly approaching. They crouched lower, breathless with apprehension.

A dark form passed by within arm's reach and mounted on a box to the fence. It was Brick himself, resetting the trap. They heard him arrange the slat and stone, then right the barrel and empty into it a couple of buckets of water. As he came down from the box to go after more water, Joe sprang upon him, tripped him up, and held him to the ground.

'Don't make any noise,' he said. 'I want you to listen to me.'

'Oh, it's you, is it?' Simpson replied, with such obvious relief in his voice as to make them feel relieved also. 'Wot d'ye want here?'

'We want to get out of here,' Joe said, 'and the shortest way's the best. There's three of us, and you're only one——'

'That's all right, that's all right,' the gang-leader interrupted. 'I'd just as soon show you the way out as not. I ain't got nothin' 'gainst you. Come on an' follow me, an' don't step to the side, an' I'll have you out in no time.'

Several minutes later they dropped from the top of a high fence into a dark alley.

'Follow this to the street,' Simpson directed; 'turn to the right two blocks, turn to the right again for three, an' yer on Union. Tra-la-loo.'

They said good-bye, and as they started down the alley received the following advice:

'Nex' time you bring kites along, you'd best leave 'em to home.'

5. HOME AGAIN

FOLLOWING Brick Simpson's directions, they came into Union Street, and without further mishap gained the Hill. From the brow they looked down into the Pit, whence arose that steady, indefinable hum which comes from crowded human places.

'I'll never go down there again, not as long as I live,' Fred said with a great deal of savagery in his voice. 'I wonder what became of the fireman.'

'We're lucky to get back with whole skins,' Joe cheered them philosophically.

'I guess we left our share, and you more than yours,' laughed Charley.

'Yes,' Joe answered. 'And I've got more trouble to face when I get home. Good-night, fellows.'

As he expected, the door on the side porch was locked, and he went around to the dining-room and entered like a burglar through a window. As he crossed the wide hall, walking softly towards the stairs, his father came out of the library. The surprise was mutual, and each halted aghast.

Joe felt a hysterical desire to laugh, for he thought that he knew precisely how he looked. In reality he looked far worse than he imagined. What Mr Bronson saw was a boy with hat and coat covered with dirt, his whole face smeared with the stains of conflict, and, in particular, a badly swollen nose, a bruised eyebrow, a cut and swollen lip, a scratched cheek, knuckles still bleeding, and a shirt torn open from throat to waist.

'What does this mean, sir?' Mr Bronson finally managed to articulate.

Joe stood speechless. How could he tell, in one brief sentence, all the whole night's happenings?—for all that must be included in the explanation of what his luckless disarray meant.

'Have you lost your tongue?' Mr Bronson demanded with an appearance of impatience.

'I've—I've——'

'Yes, yes,' his father encouraged.

'I've—well, I've been down in the Pit,' Joe succeeded in blurting out.

'I must confess that you look like it—very much like it indeed.' Mr Bronson spoke severely, but if ever by great effort he conquered a smile, that was the time. 'I presume,' he went on, 'that you do not refer to the abiding-place of sinners, but rather to some definite locality in San Francisco. Am I right?'

Joe swept his arm in a descending gesture towards Union Street, and said: 'Down there, sir.'

'And who gave it that name?'

'I did,' Joe answered, as though confessing to a specified crime.

'It's most appropriate, I'm sure, and denotes imagination. It couldn't really be bettered. You must do well at school, sir, with your English.'

This did not increase Joe's happiness, for English was the only study of which he did not have to feel ashamed.

And, while he stood thus a silent picture of misery and disgrace, Mr Bronson looked upon him through the eyes of his own boyhood with an understanding which Joe could not have believed possible.

'However, what you need just now is not a discourse, but a bath and court-plaster and witch-hazel and cold-water bandages,' Mr Bronson said; 'so to bed with you. You'll need all the sleep you can get, and you'll feel stiff and sore tomorrow morning, I promise you.'

The clock struck one as Joe pulled the bedclothes around him; and the next he knew he was being worried by a soft, insistent rapping, which seemed to continue through several centuries, until at last, unable to endure it longer, he opened his eyes and sat up.

The day was streaming in through the window—bright and sunshiny day. He stretched his arms to yawn; but a shooting pain darted through all his muscles, and his arms came down more rapidly than they had gone up. He looked at them with a bewildered stare, till suddenly the events of the night rushed in upon him, and he groaned.

The rapping still persisted, and he cried: 'Yes, I hear. What time is it?'

'Eight o'clock,' Bessie's voice came to him through the door. 'Eight o'clock, and you'll have to hurry if you don't want to be late for school.'

'Goodness!' He sprang out of bed precipitately, groaned with the pain from all his stiff muscles, and collapsed slowly and carefully on a chair. 'Why didn't you call me sooner?' he growled.

'Father said to let you sleep.'

Joe groaned again, in another fashion. Then his history book caught his eye, and he groaned yet again and in still another fashion.

'All right,' he called. 'Go on. I'll be down in a jiffy.'

He did come down in fairly brief order; but if Bessie had watched him descend the stairs she would have been astounded at the remarkable caution he observed, and at the twinges of pain that every now and then contorted his face. As it was, when she came upon him in the dining-room she uttered a frightened cry and ran over to him.

'What's the matter, Joe?' she asked tremulously. 'What has happened?'

'Nothing,' he grunted, putting sugar on his porridge.

'But surely——' she began.

'Please don't bother me,' he interrupted. 'I'm late, and I want to eat my breakfast.'

And just them Mrs Bronson caught Bessie's eye, and that young lady, still mystified, made haste to withdraw herself.

Joe was thankful to his mother for that, and thankful that she refrained from remarking upon his appearance. Father had told her; that was one thing sure. He could trust her not to worry him; it was never her way.

And, meditating in this way, he hurried through with his solitary breakfast, vaguely conscious in an uncomfortable way that his mother was fluttering anxiously about him. Tender as she always was, he noticed that she kissed him with unusual tenderness as he started out with his books swinging at the end of a strap; and he also noticed, as he turned the corner, that she was still looking after him through the window.

But of more vital importance than that, to him, was his stiffness and soreness. As he walked along, each step was an effort and a torment. Severely as the reflected sunlight from the cement side-walk hurt his bruised eye, and

severely as his various wounds pained him, still more
severely did he suffer from his muscles and joints. He
had never imagined such stiffness. Each individual muscle
in his whole body protested when called upon to move.
His fingers were badly swollen, and it was agony to clasp
and unclasp them; while his arms were sore from wrist to
elbow. This, he said to himself, was caused by the many
blows which he had warded off from his face and body.
He wondered if Brick Simpson was in similar plight, and
the thought of their mutual misery made him feel a certain
kinship for that redoubtable young ruffian.

When he entered the schoolyard he quickly became
aware that he was the centre of attraction for all eyes. The
boys crowded around in an awe-stricken way, and even his
classmates and those with whom he was well acquainted
looked at him with a certain respect he had never seen
before.

6. EXAMINATION DAY

IT WAS plain that Fred and Charley had spread the news
of their descent into the Pit, and of their battle with the
Simpson clan and the Fishes. He heard the nine o'clock
bell with feelings of relief, and passed into the school, a
mark for admiring glances from all the boys. The girls,
too, looked at him in a timid and fearful way—as they
might have looked at Daniel when he came out of the
lions' den, Joe thought, or at David after the battle with
Goliath. It made him uncomfortable and painfully self-
conscious, this hero-worshipping, and he wished heartily
that they would look in some other direction for a change.

Soon they did look in another direction. While big sheets
of foolscap were being distributed to every desk, Miss
Wilson, the teacher (an austere-looking young woman who
went through the world as though it were a refrigerator,
and who, even on the warmest days in the classroom, was

to be found with a shawl or cape about her shoulders), arose, and on the blackboard where all could see wrote the Roman numeral 'I'. Every eye, and there were fifty pairs of them, hung with expectancy upon her hand, and, in the pause that followed, the room was quiet as the grave.

Underneath the Roman numeral 'I' she wrote: '(*a*) *What were the laws of Draco?* (*b*) *Why did an Athenian orator say that they were written "not in ink, but in blood"?*'

Forty-nine heads bent down and forty-nine pens scratched lustily across as many sheets of foolscap. Joe's head alone remained up, and he regarded the blackboard with so blank a stare that Miss Wilson, glancing over her shoulder after having written 'II', stopped to look at him. Then she wrote:

'(*a*) *How did the war between Athens and Megara, respecting the Island of Salamis, bring about the reforms of Solon?* (*b*) *In what way did they differ from the laws of Draco?*'

She turned to look at Joe again. He was staring as blankly as ever.

'What is the matter, Joe?' she asked. 'Have you no paper?'

'Yes, I have, thank you,' he answered, and began moodily to sharpen a lead-pencil.

He made a fine point to it. Then he made a very fine point. Then, and with infinite patience, he proceeded to make it very much finer. Several of his classmates raised their heads inquiringly at the noise. But he did not notice. He was too absorbed in his pencil sharpening and in thinking thoughts far away from both pencil sharpening and Greek history.

'Of course you all understand that the examination papers are to be written with ink.'

Miss Wilson addressed the class in general but her eyes rested on Joe.

Just as it was about as fine as it could possibly be the point broke, and Joe began over again.

'I am afraid, Joe, that you annoy the class,' Miss Wilson said in final desperation.

He put the pencil down, closed the knife with a snap, and returned to his blank staring at the blackboard. What did he know about Draco? or Solon? or the rest of the Greeks? It was a flunk, and that was all there was to it. No need for him to look at the rest of the questions, and even if he did know the answers to two or three, there was no use in writing them down. It would not prevent the flunk. Besides, his arm hurt him too much to write. It hurt his eyes to look at the blackboard, and his eyes hurt even when they were closed; and it seemed positively to hurt him to think.

So the forty-nine pens scratched on in a race after Miss Wilson, who was covering the blackboard with question after question; and he listened to the scratching, and watched the questions growing under her chalk, and was very miserable indeed. His head seemed whirling around. It ached inside and was sore outside, and he did not seem to have any control of it at all.

He was beset with memories of the Pit, like scenes from some monstrous nightmare, and, try as he would, he could not dispel them. He would fix his mind and eyes on Miss Wilson's face, who was now sitting at her desk, and even as he looked at her the face of Brick Simpson, impudent and pugnacious, would arise before him. It was of no use. He felt sick and sore and tired and worthless. There was nothing to be done but flunk. And, when, after an age of waiting, the papers were collected, his went in a blank, save for his name, the name of the examination, and the date, which were written across the top.

After a brief interval, more papers were given out, and the examination in arithmetic began. He did not trouble himself to look at the questions. Ordinarily he might have pulled through such an examination, but in his present state of mind and body he knew it was impossible. He contented himself with burying his face in his hands and hoping for the noon hour. Once, lifting his eyes to the clock, he caught Bessie's looking anxiously at him across the room from the girls' side. This but added to his discomfort. Why was she bothering him? No need for her to trouble. She was bound to pass. Then why couldn't she leave him alone? So he gave her a particularly glowering look and buried his face in his hands again. Nor did he lift it till the twelve o'clock gong rang when he handed in a second blank paper and passed out with the boys.

Fred and Charley and he usually ate lunch in a corner of the yard which they had arrogated to themselves; but this day, by some remarkable coincidence, a score of other boys had elected to eat their lunches on the same spot. Joe surveyed them with disgust. In his present condition he did not feel inclined to receive hero-worship. His head ached too much, and he was troubled over his failure in the examinations; and there were more to come in the afternoon.

He was angry with Fred and Charley. They were chattering like magpies over the adventures of the night (in which, however, they did not fail to give him chief credit), and they conducted themselves in quite a patronizing fashion towards their awed and admiring schoolmates. But every attempt to make Joe talk was a failure. He grunted and gave short answers, and said 'yes' and 'no' to questions asked with the intention of drawing him out.

He was longing to get away somewhere by himself, to throw himself down some place on the green grass and forget his aches and pains and troubles. He got up to go and find such a place, and found half a dozen of his following tagging after him. He wanted to turn around and scream at them to leave him alone, but his pride restrained him. A great wave of disgust and despair swept over him, and then an idea flashed through his mind. Since he was sure to flunk in his examinations, why endure the afternoon's torture, which could not be worse than the morning's? And on the impulse of the moment he made up his mind.

He walked straight on to the schoolyard gate and passed out. Here his worshippers halted in wonderment, but he kept on to the corner and out of sight. For some time he wandered along aimlessly, till he came to the tracks of a cable road. A down-town car happening to stop to let off passengers, he stepped aboard and ensconced himself in an outside corner seat. The next thing he was aware of, the car was swinging around on its turn-table and he was hastily scrambling off. The big ferry building stood before him. Seeing and hearing nothing, he had been carried through the heart of the business section of San Francisco.

He glanced up at the tower clock on top of the ferry building. It was ten minutes after one—time enough to catch the quarter-past-one boat. That decided him, and without the least idea in the world as to where he was going, he paid ten cents for a ticket, passed through the gate, and was soon speeding across the bay to the pretty city of Oakland.

In the same aimless and unwitting fashion, he found himself, an hour later, sitting on the string-piece of the Oakland city wharf and leaning his aching head against a friendly timber. From where he sat he could look down upon the decks of a number of small sailing craft. Quite a crowd of curious idlers had collected to look at them and Joe found himself growing interested.

There were four boats, and from where he sat he could make out their names. The one directly beneath him had the name *Ghost* painted in large green letters on its stern. The other three, which lay beyond, were called respectively *La Caprice*, the *Oyster Queen*, and the *Flying Dutchman*.

Each of these boats had cabins built amidships, with short stovepipes projecting through the roofs, and from the pipe of the *Ghost* smoke was ascending. The cabin doors were open and the roof-slide pulled back, so that Joe could look inside and observe the inmate, a young fellow of nineteen or twenty who was engaged just then in cooking. He was clad in long seaboots which reached the hips, blue overalls, and dark woollen shirt. The sleeves, rolled back to the elbows, disclosed sturdy, sun-bronzed arms, and when the young fellow looked up his face proved to be equally bronzed and tanned.

The aroma of coffee arose to Joe's nose, and from a light iron pot came the unmistakable smell of beans nearly done. The cook placed a frying-pan on the stove, wiped it around with a piece of suet when it had heated, and tossed in a thick chunk of beef-steak. While he worked he talked with a companion on deck, who was busily engaged in filling a bucket overside and flinging the salt water over heaps of oysters that lay on the deck. This completed, he covered the oysters with wet sacks, and went into the cabin, where a place was set for him on a tiny table, and where the cook served the dinner and joined him in eating it.

All the romance of Joe's nature stirred at the sight. That was life. They were living, and gaining their living, out in the free open, under the sun and sky, with the sea rocking beneath them, and the wind blowing on them, or the rain falling on them, as the chance might be. Each day and every day he sat in a room, pent up with fifty more of his kind, racking his brains and cramming dry husks of knowledge, while they were doing all this, living glad and careless and happy, rowing boats and sailing, and cooking their own food, and certainly meeting with adventures such as one only dreams of in the crowded schoolroom.

Joe sighed. He felt that he was made for this sort of life and not for the life of a scholar. As a scholar he was undeniably a failure. He had flunked in his examinations, while at that very moment, he knew, Bessie was going triumphantly home, her last examination over and done, and with credit. Oh, it was not to be borne! His father was wrong in sending him to school. That might be well enough for boys who were inclined to study, but it was manifest that he was not so inclined. There were more careers in life than that of the schools. Men had gone down to the sea in the lowest capacity, and risen in greatness, and owned great fleets, and done great deeds, and left their names on the pages of time. And why not he, Joe Bronson?

He closed his eyes and felt immensely sorry for himself; and when he opened his eyes again he found that he had been asleep, and that the sun was sinking fast.

It was after dark when he arrived home, and he went straight to his room and to bed without meeting anyone. He sank down between the cool sheets with a sigh of satisfaction at the thought that, come what would, he need no longer worry about his history. Then another and unwelcome thought obtruded itself, and he knew that the next school term would come, and that six months thereafter, another examination in the same history awaited him.

7. FATHER AND SON

ON THE following morning, after breakfast, Joe was summoned to the library by his father, and he went in almost with a feeling of gladness that the suspense of waiting was over. Mr Bronson was standing by the window. A great chattering of sparrows outside seemed to have attracted his attention. Joe joined him in looking out, and saw a fledgling sparrow on the grass, tumbling ridiculously about in its efforts to stand on its feeble baby legs. It had fallen from the nest in the rose bush that climbed over the window, and the two parent sparrows were wild with anxiety over its plight.

'It's a way young birds have,' Mr Bronson remarked, turning to Joe with a serious smile; 'and I daresay you are on the verge of a somewhat similar predicament, my boy,' he went on. 'I am afraid things have reached a crisis, Joe. I have watched it coming on for a year now—your poor scholarship, your carelessness and inattention, your constant desire to be out of the house and away in search of adventures of one sort or another.'

He paused, as though expecting a reply; but Joe remained silent.

'I have given you plenty of liberty. I believe in liberty. The finest souls grow in such soil. So I have not hedged you in with endless rules and irksome restrictions. I have asked little of you, and you have come and gone pretty much as you pleased. In a way, I have put you on your honour, made you largely your own master, trusting to your sense of right to restrain you from going wrong, and at least to keep you up in your studies. And you have failed me. What do you want me to do? Set you certain bounds and time-limits? Keep a watch over you? Compel you by main strength to go through your books?

'I have here a note,' Mr Bronson said after another pause, in which he picked up an envelope from the table and drew forth a written sheet.

Joe recognized the stiff and uncompromising scrawl of Miss Wilson, and his heart sank.

His father began to read:

'Listlessness and carelessness have characterized his term's work, so that when the examinations came he was wholly unprepared. In neither history nor arithmetic did he attempt to answer a question, passing in his papers perfectly blank. These examinations took place in the morning. In the afternoon he did not take the trouble even to appear for the remainder.'

Mr Bronson ceased reading and looked up.

'Where were you in the afternoon?' he asked.

'I went across on the ferry to Oakland,' Joe answered, not caring to offer his aching head and body in extenuation.

'That is what is called "playing hooky", is it not?'

'Yes, sir,' Joe answered.

'The night before the examinations, instead of studying, you saw fit to wander away and involve yourself in a disgraceful fight with hoodlums. I did not say anything at the time. In my heart I think I might almost have forgiven you that, if you had done well in your school-work.'

Joe had nothing to say. He knew that there was his side to the story, but he felt that his father did not understand, and that there was little use of telling him.

'The trouble with you, Joe, is carelessness and lack of concentration. What you need is what I have not given you, and that is rigid discipline. I have been debating for some time upon the advisability of sending you to some military school, where your tasks will be set for you, and what you do every moment in the twenty-four hours will be determined for you——'

'Oh, father, you don't understand, you can't understand!' Joe broke forth at last. 'I try to study—I honestly try to study; but somehow—I don't know how—I can't study. Perhaps I am a failure. Perhaps I am not made for study. I want to go out into the world. I want to see life —to live. I don't want any military academy; I'd sooner go to sea—anywhere where I can do something and be something.'

Mr Bronson looked at him kindly. 'It is only through study that you can hope to do something and be something in the world,' he said.

Joe threw up his hand with a gesture of despair.

'I know how you feel about it,' Mr Bronson went on; 'but you are only a boy, very much like that young sparrow we were watching. If at home you have not sufficient control over yourself to study, then away from home, out in the world which you think is calling to you, you will likewise not have sufficient control over yourself to do the work of that world.

'But I am willing, Joe, I am willing, after you have finished high school and before you go into the university, to let you out into the world for a time.'

'Let me go now?' Joe asked impulsively.

'No, it is too early. You haven't your wings yet. You

are too unformed, and your ideals and standards are not yet thoroughly fixed.'

'But I shall not be able to study,' Joe threatened. 'I know I shall not be able to study.'

Mr Bronson consulted his watch and arose to go. 'I have not made up my mind yet,' he said. 'I do not know what I shall do—whether I shall give you another trial at the public school or send you to a military academy.'

He stopped a moment at the door and looked back. 'But remember this, Joe,' he said. 'I am not angry with you; I am more grieved and hurt. Think it over, and tell me this evening what you intend to do.'

His father passed out, and Joe heard the front door close after him. He leaned back in the big easy-chair and closed his eyes. A military school! He feared such an institution as the animal fears a trap. No, he would certainly never go to such a place. And as for public school—— He sighed deeply as the thought of it. He was given till evening to make up his mind as to what he intended to do. Well, he knew what he would do, and he did not have to wait till evening to find it out.

He got up with a determined look on his face, put on his hat, and went out the front door. He would show his father that he could do his share of the world's work, he thought as he walked along—he would show him.

By the time he reached the school he had his whole plan worked out definitely. Nothing remained but to put it through. It was the noon hour, and he passed in to his room and packed up his books unnoticed. Coming out through the yard, he encountered Fred and Charley.

'What's up?' Charley asked.

'Nothing,' Joe grunted.

'What are you doing there?'

'Taking my books home, of course. What did you suppose I was doing?'

'Come, come,' Fred interposed. 'Don't be so mysterious. I don't see why you can't tell us what has happened.'

'You'll find out soon enough,' Joe said significantly—more significantly than he had intended.

And, for fear that he might say more, he turned his back on his astonished chums and hurried away. He went straight home and to his room, where he busied himself at once with putting everything in order. His clothes he hung carefully away, changing the suit he had on for an older one. From his bureau he selected a couple of changes of underclothing, a couple of cotton shirts, and half a dozen pairs of socks. To these he added as many handkerchiefs, a comb, and a tooth-brush.

When he had bound the bundle in stout wrapping-paper he contemplated it with satisfaction. Then he went over to his desk and took from a small inner compartment his savings for some months, which amounted to several dollars. This sum he had been keeping for the Fourth of July, but he thrust it into his pocket with hardly a regret. Then he pulled a writing-pad over to him, sat down and wrote:

'Don't look for me. I am a failure and I am going away to sea. Don't worry about me. I am all right and able to take care of myself. I shall come back some day, and then you will all be proud of me. Good-bye, papa, and mamma, and Bessie.

JOE.'

This he left lying on his desk where it could easily be seen. He tucked the bundle under his arm, and, with a last farewell look at the room, stole out.

PART TWO

8. 'FRISCO KID AND THE NEW BOY

'FRISCO KID was discontented—discontented and disgusted. This would have seemed impossible to the boys who fished from the dock above and envied him greatly. True, they wore cleaner and better clothes, and were blessed with fathers and mothers; but his was the free floating life of the bay, the domain of moving adventure, and the companionship of men—theirs the rigid discipline and dreary sameness of home life. They did not dream that 'Frisco Kid ever looked up at them from the cockpit of the *Dazzler* and in turn envied them just those things which sometimes were the most distasteful to them and from which they suffered to repletion. Just as the romance of adventure sang its siren song in their ears and whispered vague messages of strange lands and lusty deeds, so the delicious mysteries of home enticed 'Frisco Kid's roving fancies, and his brightest day-dreams were of the things he knew not—brothers, sisters, a father's counsel, a mother's kiss.

He frowned, got up from where he had been sunning himself on top of the *Dazzler*'s cabin, and kicked off his heavy rubber boots. Then he stretched himself on the narrow side-deck and dangled his feet in the cool salt water.

'Now, that's freedom,' thought the boys who watched him. Besides, those long sea-boots, reaching to the hips and buckled to the leather strap about the waist, held a strange and wonderful fascination for them. They did not know that 'Frisco Kid did not possess such things as shoes— that the boots were an old pair of Pete Le Maire's, and were three sizes too large for him. Nor could they guess how uncomfortable they were to wear on a hot summer day.

The cause of 'Frisco Kid's discontent was those very boys who sat on the string-piece and admired him; but his disgust was the result of quite another event. The *Dazzler* was short one in its crew, and he had to do more work than was justly his share. He did not mind the cooking, nor the washing down of the decks and the pumping; but when it came to the paint-scrubbing and dish-washing he rebelled. He felt that he had earned the right to be exempt from such scullion work. That was all the green boys were fit for, while he could make or take in sail, lift anchor, steer, and make landings.

'Stan' from un'er!' Pete Le Maire or 'French Pete', captain of the *Dazzler* and lord and master of 'Frisco Kid, threw a bundle into the cockpit and came aboard by the starboard rigging.

'Come! Queeck!' he shouted to the boy who owned the bundle and who now hesitated on the dock. It was a good fifteen feet to the deck of the sloop, and he could not reach the steel stay by which he must descend.

'Now! One, two, three!' the Frenchman counted good-naturedly, after the manner of captains when their crews are short-handed.

The boy swung his body into space and gripped the rigging. A moment later he struck the deck, his hands tingling warmly from the friction.

'Kid, dis is ze new sailor. I make your acquaintance.' French Pete smirked and bowed, and stood aside. 'Mistaire Sho Bronson,' he added as an afterthought.

The two boys regarded each other silently for a moment. They were evidently about the same age, though the stranger looked the heartier and stronger of the two. 'Frisco Kid put out his hand, and they shook.

'So you're thinking of tackling the water, eh?' he said.

Joe Bronson nodded and glanced curiously about him before answering: 'Yes; I think the bay life will suit me for

a while, and then, when I've got used to it, I'm going to
sea in the forecastle.'

'In the what?'

'In the forecastle—the place where the sailors live,' he
explained, flushing and feeling doubtful of his pronunciation.

'Oh, the fo'c'sle. Know anything about going to sea?'

'Yes—no; that is, except what I've read.'

'Frisco Kid whistled, turned on his heel in a lordly
manner, and went into the cabin.

'Going to sea,' he chuckled to himself as he built the
fire and set about cooking supper; 'in the "forecastle", too;
and thinks he'll like it.'

In the meanwhile French Pete was showing the new-
comer about the sloop as though he were a guest. Such
affability and charm did he display that 'Frisco Kid, popping his head up through the scuttle to call them to supper,
nearly choked in his effort to suppress a grin.

Joe Bronson enjoyed that supper. The food was rough
but good, and the smack of the salt air and the sea-
fittings around him gave zest to his appetite. The cabin
was clean and snug, and, though not large, the accommodation surprised him. Every bit of space was utilized.
The table swung to the centreboard-case on hinges, so
that when not in use it actually occupied no room at all.
On either side, and partly under the deck, were two bunks.
The blankets were rolled back, and the boys sat on the
well-scrubbed bunk boards while they ate. A swinging sea-
lamp of brightly polished brass gave them light, which in
the daytime could be obtained through the four dead-eyes,
or small round panes of heavy glass which were fitted
into the walls of the cabin. On one side of the door was
the stove and wood-box, on the other the cupboard. The
front end of the cabin was ornamented with a couple of
rifles and a shot-gun, while exposed by the rolled back
blankets of French Pete's bunk was a cartridge-lined belt
carrying a brace of revolvers.

It all seemed like a dream to Joe. Countless times he

had imagined scenes somewhat similar to this; but here he was right in the midst of it, and already it seemed as though he had known his two companions for years. French Pete was smiling genially at him across the board. It really was a villainous countenance, but to Joe it seemed only weather-beaten. 'Frisco Kid was describing to him, between mouthfuls, the last sou'-easter the *Dazzler* had weathered, and Joe experienced an increasing awe for this boy who had lived so long upon the water and knew so much about it.

The captain, however, drank a glass of wine, and topped it off with a second and a third, and then, a vicious flush lighting his swarthy face, stretched out on top of his blankets, where he soon was snoring loudly.

'Better turn in and get a couple of hours' sleep,' 'Frisco Kid said kindly, pointing Joe's bunk out to him. 'We'll most likely be up the rest of the night.'

Joe obeyed, but he could not fall asleep so readily as the others. He lay with his eyes wide open, watching the hands of the alarm clock that hung in the cabin, and thinking how quickly event had followed event in the last twelve hours. Only that very morning he had been a schoolboy, and now he was a sailor, shipped on the *Dazzler* and bound he knew not whither. His fifteen years increased to twenty at the thought of it, and he felt every inch a man—a sailor-man at that. He wished Charley and Fred could see him now. Well, they would hear of it soon enough. He could see them talking it over, and the other boys crowding around. 'Who?' 'Oh, Joe Bronson; he's gone to sea. Used to chum with us.'

Joe pictured the scene proudly. Then he softened as the thought of his mother worrying, but hardened again at the recollection of his father. Not that his father was not good and kind; but he did not understand boys, Joe thought. That was where the trouble lay. Only that morning he had said that the world wasn't a playground, and that the boys who thought it was were liable to make sore mistakes and be glad to get home again. Well, *he* knew that there was plenty of hard work and rough experiences in the world; but *he* also thought boys had some rights. He'd show him he could take care of himself; and, anyway, he could write home after he got settled down to his new life.

9. ABOARD THE DAZZLER

A SKIFF grazed the side of the *Dazzler* softly and interrupted Joe's reveries. He wondered why he had not heard the sound of the oars in the rowlocks. Then two men jumped over the cockpit-rail and came into the cabin.

'Bli' me, if 'ere they ain't snoozin',' said the first of the new-comers, deftly rolling 'Frisco Kid out of his blankets with one hand and reaching for the wine bottle with the other.

French Pete put his head up on the other side of the centre-board, his eyes heavy with sleep, and made them welcome.

''OO's this?' asked the Cockney, as he was called, smacking his lips over the wine and rolling Joe out upon the floor. 'Passenger?'

'No, no,' French Pete made haste to answer. 'Ze new sailorman. Vaire good boy.'

'Good boy or not, he's got to keep his tongue atween his teeth,' growled the second new-comer, who had not yet spoken, glaring fiercely at Joe.

'I say,' queried the other man, ''ow does 'e whack up on the loot? I 'ope as me and Bill 'ave a square deal.'

'Ze *Dazzler* she take one share—what you call—one third; den we split ze rest in five shares. Five men, five shares. Vaire good.'

French Pete insisted in excited gibberish that the *Dazzler* had the right to have three men in its crew, and appealed to 'Frisco Kid to bear him out. But the latter left them to fight it over by themselves, and proceeded to make hot coffee.

It was all Greek to Joe, except he knew that he was in some way the cause of the quarrel. In the end French Pete had his way, and the new-comers gave in after much grumbling. After they had drunk their coffee, all hands went on deck.

'Just stay in the cockpit and keep out of their way,' 'Frisco Kid whispered to Joe. 'I'll teach you about the ropes and everything when we ain't in a hurry.'

Joe's heart went out to him in sudden gratitude, for the strange feeling came to him that of those on board, to 'Frisco Kid, and to 'Frisco Kid only, could he look for help in time of need. Already a dislike for French Pete was growing up within him. Why, he could not say; he just simply felt it.

A creaking of blocks for'ard, and the huge mainsail loomed above him in the night. Bill cast off the bowline, the Cockney followed suit with the stern, 'Frisco Kid gave her the jib as French Pete jammed up the tiller, and the *Dazzler* caught the breeze, heeling over for mid-channel. Joe heard talk of not putting up the side-lights, and of keeping a sharp lookout, though all he could comprehend was that some law of navigation was being violated.

The water-front lights of Oakland began to slip past. Soon the stretches of docks and the shadowy ships began to be broken by dim sweeps of marshland, and Joe knew that they were heading out for San Francisco Bay. The wind was blowing from the north in mild squalls, and the *Dazzler* cut noiselessly through the land-locked water.

'Where are we going?' Joe asked the Cockney, in an endeavour to be friendly and at the same time satisfy his curiosity.

'Oh, my pardner 'ere, Bill, we're goin' to take a cargo from 'is factory,' that worthy airily replied.

Joe thought he was rather a funny-looking individual to own a factory; but, conscious that even stranger things might be found in this new world he was entering, he said nothing. He had already exposed himself to 'Frisco Kid in the matter of his pronunciation of 'fo'c'sle', and he had no desire further to advertise his ignorance.

A little after that he was sent in to blow out the cabin lamp. The *Dazzler* tacked about and began to work in towards the north shore. Everybody kept silent, save for occasional whispered questions and answers which passed between Bill and the captain. Finally the sloop was run into the wind, and the jib and mainsail lowered cautiously.

'Short hawse,' French Pete whispered to 'Frisco Kid, who went for'ard and dropped the anchor, paying out the slightest quantity of slack.

The *Dazzler*'s skiff was brought alongside, as was also the small boat in which the two strangers had come aboard.

'See that that cub don't make a fuss,' Bill commanded in an undertone, as he joined his partner in his own boat.

'Can you row?' 'Frisco Kid asked as they got into the other boat.

Joe nodded his head.

'Then take these oars, and don't make a racket.'

'Frisco Kid took the second pair, while French Pete steered. Joe noticed that the oars were muffled with sennit, and that even the rowlock sockets were protected with leather. It was impossible to make a noise except by a mis-stroke, and Joe had learned to row on Lake Merrit well enough to avoid that. They followed in the wake of the first boat, and, glancing aside, he saw they were running along the length of a pier which jutted out from the land. A couple of ships, with riding-lanterns burning brightly, were moored to it, but they kept just beyond the edge of the light. He stopped rowing at the whispered command of 'Frisco Kid. Then the boats grounded like ghosts on a tiny beach, and they clambered out.

Joe followed the men, who picked their way carefully up a twenty-foot bank. At the top he found himself on a narrow railway track which ran between huge piles of rusty scrap-iron. These piles, separated by tracks, extended in every direction, he could not tell how far, though in the distance he could see the vague outlines of some great factory-like building. The men began to carry loads of the iron down to the beach, and French Pete, gripping him by the arm and again warning him not to make any noise, told him to do likewise. At the beach they turned their burden's over to 'Frisco Kid, who loaded them, first in the one skiff and then in the other. As the boats settled under the weight, he kept pushing them farther and farther out, in order that they should keep clear of the bottom.

Joe worked away steadily, though he could not help marvelling at the queerness of the whole business. Why should there be such a mystery about it? and why such care taken to maintain silence? He had just begun to ask himself these questions, and a horrible suspicion was forming itself in his mind, when he heard the hoot of an owl from the direction of the beach. Wondering at an owl being in so unlikely a place, he stopped to gather a fresh load of iron. But suddenly a man sprang out of the gloom, flashing a dark lantern full upon him. Blinded by the light, he staggered back. Then a revolver in the man's hand went off like the roar of a cannon. All Joe realized was that he was being shot at, while his legs manifested an overwhelming desire to get away. Even if he had so wished, he could not very well have stayed to explain to the excited man with the smoking revolver. So he took to his heels for the beach, colliding with another man with a dark lantern who came running around the end of one of the piles of iron. This second man quickly regained his feet, and peppered away at Joe as he flew down the bank.

He dashed out into the water for the boat. French Pete at the bow-oars and 'Frisco Kid at the stroke had the skiff's nose pointed seaward and were calmly awaiting his arrival. They had their oars ready for the start, but they held them quietly at rest, for all that both men on the bank had begun to fire at them. The other skiff lay closer inshore, partially aground. Bill was trying to shove it off, and was calling on the Cockney to lend a hand; but that gentleman had lost his head completely, and came floundering through the water hard after Joe. No sooner had Joe climbed in over the stern than he followed him. This extra weight on the stern of the heavily loaded craft nearly swamped them. As it was, a dangerous quantity of water was shipped. In the meantime the men on the bank had reloaded their pistols and opened fire again, this time with better aim. The alarm had spread. Voices and cries could be heard from the ships on the pier, along which men were running. In the distance a police whistle was being frantically blown.

'Get out!' 'Frisco Kid shouted. 'You ain't a-going to sink us, if I know it. Go and help your pardner.'

But the Cockney's teeth were chattering with fright, and he was too unnerved to move or speak.

'T'row ze crazy man out!' French Pete ordered from the bow. At this moment a bullet shattered an oar in his hand, and he coolly proceeded to ship a spare one.

'Give us a hand, Joe,' 'Frisco Kid commanded.

Joe understood, and together they seized the terror-stricken creature and flung him overboard. Two or three bullets splashed about him as he came to the surface, just in time to be picked up by Bill, who had at last succeeded in getting clear.

'Now!' French Pete called, and a few strokes into the darkness quickly took them out of the zone of fire.

So much water had been shipped that the light skiff was in danger of sinking at any moment. While the other two rowed, and by the Frenchman's orders, Joe began to throw out the iron. This saved them for the time being. But just as they swept alongside the *Dazzler* the skiff lurched, shoved a side under, and turned turtle, sending the remainder of the iron to the bottom. Joe and 'Frisco Kid came up side by side, and together they clambered aboard with the skiff's painter in tow. French Pete had already arrived, and now helped them out.

By the time they had canted the water out of the

swamped boat, Bill and his partner appeared on the scene. All hands worked rapidly, and, almost before Joe could realize, the mainsail and jib had been hoisted, the anchor broken out, and the *Dazzler* was leaping down the channel. Off a bleak piece of marshland Bill and the Cockney said good-bye and cast loose in their skiff. French Pete, in the cabin, bewailed their bad luck in various languages, and sought consolation in the wine bottle.

10. WITH THE BAY PIRATES

THE WIND freshened as they got clear of the land, and soon the *Dazzler* was heeling it with her lee-deck buried and the water churning by, half-way up the cockpit-rail. Side-lights had been hung out. 'Frisco Kid was steering, and by his side sat Joe, pondering over the events of the night.

He could no longer blind himself to the facts. His mind was in a whirl of apprehension. If he had done wrong, he reasoned, he had done it through ignorance; and he did not feel shame for the past so much as he did fear for the future. His companions were thieves and robbers—the bay pirates, of whose wild deeds he had heard vague tales. And here he was, right in the midst of them, already possessing information which could send them to State's prison. This very fact, he knew, would force them to keep a sharp watch upon him and so lessen his chances of escape. But escape he would, at the very first opportunity.

At this point his thoughts were interrupted by a sharp squall, which hurled the *Dazzler* over till the sea rushed inboard. 'Frisco Kid luffed quickly, at the same time slacking off the mainsheet. Then, single-handed—for French Pete remained below—and with Joe looking idly on, he proceeded to reef down.

The squall which had so nearly capsized the *Dazzler* was of short duration, but it marked the rising of the wind, and soon puff after puff was shrieking down upon them out of the north. The mainsail was spilling the wind, and slapping and thrashing about till it seemed it would tear itself to pieces. The sloop was rolling wildly in the quick sea which had come up. Everything was in confusion; but even Joe's untrained eye showed him that it was an orderly confusion. He could see that 'Frisco Kid knew just what to do and just how to do it. As he watched him he learned a lesson, the lack of which has made failures of the lives of many men—*the value of knowledge of one's own capacities*. 'Frisco Kid knew what he was able to do, and because of this he had confidence in himself. He was cool and self-possessed, working hurriedly but not carelessly. There was no bungling. Every reef-point was drawn down to stay. Other accidents might occur, but the next squall, or the next forty squalls, would not carry one of those reef-knots away.

He called Joe for'ard to help stretch the mainsail by means of swinging on the peak and throat-halyards. To lay out on the long bowsprit and put a single reef in the jib was a slight task compared with what had been already accomplished; so a few moments later they were again in the cockpit. Under the other lad's directions, Joe flattened down the jib-sheet, and, going into the cabin, let down a foot or so of centre-board. The excitement of the struggle had chased all unpleasant thoughts from his mind. Patterning after the other boy, he had retained his coolness. He had executed his orders without fumbling, and at the same time without undue slowness. Together they had exerted their puny strength in the face of violent nature, and together they had outwitted her.

He came back to where his companion stood at the tiller steering, and he felt proud of him and of himself; and when he read the unspoken praise in 'Frisco Kid's eyes he blushed like a girl at her first compliment. But the next instant the thought flashed across him that this boy was a thief, a common thief; and he instinctively recoiled. His whole life had been sheltered from the harsher things of the world. His reading, which had been of the best, had laid a premium upon honesty and uprightness, and he had learned to look with abhorrence upon the criminal classes. So he drew a little away from 'Frisco Kid and remained silent. But 'Frisco Kid, devoting all his energies to the handling of the sloop, had no time in which to remark this sudden change of feeling on the part of his companion.

But there was one thing Joe found in himself that surprised him. While the thought of 'Frisco Kid being a thief was repulsive to him, 'Frisco Kid himself was not. Instead of feeling an honest desire to shun him, he felt drawn towards him. He could not help liking him, though he knew not why. Had he been a little older he would have understood that it was the lad's good qualities which appealed to him—his coolness and self-reliance, his manliness and bravery, and a certain kindliness and sympathy in his nature. As it was, he thought it his own natural badness which prevented him from disliking 'Frisco Kid; but, while he felt shame at his own weakness, he could not smother the warm regard which he felt growing up for this particular bay pirate.

'Take in two or three feet on the skiff's painter,' commanded 'Frisco Kid, who had an eye for everything.

The skiff was towing with too long a painter, and was behaving very badly. Every once in a while it would hold back till the tow-rope tautened, then come leaping ahead and sheering and dropping slack till it threatened to shove its nose under the huge whitecaps which roared so hungrily on every hand. Joe climbed over the cockpit-rail to the slippery after-deck, and made his way to the bitt to which the skiff was fastened.

'Be careful,' 'Frisco Kid warned, as a heavy puff struck the *Dazzler* and careened her dangerously over on her side. 'Keep one turn round the bitt, and heave in on it when the painter slacks.'

It was ticklish work for a greenhorn. Joe threw off all the turns save the last, which he held with one hand, while with the other he attempted to bring in on the painter.

But at that instant it tightened with a tremendous jerk, the boat sheering sharply into the crest of a heavy sea. The rope slipped from his hands and began to fly out over the stern. He clutched it frantically, and was dragged after it over the sloping deck.

'Let her go! Let her go!' 'Frisco Kid shouted.

Joe let go just as he was on the verge of going over-board, and the skiff dropped rapidly astern. He glanced in a shamefaced way at his companion, expecting to be sharply reprimanded for his awkwardness. But 'Frisco Kid smiled goodnaturedly.

'That's all right,' he said. 'No bones broke and nobody overboard. Better to lose a boat than a man any day; that's what I say. Besides, I shouldn't have sent you out there. And there's no harm done. We can pick it up all right. Go in and drop some more centre-board—a couple of feet —and then come out and do what I tell you. But don't be in a hurry. Take it easy and sure.'

Joe dropped the centre-board and returned, to be stationed at the jibsheet.

'Hard a-lee!' 'Frisco Kid cried, throwing the tiller down, and following it with his body. 'Cast off! That's right. Now lend a hand on the mainsheet!'

Together, hand over hand, they came in on the reefed mainsail. Joe began to warm up with the work. The *Dazzler* turned on her heel like a racehorse, and swept into the wind, her canvas snarling and her sheets slatting like hail.

'Draw down the jib-sheet!'

Joe obeyed, and, the head-sail filling, forced her off on the other tack. This manœuvre had turned French Pete's bunk from the lee to the weather side, and rolled him out on the cabin floor, where he lay in a drunken stupor.

'Frisco Kid, with his back against the tiller and holding the sloop off that it might cover their previous course, looked at him with an expression of disgust, and muttered:

'The dog! We could well go to the bottom, for all he'd care or do!'

Twice they tacked, trying to go over the same ground; and then Joe discovered the skiff bobbing to windward in the star-lit darkness.

'Plenty of time,' 'Frisco Kid cautioned, shooting the *Dazzler* into the wind towards it and gradually losing headway. 'Now!'

Joe leaned over the side, grasped the trailing painter, and made it fast to the bitt. Then they tacked ship again and started on their way. Joe still felt ashamed for the trouble he had caused; but 'Frisco Kid quickly put him at ease.

'Oh, that's nothing,' he said. 'Everybody does that when they're beginning. Now some men forget all about the trouble they had in learning, and get mad when a greeny makes a mistake. I never do. Why, I remember——'

And then he told Joe of many of the mishaps which fell to him when, as a little lad, he first went on the water, and of some of the severe punishments for the same which were measured out to him. He had passed the running end of a lanyard over the tiller-neck, and as they talked they sat side by side and close against each other in the shelter of the cockpit.

'What place is that?' Joe asked, as they flew by a lighthouse blinking from a rocky headland.

'Goat Island. They've got a naval training station for boys over on the other side, and a torpedo-magazine. There's jolly good fishing, too—rock-cod. We'll pass to the lee of it, and make across, and anchor in the shelter of Angel Island. There's a quarantine station there. Then when French Pete gets sober we'll know where he wants to go. You can turn in now and get some sleep. I can manage all right.'

Joe shook his head. There had been too much excitement for him to feel in the least like sleeping. He could not bear to think of it with the *Dazzler* leaping and surging along and shattering the seas into the clouds of spray on her weather bow. His clothes had half dried already, and he preferred to stay on deck and enjoy it.

The lights of Oakland had dwindled till they made only a hazy flare against the sky; but to the south the San Francisco lights, topping hills and sinking into valleys, stretched miles upon miles. Starting from the great ferry building, and passing on to Telegraph Hill, Joe was soon able to locate the principal places of the city. Somewhere over in that maze of light and shadow was the home of his father, and perhaps even now they were thinking and worrying about him; and over there Bessie was sleeping cosily, to wake up in the morning and wonder why her brother Joe did not come down to breakfast. Joe shivered. It was almost morning. Then slowly his head dropped over on 'Frisco Kid's shoulder and he was fast asleep.

II. CAPTAIN AND CREW

'COME! WAKE UP! We're going in to anchor.'

Joe roused with a start, bewildered at the unusual scene; for sleep had banished his troubles for the time being, and he knew not where he was. Then he remembered. The wind had dropped with the night. Beyond, the heavy after-sea was still rolling; but the *Dazzler* was creeping up in the shelter of a rocky island. The sky was clear, and the air had the snap and vigour of early morning about it. The rippling water was laughing in the rays of the sun just shouldering above the eastern sky-line. To the south lay Alcatraz Island, and from its gun-crowned heights a flourish of trumpets saluted the day. In the west the Golden Gate yawned between the Pacific Ocean and San Francisco Bay. A full-rigged ship, with her lightest canvas, even to the sky-sails, set, was coming slowly in on the floodtide.

It was a pretty sight. Joe rubbed the sleep from his

9*

eyes and drank in the glory of it till 'Frisco Kid told him to go for'ard and make ready for dropping the anchor.

'Overhaul about fifty fathoms of chain,' he ordered, 'and then stand by.' He eased the sloop gently into the wind, at the same time casting off the jib-sheet. 'Let go the jib-halyards and come in on the downhaul!'

Joe had seen the manœuvre performed the previous night, and so was able to carry it out with fair success.

'Now! Over with the mud-hook! Watch out for turns! Lively, now!'

The chain flew out with startling rapidity and brought the *Dazzler* to rest. 'Frisco Kid went for'ard to help, and together they lowered the mainsail, furled it in shipshape manner and made all fast with the gaskets, and put the crutches under the main-boom.

'Here's a bucket,' said 'Frisco Kid, as he passed him the article in question. 'Wash down the decks, and don't be afraid of the water, nor of the dirt either. Here's a broom. Give it what for, and have everything shining. When you get that done bail out the skiff. She opened her seams a little last night. I'm going below to cook breakfast.'

The water was soon slushing merrily over the deck, while the smoke pouring from the cabin stove carried a promise of good things to come. Time and again Joe lifted his head from his task to take in the scene. It was one to appeal to any healthy boy, and he was no exception. The romance of it stirred him strangely, and his happiness would have been complete could he have escaped remembering who and what his companions were. The thought of this, and of French Pete in his bleary sleep below, marred the beauty of the day. He had been unused to such things, and was shocked at the harsh reality of life. But instead of hurting him, as it might a lad of weaker nature, it had the opposite effect. It strengthened his desire to be clean and strong, and to be unashamed of himself in his own eyes. He glanced about him and sighed. Why could not men be honest and true? It seemed too bad that he must go away and leave all this; but the events of the night were strong upon him, and he knew that in order to be true to himself he must escape.

At this juncture he was called to breakfast. He discovered that 'Frisco Kid was as good a cook as he was a sailor, and made haste to do justice to the fare. There were mush and condensed milk, beef-steak and fried potatoes, and all topped off with good French bread, butter, and coffee. French Pete did not join them, though 'Frisco Kid attempted a couple of times to rouse him. He mumbled and grunted, half opened his bleared eyes, then fell to snoring again.

'Can't tell when he's going to get those spells,' 'Frisco Kid explained, when Joe, having finished washing dishes, came on deck. 'Sometimes he won't get that way for a month, and others he won't be decent for a week at a stretch. Sometimes he's good-natured, and sometimes he's dangerous; so the best thing to do is to let him alone and keep out of his way; and don't cross him, for if you do there's liable to be trouble.

'Come on; let's take a swim,' he added, abruptly changing the subject to one more agreeable. 'Can you swim?'

Joe nodded.

'What's that place?' he asked, as he poised before diving, pointing towards a sheltered beach on the island where there were several buildings and a large number of tents.

'Quarantine station. Lots of smallpox coming in now on the China steamers, and they make them go there till the doctors say they're safe to land. I tell you, they're strict about it, too. Why——'

Splash! Had 'Frisco Kid finished his sentence just then, instead of diving overboard, much trouble might have been saved to Joe. But he did not finish it, and Joe dived after him.

'I'll tell you what,' 'Frisco Kid suggested half an hour later, while they clung to the bobstay preparatory to climbing out. 'Let's catch a mess of fish for dinner, and then turn in and make up for the sleep we lost last night. What d'you say?'

They made a race to clamber aboard, but Joe was shoved over the side again. When he finally did arrive, the other lad had brought to light a pair of heavily leaded, large-hooked lines and a mackerel-keg of salt sardines.

'Bait,' he said. 'Just shove a whole one on. They're not a bit partic'lar. Swallow the bait, hook and all, and go—that's their caper. The fellow that doesn't catch the first fish has to clean 'em.'

Both sinkers started on their long descent together, and seventy feet of line whizzed out before they came to rest. But at the instant his sinker touched the bottom Joe felt the struggling jerks of a hooked fish. As he began to haul in he glanced at 'Frisco Kid and saw that he too had evidently captured a finny prize. The race between them was exciting. Hand over hand the wet lines flashed inboard. But 'Frisco Kid was more expert, and his fish tumbled into the cockpit first. Joe's followed an instant later—a three-pound rock-cod. He was wild with joy. It was magnificent —the largest fish he had ever landed or even seen landed. Over went the lines again, and up they came with two mates of the ones already captured. It was sport royal. Joe would certainly have continued till he had fished the bay empty, had not 'Frisco Kid persuaded him to stop.

'We've got enough for three meals now,' he said, 'so there's no use in having them spoil. Besides, the more you catch the more you clean, and you'd better start in right away. I'm going to bed.'

12. JOE TRIES TO TAKE FRENCH LEAVE

JOE DID not mind. In fact, he was glad he had not caught the first fish, for it helped out a little plan which had come to him while swimming. He threw the last cleaned fish into a bucket of water and glanced about him. The quarantine station was a bare half-mile away, and he could make out a soldier pacing up and down at sentry duty on the beach. Going into the cabin, he listened to the heavy breathing of the sleepers. He had to pass so close to 'Frisco Kid to get his bundle of clothes that he decided not to take it. Returning outside, he carefully pulled the skiff alongside, got aboard with a pair of oars, and cast off.

At first he rowed very gently in the direction of the station, fearing the chance of noise if he made undue haste. But gradually he increased the strength of his strokes till he had settled down to the regular stride. When he had covered half the distance he glanced about. Escape was sure now, for he knew, even if he were discovered, that it would be impossible for the *Dazzler* to get under way and head him off before he made the land and the protection of that man who wore the uniform of Uncle Sam's soldiers.

The report of a gun came to him from the shore, but his back was in that direction, and he did not bother to turn around. A second report followed, and a bullet cut the water within a couple of feet of his oar-blade. This time he did turn around. The soldier on the beach was levelling his rifle at him for a third shot.

Joe was in a predicament, and a very tantalizing one at that. A few minutes of hard rowing would bring him to the beach and to safety; but on that beach, for some unaccountable reason, stood a United States soldier who persisted in firing at him. When Joe saw the gun aimed at him for the third time, he backed water hastily. As a result, the skiff came to a standstill, and the soldier, lowering his rifle, regarded him intently.

'I want to come ashore! Important!' Joe shouted out to him.

The man in uniform shook his head.

'But it's important, I tell you! Won't you let me come ashore?'

He took a hurried look in the direction of the *Dazzler*. The shots had evidently awakened French Pete, for the mainsail had been hoisted, and as he looked he saw the anchor broken out and the jib flung to the breeze.

'Can't land here!' the soldier shouted back. 'Smallpox!'

'But I must!' he cried, choking down a half-sob and preparing to row.

'Then I'll shoot you,' was the cheering response, and the rifle came to shoulder again.

Joe thought rapidly. The island was large. Perhaps there were no soldiers farther on, and if he only once got ashore he did not care how quickly they captured him. He might catch the smallpox, but even that was better than going back to the bay pirates. He whirled the skiff half about to the right, and threw all his strength against the oars. The cove was quite wide, and the nearest point which he must go around a good distance away. Had he been more of a sailor, he would have gone in the other direction for the opposite point, and thus had the wind on his pursuers.

As it was, the *Dazzler* had a beam wind in which to overtake him.

It was nip and tuck for a while. The breeze was light and not very steady, so sometimes he gained and sometimes they. Once it freshened till the sloop was within a hundred yards of him, and then it dropped suddenly flat, the *Dazzler*'s big mainsail flapping idly from side to side.

'Ah! you steal ze skiff, eh?' French Pete howled at him, running into the cabin for his rifle. 'I fix you! You come back queeck, or I'll kill you!' But he knew the soldier was watching them from the shore, and did not dare to fire, even over the lad's head.

Joe did not think of this, for he, who had never been shot at in all his previous life, had been under fire twice in the last twenty-four hours. Once more or less couldn't amount to much. So he pulled steadily away, while French Pete raved like a wild man, threatening him with all manner of punishments once he laid hands upon him again. To complicate matters, 'Frisco Kid waxed mutinous.

'Just you shoot him, and I'll see you hung for it—see if

I don't,' he threatened. 'You'd better let him go. He's a good boy and all right, and not raised for the dirty life you and I are leading.'

'You too, eh!' the Frenchman shrieked, beside himself with rage. 'Den I fix you, you rat!'

He made a rush for the boy, but 'Frisco Kid led him a lively chase from cockpit to bowsprit and back again. A sharp capful of wind arriving just then, French Pete abandoned the one chase for the other. Springing to the tiller and slacking away on the mainsheet—for the wind favoured—he headed the sloop down upon Joe. The latter made one tremendous spurt, then gave up in despair and hauled in his oars. French Pete let go the mainsheet, lost steerage-way as he rounded up alongside the motionless skiff, and dragged Joe out.

'Keep mum,' 'Frisco Kid whispered to him while the irate Frenchman was busy fastening the painter. 'Don't talk back. Let him say all he wants to, and keep quiet. It'll be better for you.'

But Joe's Anglo-Saxon blood was up, and he did not heed.

'Look here, Mr French Pete, or whatever your name is,' he commenced; 'I give you to understand that I want to quit, and that I'm going to quit. So you'd better put me ashore at once. If you don't, I'll put you in prison, or my name's not Joe Bronson.'

'Frisco Kid waited the outcome fearfully. French Pete was aghast. He was being defied aboard his own vessel—and by a boy! Never had such a thing been heard of. He knew he was committing an unlawful act in detaining him, but at the same time he was afraid to let him go with the information he had gathered concerning the sloop and its occupation. The boy had spoken the unpleasant truth when he said he could send him to prison. The only thing for him to do was to bully him.

'You will, eh?' His shrill voice rose wrathfully. 'Den you come too. You row ze boat last-a night—answer me dat! You steal ze iron—answer me dat! You run away—

answer me dat! And den you say you put me in jail? Bah!'

'But I didn't know,' Joe protested.

'Ha, ha! Dat is funny. You tell dat to ze judge; mebbe him laugh, eh?'

'I say I didn't,' he reiterated manfully. 'I didn't know I'd shipped along with a lot of thieves.'

'Frisco Kid winced at this epithet, and had Joe been looking at him he would have seen a red flush mount to his face.

'And now that I do know,' he continued, 'I wish to be put ashore. I don't know anything about the law, but I do know something of right and wrong; and I'm willing to take my chance with any judge for whatever wrong I have done— with all the judges in the United States, for that matter. And that's more than you can say, Mr Pete.'

'You say dat, eh? Vaire good. But you are one big t'ief——'

'I'm not—don't you dare call me that again!' Joe's face was pale, and he was trembling—but not with fear.

'T'ief!' the Frenchman taunted back.

'You lie!'

Joe had not been a boy among boys for nothing. He knew the penalty which attached itself to the words he had just spoken, and he expected to receive it. So he was not overmuch surprised when he picked himself up from the floor of the cockpit an instant later, his head still ringing from a stiff blow between the eyes.

'Say dat one time more,' French Pete bullied, his fist raised and prepared to strike.

Tears of anger stood in Joe's eyes, but he was calm and in deadly earnest. 'When you say I am a thief, Pete, you lie. You can kill me, but still I will say you lie.'

'No, you don't!' 'Frisco Kid had darted in like a cat, preventing a second blow, and shoving the Frenchman back across the cockpit.

'You leave the boy alone!' he continued, suddenly unshipping and arming himself with the heavy iron tiller,

and standing between them. 'This thing's gone just about
as far as it's going to go. You big fool, can't you see the
stuff the boy's made of? He speaks true. He's right, and he
knows it, and you could kill him and he wouldn't give in.
There's my hand on it, Joe.' He turned and extended his
hand to Joe, who returned the grip. 'You've got spunk,
and you're not afraid to show it.'

French Pete's mouth twisted itself in a sickly smile,
but the evil gleam in his eyes gave it the lie. He shrugged
his shoulders and said, 'Ah! So? He does not desire dat
I call him pet names. Ha, ha! It is only ze sailorman play.
Let us—what you call—forgive and forget, eh? Vaire
good; forgive and forget.'

He reached out his hand, but Joe refused to take it.
'Frisco Kid nodded approval, while French Pete, still
shrugging his shoulders and smiling, passed into the
cabin.

'Slack off ze mainsheet,' he called out, 'and run down for
Hunter's Point. For one time I will cook ze dinner, and den
you will say dat it is ze vaire good dinner. French Pete
is ze great cook!'

'That's the way he always does—gets real good and
cooks when he wants to make up,' 'Frisco Kid hazarded,
slipping the tiller into the rudder-head and obeying the
order. 'But even then you can't trust him.'

Joe nodded his head, but did not speak. He was in no
mood for conversation. He was still trembling from the
excitement of the last few moments, while deep down he
questioned himself on how he had behaved, and found
nothing to be ashamed of.

13. BEFRIENDING EACH OTHER

THE AFTERNOON sea-breeze had sprung up and was now
rioting in from the Pacific. Angel Island was fast dropping

astern, and the water-front of San Francisco showing up, as the *Dazzler* ploughed along before it. Soon they were in the midst of the shipping, passing in and out among the vessels which had come from the ends of the earth. Later they crossed the fairway, where the ferry steamers, crowded with passengers, passed to and fro between San Francisco and Oakland. One came so close that the passengers crowded to the side to see the gallant little sloop and the two boys in the cockpit. Joe gazed enviously at the row of down-turned faces. They were all going to their homes, while he—he was going he knew not whither, at the will of French Pete. He was half tempted to cry out for help; but the foolishness of such an act struck him, and he held his tongue. Turning his head, his eyes wandered along the smoky heights of the city, and he fell to musing on the strange way of men and ships on the sea.

'Frisco Kid watched him from the corner of his eye, following the thoughts as accurately as though he spoke them aloud.

'Got a home over there somewhere?' he queried suddenly, waving his hand in the direction of the city.

Joe started, so correctly had his thought been guessed. 'Yes,' he said simply.

'Tell us about it.'

Joe rapidly described his home, though forced to go into greater detail because of the curious questions of his companion. 'Frisco Kid was interested in everything, especially in Mrs Bronson and Bessie. Of the latter he could not seem to tire, and poured forth question after question concerning her. So peculiar and artless were some of them that Joe could hardly forbear to smile.

'Now tell me about yours,' he said when he at last had finished.

'Frisco Kid seemed suddenly to harden, and his face took on a stern look which the other had never seen there before. He swung his foot idly to and fro, and lifted a dull eye aloft to the main-peak blocks, with which, by the way, there was nothing the matter.

'Go ahead,' the other encouraged.

'I haven't no home.'

The four words left his mouth as though they had been forcibly ejected, and his lips came together after them almost with a snap.

Joe saw he had touched a tender spot, and strove to ease the way out of it again. 'Then the home you did have.' He did not dream that there were lads in the world who never had known homes, or that he had only succeeded in probing deeper.

'Never had none.'

'Oh!' His interest was aroused, and he now threw solicitude to the winds. 'Any sisters?'

'Nope.'

'Mother?'

'I was so young when she died that I don't remember her.'

'Father?'

'I never saw much of him. He went to sea—anyhow, he disappeared.'

'Oh!' Joe did not know what to say, and an oppressive silence, broken only by the churn of the *Dazzler*'s forefoot, fell upon them.

Just then Pete came out to relieve at the tiller while they went in to eat. Both lads hailed his advent with feelings of relief, and the awkwardness vanished over the dinner, which was all their skipper had claimed it to be. Afterward 'Frisco Kid relieved Pete, and while he was eating Joe washed up the dishes and put the cabin shipshape. Then they all gathered in the stern, where the captain strove to increase the general cordiality by entertaining them with descriptions of life among the pearl-divers of the South Seas.

In this fashion the afternoon wore away, They had long since left San Francisco behind, rounded Hunter's Point, and were now skirting the San Mateo shore. Joe caught a glimpse, once, of a party of cyclists rounding a cliff on the San Bruno Road, and remembered the time when he had gone over the same ground on his own wheel. It was only a month or two before, but it seemed an age to him now, so much had there been to come between.

By the time supper had been eaten and the things cleared away, they were well down the bay, off the marshes behind which Redwood City clustered. The wind had gone down with the sun, and the *Dazzler* was making but little headway, when they sighted a sloop bearing down upon them on the dying wind. 'Frisco Kid instantly named it as the *Reindeer*, to which French Pete, after a deep scrutiny, agreed. He seemed very much pleased at the meeting.

'Red Nelson runs her,' 'Frisco Kid informed Joe. 'And he's a terror and no mistake. I'm always afraid of him when he comes near. They've got something big down here, and they're always after French Pete to tackle it with them. He knows more about it, whatever it is.'

Joe nodded, and looked at the approaching craft curiously. Though somewhat larger, it was built on about the same lines as the *Dazzler*—which meant, above everything else, that it was built for speed. The mainsail was so large that it was more like that of a racing yacht, and it carried the points for no less than three reefs in case of rough weather. Aloft and on deck everything was in place—nothing was untidy or useless. From running-gear to standing rigging, everything bore evidence of thorough order and smart seamanship.

The *Reindeer* came up slowly in the gathering twilight and went to anchor a biscuit-toss away. French Pete followed suit with the *Dazzler*, and then went in the skiff to pay them a visit. The two lads stretched themselves out on top of the cabin and awaited his return.

'Do you like the life?' Joe broke silence.

The other turned on his elbow. 'Well—I do, and then again I don't. The fresh air, and the salt water, and all that, and the freedom—that's all right; but I don't like the —the——' He paused a moment, as though his tongue had failed in its duty, and then blurted out: 'the stealing.'

'Then why don't you quit it?' Joe liked the lad more than he dare confess to himself, and he felt a sudden missionary zeal come upon him.

'I will just as soon as I can turn my hand to something else.'

'But why not now?'

Now is the accepted time was ringing in Joe's ears, and if the other wished to leave, it seemed a pity that he did not, and at once.

'Where can I go? What can I do? There's nobody in all the world to lend me a hand, just as there never has been. I tried it once, and learned my lesson too well to do it again in a hurry.'

'Well, when I get out of this I'm going home. Guess my father was right, after all. And I don't see, maybe—what's the matter with you going with me?' He said this last without thinking, impulsively, and 'Frisco Kid knew it.

'You don't know what you're talking about,' he answered. 'Fancy me going off with you! What'd your father say? and—and the rest? How would he think of me? And what'd he do?'

Joe felt sick at heart. He realized that in the spirit of the moment he had given an invitation which, on sober thought, he knew would be impossible to carry out. He tried to imagine his father receiving in his own house a stranger like 'Frisco Kid—no, that was not to be thought of. Then, forgetting his own plight, he fell to racking his brains for some other method by which 'Frisco Kid could get away from his present surroundings.

'He might turn me over to the police,' the other went on, 'and send me to a refuge. I'd die first, before I'd let that happen to me. And besides, Joe, I'm not of your kind, and you know it. Why, I'd be like a fish out of water, what with all the things I didn't know. Nope; I guess I'll have to wait a little before I strike out. But there's only one thing for you to do, and that's to go straight home. First chance I get I'll land you, and then I'll deal with French Pete——'

'No, you don't,' Joe interrupted hotly. 'When I leave I'm not going to leave you in trouble on my account. So don't you try anything like that. I'll get away, never fear, and if I can figure it out I want you to come along too; come along anyway, and figure it out afterward. What d'you say?'

'Frisco Kid shook his head, and, gazing up at the starlit heavens, wandered off into dreams of the life he would like to lead, but from which he seemed inexorably shut out. The seriousness of life was striking deeper than ever into Joe's heart, and he lay silent, thinking hard. A mumble of heavy voices came to them from the *Reindeer*; and from the land the solemn notes of a church bell floated across the water while the summer night wrapped them slowly in its warm darkness.

14. AMONG THE OYSTER-BEDS

TIME AND the world slipped away, and both boys were aroused by the harsh voice of French Pete from the sleep into which they had fallen.

'Get under way!' he was bawling. 'Here, you, Sho! Cast off ze gaskets! Queeck! Lively! You, Kid, ze jib!'

Joe was clumsy in the darkness, not knowing the names of things and the places where they were to be found; but he made fair progress, and when he had tossed the gaskets into the cockpit was ordered forward to help hoist the mainsail. After that the anchor was hove in and the jib set. Then they coiled down the halyards and put everything in order before they returned aft.

'Vaire good, vaire good,' the Frenchman praised, as Joe dropped in over the rail. 'Splendeed! You make ze good sailorman, I know for sure.'

'Frisco Kid lifted the cover of one of the cockpit lockers and glanced questioningly at French Pete.

'For sure,' that mariner replied. 'Put up ze side-lights.'

'Frisco Kid took the red and green lanterns into the cabin to light them, and then went forward with Joe to hang them in the rigging.

'They're not goin' to tackle it,' 'Frisco Kid said in an undertone.

'What?' Joe asked.

'That big thing I was tellin' you was down here some-where. It's so big, I guess, that French Pete's 'most afraid to go in for it. Red Nelson'd go in quicker'n a wink, but don't know enough about it. Can't go in, you see, till Pete gives the word.'

'Where are we going now?' Joe questioned.

'Don't know; oyster-beds most likely, from the way we're heading.'

It was an uneventful trip. A breeze sprang up out of the night behind them, and held steady for an hour or more. Then it dropped and became aimless and erratic, puffing gently first from one quarter and then another. French Pete remained at the tiller, while occasionally Joe or 'Frisco Kid took in or slacked off a sheet.

Joe sat and marvelled that the Frenchman should know where he was going. To Joe it seemed that they were lost in the impenetrable darkness which shrouded them. A high fog had rolled in from the Pacific, and though they were beneath, it came between them and the stars, depriving them of the little light from that source.

But French Pete seemed to know instinctively the direction he should go, and once, in reply to a query from Joe, bragged of his ability to go by the 'feel' of things.

'I feel ze tide, ze wind, ze speed,' he explained. 'Even do I feel ze land. Dat I tell you for sure. How? I do not know. Only do I know dat I feel ze land, just like my arm grow long, miles and miles long, and I put my hand upon ze land and feel it, and know dat it is there.'

Joe looked incredulously at 'Frisco Kid.

'That's right,' he affirmed. 'After you've been on the

water a good while you come to feel the land. And if your nose is any account, you can usually smell it.'

An hour or so later, Joe surmised from the Frenchman's actions that they were approaching their destination. He seemed on the alert, and was constantly peering into the darkness ahead as though he expected to see something at any moment. Joe looked very hard, but saw only the darkness.

'Try ze stick, Kid,' French Pete ordered. 'I t'ink it is about ze time.'

'Frisco Kid unlashed a long and slender pole from the top of the cabin, and, standing on the narrow deck amidships, plunged one end of it into the water and drove it straight down.

'About fifteen feet,' he said.

'What ze bottom?'

'Mud,' was the answer.

'Wait one while, den we try some more.'

Five minutes afterwards the pole was plunged overside again.

'Two fathoms,' Joe answered—'shells.'

French Pete rubbed his hands with satisfaction. 'Vaire good, vaire well,' he said. 'I hit ze ground every time. You can't fool-a ze old man; I tell you dat for sure.'

'Frisco Kid continued operating the pole and announcing the results, to the mystification of Joe, who could not comprehend their intimate knowledge of the bottom of the bay.

'Ten feet—shells,' 'Frisco Kid went on in a monotonous voice. ''Leven feet—shells. Fourteen feet—soft. Sixteen feet—mud. No bottom.'

'Ah, ze channel,' said French Pete at this.

For a few minutes it was 'No bottom'; and then, suddenly, came 'Frisco Kid's cry: 'Eight feet—hard!'

'Dat'll do,' French Pete commanded. 'Run for'ard, you, Sho, an' let go ze jib. You, Kid, get all ready ze hook.'

Joe found the jib-halyard and cast it off the pin, and, as

the canvas fluttered down, came in hand over hand on the down haul.

'Let 'er go!' came the command, and the anchor dropped into the water, carrying but little chain after it.

'Frisco Kid threw over plenty of slack and made fast. Then they furled the sails, made things tidy, and went below and to bed.

It was six o'clock when Joe awoke and went out into the cockpit to look about. Wind and sea had sprung up, and the *Dazzler* was rolling and tossing, and now and again fetching up on the anchor-chain with a savage jerk. He was forced to hold on to the boom overhead to steady himself. It was a grey and leaden day, with no signs of the rising sun, while the sky was obscured by great masses of flying clouds.

Joe sought for the land. A mile and a half away it lay —a long, low stretch of sandy beach with a heavy surf thundering upon it. Behind appeared desolate marshlands, while far beyond towered the Contra Costa Hills.

Changing the direction of his gaze, Joe was startled by the sight of a small sloop rolling and plunging at her anchor not a hundred yards away. She was nearly to windward, and as she swung off slightly he read her name on the stern, the *Flying Dutchman*, one of the boats he had seen lying at the city wharf in Oakland. A little to the left of her he discovered the *Ghost*, and beyond were half a dozen other sloops at anchor.

'What I tell you?'

Joe looked quickly over his shoulder. French Pete had come out of the cabin and was triumphantly regarding the spectacle.

'What I tell you? Can't fool-a ze old man, dat's what I hit it in ze dark just so well as in ze sunshine. I know—I know.'

'Is she goin' to howl?' 'Frisco Kid asked from the cabin, where he was starting the fire.

The Frenchman gravely studied sea and sky for a couple of minutes.

'Mebbe blow over—mebbe blow up,' was his doubtful verdict. 'Get breakfast queeck, and we try ze dredging.'

Smoke was rising from the cabins of the different sloops, denoting that they were all bent on getting the first meal of the day. So far as the *Dazzler* was concerned, it was a simple matter, and soon they were putting a single reef in the mainsail and getting ready to weigh anchor.

Joe was curious. These were undoubtedly the oyster-beds; but how under the sun, in that wild sea, were they to get oysters? He was quickly to learn the way. Lifting a section of the cockpit flooring, French Pete brought out two triangular frames of steel. At the apex of one of these triangles, in a ring for the purpose, he made fast a piece of stout rope. From this the sides (inch rods) diverged at almost right-angles, and extended down for a distance of four feet or more, where they were connected by the third side of the triangle, which was the bottom of the dredge. This was a flat plate of steel over a yard in length, to which was bolted a row of long, sharp teeth, likewise of steel. Attached to the toothed plate and to the sides of the frame was a net of very coarse fishing-twine, which Joe correctly surmised was there to catch the oysters raked loose by the teeth from the bottom of the bay.

A rope being made fast to each of the dredges, they were dropped overboard from either side of the *Dazzler*. When they had reached the bottom, and were dragging with the proper length of line out, they checked her speed quite noticeably. Joe touched one of the lines with his hands, and could feel plainly the shock and jar and grind as it tore over the bottom.

''Aul in!' French Pete shouted.

The boys laid hold of the line and hove in the dredge. The net was full of mud and slime and small oysters, with here and there a large one. This mess they dumped on the deck and picked over while the dredge was dragging again. The large oysters they threw into the cockpit, and shovelled the rubbish overboard. There was no rest, for by this time the other dredge required emptying. And when this was done and the oysters sorted, both dredges had to be hauled aboard, so that French Pete could put the *Dazzler* about on the other tack.

The rest of the fleet was under way and dredging back in similar fashion. Sometimes the different sloops came quite close to them, and they hailed them and exchanged snatches of conversation and rough jokes. But in the main it was hard work, and at the end of an hour Joe's back was aching from the unaccustomed strain, and his fingers were cut and bleeding from his clumsy handling of the sharp-edged oysters.

'Dat's right,' French Pete said approvingly. 'You learn queeck. Vaire soon you know how.'

Joe grinned ruefully and wished it was dinner-time. Now and then, when a light dredge was hauled, the boys managed to catch breath and say a couple of words.

'That's Asparagus Island,' 'Frisco Kid said, indicating the shore. 'At least, that's what the fishermen and scow-sailors call it. The people who live there call it Bay Farm Island.' He pointed more to the right. 'And over there is San Leandro. You can't see it, but it's there.'

'Ever been there?' Joe asked.

'Frisco Kid nodded his head and signed to him to help heave in the starboard dredge.

'These are what they call the deserted beds,' he said again. 'Nobody owns them, so the oyster pirates come down and make a bluff at working them.'

'Why a bluff?'

''Cause they're pirates, that's why, and because there's more money in raiding the private beds.'

He made a sweeping gesture toward the east and south-east. 'The private beds are over yonder, and if it don't storm, the whole fleet'll be raidin' 'em tonight.'

'And if it does storm?' Joe asked.

'Why, we won't raid them, and French Pete 'll be mad, that's all. He always hates being put out by the weather. But it don't look like lettin' up, and this is the worst possible shore in a sou'-wester. Pete may try to hang on, but it's best to get out before she howls.'

At first it did seem as though the weather were growing better. The stiff south-west wind dropped perceptibly, and by noon, when they went to anchor for dinner, the sun was breaking fitfully through the clouds.

'That's all right,' 'Frisco Kid said prophetically. 'But I ain't been on the bay for nothing. She's just gettin' ready to let us have it good an' hard.'

'I t'ink you're right, Kid,' French Pete agreed; 'but ze *Dazzler* hang on all ze same. Last-a time she run away, an' fine night come. Dis time she run not away. Eh? Vaire good.'

15. GOOD SAILORS
IN A WILD ANCHORAGE

ALL AFTERNOON the *Dazzler* pitched and rolled at her anchorage, and as evening drew on the wind deceitfully eased down. This, and the example set by French Pete, encouraged the rest of the oyster-boats to attempt to ride out the night; but they looked carefully to their moorings and put out spare anchors.

French Pete ordered the two boys into the skiff, and, at the imminent risk of swamping, they carried out a second anchor, at nearly right-angles to the first one, and dropped it over. French Pete then ran out a great quantity of chain and rope, so that the *Dazzler* dropped back a hundred feet or more, where she rode more easily.

It was a wild stretch of water which Joe looked upon from the shelter of the cockpit. The oyster-beds were out in the open bay, utterly unprotected, and the wind, sweeping the water for a clean twelve miles, kicked up so tremendous a sea that at every moment it seemed as though the wallowing sloops would roll their masts overside. Just before twilight a patch of sail sprang up to windward, and grew and grew until it resolved itself into the huge mainsail of the *Reindeer*.

'Ze beeg fool!' French Pete cried, running out of the cabin to see. 'Sometime—ah, sometime, I tell you—he crack on like dat, an' he go, pouf! just like dat, pouf!—an' no more Nelson, no more *Reindeer*, no more nothing.'

Joe looked inquiringly at 'Frisco Kid.

'That's right,' he answered. 'Nelson ought to have at least one reef in. Two'd be better. But there he goes, every inch spread, as though some fiend was after 'im. He drives too hard; he's too reckless, when there ain't the smallest need for it. I've sailed with him, and I know his ways.'

Like some huge bird of the air, the *Reindeer* lifted and soared down on them on the foaming crest of a wave.

'Don't mind,' 'Frisco Kid warned. 'He's only tryin' to see how close he can come to us without hittin' us.'

Joe nodded, and stared with wide eyes at the thrilling sight. The *Reindeer* leaped up in the air, pointing her nose to the sky till they could see her whole churning forefoot; then she plunged downward till her for'ard deck was flush with the foam, and with a dizzying rush she drove past them, her main-boom missing the *Dazzler*'s rigging by scarcely a foot.

Nelson, at the wheel, waved his hand to them as he hurtled past, and laughed joyously in French Pete's face, who was angered by the dangerous trick.

When to leeward, the splendid craft rounded to the wind, rolling once till her brown bottom showed to the centre-board and they thought she was over, then righting and dashing ahead again like a thing possessed. She passed abreast of them on the starboard side. They saw the jib run down with a rush and an anchor go overboard as she shot into the wind; and as she fell off and back and off and back with a spilling mainsail, they saw a second anchor go overboard, wide apart from the first. Then the mainsail came down on the run, and was furled and fastened by the time she had tightened to her double hawsers.

'Ah, ah! Never was there such a man!'

The Frenchman's eyes were glistening with admiration for such perfect seamanship, and 'Frisco Kid's were likewise moist.

'Just like a yacht,' he said as he went back into the cabin. 'Just like a yacht, only better.'

As night came on the wind began to rise again, and by eleven o'clock had reached the stage which 'Frisco Kid described as 'howlin''. There was little sleep on the *Dazzler*. He alone closed his eyes. French Pete was up and down every few minutes. Twice, when he went on deck, he paid out more chain and rope. Joe lay in his blankets and listened, the while vainly courting sleep. He was not frightened, but he was untrained in the art of sleeping in the midst of such turmoil and uproar and violent commotion. Nor had he imagined a boat could play as wild antics as did the *Dazzler* and still survive. Often she wallowed over on her beam till he thought she would surely capsize. At other times she leaped and plunged in the air and fell upon the seas with thunderous crashes as though her bottom were shattered to fragments. Again, she would fetch up taut on her hawsers so suddenly and so fiercely as to reel from the shock and to groan and protest through every timber.

'Frisco Kid awoke once, and smiled at him, saying:

'This is what they call hangin' on. But just you wait till daylight comes, and watch us clawin' off. If some of the sloops don't go ashore, I'm not me, that's all.'

And thereat he rolled over on his side and was off to sleep. Joe envied him. About three in the morning he heard French Pete crawl up for'ard and rummage around in the eyes of the boat. Joe looked on curiously, and by the dim light of the wildly swinging sea-lamp saw him drag out two spare coils of line. These he took up on deck, and Joe knew he was bending them on to the hawsers to make them still longer.

At half-past four French Pete had the fire going, and at five he called the boys for coffee. This over, they crept into the cockpit to gaze on the terrible scene. The dawn was breaking bleak and grey over a wild waste of tumbling water. They could faintly see the beach-line of Asparagus Island, but they could distinctly hear the thunder of the surf upon it; and as the day grew stronger they made out that they had dragged fully half a mile during the night.

The rest of the fleet had likewise dragged. The *Reindeer* was almost abreast of them; *La Caprice* lay a few hundred yards away; and to leeward, straggling between them and shore, were five more of the struggling oyster-boats.

'Two missing,' 'Frisco Kid announced, putting the glasses to his eyes and searching the beach.

'And there's one!' he cried. And after studying it carefully he added: 'The *Go Ask Her*. She'll be in pieces in no time. I hope they got ashore.'

French Pete looked through the glasses, and then Joe. He could clearly see the unfortunate sloop lifting and pounding in the surf, and on the beach he spied the men who made up her crew.

'Where's ze *Ghost*?' French Pete queried.

'Frisco Kid looked for her in vain along the beach; but when he turned the glass seaward he quickly discovered her riding safely in the growing light, half a mile or more to windward.

'I'll bet she didn't drag a hundred feet all night,' he said. 'Must've struck good holding-ground.'

'Mud,' was French Pete's verdict. 'Just one vaire small patch of mud right there. If she get t'rough it she's a sure-enough goner, I tell you dat. Her anchors vaire light, only good for mud. I tell ze boys get more heavy anchors, but dey laugh. Some day be sorry, for sure.'

One of the sloops to leeward raised a patch of sail and began the terrible struggle out of the jaws of destruction and death. They watched her for a space, rolling and plunging fearfully, and making very little headway.

French Pete put a stop to their gazing. 'Come on!' he shouted. 'Put two reef in ze mainsail! We get out queeck!'

While occupied with this a shout aroused them. Looking up, they saw the *Ghost* dead ahead and right on top of them, and dragging down upon them at a furious rate.

French Pete scrambled forward like a cat, at the same time drawing his knife, with one stroke of which he severed the rope that held them to the spare anchor. This threw the whole weight of the *Dazzler* on the chain-anchor. In consequence, she swung off to the left, and just in time; for the next instant, drifting stern foremost, the *Ghost* passed over the spot she had vacated.

'Why, she's got four anchors out!' Joe exclaimed, at sight of four taut ropes entering the water almost horizontally from her bow.

'Two of 'em's dredges,' 'Frisco Kid grinned; 'and there goes the stove.'

As he spoke, two young fellows appeared on deck and dropped the cooking-stove overside with a line attached.

'Phew!' 'Frisco Kid cried. 'Look at Nelson. He's got one reef in, and you can just bet that's a sign she's howlin'!'

The *Reindeer* came foaming toward them, breasting the storm like some magnificent sea-animal. Red Nelson waved to them as he passed astern, and fifteen minutes later, when they were breaking out the one anchor that remained to them, he passed well to windward on the other tack.

French Pete followed her admiringly, though he said ominously: 'Some day, pouf! he go just like dat, I tell you, sure.'

A moment later the *Dazzler's* reefed jib was flung out, and she was straining and struggling in the thick of the fight. It was slow work, and hard and dangerous, clawing off that leeshore, and Joe found himself marvelling often that so small a craft could possibly endure a minute in such elemental fury. But little by little she worked off the shore and out of the ground-swell into the deeper waters of the bay, where the mainsheet was slacked away a bit, and she ran for shelter behind the rock wall of the Alameda Mole a few miles away. Here they found the *Reindeer* calmly at anchor; and here, during the next several hours, straggled in the remainder of the fleet, with the exception of the *Ghost*, which had evidently gone ashore to keep the *Go Ask Her* company.

By afternoon the wind had dropped away with surprising suddenness, and the weather had turned almost summer-like.

'It doesn't look right,' 'Frisco Kid said in the evening, after French Pete had rowed over in the skiff to visit Nelson.

'What doesn't look right?' Joe asked.

'Why, the weather. It went down too sudden. It didn't have a chance to blow itself out, and it ain't going to quit till it does blow itself out. It's likely to puff up and howl at any moment, if I know anything about it.'

'Where will we go from here?' Joe asked. 'Back to the oyster-beds?'

'Frisco Kid shook his head. 'I can't say what French Pete'll do. He's been fooled on the iron, and fooled on the oysters, and he's that disgusted he's liable to do 'most anything desperate. I wouldn't be surprised to see him go off with Nelson towards Redwood City, where that big thing is that I was tellin' you about. It's somewhere over there.'

'Well, I won't have anything to do with it,' Joe announced decisively.

'Of course not,' 'Frisco Kid answered. 'And with Nelson and his two men and French Pete, I don't think there'll be any need for you anyway.'

16. 'FRISCO KID'S DITTY-BOX

AFTER THE conversation died away, the two lads lay upon the cabin for perhaps an hour. Then, without saying a word, 'Frisco Kid went below and struck a light. Joe could hear him fumbling about, and a little later heard his own name called softly. On going into the cabin, he saw 'Frisco Kid sitting on the edge of the bunk, a sailor's ditty-box on his knees, and in his hand a carefully folded page from a magazine.

'Does she look like this?' he asked, smoothing it out and turning it that the other might see.

It was a half-page illustration of two girls and a boy, grouped evidently, in an old-fashioned roomy attic, and holding a council of some sort. The girl who was talking faced the onlooker, while the backs of the other two were turned.

'Who?' Joe queried, glancing in perplexity from the picture to 'Frisco Kid's face.

'Your—your sister—Bessie.'

The word seemed reluctant in coming to his lips, and he expressed himself with a certain shy reverence, as though it were something unspeakably sacred.

Joe was nonplussed for the moment. He could see no bearing between the two in point, and, anyway, girls were rather silly creatures to waste one's time over. "He's actually blushing,' he thought, regarding the soft glow on the other's cheeks. He felt an irresistible desire to laugh, and tried to smother it down.

'No, no; don't!' 'Frisco Kid cried snatching the paper away and putting it back in the ditty-box with shaking fingers. Then he added more slowly: 'I thought—I—I kind o' thought you would understand and—and——'

His lips trembled and his eyes glistened with unwanted moistness as he turned hastily away.

The next instant Joe was by his side on the bunk, his arm around him. Prompted by some instinctive monitor, he had done it before he thought. A week before he could not have imagined himself in such an absurd situation— his arm around a boy; but now it seemed the most natural thing in the world. He did not comprehend, but he knew, whatever it was, that it was of deep importance to his companion.

'Go ahead and tell us,' he urged. 'I'll understand.'

'No, you won't. You can't.'

'Yes, sure. Go ahead.'

'Frisco Kid choked and shook his head. 'I don't think I could, anyway. It's more the things I feel, and I don't know how to put them in words.' Joe's hand patted his shoulder reassuringly, and he went on: 'Well, it's this way. You see, I don't know much about the land, and people, and things, and I never had any brothers or sisters or playmates. All the time I didn't know it, but I was lonely—sort of missed them down in here somewheres.' He placed a hand over his breast. 'Did you ever feel downright hungry? Well, that's just the way I used to feel, only a different kind of hunger, and me not knowing what it was. But one day, oh, a long time back, I got a hold of a magazine and saw a picture—that picture, with the two girls and the boy talking together. I thought it must be fine to be like them, and I got to thinking about the things they said and did, till it came to me all of a sudden like, and I knew it was just loneliness was the matter with me.

'But, more than anything else, I got to wondering about the girl who looks out of the picture right at you. I was thinking about her all the time, and by and by she became real to me. You see, it was making believe, and I knew it all the time, and then again I didn't. Whenever I'd think of the men, and the work, and the hard life, I'd know it was make-believe; but when I'd think of her, it wasn't. I don't know; I can't explain it.'

Joe remembered all his own adventures which he had imagined on land and sea, and nodded. He at least understood that much.

'Of course it was all foolishness, but to have a girl like that for a comrade or friend seemed more like heaven to me than anything else I knew of. As I said, it was a long while back, and I was only a little kid—that was when Red Nelson gave me my name, and I've never been anything but 'Frisco Kid ever since. But the girl in the picture: I was always getting that picture out to look at her, and before long, if I wasn't square—why, I felt ashamed to look at her. Afterwards, when I was older, I came to look at it in another way. I thought, 'Suppose, Kid, some day you were to meet a girl like that, what would she think of you? Could she like you? Could she be even the least bit of a friend to you?' And then I'd make up my mind to be better, to try and do something with myself so that she or any of her kind of people would not be ashamed to know me.

'That's why I learned to read. That's why I ran away. Nicky Perrata, a Greek boy, taught me my letters, and it wasn't till after I learned to read that I found out there was anything really wrong with bay-pirating. I'd been used to it ever since I could remember, and almost all the people I knew made their living that way. But when I did find out, I ran away, thinking to quit it for good. I'll tell you about it sometime, and how I'm back at it again.

'Of course she seemed a real girl when I was a youngster, and even now she sometimes seems that way, I've thought so much about her. But while I'm talking to you it all clears up and she comes to me in this light: she stands just for a plain idea, a better, cleaner life than this, and one I'd like to live; and if I could live it, why, I'd come to know that kind of girls, and their kind of people—your kind, that's what I mean. So I was wondering about your sister and you, and that's why—I don't know; I guess I was just wondering. But I suppose you know lots of girls like that, don't you?'

Joe nodded his head.

'Then tell me about them—something, anything,' he added as he noted the fleeting expression of doubt in the other's eyes.

'Oh, that's easy,' Joe began valiantly. To a certain extent he did understand the lad's hunger, and it seemed a simple enough task to at least partially satisfy him. 'To begin with,

they're like—hem!—why, they're like—girls, just girls.'
He broke off with a miserable sense of failure.

'Frisco Kid waited patiently, his face a study in expectancy.

Joe struggled valiantly to marshal his forces. To his mind, in quick succession, came the girls with whom he had gone to school—the sisters of the boys he knew, and those who were his sister's friends: slim girls and plump girls, tall girls and short girls, blue-eyed and brown-eyed, curly-haired, black-haired, golden-haired; in short, a procession of all sorts and descriptions. But, to save himself, he could say nothing about them. Anyway, he'd never been a 'sissy', and why should he be expected to know anything about them? 'All girls are alike,' he concluded desperately. 'They're just the same as the ones you know, Kid—sure they are.'

'But I don't know any.'

Joe whistled. 'And never did?'

'Yes, one. Carlotta Gispardi. But she couldn't speak English, and I couldn't speak Dago; and she died. I don't care; though I never knew any, I seem to know as much about them as you do.'

'And I guess I know more about adventures all over the world than you do,' Joe retorted.

Both boys laughed. But a moment later, Joe fell into deep thought. It had come upon him quite swiftly that he had not been duly grateful for the good things of life he did possess. Already home, father and mother had assumed a greater significance to him; but he now found himself placing a higher personal value upon his sister and his chums and friends. He had never appreciated them properly, he thought, but henceforth—well, there would be a different tale to tell.

The voice of French Pete hailing them put a finish to the conversation, for they both ran on deck.

17. 'FRISCO KID TELLS HIS STORY

'GET UP ze mainsail and break out ze hook!' the French-man shouted. 'And den tail on to ze *Reindeer*! No side-lights!'

'Come! Cast off those gaskets—lively!' 'Frisco Kid ordered. 'Now lay on to the peak halyards—there, that rope—cast it off the pin. And don't hoist ahead of me. There! Make fast! We'll stretch it afterwards. Run aft and come in on the mainsheet! Shove the helm up!'

Under the sudden driving power of the mainsail, the *Dazzler* strained and tugged at her anchor like an impatient horse till the muddy iron left the bottom with a rush and she was free.

'Let go the sheet! Come for'ard again and lend a hand on the chain! Stand by to give her the jib!' 'Frisco Kid the boy who mooned over girls in pictorial magazines had vanished, and 'Frisco Kid the sailor, strong and dominant, was on deck. He ran aft and tacked about as the jib rattled aloft in the hands of Joe, who quickly joined him. Just then the *Reindeer*, like a monstrous bat, passed to leeward of them in the gloom.

'Ah, dose boys! Dey take all-a night!' they heard French Pete exclaim, and then the gruff voice of Red Nelson, who said: 'Never you mind, Frenchy. I taught the Kid his sailorizing, and I ain't never been ashamed of him yet.'

The *Reindeer* was the faster boat, but by spilling the wind from her sails they managed so that the boys could keep them in sight. The breeze came steadily in from the west, with a promise of early increase. The stars were being blotted out by masses of driving clouds, which indicated a greater velocity in the upper strata. 'Frisco Kid surveyed the sky.

'Going to have it good and stiff before morning,' he said, 'just as I told you.'

Several hours later, both boats stood in for San Mateo shore, and dropped anchor not more than a cable's length away. A little wharf ran out, the bare end of which was perceptible to them, though they could discern a small yacht lying moored to a buoy a short distance away.

According to their custom, everything was put in readiness for hasty departure. The anchors could be tripped and the sails flung out on a moment's notice. Both skiffs came over noiselessly from the *Reindeer*. Red Nelson had given one of his two men to French Pete, so that each skiff was doubly manned. They were not a very prepossessing group of men—at least, Joe did not think so—for their faces bore a savage seriousness which almost made him shiver. The captain of the *Dazzler* buckled on his pistol-belt, and place a rifle and a stout double-block tackle in the boat. Then he poured out wine all around, and, standing in the darkness of the little cabin, they pledged success to the expedition. Red Nelson was also armed, while his men wore at their hips the customary sailor's sheath-knife. They were very slow and careful to avoid noise in getting into the boats, French Pete pausing long enough to warn the boys to remain quietly aboard and not try any tricks.

'Now'd be your chance, Joe, if they hadn't taken the skiff,' 'Frisco Kid whispered, when the boats had vanished into the loom of the land.

'What's the matter with the *Dazzler*?' was the unexpected answer. 'We could up sail and away before you could say Jack Robinson.'

'Frisco Kid hesitated. The spirit of comradeship was strong in the lad, and deserting a companion in a pinch could not but be repulsive to him.

'I don't think it'd be exactly square to leave them in the lurch ashore,' he said. 'Of course,' he went on hurriedly, 'I know the whole thing's wrong; but you remember that first night, when you came running through the water for the skiff, and those fellows on the bank busy popping away? We didn't leave you in the lurch, did we?'

Joe assented reluctantly, and then a new thought flashed across his mind. 'But they're pirates—and thieves—and criminals. They're breaking the law, and you and I are not willing to be law-breakers. Besides, they'll not be left. There's the *Reindeer*. There's nothing to prevent them from getting away on her, and they'll never catch us in the dark.'

'Come on, then.' Though he had agreed, 'Frisco Kid did not quite like it, for it still seemed to savour of desertion.

They crawled forward and began to hoist the mainsail. The anchor they could slip, if necessary, and save the time of pulling it up. But at the first rattle of the halyards on the sheaves a warning 'Hist!' came to them through the darkness, followed by a loudly whispered 'Drop that!'

Glancing in the direction from which these sounds proceeded they made out a white face peering at them from over the rail of the other sloop.

'Aw, it's only the *Reindeer*'s boy,' 'Frisco Kid said. 'Come on.'

Again they were interrupted at the first rattling of the blocks.

'I say, you fellers, you'd better let go them halyards pretty quick, I'm a-tellin' you, or I'll give you what for!'

This threat being dramatically capped by the click of a cocking pistol, 'Frisco Kid obeyed and went grumblingly back to the cockpit. 'Oh, there's plenty more chances to come,' he whispered consolingly to Joe. 'French Pete was cute, wasn't he? He thought you might be trying to make a break, and put a guard on us.'

Nothing came from the shore to indicate how the pirates were faring. Not a dog barked, not a light flared. Yet the air seemed quivering with an alarm about to burst forth. The night had taken on a strained feeling of intensity, as though it held in store all kinds of terrible things. The boys felt this keenly as they huddled against each other in the cockpit and waited.

'You were going to tell me about your running away,' Joe ventured finally, 'and why you came back again.'

'Frisco Kid took up the tale at once, speaking in a muffled undertone close to the other's ear.

'You see, when I made up my mind to quit the life, there wasn't a soul to lend me a hand; but I knew that the only thing for me to do was to get ashore and find some kind of work, so I could study. Then I figured there'd be more chance in the country than in the city; so I gave Red Nelson the slip. I was on the *Reindeer* then. One night on the Alameda oyster-beds, I got ashore and headed back from the bay as fast as I could sprint. Nelson didn't catch me. But they were all Portuguese farmers thereabouts, and none of them had work for me. Besides, it was in the wrong time of the year—winter. That shows how much I knew about the land.

'I'd saved up a couple of dollars, and I kept travelling back, deeper and deeper into the country, looking for work, and buying bread and cheese and such things from the storekeepers. I tell you, it was cold, nights, sleeping out without blankets, and I was always glad when morning came. But worse than that was the way everybody looked on me. They were all suspicious, and not a bit afraid to show it, and sometimes they'd set their dogs on me and tell me to get along. Seemed as though there wasn't any place for me on the land. Then my money gave out, and just about the time I was good and hungry I got captured.'

'Captured! What for?'

'Nothing. Living, I suppose. I crawled into a haystack to sleep one night, because it was warmer, and along comes a village constable and arrests me for being a tramp. At first they thought I was a runaway, and telegraphed my description all over. I told them I didn't have any people, but they wouldn't believe me for a long while. And then,

10*

when nobody claimed me, the judge sent me to a boys' "refuge" in San Francisco.'

He stopped and peered intently in the direction of the shore. The darkness and the silence in which the men had been swallowed up were profound. Nothing was stirring save the rising wind.

'I thought I'd die in that "refuge". It was just like being in jail. We were locked up and guarded like prisoners. Even then, if I could have liked the other boys it might have been all right. But they were mostly street boys of the worst kind—lying, and sneaking, and cowardly, without one spark of manhood or one idea of square dealing and fair play. There was only one thing I did like, and that was the books. Oh, I did lots of reading, I tell you! But that couldn't make up for the rest. I wanted the freedom and the sunlight and the salt water. And what had I done to be kept in prison and herded with such a gang? Instead of doing wrong, I had tried to do right, to make myself better, and that's what I got for it. I wasn't old enough, you see, to reason anything out.

'Sometimes I'd see the sunshine dancing on the water and showing white on the sails, and the *Reindeer* cutting through it just as you please, and I'd get that sick I would know hardly what I did. And then the boys would come against me with some of their meannesses, and I'd start in to lick the whole kit of them. Then the men in charge would lock me up and punish me. Well, I couldn't stand it any longer; I watched my chance and ran for it. Seemed as though there wasn't any place on the land for me, so I picked up with French Pete and went back on the bay. That's about all there is to it, though I'm going to try it again when I get a little older—old enough to get a square deal for myself.'

'You're going back on the land with me,' Joe said authoritatively, laying a hand on his shoulder. 'That's what you're going to do. As for ——'

Bang! a revolver-shot rang out from the shore. Bang! bang! More guns were speaking sharply and hurriedly.

A man's voice rose wildly on the air and died away. Somebody began to cry for help. Both boys were on their feet on the instant, hoisting the mainsail and getting everything ready to run. The *Reindeer* boy was doing likewise. A man, roused from his sleep on the yacht, thrust an excited head through the sky-light, but withdrew it hastily at sight of the two strangers' sloops. The intensity of waiting was broken, the time for action come.

18. A NEW RESPONSIBILITY FOR JOE

HEAVING IN on the anchor-chain till it was up and down, 'Frisco Kid and Joe ceased from their exertions. Everything was in readiness to give the *Dazzler* the jib, and go. They strained their eyes in the direction of the shore. The clamour had died away, but here and there lights were beginning to flash. The creaking of a block and tackle came to their ears, and they heard Red Nelson's voice singing out: 'Lower away!' and 'Cast-off!'

'French Pete forgot to oil it,' 'Frisco Kid commented, referring to the tackle.

'Takin' their time about it, ain't they?' the boy on the *Reindeer* called over to them, sitting down on the cabin and mopping his face after the exertion of hoisting the mainsail single-handed.

'Guess they're all right,' 'Frisco Kid rejoined. 'All ready?'

'Yes—all right here.'

'Say, you,' the man on the yacht cried through the sky-light, not venturing to show his head. 'You'd better go away.'

'And you'd better stay below and keep quiet,' was the response. 'We'll take care of ourselves. You do the same.'

'If I was only out of this, I'd show you!' he threatened.

'Lucky for you you're not,' responded the boy on the *Reindeer*; and thereat the man kept quiet.

'Here they come!' said 'Frisco Kid suddenly to Joe.

The two skiffs shot out of the darkness and came alongside. Some kind of an altercation was going on, as French Pete's voice attested.

'No, no!' he cried. 'Put it on ze *Dazzler*. Ze *Reindeer* she sails too fast-a, and run away, oh, so queeck, and never more I see it. Put it on ze *Dazzler*. Eh? Wot you say?'

'All right then,' Red Nelson agreed. 'We'll whack up afterwards. But, say, hurry up. Out with you, lads, and heave her up! My arm's broke.'

The men tumbled out, ropes were cast inboard, and all hands, with the exception of Joe, tailed on. The shouting of men, the sound of oars, and the rattling and slapping of blocks and sails, told that the men on shore were getting under way for the pursuit.

'Now!' Red Nelson commanded. 'All together! Don't let her come back or you'll smash the skiff. There she takes it! A long pull and a strong pull! Once again! And yet again! Get a turn there somebody, and take a spell.'

Though the task was but half accomplished, they were exhausted by the strenuous effort, and hailed the rest eagerly. Joe glanced over the side to discover what the heavy object might me, and saw the vague outlines of a small office safe.

'Now all together!' Red Nelson began again. 'Take her on the run and don't let her stop! Yo, ho; heave, ho! Once again! And another! Over with her!'

Straining and gasping, with tense muscles and heaving chests, they brought the cumbersome weight over the side, rolled it on top of the rail, and lowered it into the cockpit on the run. The cabin doors were thrown apart, and it was moved along, end for end, till it lay on the cabin floor, snug against the end of the centreboard-case. Red Nelson had followed it aboard to superintend. His left arm hung helpless at his side, and from the finger-tips blood dripped with monotonous regularity. He did not seem to mind it, however, nor even the mutterings of the human storm he had raised ashore, and which, to judge by the sounds, was even then threatening to break upon them.

'Lay your course for the Golden Gate,' he said to French Pete, as he turned to go. 'I'll try to stand by you, but if you get lost in the dark I'll meet you outside, off the Farralones, in the morning.' He sprang into the skiff after the men, and, with a wave of his uninjured arm, cried heartily: 'And then it's for Mexico, my lads—Mexico and summer weather!'

Just as the *Dazzler*, freed from her anchor, paid off under the jib and filled away, a dark sail loomed under their stern, barely missing the skiff in tow. The cockpit of the stranger was crowded with men, who raised their voices angrily at sight of the pirates. Joe had half a mind to run forward and cut the halyards so that the *Dazzler* might be captured. As he had told French Pete the day before, he had done nothing to be ashamed of, and was not afraid to go before a court of justice. But the thought of 'Frisco Kid restrained him. He wanted to take him ashore with him, but in so doing he did not wish to take him to jail. So he, too, began to experience a keen interest in the escape of the *Dazzler*.

The pursuing sloop rounded up hurriedly to come about after them, and in the darkness fouled the yacht which lay at anchor. The man aboard of her, thinking that at last his time had come, gave one wild yell, ran on deck, and leaped overboard. In the confusion of the collision, and while they were endeavouring to save him, French Pete and the boys slipped away into the night.

The *Reindeer* had already disappeared, and by the time Joe and 'Frisco Kid had the running-gear coiled down and everything in shape, they were standing out in open water. The wind was freshening constantly, and the *Dazzler* heeled a lively clip through the comparatively smooth stretch. Before an hour had passed, the lights of Hunter's Point were well on her starboard beam. 'Frisco Kid went below to make coffee, but Joe remained on deck, watching the lights of South San Francisco grow, and speculating on their destination. Mexico! They were going to sea in such a frail craft! Impossible! At least, it seemed so to him, for his conceptions of ocean travel were limited to steamers and full-rigged ships. He was beginning to feel half sorry he had not cut the halyards, and longed to ask French Pete a thousand questions; but just as the first was on his lips that worthy ordered him to go below and get some coffee and then to turn in. He was followed shortly afterwards by 'Frisco Kid, French Pete remaining at his lonely task of beating down the bay and out to sea. Twice he heard the waves buffeted back from some flying forefoot, and once he saw a sail to leeward on the opposite tack, which luffed sharply and came about at sight of him. But the darkness favoured, and he heard no more of it— perhaps because he worked into the wind closer by a point, and held on his way with a shaking after-leech.

Shortly after dawn, the two boys were called and came sleepily on deck. The day had broken cold and grey, while the wind had attained half a gale. Joe noted with astonishment the white tents of the quarantine station on Angel Island. San Francisco lay a smoky blur on the southern horizon, while the night, still lingering on the western edge of the world, slowly withdrew before their eyes. French Pete was just finishing a long reach into the Raccoon Straits, and at the same time studiously regarding a plunging sloop-yacht half a mile astern.

'Dey t'ink to catch ze *Dazzler*, eh? Bah!' And he brought the craft in question about, laying a course straight for the Golden Gate.

The pursuing yacht followed suit. Joe watched her a few moments. She held an apparently parallel course to them, and forged ahead much faster.

'Why, at this rate they'll have us in no time!' he cried.

French Pete laughed. 'You t'ink so? Bam! Dey outfoot; we outpoint. Dey are scared of ze wind; we wipe ze eye of ze wind. Ah! you wait, you see.'

'They're travelling ahead faster,' 'Frisco Kid explained; 'but we're sailing closer to the wind. In the end we'll beat them, even if they have the nerve to cross the bar—which I don't think they have. Look! See!'

Ahead could be seen the great ocean surges, flinging themselves skyward and bursting into roaring caps of smother. In the midst of it, now rolling her dripping bottom clear, now sousing her deck-load of lumber far above the guards, a coasting steam-schooner was lumbering drunkenly into port. It was magnificent—this battle between man and the elements. Whatever timidity he had entertained fled away, and Joe's nostrils began to dilate and his eyes to flash at the nearness of the impending struggle.

French Pete called for his oilskins and sou'-wester, and Joe also was equipped with a spare suit. Then he and 'Frisco Kid were sent below to lash and cleat the safe in place. In the midst of this task Joe glanced at the firm-name, gilt-lettered on the face of it, and read: 'Bronson & Tate.' Why, that was his father and his father's partner. That was their safe, their money! 'Frisco Kid, nailing the last cleat on the floor of the cabin, looked up and followed his fascinated gaze.

'That's rough, isn't it,' he whispered. 'Your father?'

Joe nodded. He could see it all now. They had run into San Andreas, where his father worked the big quarries, and most probably the safe contained the wages of the thousand men or more whom he employed. 'Don't say anything,' he cautioned.

'Frisco Kid agreed knowingly. 'French Pete can't read, anyway.' he muttered; 'and the chances are that Red Nelson won't know what *your* name is. But, just the same, it's pretty rough. They'll break it open and divide up as soon as they can, so I don't see what you're going to do about it.'

'Wait and see.'

Joe had made up his mind that he would do his best to stand by his father's property. At the worst, it could only be lost; and that would surely be the case were he not along, while, being along, he at least had a fighting chance to save it, or to be in position to recover it. Responsibilities were showering upon him thick and fast. But a few days back he had had but himself to consider; then, in some subtle way, he had felt a certain accountability for 'Frisco Kid's future welfare; and after that, and still more subtly, he had become aware of duties which he owed to his position, to his sister, to his chums and friends; and now, by a most unexpected chain of circumstances, came the pressing need of service for his father's sake. It was a call upon his deepest strength, and he responded bravely. While the future might be doubtful, he had no doubt of himself; and this very state of mind, this self-confidence, by a generous alchemy, gave him added resolution. Nor did he fail to be vaguely aware of it, and to grasp dimly at the truth that confidence breeds confidence—strength, strength.

19. THE BOYS PLAN AN ESCAPE

'Now she takes it!' French Pete cried.

Both lads ran into the cockpit. They were on the edge of the breaking bar. A huge forty-footer reared a foam-crested head far above them, stealing their wind for the moment and threatening to crush the tiny craft like an egg-shell. Joe held his breath. It was the supreme moment. French Pete luffed straight into it, and the *Dazzler* mounted the steep slope with a rush, poised a moment on the giddy summit, and fell into the yawning valley beyond. Keeping off in the intervals to fill the mainsail, and luffing into the combers, they worked their way across the dangerous stretch. Once they caught the tail-end of a whitecap and were well-nigh smothered in the froth, but otherwise the sloop bobbed and ducked with the happy facility of a cork.

To Joe it seemed as though he had been lifted out of himself—out of the world. Ah, this was life! this was action! Surely it could not be the old, commonplace world he had lived in so long! The sailors, grouped on the streaming deck-load of the steamer, waved their sou'-westers, and, on the bridge, even the captain was expressing his admiration for the plucky craft.

'Ah, you see! you see!' French Pete pointed astern.

The sloop-yacht had been afraid to venture it, and was skirting back and forth on the inner edge of the bar. The chase was over. A pilot-boat, running for shelter from the coming storm, flew by them like a frightened bird, passing the steamer as though the latter were standing still.

Half an hour later the *Dazzler* sped beyond the last smoking sea and was sliding up and down on the long Pacific swell. The wind had increased its velocity and necessitated a reefing down of jib and mainsail. Then they laid off again full and free on the starboard tack, for the Farralones, thirty miles away. By the time breakfast was cooked and eaten they picked up the *Reindeer*, which was hove-to and working offshore to the south and west. The wheel was lashed down, and there was not a soul on deck.

French Pete complained bitterly against such recklessness. 'Dat is ze one fault of Red Nelson. He no care. He is afraid of not'ing. Some day he will die, oh, so vaire queeck! I know he will.'

Three times they circled about the *Reindeer*, running under her weather quarter and shouting in chorus, before they brought anybody on deck. Sail was then made at once, and together the two cockle-shells plunged away into the vastness of the Pacific. This was necessary, as 'Frisco Kid informed Joe, in order to have an offing before the whole fury of the storm broke upon them. Otherwise they would be driven on the lee-shore of the California coast. Grub and water, he said, could be obtained by running into the land when fine weather came. He congratulated Joe upon the fact that he was not seasick, which circumstances like-wise brought praise from French Pete, and put him in better humour with his mutinous young sailor.

'I'll tell you what we'll do,' 'Frisco Kid whispered, while cooking dinner. 'Tonight we'll drag French Pete down——'

'Drag French Pete down?'

'Yes, and tie him up good and snug, as soon as it gets dark; then put out the lights and make a run for land; get to port anyway, anywhere, just so long as we shake loose from Red Nelson.'

'Yes,' Joe deliberated: 'that would be all right—if I could do it alone. But as for asking you to help me—why, that would be treason to French Pete.'

'That's what I'm coming to. I'll help you if you promise me a few things. French Pete took me aboard when I ran away from the "refuge", when I was starving and had no place to go, and I just can't repay him for that by sending him to jail. 'Twouldn't be square. Your father wouldn't have you break your word, would he?'

'No; of course not.' Joe knew how sacredly his father held his word of honour.

'Then you must promise, and your father must see it carried out, not to press any charge against French Pete.'

'All right. And now, what about yourself? You can't very well expect to go away with him again on the *Dazzler!*'

'Oh, don't bother about me. There's nobody to miss me. I'm strong enough, and know enough about it, to ship to sea as ordinary seaman. I'll go away somewhere over on the other side of the world, and begin all over again.'

'Then we'll have to call it off, that's all.'

'Call what off?'

'Tying French Pete up and running for it.'

'No, sir. That's decided upon.'

'Now listen here: I'll not have a thing to do with it. I'll go on to Mexico first, if you don't make me one promise.'

'And what's the promise?'

'Just this: you place yourself in my hands from the moment we get ashore, and trust to me. You don't know anything about the land, anyway—you said so. And I'll fix it with my father—I know I can—so that you can get to know people of the right sort, and study and get an education, and be something else than a bay pirate or a sailor. That's what you'd like, isn't it?'

Though he said nothing, 'Frisco Kid showed how well he liked it by the expression of his face.

'And it'll be no more than your due, either,' Joe continued. 'You will have stood by me, and you'll have recovered my father's money. He'll owe it to you.'

'But I don't do things that way. I don't think much of a man who does a favour just to be paid for it.'

'Now you keep quiet. How much do you think it would cost my father for detectives and all that to recover that safe? Give me your promise, that's all, and when I've got things arranged, if you don't like them you can back out. Come on; that's fair.'

They shook hands on the bargain, and proceeded to map out their line of action for the night.

But the storm, yelling down out of the north-west, had something entirely different in store for the *Dazzler* and her crew. By the time dinner was over they were forced to put double reefs in mainsail and jib, and still the gale had not reached its height. The sea, also, had been kicked up till it was a continuous succession of water-mountains, frightful and withal grand to look upon from the low deck of the sloop. It was only when the sloops were tossed upon the crest of the waves at the same time that they caught sight of each other. Occasional fragments of seas swashed into the cockpit or dashed aft over the cabin, and Joe was stationed at the small pump to keep the well dry.

At three o'clock, watching his chance, French Pete motioned to the *Reindeer* that he was going to heave-to and get out a sea-anchor. This latter was of the nature of a large shallow canvas bag, with the mouth held open by triangularly lashed spars. To this the towing-ropes were attached, on the kite principle, so that the greatest resisting surface was presented to the water. The sloop, drifting so much faster, would thus be held bow on to both wind and sea—the safest possible position in a storm. Red Nelson waved his hand in response that he understood and to go ahead.

French Pete went forward to launch the sea-anchor himself, leaving it to 'Frisco Kid to put the helm down at the proper moment and run into the wind. The Frenchman poised on the slippery foredeck, waiting an opportunity. But at that moment the *Dazzler* lifted into an unusually large sea, and, as she cleared the summit, caught a heavy snort of the gale at the very instant she was righting herself to an even keel. Thus there was not the slightest yield to this sudden pressure on her sails and mast-gear.

There was a quick snap, followed by a crash. The steel weather-rigging carried away at the lanyards, and mast, jib, mainsail, blocks, stays, sea-anchor, French Pete—everything—went over the side. Almost by a miracle, the captain clutched at the bobstay and managed to get one hand up and over the bowsprit. The boys ran forward to drag him into safety, and Red Nelson, observing the disaster, put up his helm and ran down to the rescue.

20. PERILOUS HOURS

FRENCH PETE was uninjured from the fall overboard with the *Dazzler*'s mast; but the sea-anchor, which had gone with him, had not escaped so easily. The gaff of the mainsail had been driven through it, and it refused to work. The wreckage, thumping alongside, held the sloop in a quartering slant to the seas—not so dangerous a position as it might be, nor so safe, either.

'Good-bye, old-a *Dazzler*. Never no more you wipe ze eye of ze wind. Never no more you kick your heels at ze crack gentlemen yachts.'

So the captain lamented, standing in the cockpit and surveying the ruin with wet eyes. Even Joe, who bore him great dislike, felt sorry for him at this moment. A heavier blast of the wind caught the jagged crest of a wave and hurled it upon the helpless craft.

'Can't we save her?' Joe spluttered.

'Frisco Kid shook his head.

'Nor the safe?'

'Impossible,' he answered. 'Couldn't lay another boat alongside for a United States mint. As it is, it'll keep us guessing to save ourselves.'

Another sea swept over them, and the skiff, which had long since been swamped, dashed itself to pieces against the stern. Then the *Reindeer* towered above them on a mountain of water. Joe caught himself half shrinking back, for it seemed she would fall down squarely on top of them; but the next instant she dropped into the gaping trough, and they were looking down upon her far below. It was a striking picture—one Joe was destined never to forget. The *Reindeer* was wallowing in the snow-white smother, her rails flush with the sea, the water scudding across her deck in foaming cataracts. The air was filled with flying spray, which made the scene appear hazy and unreal. One of the men was clinging to the perilous after-deck and striving to cast off the water-logged skiff. The boy, leaning far over the cockpit-rail and holding on for dear life, was passing him a knife. The second man stood at the wheel, putting it up with flying hands and forcing the sloop to pay off. Besides him, his injured arm in a sling, was Red Nelson, his sou'-wester gone and his fair hair plastered in wet, wind-blown ringlets about his face. His whole attitude breathed indomitability, courage, strength. It seemed almost as though the divine were blazing forth from him.

Joe looked upon him in sudden awe, and, realizing the enormous possibilities of the man, felt sorrow for the way in which they had been wasted. A thief and a robber! In that flashing moment Joe caught a glimpse of human truth, grasped at the mystery of success and failure. Life threw back its curtains that he might read it and understand. Of such stuff as Red Nelson were heroes made; but they possessed wherein he lacked—the power of choice, the careful poise of mind, the sober control of soul: in short, the very things his father had so often 'preached' to him about.

These were the thoughts which came to Joe in the flight of a second. Then the *Reindeer* swept skyward and hurtled across their bow to leeward on the breast of a mighty billow.

'Ze wild man! ze wild man!' French Pete shrieked, watching her in amazement. 'He t'inks he can jibe! He will die! we will all die! He must come about. Oh, ze fool, ze fool!'

But time was precious, and Red Nelson ventured the chance. At the right moment he jibed the mainsail over and hauled back on the wind.

'Here she comes! Make ready to jump for it,' 'Frisco Kid cried to Joe.

The *Reindeer* dashed by their stern, heeling over till the cabin windows were buried, and so close that it appeared she must run them down. But a freak of the waters lurched the two crafts apart. Red Nelson, seeing that the manœuvre had miscarried, instantly instituted another. Throwing the helm hard up, the *Reindeer* whirled on her heel, thus swinging her overhanging main-boom closer to the *Dazzler*. French Pete was the nearest, and the opportunity could last no longer than a second. Like a cat he sprang, catching the foot-rope with both hands. Then the *Reindeer* forged ahead, dipping him into the sea at every plunge. But he clung on, working inboard every time he emerged, till he dropped into the cockpit as Red Nelson squared off to run down to leeward and repeat the manœuvre.

'Your turn next,' 'Frisco Kid said.

'No; yours,' Joe replied.

'But I know more about the water,' 'Frisco Kid insisted.

'And I can swim as well as you,' the other retorted.

It would have been hard to forecast the outcome of this dispute; but, as it was, the swift rush of events made any settlement needless. The *Reindeer* had jibed over and was ploughing back at breakneck speed, careening at such an angle that it seemed she must surely capsize. It was a gallant sight. Just then the storm burst in all its fury, the shouting wind flattening the ragged crests till they boiled. The *Reindeer* dipped from view behind an immense wave. The wave rolled on, but the next moment, where the sloop had been, the boys noted with startled eyes only the angry waters! Doubting they looked a second time. There was no *Reindeer*. They were alone on the torn crest of the ocean!

'God have mercy on their souls!' 'Frisco Kid said solemnly.

Joe was too horrified at the suddenness of the catastrophe to utter a sound.

'Sailed her clean under, and, with the ballast she carried, went straight to bottom,' 'Frisco Kid gasped. Then, turning to their own pressing need, he said: 'Now we've got to look out for ourselves. The back of the storm broke in that puff, but the sea'll kick up worse yet as the wind eases down. Lend a hand and hang on with the other. We've got to get her head-on.'

Together, knives in hand, they crawled forward to where the pounding wreckage hampered the boat sorely. 'Frisco Kid took the lead in the ticklish work, but Joe obeyed orders like a veteran. Every minute or two the bow was swept by the sea, and they were pounded and buffeted about like a pair of shuttlecocks. First the main portion of the wreckage was securely fastened to the forward bitts; then, breathless and gasping, more often under the water than out, they cut and hacked at the tangle of halyards, sheets, stays, and tackles. The cockpit was taking water rapidly, and it was a race between swamping and completing the task. At last, however, everything stood clear save the lee rigging. 'Frisco Kid slashed the lanyards. The storm did the rest. The *Dazzler* drifted swiftly to leeward of the wreckage till the strain on the line fast to the forward bitts jerked her bow into place and she ducked dead into the eye of the wind and sea.

Pausing only for a cheer at the success of their undertaking, the two lads raced aft, where the cockpit was half full and the dunnage of the cabin all afloat. With a couple of buckets procured from the stern lockers, they proceeded to fling the water overboard. It was heartbreaking work, for many a barrelful was flung back upon them again; but they persevered, and when night fell the *Dazzler*, bobbing merrily at her sea-anchor, could boast that her pumps sucked once more. As 'Frisco Kid had said, the backbone of the storm was broken, though the wind had veered to the west, where it still blew stiffly.

'If she holds,' 'Frisco Kid said, referring to the breeze, 'we'll drift to the California coast sometime tomorrow. Nothing to do now but wait.'

They said little, oppressed by the loss of their comrades and overcome with exhaustion, preferring to huddle against each other for the sake of warmth and companionship. It was a miserable night, and they shivered constantly from the cold. Nothing dry was to be obtained aboard, food, blankets, everything being soaked with the salt water. Sometimes they dozed; but these intervals were short and harassing, for it seemed each took turn in waking with such sudden starts as to rouse the other.

At last day broke, and they looked about. Wind and sea had dropped considerably, and there was no question as to the safety of the *Dazzler*. The coast was nearer than they had expected, its cliffs showing dark and forbidding in the grey of dawn. But with the rising of the sun they could see the yellow beaches, flanked by the white surf, and beyond—it seemed too good to be true—the clustering houses and smoking chimneys of a town.

'Santa Cruz!' 'Frisco Kid cried, 'and no chance of being wrecked in the surf!'

'Then the safe *is* safe?' Joe queried.

'Safe! I should say so. It ain't much of a sheltered harbour for large vessels, but with this breeze we'll run right up the mouth of the San Lorenzo River. Then there's a little lake like, and a boathouse. Water smooth as glass and hardly over your head. You see, I was down here once before, with Red Nelson. Come on. We'll be in in time for breakfast.'

Bringing to light some spare coils of rope from the lockers, he put a clove-hitch on the standing part of the sea-anchor hawser, and carried the new running-line aft, making it fast to the stern bitts. Then he cast off from the forward bitts. The *Dazzler* swung off into the trough, completed the evolution, and pointed her nose toward shore. A couple of spare oars from below, and as many water-soaked blankets, sufficed to make a jury-mast and sail. When this was in place, Joe cast loose from the wreckage, which was now towing astern, while 'Frisco Kid took the tiller.

21. JOE AND HIS FATHER

'HOW'S THAT?' cried 'Frisco Kid, as he finished making the *Dazzler* fast fore and aft, and sat down on the stringpiece of the tiny wharf. 'What'll we do next, captain?'

Joe looked up in quick surprise. 'Why—I—what's the matter?'

'Well, ain't you captain now? Haven't we reached land? I'm crew from now on, ain't I? What's your orders?'

Joe caught the spirit of it. 'Pipe all hands for breakfast —that is—wait a minute.'

Diving below, he possessed himself of the money he had stowed away in his bundle when he came aboard.

Then he locked the cabin door, and they went up town in search of a restaurant. Over the breakfast Joe planned the next move, and, when they had done, communicated it to 'Frisco Kid.

In response to his inquiry, the cashier told him when the morning train started for San Francisco. He glanced at the clock.

'Just time to catch it,' he said to 'Frisco Kid. 'Keep the cabin doors locked, and don't let anybody come aboard. Here's money. Eat at the restaurants. Dry your blankets and sleep in the cockpit. I'll be back tomorrow. And don't let anybody into the cabin. Good-bye.'

With a hasty hand-grip, he sped down the street to the depôt. The conductor looked at him with surprise when he punched his ticket. And well he might, for it was not the custom of his passengers to travel in sea-boots and sou'-westers. But Joe did not mind. He did not even notice. He had bought a paper and was absorbed in its contents. Before long his eyes caught an interesting paragraph:

SUPPOSED TO HAVE BEEN LOST

The tug *Sea Queen*, chartered by Bronson & Tate, has returned from a fruitless cruise outside the Heads. No news of value could be obtained concerning the pirates who so daringly carried off their safe at San Andreas last Tuesday night. The lighthouse-keeper at the Farralones mentions having sighted the two sloops Wednesday morning, clawing offshore in the teeth of the gale. It is supposed by shipping men that they perished in the storm with their ill-gotten treasure. Rumour has it that, in addition to the ten thousand dollars in gold, the safe contained papers of great importance.

When Joe had read this he felt a great relief. It was evident no one had been killed at San Andreas the night of the robbery, else there would have been some comment on it in the paper. Nor, if they had had any clue to his own whereabouts, would they have omitted such a striking bit of information.

At the depot in San Francisco the curious onlookers were surprised to see a boy clad conspicuously in sea-boots and sou'-wester hail a cab and dash away. But Joe was in a hurry. He knew his father's hours, and was fearful lest he should not catch him before he went to lunch.

The office-boy scowled at him when he pushed open the door and asked to see Mr Bronson; nor could the head clerk, when summoned by this disreputable intruder, recognize him.

'Don't you know me, Mr Willis?'

Mr Willis looked a second time. 'Why, it's Joe Bronson! Of all things under the sun, where did you drop from? Go right in. Your father's in there.'

Mr Bronson stopped dictating to his stenographer and looked up. 'Hello! Where have you been?' he said.

'To sea,' Joe answered demurely, not sure of just what kind of a reception he was to get, and fingering his sou'-wester nervously.

'Short trip, eh? How did you make out?'

'Oh, so-so.' He had caught the twinkle of his father's eye and knew that it was all clear sailing. 'Not so bad—er—that is, considering.'

'Considering?'

'Well, not exactly that; rather, it might have been worse, while it couldn't have been better.'

'That's interesting. Sit down.' Then turning to the stenographer: 'You may go, Mr Brown, and—hum!—I won't need you any more today.'

It was all Joe could do to keep from crying, so kindly and naturally had his father received him, making him feel at once as if not the slightest thing uncommon had occurred. It seemed as if he had just returned from a vacation, or, man-grown, had come back from some business trip.

'Now go ahead, Joe. You were speaking to me a moment

ago in conundrums, and you have aroused my curiosity to a most uncomfortable degree.'

Whereupon Joe sat down and told what had happened —all that had happened—from Monday night to that very moment. Each little incident he related—every detail— not forgetting his conversations with 'Frisco Kid nor his plans concerning him. His face flushed, and he was carried away with the excitement of the narrative, while Mr Bronson was almost as eager, urging him on whenever he slackened his pace, but otherwise remaining silent.

'So you see,' Joe concluded, 'it couldn't possible have turned out any better.'

'Ah, well,' Mr Bronson deliberated judiciously, 'it may be so, and then again it may not.'

'I don't see it.' Joe felt sharp disappointment at his father's qualified approval. It seemed to him that the return of the safe merited something stronger.

That Mr Bronson fully comprehended the way Joe felt about it was clearly in evidence, for he went on: 'As to the matter of the safe, all hail to you, Joe! Credit, and plenty of it, is your due. Mr Tate and myself have already spent five hundred dollars in attempting to recover it. So important was it that we have also offered five thousand dollars reward, and but this morning were considering the advisability of increasing the amount. But, my son'—Mr Bronson stood up, resting a hand affectionately on his boy's shoulder—'there are certain things in this world which are of still greater importance than gold, or papers which represent what gold may buy. How about *yourself*? That's the point. Will you sell the best possibilities of your life right now for a million dollars?'

Joe shook his head.

'As I said, that's the point. A human life the money of the world cannot buy; nor can it redeem one which is misspent; nor can it make full and complete and beautiful a life which is dwarfed and warped and ugly. How about yourself? What is to be the effect of all these strange adventures on your life—*your* life, Joe? Are you going to pick yourself up tomorrow and try it over again? or the next day? or the day after? Do you understand? Why, Joe, do you think for one moment that I would place against the best value of my son's life the paltry value of a safe? And *can* I say, until time has told me, whether this trip of yours could not possibly have been better? Such an experience is as potent for evil as for good. One dollar is exactly like another—there are many in the world: but no Joe is like my Joe, nor can there be any others in the world to take his place. Don't you see, Joe? Don't you understand?'

Mr Bronson's voice broke slightly, and the next instant Joe was sobbing as though his heart would break. He had never understood this father of his before, and he knew now the pain he must have caused him, to say nothing of his mother and sister. But the four stirring days he had lived had given him a clearer view of the world and humanity, and he had always possessed the power of putting his thoughts into speech; so he spoke of these things and the lessons he had learned—the conclusions he had drawn from his conversations with 'Frisco Kid, from his intercourse with French Pete, from the graphic picture he retained of the *Reindeer* and Red Nelson as they wallowed in the trough beneath him. And Mr Bronson listened and, in turn, understood.

'But what of 'Frisco Kid, father?' Joe asked when he had finished.

'Hum! there seems to be a great deal of promise in the boy, from what you say of him.' Mr Bronson hid the twinkle in his eye this time. 'And, I must confess, he seems perfectly capable of shifting for himself.'

'Sir?' Joe could not believe his ears.

'Let us see, then. He is at present entitled to the half of five thousand dollars, the other half of which belongs to you. It was you two who preserved the safe from the bottom of the Pacific, and if you only had waited a little longer, Mr Tate and myself would have increased the reward.'

'Oh!' Joe caught a glimmering of the light. 'Part of that is easily arranged. I simply refuse to take my half. As to the other—that isn't exactly what 'Frisco Kid desires. He wants friends—and—and—though you didn't say so, they are far higher than money, nor can money buy them. He wants friends and a chance for an education, not twenty-five hundred dollars.'

'Don't you think it would be better for him to choose for himself?'

'Ah, no. That's all arranged.'

'Arranged?'

'Yes, sir. He's captain on sea, and I'm captain on land. So he's under my charge now.'

'Then you have the power of attorney for him in the present negotiations? Good. I'll make you a proposition. The twenty-five hundred dollars shall be held in trust by me, on his demand at any time. We'll settle about your affairs afterward. Then he shall be put on probation for, say, a year—in our office. You can either coach him in his studies, for I am confident now that you will be up in yours hereafter, or he can attend night-school. And after that, if he comes through his period of probation with flying colours, I'll give him the same opportunities for an education that you possess. It all depends on himself. And now, Mr Attorney, what have you to say to my offer in the interests of your client?'

'That I close with it at once.'

Father and son shook hands.

'And what are you going to do now, Joe?'

'Send a telegram to 'Frisco Kid first, and then hurry home.'

'Then wait a minute till I call up San Andreas and tell Mr Tate the good news, and then I'll go with you.'

'Mr Willis,' Mr Bronson said as they left the outer office, 'the San Andreas safe is recovered, and we'll all take a holiday. Kindly tell the clerks that they are free for the rest of the day. And, I say,' he called back as they entered the elevator, 'don't forget the office-boy.'

THE ROAD

' Speakin' in general, I 'ave tried 'em all,
The 'appy roads that take you o'er the world.
Speakin' in general, I 'ave found them good
For such as cannot use one bed too long,
But must get 'ence, the same as I 'ave done,
An' go observin' matters till they die.'

Sestina of the Tramp-Royal

TO
JOSIAH FLYNT
THE REAL THING
BLOWED IN THE GLASS

CONTENTS

ROAD-KIDS AND GAY-CATS

EVERY ONCE in a while, in newspapers, magazines, and biographical dictionaries, I run upon sketches of my life, wherein, delicately phrased, I learn that it was in order to study sociology that I became a tramp. This is very nice and thoughtful of the biographers, but it is inaccurate. I became a tramp—well, because of the life that was in me, of the wander-lust in my blood that would not let me rest. Sociology was merely incidental; it came afterward, in the same manner that a wet skin follows a ducking. I went on 'The Road' because I couldn't keep away from it; because I hadn't the price of the railroad fare in my jeans; because I was so made that I couldn't work all my life on 'one same shift'; because—well, just because it was easier to than not to.

It happened in my own town, in Oakland, when I was sixteen. At that time I had attained a dizzy reputation in my chosen circle of adventurers, by whom I was kown as the Prince of the Oyster Pirates. It is true, those immediately outside my circle, such as honest bay-sailors, longshore-men, yachtsmen, and the legal owners of the oysters, called me 'tough', 'hoodlum', 'smoudge', 'thief', 'robber', and various other not nice things—all of which was complimentary and but served to increase the dizziness of the high place in which I sat. At that time I had not read *Paradise Lost*, and later, when I read Milton's *Better to reign in hell than serve in heaven*, I was fully convinced that great minds run in the same channels.

It was at this time that the fortuitous concatenation of events sent me upon my first adventure on The Road. It happened that there was nothing doing in oysters just then; that at Benicia, forty miles away, I had some blankets I wanted to get; and that at Port Costa, several miles from Benicia, a stolen boat lay at anchor in charge of the constable. Now this boat was owned by a friend of mine, by name Dinny McCrea. It had been stolen and left at Port Costa by Whiskey Bob, another friend of mine. (Poor Whiskey Bob! Only last winter his body was picked up on the beach shot full of holes by nobody knows whom.) I had come down from 'up river' some time before, and reported to Dinny McCrea the whereabouts of his boat; and Dinny McCrea had promptly offered ten dollars to me if I should bring it down to Oakland to him.

Time was heavy on my hands. I sat on the dock and talked it over with Nickey the Greek, another idle oyster pirate. 'Let's go,' said I, and Nickey was willing. He was 'broke'. I possessed fifty cents and a small skiff. The former I invested and loaded into the latter in the form of crackers, canned corned beef, and a ten-cent bottle of French mustard. (We were keen on French mustard in those days.) Then, late in the afternoon, we hoisted our small spritsail and started. We sailed all night, and next morning, on the first of a glorious flood-tide, a fair wind behind us, we came booming up the Carquinez Straits to Port Costa. There lay the stolen boat, not twenty-five feet from the wharf. We ran alongside and doused our little spritsail. I sent Nickey forward to lift the anchor, while I began casting off the gaskets.

A man ran out on the wharf and hailed us. It was the constable. It suddenly came to me that I had neglected to get a written authorization from Dinny McCrea to take possession of his boat. Also, I knew that constable wanted to charge at least twenty-five dollars in fees for capturing the boat from Whiskey Bob and subsequently taking care of it. And my last fifty cents had been blown in for corned beef and French mustard, and the reward was only ten dollars anyway. I shot a glance forward to Nickey. He had the anchor up-and-down and was straining at it. 'Break her out,' I whispered to him, and turned and shouted back to the constable. The result was that he and I were talking at the same time, our spoken thoughts colliding in mid-air and making gibberish.

The constable grew more imperative, and perforce I had to listen. Nickey was heaving on the anchor till I thought he'd burst a blood-vessel. When the constable got done with his threats and warnings, I asked him who he was. The time he lost in telling me enabled Nickey to break out the anchor. I was doing some quick calculating. At the feet of the constable a ladder ran down the dock to the water, and to the ladder was moored a skiff. The oars were in it. But it was padlocked. I gambled everything on that padlock. I felt the breeze on my cheek, saw the surge of the tide, looked at the remaining gaskets that confined the sail, ran my eyes up the halyards to the blocks and knew that all was clear, and then threw off all dissimulation.

'In with her!' I shouted to Nickey, and sprang to the gaskets, casting them loose and thanking my stars that Whiskey Bob had tied them in square-knots instead of 'grannies'.

The constable had slid down the ladder and was fumbling with a key at the padlock. The anchor came aboard and the last gasket was loosed at the same instant that the constable freed the skiff and jumped to the oars.

'Peak-halyards!' I commanded my crew, at the same time swinging on to the throat-halyards. Up came the sail on the run. I belayed and ran aft to the tiller.

'Stretch her!' I shouted to Nickey at the peak. The constable was just reaching for our stern. A puff of wind caught us, and we shot away. It was great. If I'd had a black flag, I know I'd have run it up in triumph. The constable stood up in the skiff, and paled the glory of the day with the vividness of his language. Also, he wailed for a gun. You see, that was another gamble we had taken.

Anyway, we weren't stealing the boat. It wasn't the constable's. We were merely stealing his fees, which was his particular form of graft. And we weren't stealing the fees for ourselves, either; we were stealing them for my friend, Dinny McCrea.

Benicia was made in a few minutes, and a few minutes later my blankets were aboard. I shifted the boat down to the far end of Steamboat Wharf, from which point of vantage we could see anybody coming after us. There was no telling. Maybe the Port Costa constable would telephone to the Benicia constable. Nickey and I held a council of war. We lay on deck in the warm sun, the fresh breeze on our cheeks, the flood-tide rippling and swirling past. It was impossible to start back to Oakland till afternoon, when the ebb would begin to run. But we figured that the constable would have an eye out on the Carquinez Straits when the ebb started, and that nothing remained for us but to wait for the following ebb, at two o'clock next morning, when we could slip by Cerberus in the darkness.

So we lay on deck, smoked cigarettes, and were glad that we were alive. I spat over the side and gauged the speed of the current.

'With this wind, we could run this flood clear to Rio Vista,' I said.

'And it's fruit-time on the river,' said Nickey.

'And low water on the river,' said I. 'It's the best time of the year to make Sacramento.'

We sat up and looked at each other. The glorious west wind was pouring over us like wine. We both spat over the side and gauged the current. Now I contend that it was all the fault of that flood-tide and fair wind. They appealed to our sailor instinct. If it had not been for them, the whole chain of events that was to put me upon The Road would have broken down.

We said no word, but cast off our moorings and hoisted sail. Our adventures up the Sacramento River are no part of this narrative. We subsequently made the city of Sacramento and tied up at a wharf. The water was fine, and we spent most of our time in swimming. On the sandbar above the railroad bridge we fell in with a bunch of boys likewise in swimming. Between swims we lay on the

bank and talked. They talked differently from the fellows
I had been used to herding with. It was a new vernacular.
They were road-kids, and with every word they uttered
the lure of The Road laid hold of me more imperiously.

'When I was down in Alabama,' one kid would begin;
or, another, 'Coming up on the C. & A. from K.C.'; whereat, a third kid, 'On the C. and A. there ain't no steps to the
"blinds".' And I would lie silently in the sand and listen.
'It was at a little town in Ohio on the Lake Shore and
Michigan Southern,' a kid would start; and another, 'Ever
ride the Cannon-ball on the Wabash?'; and yet another,
'Nope, but I've been on the White Mail out of Chicago.'
'Talk about railroadin'—wait till you hit the Pennsylvania,
four tracks, no water tanks, take water on the fly, that's
goin' some.' 'The Northern Pacific's a bad road now.'
'Salinas is on the "hog", the "bulls" is "horstile".' I got
"pinched" at El Paso, along with Moke Kid.' 'Talkin' of
"pokeouts", wait till you hit the French country out of
Montreal—not a word of English—you say, "*Mongee,
Madame, mongee, no spika da French*," an' rub your
stomach an' look hungry, an' she gives you a slice of
sow-belly an' a chunk of dry "punk".'

And I continued to lie in the sand and listen. These
wanderers made my oyster-piracy look like thirty cents. A
new world was calling to me in every word that was
spoken—a word of rods and gunnels, blind baggages and
'side-door Pullmans', 'bulls' and 'shacks', 'floppings', and
'chewin's', 'pinches' and 'get-aways', 'strong-arms' and
'bindle-stiffs', 'punks', and 'profesh'. And it all spelled
Adventure. Very well; I would tackle this new world. I
'lined' myself up alongside those road-kids. I was just as
strong as any of them, just as quick, just as nervy, and
my brain was just as good.

After the swim, as evening came on, they dressed and
went up town. I went along. The kids began 'battering'
the 'mainstem' for 'light pieces', or, in other words, begging for money on the main street. I had never begged in
my life, and this was the hardest thing for me to stomach

when I first went on The Road. I had absurd notions about begging. My philosophy, up to that time, was that it was finer to steal than to beg; and that robbery was finer still because the risk and the penalty were proportionately greater. As an oyster pirate I had already earned convictions at the hands of justice, which, if I had tried to serve them, would have required a thousand years in State's prison. To rob was manly; to beg was sordid and despicable. But I developed in the days to come all right, all right, till I came to look upon begging as a joyous prank, a game of wits, a nerve-exerciser.

That first night, however, I couldn't rise to it; and the result was that when the kids were ready to go to a restaurant and eat, I wasn't. I was broke. Meeny Kid, I think it was, gave me the price, and we all ate together. But while I ate, I meditated. The receiver, it was said, was as bad as the thief; Meeny Kid had done the begging, and I was profiting by it. I decided that the receiver was a whole lot worse than the thief, and that it shouldn't happen again. And it didn't. I turned out next day and threw my feet as well as the next one.

Nickey the Greek's ambition didn't run to The Road. He was not a success at throwing his feet, and he stowed away one night on a barge and went down river to San Francisco. I met him, only a week ago, at a pugilistic carnival. He has progressed. He sat in a place of honour at the ring-side. He is now a manager of prize-fighters and proud of it. In fact, in a small way, in local sportdom, he is quite a shining light.

'No kid is a road-kid until he has gone over "the hill"'— such was the law of The Road I heard expounded in Sacramento. All right, I'd go over the hill and matriculate. 'The hill', by the way, was the Sierra Nevadas. The whole gang was going over the hill on a jaunt, and of course I'd go along. It was French Kid's first adventure on The Road. He had just run away from his people in San Francisco. It was up to him and me to deliver the goods. In passing, I may remark that my old title of 'Prince' had vanished. I had received my 'monica'. I was now 'Sailor Kid', later to be known as "'Frisco Kid', when I had put the Rockies between me and my native state.

At 10.20 p.m. the Central Pacific overland pulled out of the depot at Sacramento for the East—that particular item of time-table is indelibly engraved on my memory. There were about a dozen in our gang, and we strung out in the darkness ahead of the train ready to take her out. All the local road-kids that we knew came down to see us off—also, to 'ditch' us if they could. That was their idea of a joke, and there were only about forty of them to carry it out. Their ring-leader was a crackerjack road-kid named Bob. Sacramento was his home town, but he'd hit The Road pretty well everywhere over the whole country. He took French Kid and me aside and gave us advice something like this: 'We're goin' to try an' ditch your bunch, see? Youse two are weak. The rest of the push can take care of itself. So, as soon as youse two nail a blind, deck her. An' stay on the decks till youse pass Roseville Junction, at which burgh the constables are horstile, sloughin' in everybody on sight.'

The engine whistled and the overland pulled out. There were three blinds on her—room for all of us. The dozen of us who were trying to make her out would have preferred to slip aboard quietly; but our forty friends crowded on with the most amazing and shameless publicity and advertisement. Following Bob's advice, I immediately 'decked her', that is, climbed up on the top of the roof of one of the mail-cars. There I lay down, my heart jumping a few extra beats, and listened to the fun. The whole train crew was forward, and the ditching went on fast and furious. After the train had run half a mile, it stopped, and the crew came forward again and ditched the survivors. I, alone, had made the train out.

Back at the depot, about him two or three of the push that had witnessed the accident, lay French Kid with both legs off. French Kid had slipped or stumbled—that was all, and the wheels had done the rest. Such was my initiation to The Road. It was two years afterward when I next saw French Kid and examined his 'stumps'. This was an act of courtesy. 'Cripples' always like to have their stumps examined. One of the entertaining sights on The Road is to witness the meeting of two cripples. Their common disability is a fruitful source of conversation; and they tell how it happened, describe what they know of the amputation, pass critical judgment on their own and each other's surgeons, and wind up by withdrawing to one side, taking off bandages and wrappings, and comparing stumps.

But it was not until several days later, over in Nevada, when the push caught up with me, that I learned of French Kid's accident. The push itself arrived in bad condition. It had gone through a train-wreck in the snow-sheds; Happy Joe was on crutches with two mashed legs, and the rest were nursing skins and bruises.

In the meantime, I lay on the roof of the mail-car, trying to remember whether Roseville Junction, against which burg Bob had warned me, was the first stop or the second stop. To make sure, I delayed descending to the platform of the blind until after the second stop. And then I didn't descend. I was new to the game, and I felt safer where I was. But I never told the push that I held down the decks the whole night, clear across the Sierras, through snow-sheds and tunnels, and down to Truckee on the other side, where I arrived at seven in the morning. Such a thing was disgraceful, and I'd have been a common laughing-stock. This is the first time I have confessed the truth about that first ride over the hill. As for the push, it decided that I was all right, and when I came back over the hill to Sacramento, I was a full-fledged road-kid.

Yet I had much to learn. Bob was my mentor, and he was all right. I remember one evening (it was fair-time in Sacramento, and we were knocking about and having a good time) when I lost my hat in a fight. There was I bare-headed in the street, and it was Bob to the rescue. He took me to one side from the push and told me what to do. I was a bit timid of his advice. I had just come out of jail, where I had been three days, and I knew that if the police 'pinched' me again, I'd get good and 'soaked'. On the other hand, I couldn't show the white feather. I'd been over the hill, I was running full-fledged with the push, and it was up to me to deliver the goods. So I accepted Bob's advice, and he came along with me to see that I did it up brown.

We took our position on K Street, on the corner, I think, of Fifth. It was early in the evening and the street was crowded. Bob studied the head-gear of every China-man that passed. I used to wonder how the road-kids all managed to wear 'five-dollar Stetson stiff-rims', and now I knew. They got them, the way I was going to get mine, from the Chinese. I was nervous—there were so many people about; but Bob was cool as an iceberg. Several times, when I started forward toward a Chinaman, all nerved and keyed up, Bob dragged me back. He wanted me to get a good hat, and one that fitted. Now a hat came by that was the right size but not new; and, after a dozen impossible hats, along would come one that was new but not the right size. And when one did come by that was new and the right size, the rim was too large or not large enough. My, Bob was finicky. I was so wrought up that I'd have snatched any kind of a head-covering.

At last came that hat, the one hat in Sacramento for me. I knew it was a winner as soon as I looked at it. I glanced at Bob. He sent a sweeping look-about for police, then nodded his head. I lifted the hat from the Chinaman's head and pulled it down on my own. It was a perfect fit. Then I started. I heard Bob crying out, and I caught a glimpse of him blocking the irate Mongolian and tripping him up. I ran on. I turned up the next corner, and around the next. This street was not so crowded as K, and I walked along in quietude, catching my breath and congratulating myself upon my hat and my get-away.

And then, suddenly, around the corner at my back, came the bare-headed Chinaman. With him were a couple more Chinamen, and at their heels were half a dozen men

II*

and boys. I sprinted to the next corner, crossed the street, and rounded the following corner. I decided that I had surely played him out, and I dropped into a walk again. But around the corner at my heels came that persistent Mongolian. It was the old story of the hare and the tortoise. He could not run so fast as I, but he stayed with it, plodding along at a shambling and deceptive trot, and wasting much good breath in noisy imprecations. He called all Sacramento to witness the dishonour that had been done him, and a goodly portion of Sacramento heard and flocked at his heels. And I ran on like the hare, and ever that persistent Mongolian, with the increasing rabble, overhauled me. But finally, when a policeman had joined his following, I let out all my links. I twisted and turned, and I swear I ran at least twenty blocks on the straight away. And I never saw that Chinaman again. The hat was a dandy, a brand-new Stetson, just out of the shop, and it was the envy of the whole push. Furthermore, it was the symbol that I had delivered the goods. I wore it for over a year.

Road-kids are nice little chaps—when you get them alone and they are telling you 'how it happened'; but take my word for it, watch out for them when they run in pack. Then they are wolves, and like wolves they are capable of dragging down the strongest man. At such times they are not cowardly. They will fling themselves upon a man and hold on with every ounce of strength in their wiry bodies, till he is thrown and helpless. More than once have I seen them do it, and I know whereof I speak. Their motive is usually robbery. And watch out for the 'strong arm'. Every kid in the push I travelled with was expert at it. Even French Kid mastered it before he lost his legs.

I have strong upon me now a vision of what I once saw in 'The Willows'. The Willows was a clump of trees in a waste piece of land near the railway depot and not more than five minutes walk from the heart of Sacramento. It is night-time, and the scene is illuminated by the thin light of stars. I see a husky labourer in the midst of a pack of road-kids. He is infuriated and cursing them, not a bit afraid, confident of his own strength. He weighs about one hundred and eighty pounds, and his muscles are hard; but he doesn't know what he is up against. The kids are snarling. It is not pretty. They make a rush from all sides, and he lashes out and whirls. Barber Kid is standing beside me. As the man whirls, Barber Kid leaps forward and does the trick. Into the man's back goes his knee; around the man's neck, from behind, passes his right hand, the bone of the wrist pressing against the jugular vein. Barber Kid throws his whole weight backward. It is a powerful leverage. Besides, the man's wind has been shut off. It is the strong arm.

The man resists, but he is already practically helpless. The road-kids are upon him from every side, clinging to arms and legs and body, and like a wolf at the throat of a moose Barber Kid hangs on and drags backward. Over the man goes, and down under the heap. Barber Kid changes the position of his own body, but never lets go. While some of the kids are 'going through' the victim, others are holding his legs so that he cannot kick and thresh about. They improve the opportunity by taking off the man's shoes. As for him, he has given in. He is beaten. Also, what of the strong arm at his throat, he is short of wind. He is making ugly choking noises, and the kids hurry. They really don't want to kill him. All is done. At a word all holds are released at once, and the kids scatter, one of them lugging the shoes—he knows where he can get half a dollar for them. The man sits up and looks about him, dazed and helpless. Even if he wanted to, bare-footed pursuit in the darkness would be hopeless. I linger a moment and watch him. He is feeling at his throat, making dry, hawking noises, and jerking his head in a quaint way as though to assure himself that the neck is not dislocated. Then I slip away to join the push, and see that man no more—though I shall always see him, sitting there in the starlight, somewhat dazed, a bit frightened, greatly dishevelled, and making quaint jerking movements of head and neck.

Drunken men are the especial prey of the road-kids. Robbing a drunken man they call 'rolling a stiff'; and wherever they are, they are on the constant lookout for drunks. The drunk is their particular meat, as the fly is the particular meat of the spider. The rolling of a stiff is oft-times an amusing sight, especially when the stiff is helpless and when interference is unlikely. At the first sweep the stiff's money and jewellery go. Then the kids sit around their victim in a sort of pow-wow. A kid generates a fancy for the stiff's necktie. Off it comes. Another kid is after underclothes. Off they come, and a knife quickly abbreviates arms and legs. Friendly hoboes may be called in to take the coat and trousers, which are too large for the kids. And in the end they depart, leaving beside the stiff the heap of their discarded rags.

Another vision comes to me. It is a dark night. My push is coming along the sidewalk in the suburbs. Ahead of us, under the electric light, a man crosses the street diagonally. There is something tentative and desultory in his walk. The kids scent the game on the instant. The man is drunk. He blunders across the opposite sidewalk and is lost in the darkness as he takes a short-cut through a vacant lot. No hunting cry is raised, but the pack flings itself forward in quick pursuit. In the middle of the vacant lot it comes upon him. But what is this?—snarling and strange forms, small and dim and menacing, are between the pack and its prey. It is another pack of road-kids, and in the hostile pause we learn that it is their meat, that they have been trailing it a dozen blocks and more and that we are butting in. But it is the world primeval. These wolves are baby wolves. (As a matter of fact, I don't think one of them was over twelve or thirteen years of age. I met some of them afterward, and learned that they had just arrived that day over the hill, and that they hailed from Denver and Salt Lake City.) Our pack flings forward. The baby wolves squeal and screech and fight like little demons. All about the drunken man rages the struggle for the possession of him. Down he goes in the thick of it, and the combat rages over his body after the fashion of the Greeks and Trojans over the body and armour of a fallen hero. Amid cries and tears and wailings the baby wolves are dispossessed, and my pack rolls the stiff. But always I remember the poor stiff and his befuddled amazement at the abrupt eruption of battle in the vacant lot. I see him now, dim in the darkness, titubating in stupid wonder, good-naturedly essaying the rôle of peacemaker in that multitudinous scrap the significance of which he did not understand, and the really hurt expression on his face when he, unoffending he, was clutched at by many hands and dragged down in the thick of the press.

'Bindle-stiffs' are favourite prey of the road-kids. A bindle-stiff is a working tramp. He takes his name from the roll of blankets he carries, which is known as a 'bindle'. Because he does work, a bindle-stiff is expected usually to have some small change about him, and it is after that small change that the road-kids go. The best hunting-ground for bindle-stiffs is in the sheds, barns, lumber-yards, railroad-yards, etc., on the edges of a city, and the time for hunting is the night, when the bindle-stiff seeks these places to roll up in his blankets and sleep.

'Gay-cats' also come to grief at the hands of the road-kids. In more familiar parlance, gay-cats are short-horns, *chechaquos*, new chums, or tenderfeet. A gay-cat is a newcomer on The Road who is man-grown, or, at least, youth-grown. A boy on The Road, on the other hand, no matter how green he is, is never a gay-cat; he is a road-kid or a 'punk', and if he travels with a 'profesh', he is known possessively as a 'prushun'. I was never a prushun, for I did not take kindly to possession. I was first a road-kid and then a profesh. Because I started in young, I practically skipped my gay-cat apprenticeship. For a short period, during the time I was exchanging my 'Frisco Kid monica for that of Sailor Jack, I laboured under the suspicion of being a gay-cat. But closer acquaintance on the part of those that suspected me quickly disabused their minds, and in a short time I acquired the unmistakable airs and ear-marks of the blowed-in-the-glass profesh. And be it known, here and now, that the profesh are the aristocracy of The Road. They are the lords and masters, the aggressive men, the primordial noblemen, the *blond beasts* so beloved of Nietzsche.

When I came back over the hill from Nevada, I found that some river pirate had stolen Dinny McCrea's boat. (A funny thing at this day is that I cannot remember what became of the skiff in which Nickey the Greek and I sailed from Oakland to Port Costa. I know that the constable didn't get it, and I know that it didn't go with us up the Sacramento River, and that is all I do know.) With the loss of Dinny McCrea's boat, I was pledged to The Road; and when I grew tired of Sacramento, I said good-bye to the push (which, in its friendly way, tried to ditch me from a freight as I left town) and started on a *passear* down the valley of the San Joaquin. The Road had gripped me and would not let me go; and later, when I had voyaged to sea and done one thing and another, I returned to The Road to make longer flights, to be a 'comet' and a profesh, and to plump into the bath of sociology that wet me to the skin.

CONFESSION

THERE IS a woman in the state of Nevada to whom I once lied continuously, consistently, and shamelessly, for the matter of a couple of hours. I don't want to apologize to her. Far be it from me. But I do want to explain. Unfortunately, I do not know her name, much less her present address. If her eyes should chance upon these lines, I hope she will write to me.

It was in Reno, Nevada, in the summer of 1892. Also,

it was fair-time, and the town was filled with petty crooks and tin-horns, to say nothing of a vast and hungry horde of hoboes. It was the hungry hoboes that made the town a 'hungry' town. They 'battered' the back doors of the homes of the citizens until the back doors became unresponsive.

A hard town for 'scoffings', was what the hoboes called it at that time. I know that I missed many a meal, in spite of the fact that I could 'throw my feet' with the next one when it came to 'slamming a gate' for a 'poke-out' or a 'set-down', or hitting for a 'light piece' on the street. Why, I was so hard put in that town, one day, that I gave the porter the slip and invaded the private car of some itinerant millionaire. The train started as I made the plat-form, and I headed for the aforesaid millionaire with the porter one jump behind and reaching for me. It was a dead heat, for I reached the millionaire at the same instant that the porter reached me. I had no time for formalities. 'Gimme a quarter to eat on,' I blurted out. And as I live, that millionaire dipped into his pocket and gave me ... just ... precisely ... a quarter. It is my conviction that he was so flabbergasted that he obeyed automatically, and it has been a matter of keen regret ever since, on my part, that I didn't ask him for a dollar. I know that I'd have got it. I swung off the platform of that private car with the porter manœuvring to kick me in the face. He missed me. One is at a terrible disadvantage when trying to swing off the lowest step of a car and not break his neck on the right of way, with, at the same time, an irate Ethiopian on the platform above trying to land him in the face with a number eleven. But I got the quarter! I got it!

But to return to the woman to whom I so shamelessly lied. It was in the evening of my last day in Reno. I had been out to the race-track watching the ponies run, and had missed my dinner (i.e. the mid-day meal). I was hungry, and, furthermore, a committee of public safety had just been organized to rid the town of just such hungry mor-tals as I. Already a lot of my brother hoboes had been gathered in by John Law, and I could hear the sunny valleys of California calling to me over the cold crests of the Sierras. Two acts remained for me to perform before I shook the dust of Reno from my feet. One was to catch the blind baggage on the west-bound overland that night. The other was first to get something to eat. Even youth will hesitate at an all-night ride, on an empty stomach, outside a train that is tearing the atmosphere through the snowsheds, tunnels, and eternal snows of heaven-aspiring mountains.

But that something to eat was a hard proposition. I was 'turned down' at a dozen houses. Sometimes I received insulting remarks and was informed of the barred domicile that should be mine if I had my just deserts. The worst of it was that such assertions were only too true. That was why I was pulling west that night. John Law was abroad in the town, seeking eagerly for the hungry and homeless, for by such was his barred domicile tenanted.

At other houses the doors were slammed in my face, cutting short my politely and humbly couched request for something to eat. At one house they did not open the door. I stood on the porch and knocked, and they looked out at me through the window. They even held one sturdy little boy aloft so that he could see, over the shoulders of his elders, the tramp who wasn't going to get anything to eat at their house.

It began to look as if I should be compelled to go to the very poor for my food. The very poor constitute the last sure recourse of the hungry tramp. The very poor can always be depended upon. They never turn away the hungry. Time and again, all over the United States, have I been refused food by the big house on the hill; and always have I received food from the little shack down by the creek or marsh, with its broken windows stuffed with rags and its tired-faced mother broken with labour. Oh, you charity-mongers! Go to the poor and learn, for the poor alone are the charitable. They neither give nor withhold from their excess. They have no excess. They give, and they withhold never, from what they need for themselves, and very often from what they cruelly need for themselves. A bone to the dog is not charity. Charity is the bone shared with the dog when you are just as hungry as the dog.

There was one house in particular where I was turned down that evening. The porch windows opened on the dining room, and through them I saw a man eating pie— a big meat-pie. I stood in the open door, and while he talked with me, he went on eating. He was prosperous, and out of his prosperity had been bred resentment against his less fortunate brothers.

He cut short my request for something to eat, snapping out, 'I don't believe you want to work'.

Now this was irrelevant. I hadn't said anything about work. The topic of conversation I had introduced was 'food'. In fact, I didn't want to work. I wanted to take the westbound overland that night.

'You wouldn't work if you had a chance,' he bullied.

I glanced at his meek-faced wife, and knew that but for the presence of this Cerberus I'd have a whack at that meat-pie myself. But Cerberus sopped himself in the pie, and I saw that I must placate him if I were to get a share of it. So I sighed to myself and accepted his work-morality.

'Of course I want work,' I bluffed.

'Don't believe it,' he snorted.

'Try me,' I answered, warming to the bluff.

'All right,' he said. 'Come to the corner of blank and blank street'—(I have forgotten the address)—'tomorrow morning. You know where that burned building is, and I'll put you to work tossing bricks.'

'All right, sir; I'll be there.'

He grunted and went on eating. I waited. After a couple of minutes he looked up with an I-thought-you-were-gone expression on his face, and demanded:—

'Well?'

'I . . . I am waiting for something to eat,' I said gently.

'I knew you wouldn't work!' he roared.

He was right, of course; but his conclusion must have

been reached by mind-reading, for his logic wouldn't bear it out. But the beggar at the door must be humble, so I accepted his logic as I had accepted his morality.

'You see, I am now hungry,' I said still gently. 'To-morrow morning I shall be hungrier. Think how hungry I shall be when I have tossed bricks all day without anything to eat. Now if you will give me something to eat, I'll be in great shape for those bricks.'

He gravely considered my plea, at the same time going on eating, while his wife nearly trembled into propitiatory speech, but refrained.

'I'll tell you what I'll do,' he said, between mouthfuls. 'You come to work tomorrow, and in the middle of the day I'll advance you enough for your dinner. That will show whether you are in earnest or not.'

'In the meantime——' I began; but he interrupted.

'If I gave you something to eat now, I'd never see you again. Oh, I know your kind. Look at me. I owe no man. I have never descended so low as to ask anyone for food. I have always earned my food. The trouble with you is that you are idle and dissolute. I can see it in your face. I have worked and been honest. I have made myself what I am. And you can do the same, if you work and are honest.'

'Like you?' I queried.

Alas, no ray of humour had even penetrated the sombre work-sodden soul of that man.

'Yes, like me,' he answered.

'All of us?' I queried.

'Yes, all of you,' he answered, conviction vibrating in his voice.

'But if we all became like you,' I said, 'allow me to point out that there'd be nobody to toss bricks for you.'

I swear there was a flicker of a smile in his wife's eye. As for him, he was aghast—but whether at the awful possibility of a reformed humanity that would not enable him to get anybody to toss bricks for him, or at my impudence, I shall never know.

'I'll not waste words on you,' he roared. 'Get out of here, you ungrateful whelp.'

I scraped my feet to advertise my intention of going, and queried:

'And I don't get anything to eat?'

He arose suddenly to his feet. He was a large man. I was a stranger in a strange land, and John Law was looking for me. I went away hurriedly. 'But why ungrateful?' I asked myself as I slammed his gate. 'What in the dickens did he give me to be ungrateful about?' I looked back. I could still see him through the window. He had returned to his pie.

By this time I had lost heart. I passed many houses by without venturing up to them. All houses looked alike, and none looked 'good'. After walking half a dozen blocks I shook off my despondency and gathered my 'nerve'. This begging for food was all a game, and if I didn't like the cards, I could always call for a new deal. I made up my mind to tackle the next house. I approached it in the deepening twilight, going around to the kitchen door.

I knocked softly, and when I saw the kind face of the middle-aged woman who answered, as by inspiration came to me the 'story' I was to tell. For know that upon his ability to tell a good story depends the success of the beggar. First of all, and on the instant, the beggar must 'size up' his victim. After that, he must tell a story that will appeal to the peculiar personality and temperament of that particular victim. And right here arises the great difficulty: in the instant that he is sizing up the victim he must begin his story. Not a minute is allowed for preparation. As in a lightning flash he must divine the nature of the victim and conceive a tale that will hit home. The successful hobo must be an artist. He must create spontaneously and instantaneously—and not upon a theme selected from the plenitude of his own imagination, but upon the theme he reads in the face of the person who opens the door, be it man, woman, or child, sweet or crabbed, generous or miserly, good-natured or cantankerous, Jew or Gentile, black or white, race-prejudiced or brotherly, provincial or universal, or whatever else it may be. I have often thought that to this training of my tramp days is due much of my success as a story-writer. In order to get the food whereby I lived, I was compelled to tell tales that rang true. At the back door, out of inexorable necessity, is developed the convincingness and sincerity laid down by all authorities on the art of the short story. Also, I quite believe it was my tramp-apprenticeship that made a realist out of me. Realism constitutes the only goods one can exchange at the kitchen door for grub.

After all, art is only consummate artfulness, and artfulness saves many a 'story'. I remember lying in a police station at Winnipeg, Manitoba. I was bound west over the Canadian Pacific. Of course, the police wanted my story, and I gave it to them—on the spur of the moment. They were landlubbers, in the heart of the continent, and what better story for them than a sea story? They could never trip me up on that. And so I told a fearful tale of my life on the hell ship *Glenmore*. (I had once seen the *Glenmore* lying at anchor in San Francisco Bay.)

I was an English apprentice, I said. And they said that I didn't talk like an English boy. It was up to me to create on the instant. I had been born and reared in the United States. On the death of my parents, I had been sent to England to my grandparents. It was they who had apprenticed me on the *Glenmore*. I hope the captain of the *Glenmore* will forgive me, for I gave him a character that night in the Winnipeg police station. Such cruelty! Such brutality! Such diabolical ingenuity of torture! It explained why I had deserted the *Glenmore* at Montreal.

But why was I in the middle of Canada going west, when my grandparents lived in England? Promptly I created a married sister who lived in California. She would take care of me. I developed at great length her loving nature. But they were not done with me, those hard-hearted policemen. I had joined the *Glenmore* in England; in the two years that had elapsed before my desertion at

Montreal, what had the *Glenmore* done and where had she been? And thereat I took those landlubbers around the world with me. Buffeted by pounding seas and stung with flying spray, they fought a typhoon with me off the coast of Japan. They loaded and unloaded cargo with me in all the ports of the Seven Seas. I took them to India, and Rangoon, and China, and had them hammer ice with me around the Horn and at last come to moorings at Montreal.

And then they said to wait a moment, and one policeman went forth into the night while I warmed myself at the stove, all the while racking my brains for the trap they were going to spring on me.

I groaned to myself when I saw him come in the door at the heels of the policeman. No gypsy prank had thrust those tiny hoops of gold through the ears; no prairie winds had beaten that skin into wrinkled leather; nor had snow-drift and mountain-slope put in his walk that reminiscent roll. And in those eyes, when they looked at me, I saw the unmistakable sunwash of the sea. Here was a theme, alas! with half a dozen policemen to watch me read—I who had never sailed the China seas, nor been around the Horn, nor looked with my eyes upon India and Rangoon.

I was desperate. Disaster stalked before me incarnate in the form of that gold-ear-ringed, weather-beaten son of the sea. Who was he? What was he? I must solve him ere he solved me. I must take a new orientation, or else those wicked policemen would orientate me to a cell, a police court, and more cells. If he questioned me first, before I knew how much he knew, I was lost.

But did I betray my desperate plight to those lynx-eyed guardians of the public welfare of Winnipeg? Not I. I met that aged sailorman glad-eyed and beaming, with all the simulated relief at deliverance that a drowning man would display on finding a life-preserver in his last despairing clutch. Here was a man who understood and who would verify my true story to the faces of those sleuth-hounds who did not understand, or, at least, such was what I endeavoured to play-act. I seized upon him; I volleyed him with questions about himself. Before my judges I would prove the character of my saviour before he saved me.

He was a kindly sailorman—an 'easy mark'. The policemen grew impatient while I questioned him. At last one of them told me to shut up. I shut up; but while I remained shut up, I was busy creating, busy sketching the scenario of the next act. I had learned enough to go on with. He was a Frenchman. He had sailed always on French merchant vessels, with the one exception of a voyage on a 'lime-juicer'. And last of all—blessed fact!—he had not been on the sea for twenty years.

The policeman urged him on to examine me.

'You called in at Rangoon?' he queried.

I nodded. 'We put our third mate ashore there. Fever.'

If he had asked me what kind of fever, I should have answered, 'Enteric', though for the life of me I didn't know what enteric was. But he didn't ask me. Instead, his next question was:

'And how is Rangoon?'

'All right. It rained a whole lot when we were there.'

'Did you get shore-leave?'

'Sure,' I answered. 'Three of us apprentices went ashore together.'

'Do you remember the temple?'

'Which temple?' I parried.

'The big one, at the top of the stairway.'

If I remembered that temple, I knew I'd have to describe it. The gulf yawned for me.

I shook my head.

'You can see it from all over the harbour,' he informed me. 'You don't need shore-leave to see that temple.'

I never loathed a temple so in my life. But I fixed that particular temple at Rangoon.

'You can't see it from the harbour,' I contradicted. 'You can't see it from the town. You can't see it from the top of the stairway. Because——' I paused for the effect. 'Because there isn't any temple there.'

'But I saw it with my own eyes' he cried.

'That was in ——?' I queried.

'Seventy-one.'

'It was destroyed in the great earthquake of 1887,' I explained. 'It was very old.'

There was a pause. He was busy reconstructing in his old eyes the youthful vision of that fair temple by the sea.

'The stairway is still there,' I aided him. 'You can see it from all over the harbour. And you remember that little island on the right-hand side coming into the harbour?' I guess there must have been one there (I was prepared to shift it over to the left-hand side), for he nodded. 'Gone,' I said. 'Seven fathoms of water there now.'

I had gained a moment for breath. While he pondered on time's changes, I prepared the finishing touches of my story.

'You remember the custom-house at Bombay?'

He remembered it.

'Burned to the ground,' I announced.

'Do you remember Jim Wan?' he came back at me.

'Dead,' I said; but who the devil Jim Wan was I hadn't the slightest idea.

I was on thin ice again.

'Do you remember Billy Harper, at Shanghai?' I queried back at him quickly.

That aged sailorman worked hard to recollect, but the Billy Harper of my imagination was beyond his faded memory.

'Of course you remember Billy Harper,' I insisted. 'Everybody knows him. He's been there forty years. Well, he's still there, that's all.'

And then the miracle happened. The sailorman remembered Billy Harper. Perhaps there was a Billy Harper, and perhaps he had been in Shanghai for forty years and was still there; but it was news to me.

For fully half-an-hour longer, the sailorman and I talked on in similar fashion. In the end he told the policemen that I was what I represented myself to be, and after a night's lodging and a breakfast I was released to wander on westward to my married sister in San Francisco.

But to return to the woman in Reno who opened her door to me in the deepening twilight. At the first glimpse of her kindly face I took my cue. I became a sweet, inno-cent, unfortunate lad. I couldn't speak. I opened my mouth and closed it again. Never in my life before had I asked anyone for food. My embarrassment was painful, extreme. I was ashamed. I, who looked upon begging as a delightful whimsicality, thumbed myself over into a true son of Mrs Grundy, burdened with all her bourgeois morality. Only the harsh pangs of the belly-need could compel me to do so degraded and ignoble a thing as beg for food. And into my face I strove to throw all the wan wistfulness of famished and ingenuous youth unused to mendicancy.

'You are hungry, my poor boy,' she said.

I had made her speak first.

I nodded my head and gulped.

'It is the first time I have ever . . . asked,' I faltered.

'Come right in.' The door swung open. 'We have already finished eating, but the fire is burning and I can get some-thing up for you.'

She looked at me closely when she got me into the light.

'I wish my boy were as healthy and strong as you,' she said. 'But he is not strong. He sometimes falls down. He just fell down this afternoon and hurt himself badly, the poor dear.'

She mothered him with her voice, with an ineffable tenderness in it that I yearned to appropriate. I glanced at him. He sat across the table, slender and pale, his head swathed in bandages. He did not move, but his eyes, bright in the lamplight, were fixed upon me in a steady and wondering stare.

'Just like my poor father,' I said. 'He had the falling sickness. Some kind of vertigo. It puzzled the doctors. They never could make out what was the matter with him.'

'He is dead?' she queried gently, setting before me half a dozen soft-boiled eggs.

'Dead,' I gulped. 'Two weeks ago. I was with him when it happened. We were crossing the street together. He fell right down. He was never conscious again. They carried him into a drug-store. He died there.'

And thereat I developed the pitiful tale of my father—how, after my mother's death, he and I had gone to San Francisco from the ranch; how his pension (he was an old soldier), and the little other money he had, was not enough; and how he had tried book-canvassing. Also, I narrated my own woes during the few days after his death that I had spent alone and forlorn on the streets of San Francisco. While that good woman warmed up biscuits, fried bacon, and cooked more eggs, and while I kept pace with her in taking care of all that she placed before me, I enlarged the picture of that poor orphan boy and filled in the details. I became that poor boy. I believed in him as I believed in the beautiful eggs I was devouring. I could have wept for myself. I know the tears did get into my voice at times. It was very effective.

In fact, with every touch I added to the picture, that kind soul gave me something also. She made up a lunch for me to carry away. She put in many boiled eggs, pepper and salt, and other things, and a big apple. She provided me with three pairs of thick red woollen socks. She gave me clean handkerchiefs and other things which I have since forgotten. And all the time she cooked more and more and I ate more and more. I gorged like a savage; but then it was a far cry across the Sierras on a blind baggage, and I knew not when nor where I should find my next meal. And all the while, like a death's-head at the feast, silent and motionless, her own unfortunate boy sat and stared at me across the table. I suppose I represented to him mystery, and romance, and adventure—all that was denied the feeble flicker of life that was in him. And yet I could not forbear, once or twice, from wondering if he saw through me down to the bottom of my mendacious heart.

'But where are you going to?' she asked me.

'Salt Lake City,' said I. 'I have a sister there—a married

sister.' (I debated if I should make a Mormon out of her, and decided against it.) 'Her husband is a plumber—a contracting plumber.'

Now I knew that contracting plumbers were usually credited with making lots of money. But I had spoken. It was up to me to qualify.

'They would have sent me the money for my fare if I had asked for it,' I explained, 'but they have had sickness and business troubles. His partner cheated him. And so I wouldn't write for the money. I knew I could make my way there somehow. I let them think I had enough to get me to Salt Lake City. She is lovely, and so kind. She was always kind to me. I guess I'll go into the shop and learn the trade. She has two daughters. They are younger than I. One is only a baby.'

Of all my married sisters that I have distributed among the cities of the United States, that Salt Lake sister is my favourite. She is quite real, too. When I tell about her, I can see her, and her two little girls, and her plumber husband. She is a large, motherly woman, just verging on beneficent stoutness—the kind, you know, that always cooks nice things and that never gets angry. She is a brunette. Her husband is a quiet, easy-going fellow. Sometimes I almost know him quite well. And who knows but some day I may meet him? If that aged sailorman could remember Billy Harper, I see no reason why I should not some day meet the husband of my sister who lives in Salt Lake City.

On the other hand, I have a feeling of certitude within me that I shall never meet in the flesh my many parents and grandparents—you see, I invariably killed them off. Heart disease was my favourite way of getting rid of my mother, though on occasion I did away with her by means of consumption, pneumonia, and typhoid fever. It is true, as the Winnipeg policemen will attest, that I have grandparents living in England; but that was a long time ago and it is a fair assumption that they are dead by now. At any rate, they have never written to me.

I hope that woman in Reno will read these lines and forgive me my gracelessness and unveracity. I do not apologize, for I am unashamed. It was youth, delight in life, zest for experience, that brought me to her door. It did me good. It taught me the intrinsic kindliness of human nature. I hope it did her good. Anyway, she may get a good laugh out of it now that she learns the real inwardness of the situation.

To her my story was 'true'. She believed in me and all my family, and she was filled with solicitude for the dangerous journey I must make ere I won to Salt Lake City. This solicitude nearly brought me to grief. Just as I was leaving, my arms full of lunch and my pockets bulging with fat woollen socks, she bethought herself of a nephew, or uncle, or relative of some sort, who was in the railway mail service, and who, moreover, would come through that night on the very train on which I was going to steal my ride. The very thing! She would take me down to the depot, tell him my story, and get him to hide me in the mail car. Thus, without danger or hardship, I would be carried straight through to Ogden. Salt Lake City was only a few miles farther on. My heart sank. She grew excited as she developed the plan and with my sinking heart I had to feign unbounded gladness and enthusiasm at this solution of my difficutlies.

Solution! Why, I was bound west that night, and here was I being trapped into going east. It was a *trap*, and I hadn't the heart to tell her that it was all a miserable lie. And while I made believe that I was delighted, I was busy cudgelling my brains for some way to escape. But there was no way. She would see me into the mail-car—she said so herself—and then that mail-clerk relative of hers would carry me to Ogden. And then I would have to beat my way back over all those hundreds of miles of desert.

But luck was with me that night. Just about the time she was getting ready to put on her bonnet and accompany me, she discovered that she had make a mistake. Her mail-clerk relative was not scheduled to come through that night. His run had been changed. He would not come through until two nights afterwards. I was saved, for of course my boundless youth would never permit me to wait those two days. I optimistically assured her that I'd get to Salt Lake City quicker if I started immediately, and I departed with her blessings and best wishes ringing in my ears.

But those woollen socks were great. I know. I wore a pair of them that night on the blind baggage of the overland, and that overland went west.

TWO THOUSAND STIFFS

A 'STIFF' is a tramp. It was once my fortune to travel a few weeks with a 'push' that numbered two thousand. This was known as 'Kelly's Army'. Across the wild and woolly West, clear from California, General Kelly and his heroes had captured trains; but they fell down when they crossed the Missouri and went up against the effete East. The East hadn't the slightest intention of giving free transportation to two thousand hoboes. Kelly's Army lay helplessly for some time at Council Bluffs. The day I joined it, made desperate by delay, it marched out to capture a train.

It was quite an imposing sight. General Kelly sat a magnificent black charger, and with waving banners, to the martial music of fife and drum corps, company by company, in two divisions, his two thousand stiffs countermarched before him and hit the wagon-road to the little burg of Weston, seven miles away. Being the latest recruit, I was in the last company, of the last regiment, of the Second Division, and, furthermore, in the last rank of the rear-guard. The army went into camp at Weston beside the railroad track—beside the tracks, rather, for two roads went through: the Chicago, Milwaukee, and St Paul, and the Rock Island.

Our intention was to take the first train out, but the railroad officials 'coppered' our play—and won. There was no first train. They tied up the two lines and stopped running trains. In the meantime, while we lay by the dead tracks, the good people of Omaha and Council Bluffs were bestirring themselves. Preparations were making to form a mob, capture a train in Council Bluffs, run it down to us, and make us a present of it. The railroad officials coppered that play, too. They didn't wait for the mob. Early in the morning of the second day, an engine, with a single private car attached, arrived at the station and side-tracked. At this sign that life had renewed in the dead roads, the whole army lined up beside the track.

But never did life renew so monstrously on a dead railroad as it did on those two roads. From the west came the whistle of a locomotive. It was coming in our direction, bound east. We were bound east. A stir of preparation ran down our ranks. The whistle tooted fast and furiously, and the train thundered at top speed. The hobo didn't live that could have boarded it. Another locomotive whistled, and another train came through at top speed, and another, and another, train after train, train after train, till toward the last the trains were composed of passenger coaches, box-cars, flat-cars, dead engines, cabooses, mail-cars, wrecking appliances, and all the riff-raff of worn-out and abandoned rolling-stock that collects in the yards of great railways. When the yards at Council Bluffs had been completely cleaned, the private car and engine went east, and the tracks died for keeps.

That day went by, and the next, and nothing moved, and in the meantime, pelted by sleet, and rain, and hail, the two thousand hoboes lay beside the track. But that night the good people of Council Bluffs went the railroad officials one better. A mob formed in Council Bluffs, crossed the river to Omaha, and there joined with another mob in a raid on the Union Pacific yards. First they captured an engine, next they knocked a train together, and then the united mobs piled aboard, crossed the Missouri, and ran down the Rock Island right of way to turn the train over to us. The railway officials tried to copper this play, but fell down, to the mortal terror of the section boss and one member of the section gang at Weston. This pair, under secret telegraphic orders, tried to wreck our train-load of sympathizers by tearing up the track. It happened that we were suspicious and had our patrols out. Caught red-handed at train-wrecking, and surrounded by twenty hundred infuriated hoboes, that section-gang boss and assistant prepared to meet death. I don't remember what saved them, unless it was the arrival of the train.

It was our turn to fall down, and we did, hard. In their haste, the two mobs had neglected to make up a sufficiently long train. There wasn't room for two thousand hoboes to ride. So the mobs and the hoboes had a talkfest, fraternized, sang songs, and parted, the mobs going back on their captured train to Omaha, the hoboes pulling out next morning on a hundred-and-forty-mile march to Des Moines. It was not until Kelly's Army crossed the Missouri that it began to walk, and after that it never rode again. It cost the railroads slathers of money, but they were acting on principle, and they won.

Underwood, Leola, Menden, Avoca, Walnut, Marno, Atlantic, Wyoto, Anita, Adair, Adam, Casey, Stuart, Dexter, Carlham, De Soto, Van Meter, Booneville, Commerce, Valley Junction—how the names of the towns come back to me as I con the map and trace our route through the fat Iowa country! And the hospitable Iowa farmer-folk! They turned out with their wagons and carried our baggage; gave us hot lunches at noon by the way side; mayors of comfortable little towns made speeches of welcome and hastened us on our way; deputations of little girls and maidens came out to meet us, and the good citizens turned out by hundreds, locked arms, and marched with us down their main streets. It was circus day when we came to town, and every day was circus day, for there were many towns.

In the evenings our camps were invaded by whole

populations. Every company had its camp-fire, and around each fire something was doing. The cooks in my company, Company L, were song-and-dance artists and contributed most of our entertainment. In another part of the encampment the glee club would be singing—one of its star voices was the 'Dentist', drawn from Company L, and we were mighty proud of him. Also, he pulled teeth for the whole army, and, since the extractions usually occurred at meal-time, our digestions were stimulated by variety of incident. The Dentist had no anæsthetics, but two or three of us were always on tap to volunteer to hold down the patient. In addition to the stunts of the companies and the glee club, church services were usually held, local preachers officiating, and always there was a great making of political speeches. All these things ran neck and neck; it was a full-blown Midway. A lot of talent can be dug out of two thousand hoboes. I remember we had a picked baseball nine, and on Sundays we made a practice of putting it all over the local nines. Sometimes we did it twice on Sundays.

Last year, while on a lecturing trip, I rode into Des Moines in a Pullman—I don't mean a 'side-door Pullman', but the real thing. On the outskirts of the city I saw the old stove-works, and my heart leaped. It was there, at the stove-works, a dozen years before, that the army lay down and swore a mighty oath that its feet were sore and that it would walk no more. We took possession of the stove-works and told Des Moines that we had come to stay—that we'd walked in, but we'd be blessed if we'd walk out. Des Moines was hospitable, but this was too much of a good thing. Do a little mental arithmetic, gentle reader. Two thousand hoboes, eating three square meals, make six thousand meals per day, forty-two thousand meals per week, or one hundred and sixty-eight thousand meals per shortest month in the calendar. That's going some. We had no money. It was up to Des Moines.

Des Moines was desperate. We lay in camp, made political speeches, held sacred concerts, pulled teeth, played baseball and seven-up, and ate our six thousand meals per day, and Des Moines paid for it. Des Moines pleaded with the railroads, but they were obdurate; they had said we shouldn't ride, and that settled it. To permit us to ride would be to establish a precedent, and there weren't going to be any precedents. And still we went on eating. That was the terrifying factor in the situation. We were bound for Washington, and Des Moines would have had to float municipal bonds to pay all our railroad fares, even at special rates, and if we remained much longer, she'd have to float bonds anyway to feed us.

Then some local genius solved the problem. We wouldn't walk. Very good. We should ride. From Des Moines to Keokuk on the Mississippi flowed the Des Moines River. This particular stretch of river was three hundred miles long. We could ride on it, said the local genius; and, once equipped with floating stock, we could ride on down the Mississippi to the Ohio, and thence up the Ohio, winding up with a short portage over the mountains to Washington.

Des Moines took up a subscripton. Public-spirited citizens contributed several thousand dollars. Lumber, rope, nails, and cotton for caulking were brought in large quantities, and on the banks of the Des Moines was inaugurated a tremendous era of shipbuilding. Now the Des Moines is a picayune stream, unduly dignified by the appellation of 'river'. In our spacious western land it would be called a 'creek'. The oldest inhabitants shook their heads and said we couldn't make it, that there wasn't enough water to float us. Des Moines didn't care, so long as it got rid of us, and we were such well-fed optimists that we didn't care either.

On Wednesday, May 9, 1894, we got under way and started on our colossal picnic. Des Moines had got off pretty easily, and she certainly owes a statue in bronze to the local genius who got her out of her difficulty. True, Des Moines had to pay for our boats; we had eaten sixty-six thousand meals at the stove-works; and we took twelve

thousand additional meals along with us in our commissary—as a precaution against famine in the wilds; but
then, think what it would have meant if we had remained
at Des Moines eleven months instead of eleven days. Also,
when we departed, we promised Des Moines we'd come
back if the river failed to float us.

It was all very well having twelve thousand meals in the
commissary, and no doubt the commissary 'ducks' enjoyed
them; for the commissary promptly got lost, and my boat,
for one, never saw it again. The company formation was
hopelessly broken up during the river-trip. In any camp
of men there will always be found a certain percentage
of shirks, of helpless, of just ordinary, and of hustlers.
There were ten men in my boat, and they were the cream
of Company L. Every man was a hustler. For two reasons
I was included in the ten. First, I was as good a hustler
as ever 'threw his feet', and next, I was 'Sailor Jack'. I
understood boats and boating. The ten of us forgot the
remaining forty men of Company L, and by the time we
had missed one meal we promptly forgot the commissary.
We were independent. We went down the river 'on our
own', hustling our 'chewin's', beating every boat in the
fleet, and, alas that I must say it, sometimes taking possession of the stores the farmer-folk had collected for the
Army.

For a good part of the three hundred miles we were
from half a day to a day or so in advance of the Army. We
had managed to get hold of several American flags. When
we approached a small town, or when we saw a group
of farmers gathered on the bank, we ran up our flags,
called ourselves the 'advance boat', and demanded to
know what provisions had been collected for the Army.
We represented the Army, of course, and the provisions
were turned over to us. But there wasn't anything small
about us. We never took more than we could get away
with. But we did take the cream of everything. For instance, if some philanthropic farmer had donated several
dollars' worth of tobacco, we took it. So, also, we took

butter and sugar, coffee and canned goods; but when the stores consisted of sacks of beans and flour, or two or three slaughtered steers, we resolutely refrained and went our way, leaving orders to turn such provisions over to the commissary boats whose business was to follow behind us.

My, but the ten of us did live on the fat of the land! For a long time General Kelly vainly tried to head us off. He sent two rowers, in a light, round-bottomed boat, to overtake us and put a stop to our piratical careers. They overtook us all right, but they were two and we were ten. They were empowered by General Kelly to make us prisoners, and they told us so. When we expressed disinclination to become prisoners, they hurried ahead to the next town to invoke the aid of the authorities. We went ashore immediately and cooked an early supper; and under the cloak of darkness we ran by the town and its authorities.

I kept a diary on part of the trip, and as I read it over now I note one persistently recurring phrase, namely, 'Living fine'. We did live fine. We even disdained to use coffee boiled in water. We made our coffee out of milk, calling the wonderful beverage, if I remember rightly, 'pale Vienna'.

While we were ahead, skimming the cream, and while the commissary was lost far behind, the main Army, coming along in the middle, starved. This was hard on the Army, I'll allow; but then, the ten of us were individualists. We had initiative and enterprise. We ardently believed that the grub was to the man who got there first, the pale Vienna to the strong. On one stretch the Army went forty-eight hours without grub; and then it arrived at a small village of some three hundred inhabitants, the name of which I do not remember, though I think it was Red Rock. This town, following the practice of all towns through which the Army passed, had appointed a committee of safety. Counting five to a family, Red Rock consisted of sixty households. Her committee of safety was scared stiff by the eruption of two thousand hungry hoboes who lined their boats two and three deep along the river bank. General Kelly was a fair man. He had no intention of working a hardship on the village. He did not expect sixty households to furnish two thousand meals. Besides, the Army had its treasure-chest.

But the committee of safety lost its head. 'No encouragement to the invader' was its programme, and when General Kelly wanted to buy food, the committee turned him down. It had nothing to sell; General Kelly's money was 'no good' in their burg. And then General Kelly went into action. The bugles blew. The Army left the boats and on top of the bank formed in battle array. The committee was there to see. General Kelly's speech was brief.

'Boys,' he said, 'when did you eat last?'

'Day before yesterday,' they shouted.

'Are you hungry?'

A mighty affirmation from two thousand throats shook the atmosphere. Then General Kelly turned to the committee of safety:

'You see, gentlemen, the situation. My men have eaten nothing in forty-eight hours. If I turn them loose upon your town, I'll not be responsible for what happens. They are desperate. I offered to buy food for them, but you refused to sell. I now withdraw my offer. Instead, I shall demand. I give you five minutes to decide. Either kill me six steers and give me four thousand rations, or I turn the men loose. Five minutes, gentlemen.'

The terrified committee of safety looked at the two thousand hungry hoboes and collapsed. It didn't wait the five minutes. It wasn't going to take any chances. The killing of the steers and the collecting of the requisition began forthwith, and the Army dined.

And still the ten graceless individualists soared along ahead and gathered in everything in sight. But General Kelly fixed us. He sent horsemen down each bank, warning farmers and townspeople against us. They did their work thoroughly, all right. The erstwhile hospitable farmers met us with the icy mit. Also, they summoned the constables when we tied up to the bank, and loosed the dogs. I know. Two of the latter caught me with a barbed wire fence between me and the river. I was carrying two buckets of milk for the pale Vienna. I didn't damage the fence any; but we drank plebian coffee boiled with vulgar water, and it was up to me to throw my feet for another pair of trousers. I wonder, gentle reader, if you ever essayed hastily to climb a barbed-wire fence with a bucket of milk in each hand. Ever since that day I have had a prejudice against barbed wire, and I have gathered statistics on the subject.

Unable to make an honest living so long as General Kelly kept his two horsemen ahead of us, we returned to the Army and raised a revolution. It was a small affair, but it devastated Company L of the Second Division. The Captain of Company L refused to recognize us; said we were deserters, and traitors, and scalawags; and when he drew rations for Company L from the commissary, he wouldn't give us any. That Captain didn't appreciate us, or he wouldn't have refused us grub. Promptly we intrigued with the first lieutenant. He joined us with the ten men in his boat, and in return we elected him captain of Company M. The captain of Company L raised a roar. Down upon us came General Kelly, Colonel Speed, and Colonel Baker. The twenty of us stood firm, and our revolution was ratified.

But we never bothered with the commissary. Our hustlers drew better rations from the farmers. Our new captain, however, doubted us. He never knew when he'd see the ten of us again, once we got under way in the morning, so he called in a blacksmith to clinch his captaincy. In the stern of our boat, one on each side, were driven two heavy eye-bolts of iron. Correspondingly, on the bow of his boat, were fastened two huge iron hooks. The boats were brought together, end on, the hooks dropped into the eye-bolts, and there we were, hard and fast. We couldn't lose that captain. But we were irrepressible. Out of our very manacles we wrought an invincible device that enabled us to put it all over every other boat in the fleet.

Like all great inventions, this one of ours was accidental. We discovered it the first time we ran on a snag in a bit of a rapid. The head-boat hung up and anchored, and the tail-boat swung around in the current, pivoting the head-boat on the snag. I was at the stern of the tail-boat, steering. In vain we tried to shove off. Then I ordered the men from the head-boat into the tail-boat. Immediately the head-boat floated clear, and its men returned into it. After that, snags, reefs, shoals, and bars had no terrors for us. The instant the head-boat struck, the men in it leaped into the tail-boat. Of course, the head-boat floated over the obstruction and the tail-boat then struck. Like automatons, the twenty men now in the tail-boat leaped into the head-boat, and the tail-boat floated past.

The boats used by the Army were all alike, made by the mile and sawed off. They were flat-boats, and their lines were rectangles. Each boat was six feet wide, ten feet long, and a foot and a half deep. Thus, when our two boats were hooked together, I sat at the stern steering a craft twenty feet long, containing twenty husky hoboes who 'spelled' each other at the oars and paddles, and loaded with blankets, cooking outfit, and our own private commissary.

Still we caused General Kelly trouble. He had called in his horsemen, and substituted three police-boats that travelled in the van and allowed no boats to pass them. The craft containing Company M crowded the police-boats hard. We could have passed them easily, but it was against the rules. So we kept a respectable distance astern and waited. Ahead we knew was virgin farming country, unbegged and generous; but we waited. White water was all we needed, and when we rounded a bend and a rapid showed up we knew what would happen. Smash! Police-boat number one goes on a boulder and hangs up. Bang! Police-boat number two follows suit. Whop! Police-boat number three encounters the common fate of all. Of course our boat does the same things; but one, two, the men are out of the head-boat and into the tail-boat; one, two, they are out of the tail-boat and into the head-boat; and one, two, the men who belong in the tail-boat are back in it and we are dashing on. 'Stop! you blankety-blank-blanks!' shriek the police-boats. 'How can we?—blank the blankety-blank river, anyway!' we wail plaintively as we surge past, caught in that remorseless current that sweeps us on out of sight and into the hospitable farmer-country that replenishes our private commissary with the cream of its contributions. Again we drink pale Vienna and realize that the grub is to the man who gets there.

Poor General Kelly! He devised another scheme. The whole fleet started ahead of us. Company M of the Second Division started in its proper place in the line, which was last. And it took us only one day to put the 'kibosh' on that particular scheme. Twenty-five miles of bad water lay before us—all rapids, shoals, bars, and boulders. It was over that stretch of water that the oldest inhabitants of Des Moines had shaken their heads. Nearly two hundred boats entered the bad water ahead of us, and they piled up in the most astounding manner. We went through that stranded fleet like hemlock through the fire. There was no avoiding the boulders, bars, and snags except by getting out on the bank. We didn't avoid them. We went right over them, one, two, one, two, head-boat, tail-boat, head-boat, tail-boat, all hands back and forth and back again. We camped that night alone, and loafed in camp all of the next day while the Army patched and repaired its wrecked boats and straggled up to us.

There was no stopping our cussedness. We rigged up a mast, piled on the canvas (blankets), and travelled short hours while the Army worked over-time to keep us in sight. Then General Kelly had recourse to diplomacy. No boat could touch us in the straight-away. Without discussion, we were the hottest bunch that ever came down the Des Moines. The ban of the police-boats was lifted. Colonel Speed was put aboard, and with this distinguished officer we had the honour of arriving first at Keokuk on the Mississippi. And right here I want to say to General Kelly and Colonel Speed that here's my hand. You were heroes, both of you, and you were men. And I'm sorry for at least ten per cent. of the trouble that was given you by the head-boat of Company M.

At Keokuk the whole fleet was lashed together in a huge raft, and, after being wind-bound a day, a steamboat took us in tow down the Mississippi to Quincy, Illinois, where we camped across the river on Goose Island. Here the raft idea was abandoned, the boats being joined together in groups of four and decked over. Somebody told me that Quincy was the richest town of its size in the United States. When I heard this, I was immediately overcome by an irresistible impulse to throw my feet. No 'blowed-in-the-glass profesh' could possibly pass up such a promising burg. I crossed the river to Quincy in a small dug-out; but I came back in a large river-boat, down to the gunwales with the results of my thrown feet. Of course I kept all the money I had collected, though I paid the boat-hire; also I took my pick of the underwear, socks, cast-off clothes, shirts, 'kicks', and 'sky-pieces'; and when Company M had taken all it wanted there was still a respectable heap that was turned over to Company L. Alas, I was young and prodigal in those days! I told a thousand 'stories' to the good people of Quincy, and every story was 'good'; but since I have come to write for the magazines I have often regretted the wealth of story, the fecundity of fiction, I lavished that day in Quincy, Illinois.

It was at Hannibal, Missouri, that the ten invincibles went to pieces. It was not planned. We just naturally flew apart. The Boiler-Maker and I deserted secretly. On the same day Scotty and Davy made a swift sneak for the Illinois shore; also McAvoy and Fish achieved their get-away. This accounts for six of the ten; what became of the remaining four I do not know. As a sample of life on The Road, I make the following quotation from my diary of the several days following my desertion:

'Friday, May 25th. Boiler-Maker and I left the camp on the island. We went ashore on the Illinois side in a skiff and walked six miles on the C. B. & Q. to Fell Creek. We had gone six miles out of our way, but we got on a hand-car and road six miles to Hull's, on the Wabash. While there, we met McAvoy, Fish, Scotty, and Davy, who had also pulled out from the Army.

'Saturday, May 26th. At 2.11 a.m. we caught the Cannon-ball as she slowed up at the crossing. Scotty and Davy were ditched. The four of us were ditched at the Bluffs, forty miles farther on. In the afternoon Fish and McAvoy caught a freight while Boiler-Maker and I were away getting something to eat.

'Sunday, May 27th. At 3.21 a.m. we caught the Cannon-ball and found Scotty and Davy on the blind. We were all ditched at daylight at Jacksonville. The C. & A. runs through here, and we're going to take that. Boiler-Maker went off, but didn't return. Guess he caught a freight.

'Monday, May 28th. Boiler-Maker didn't show up. Scotty and Davy went off to sleep somewhere, and didn't get back in time to catch the K.C. passenger at 3.30 a.m. I caught her and rode her till after sunrise to Masson City, 25,000 inhabitants. Caught a cattle train and rode all night.

'Tuesday, May 29th. Arrived in Chicago at 7 a.m. . . .'

And years afterwards, in China, I had the grief of learning that the device we employed to navigate the rapids of the Des Moines—the one-two-one-two, head-boat-tail-boat proposition—was not originated by us. I learned that the Chinese river-boatmen had for thousands of years used a similar device to negotiate 'bad water'. It is a good stunt all right, even if we don't get the credit. It answers Dr Jordan's test of truth: 'Will it work? Will you trust your life to it?'

PICTURES

' What do it matter where or 'ow we die,
    So long as we've our 'ealth to watch it all?'
        Sestina of the Tramp-Royal

PERHAPS THE greatest charm of tramp-life is the
absence of monotony. In Hobo Land the face of life is protean—an ever-changing phantasmagoria, where the impossible happens and the unexpected jumps out of the
bushes at every turn of the road. The hobo never knows
what is going to happen the next moment; hence he lives
only in the present moment. He has learned the futility of
telic endeavour, and knows the delight of drifting along
with the whimsicalities of Chance.

Often I think over my tramp days, and ever I marvel at
the swift succession of pictures that flash up in my
memory. It matters not where I begin to think; any day of
all the days is a day apart, with a record of swift-moving
pictures all its own. For instance, I remember a sunny
summer morning in Harrisburg, Pennsylvania, and immediately comes to my mind the auspicious beginning of
the day—a 'set-down' with two maiden ladies, and not in
their kitchen, but in their dining-room, with them beside
me at the table. We ate eggs, out of egg-cups! It was the
first time I had ever seen egg-cups, or heard of egg-cups!
I was a bit awkward at first, I'll confess; but I was hungry
and unabashed. I mastered the egg-cup, and I mastered
the eggs in a way that made those two maiden ladies sit up.

Why, they ate like a couple of canaries, dabbing with the
one egg each they took, and nibbling at tiny wafers of
toast. Life was low in their bodies; their blood ran thin;
and they had slept warm all night. I had been out all night,
consuming much fuel of my body to keep warm, beating
my way down from a place called Emporium, in the

12*

northern part of the State. Wafers of toast! Out of sight! But each wafer was no more than a mouthful to me—nay, no more than a bite. It is tedious to have to reach for another piece of toast each bite when one is potential with many bites.

When I was a very little lad, I had a very little dog called Punch. I saw to his feeding myself. Some one in the household had shot a lot of ducks, and we had a fine meat dinner. When I had finished, I prepared Punch's dinner— a large plateful of bones and tidbits. I went outside to give it to him. Now it happened that a visitor had ridden over from a neighbouring ranch, and with him had come a New-foundland dog as big as a calf. I set the plate on the ground. Punch wagged his tail and began. He had before him a blissful half-hour at least. There was a sudden rush. Punch was brushed aside like a straw in the path of a cyclone, and that Newfoundland swooped down upon the plate. In spite of his huge maw he must have been trained to quick lunches, for, in the fleeting instant before he received the kick in the ribs I aimed at him, he completely engulfed the contents of the plate. He swept it clean. One last lingering lick of his tongue removed even the grease stains.

As that big Newfoundland behaved at the plate of my dog Punch, so behaved I at the table of those two maiden ladies of Harrisburg. I swept it bare. I didn't break anything, but I cleaned out the eggs and the toast and the coffee. The servant brought more, but I kept her busy, and ever she brought more and more. The coffee was delicious, but it needn't have been served in such tiny cups. What time had I to eat when it took all my time to prepare the many cups of coffee for drinking?

At any rate, it gave my tongue time to wag. Those two maiden ladies, with their pink-and-white complexions and grey curls, had never looked upon the bright face of adventure. As the 'Tramp-Royal' would have it, they had worked all their lives 'on one same shift'. Into the sweet scents and narrow confines of their uneventful existence I brought the large airs of the world, freighted with the lusty smells of sweat and strife, and with the tangs and odours of strange lands and soils. And right well I scratched their soft palms with the callous on my own palms—the half-inch horn that comes of pull-and-haul of rope and long and arduous hours of caressing shovel-handles. This I did, not merely in the braggadocio of youth, but to prove, by toil performed, the claim I had upon their charity.

Ah, I can see them now, those dear, sweet ladies, just as I sat at their breakfast table twelve years ago, discoursing upon the way of my feet in the world, brushing aside their kindly counsel as a real devilish fellow should, and thrilling them, not alone with my own adventures, but with the adventures of all the other fellows with whom I had rubbed shoulders and exchanged confidences. I appropriated them all, the adventures of the other fellows, I mean; and if those maiden ladies had been less trustful and guileless, they could have tangled me up beautifully in my chronology. Well, well, and what of it? It was fair exchange. For their many cups of coffee, and eggs, and bites of toast, I gave full value. Right royally I gave them entertainment. My coming to sit at their table was their adventure, and adventure is beyond price anyway.

Coming along the street, after parting from the maiden ladies, I gathered in a newspaper from the doorway of some late-riser, and in a grassy park lay down to get in touch with the last twenty-four hours of the world. There, in the park, I met a fellow-hobo who told me his life-story and who wrestled with me to join the United States Army. He had given in to the recruiting officer and was just about to join, and he couldn't see why I shouldn't join with him. He had been a member of Coxey's Army in the march to Washington several months before, and that seemed to have given him a taste for army life. I, too, was a veteran, for had I not been a private in Company L of the Second Division of Kelly's Industrial Army? —said Company L being commonly known as the

'Nevada push'. But my army experience had had the opposite effect on me; so I left that hobo to go his way to the
dogs of war, while I 'threw my feet' for dinner.

This duty performed, I started to walk across the bridge
over the Susquehanna to the west shore. I forget the name
of the railroad that ran down that side, but while lying
in the grass in the morning the idea had come to me to go
to Baltimore; so to Baltimore I was going on that railroad,
whatever its name was. It was a warm afternoon, and part
way across the bridge I came to a lot of fellows who were
in swimming off one of the piers. Off went my clothes and
in went I. The water was fine; but when I came out and
dressed, I found I had been robbed. Someone had gone
through my clothes. Now I leave it to you if being robbed
isn't in itself adventure for one day. I have known men
who have been robbed and who have talked all the rest
of their lives about it. True, the thief that went through
my clothes didn't get much—some thirty or forty cents in
nickels and pennies, and my tobacco and cigarette papers;
but it was all I had, which is more than most men can
be robbed of, for they have something left at home, while I
had no home. It was a pretty tough gang in swimming
there. I sized up, and knew better than to squeal. So I
begged 'the makings', and I could have sworn it was one
of my own papers I rolled the tobacco in.

Then on across the bridge I hiked to the west shore.
Here ran the railroad I was after. No station was in
sight. How to catch a freight without walking to a
station was the problem. I noticed that the track came up
a steep grade, culminating at the point where I had tapped
it, and I knew that a heavy freight couldn't pull up there
any too lively. But how lively? On the opposite side of
the track rose a high bank. On the edge, at the top, I saw
a man's head sticking up from the grass. Perhaps he knew
how fast the freights took the grade, and when the next
one went south. I called out my questions to him, and he
motioned to me to come up.

I obeyed, and when I reached the top, I found four

other men lying in the grass with him. I took in the scene and knew them for what they were—American gypsies. In the open space that extended back among the trees from the edge of the bank were several nondescript wagons. Ragged, half-naked children swarmed over the camp, though I noticed that they took care not to come near and bother the men-folk. Several lean, unbeautiful, and toil-degraded women were pottering about with camp-chores, and one I noticed who sat by herself on the seat of one of the wagons, her head drooped forward, her knees drawn up to her chin and clasped limply by her arms. She did not look happy. She looked as if she did not care for anything—in this I was wrong, for later I was to learn that there was something for which she did care. The full measure of human suffering was in her face, and, in addition, there was the tragic expression of incapacity for further suffering. Nothing could hurt any more, was what her face seemed to portray; but in this, too, I was wrong.

I lay in the grass on the edge of the steep and talked with the men-folk. We were kin—brothers. I was the American hobo, and they were the American gypsy. I knew enough of their argot for conversation, and they knew enough of mine. There were two more in their gang, who were across the river 'mushing' in Harrisburg. A 'musher' is an itinerant fakir. This word is not to be confounded with the Klondike 'musher', though the origin of both terms may be the same; namely, the corruption of the French *marcher*, to march, to walk, to 'mush'. The particular graft of the two mushers who had crossed the river was umbrella-mending; but what real graft lay behind their umbrella-mending, I was not told, nor would it have been polite to ask.

It was a glorious day. Not a breath of wind was stirring, and we basked in the shimmering warmth of the sun. From everywhere arose the drowsy hum of insects, and the balmy air was filled with scents of the sweet earth and the green growing things. We were too lazy to do more than mumble on in intermittent conversation. And then, all abruptly, the peace and quietude was jarred awry by man.

Two bare-legged boys of eight or nine in some minor way broke some rule of the camp—what it was I did not know; and a man who lay beside me suddenly sat up and called to them. He was chief of the tribe, a man with narrow forehead and narrow-slitted eyes, whose thin lips and twisted sardonic features explained why the two boys jumped and tensed like startled deer at the sound of his voice. The alertness of fear was in their faces, and they turned, in a panic, to run. He called to them to come back, and one boy lagged behind reluctantly, his meagre little frame portraying in pantomime the struggle within him between fear and reason. He wanted to come back. His intelligence and past experience told him that to come back was a lesser evil than to run on; but lesser evil that it was, it was great enough to put wings to his fear and urge his feet to flight.

Still he lagged and struggled until he reached the shelter of the trees, where he halted. The chief of the tribe did not pursue. He sauntered over to a wagon and picked up a heavy whip. Then he came back to the centre of the open space and stood still. He did not speak. He made no gestures. He was the Law, pitiless and omnipotent. He merely stood there and waited. And I knew, and all knew, and the two boys in the shelter of the trees knew, for what he waited.

The boy who had lagged slowly came back. His face was stamped with quivering resolution. He did not falter. He had made up his mind to take his punishment. And mark you, the punishment was not for the original offence, but for the offence of running away. And in this, that tribal chieftain but behaved as behaves the exalted society in which he lived. We punish our criminals, and when they escape and run away, we bring them back and add to their punishment.

Straight up to the chief the boy came, halting at the

proper distance for the swing of the lash. The whip hissed through the air, and I caught myself with a start of surprise at the weight of the blow. The thin little leg was so very thin and little. The flesh showed white where the lash had curled and bitten, and then, where the white had shown, sprang up the savage welt, with here and there along its length little scarlet oozings where the skin had broken. Again the whip swung, and the boy's whole body winced in anticipation of the blow, though he did not move from the spot. His will held good. A second welt sprang up, and a third. It was not until the fourth landed that the boy screamed. Also, he could no longer stand still, and from then on, blow after blow, he danced up and down in his anguish, screaming; but he did not attempt to run away. If his involuntary dancing took him beyond the reach of the whip, he danced back into range again. And when it was all over—a dozen blows—he went away, whimpering and squealing, among the wagons.

The chief stood still and waited. The second boy came out from the trees. But he did not come straight. He came like a cringing dog, obsessed by little panics that made him turn and dart away for half a dozen steps. But always he turned and came back, circling nearer and nearer to the man, whimpering, making inarticulate animal-noises in his throat. I saw that he never looked at the man. His eyes always were fixed upon the whip, and in his eyes was a terror that made me sick—the frantic terror of an inconceivably maltreated child. I have seen strong men dropping right and left out of battle and squirming in their death-throes, I have seen them by scores blown into the air by bursting shells and their bodies torn asunder; believe me, the witnessing was as merrymaking and laughter and song to me in comparison with the way the sight of that poor child affected me.

The whipping began. The whipping of the first boy was as play compared with this one. In no time the blood was running down his thin little legs. He danced and squirmed and doubled up till it seemed almost that he was some grotesque marionette operated by strings. I say 'seemed', for his screaming gave the lie to the seeming and stamped it with reality. His shrieks were shrill and piercing; within them no hoarse notes, but only the thin sexlessness of the voice of a child. The time came when the boy could stand it no more. Reason fled, and he tried to run away. But now the man followed up, curbing his flight, herding him with blows back always into the open space.

Then came interruption. I heard a wild smothered cry. The woman who sat in the wagon seat had got out and was running to interfere. She sprang between the man and boy.

'You want some, eh?' said he with the whip. 'All right, then.'

He swung the whip upon her. Her skirts were long, so he did not try for her legs. He drove the lash for her face, which she shielded as best she could with her hands and forearms, drooping her head forward between her lean shoulders, and on the lean shoulders and arms receiving the blows. Heroic mother! She knew just what she was doing. The boy, still shrieking, was making his get-away to the wagons.

And all the while the four men lay beside me and watched and made no move. Nor did I move, and without shame I say it; though my reason was compelled to struggle hard against my natural impulse to rise up and interfere. I knew life. Of what use to the woman, or to me, would be my being beaten to death by five men there on the bank of the Susquehanna? I once saw a man hanged, and though my whole soul cried protest, my mouth cried not. Had it cried, I should most likely have had my skull crushed by the butt of a revolver, for it was the law that the man should hang. And here, in this gypsy group, it was the law that the woman should be whipped.

Even so, the reason in both cases that I did not interfere was not that it was the law, but that the law was stronger than I. Had it not been for those four men beside me in the grass, right gladly would I have waded into the man with the whip. And, barring the accident of the landing on me with a knife or a club in the hands of some of the various women of the camp, I am confident that I should have beaten him into a mess. But the four men *were* beside me in the grass. They made their law stronger than I.

Oh, believe me, I did my own suffering. I had seen women beaten before, often, but never had I seen such a beating as this. Her dress across the shoulders was cut into shreds. One blow that had passed her guard had raised a bloody welt from cheek to chin. Not one blow, nor two, not one dozen, not two dozen, but endlessly, infinitely, that whip-lash smote and curled about her. The sweat poured from me, and I breathed hard, clutching at the grass with my hands until I strained it out by the roots. And all the time my reason kept whispering, 'Fool! Fool!' That welt on the face nearly did for me. I started to rise to my feet; but the hand of the man next to me went to my shoulder and pressed me down.

'Easy, pardner, easy,' he warned me in a low voice. I looked at him. His eyes met mine unwaveringly. He was a large man, broad-shouldered and heavy-muscled; and his face was lazy, phlegmatic, slothful, withal kindly, yet without passion, and quite soulless—a dim soul, unmalicious, unmoral, bovine, and stubborn. Just an animal he was, with no more than a faint flickering of intelligence, a good-natured brute with the strength and mental calibre of a gorilla. His hand pressed heavily upon me, and I knew the weight of the muscles behind. I looked at the other brutes, two of them unperturbed and incurious, and one of them that gloated over the spectacle; and my reason came back to me, my muscles relaxed, and I sank down in the grass.

My mind went back to the two maiden ladies with whom I had had breakfast that morning. Less than two miles, as the crow flies, separated them from this scene. Here, in the windless day, under a beneficent sun, was a sister of theirs being beaten by a brother of mine. Here was a page of life they could never see—and better so, though for lack of seeing they would never be able to understand their sisterhood, nor themselves, nor know the clay of which they were made. For it is not given to woman to live in sweet-scented narrow rooms and at the same time be a little sister to all the world.

The whipping was finished, and the woman, no longer screaming, went back to her seat in the wagon. Nor did the other women come to her—just then. They were afraid. But they came afterward, when a decent interval had elapsed. The man put the whip away and rejoined us, flinging himself down on the other side of me. He was breathing hard from his exertions. He wiped the sweat from his eyes on his coat-sleeve, and looked challengingly at me. I returned his look carelessly; what he had done was no concern of mine. I did not go away abruptly. I lay there half an hour longer, which, under the circumstances, was tact and etiquette. I rolled cigarettes from tobacco I borrowed from them, and when I slipped down the bank to the railroad, I was equipped with the necessary information for catching the next freight bound south.

Well, and what of it? It was a page out of life, that's all; and there are many pages worse, far worse, that I have seen. I have sometimes held forth (facetiously, so my listeners believed) that the chief distinguishing trait between man and the other animals is that man is the only animal that maltreats the females of his kind. It is something of which no wolf nor cowardly coyote is ever guilty. It is something that even the dog, degenerated by domestication, will not do. The dog still retains the wild instinct in this matter, while man has lost most of his wild instincts—at least, most of the good ones.

Worse pages of life than what I have described? Read the reports on child labour in the United States,—east, west, north, and south, it doesn't matter where,—and know that all of us, profit-mongers that we are, are typesetters and printers of worse pages of life than that mere page of wife-beating on the Susquehanna.

I went down the grade a hundred yards to where the footing beside the track was good. Here I could catch my freight as it pulled slowly up the hill, and here I found half a dozen hoboes waiting for the same purpose. Several were playing seven-up with an old pack of cards. I took a hand. A coon began to shuffle the deck. He was fat, and young, and moon-faced. He beamed with good-nature. It fairly oozed from him. As he dealt the first card to me, he paused and said:

'Say, Bo, ain't I done seen you befo'?'

'You sure have,' I answered. 'An' you didn't have those same duds on, either.'

He was puzzled.

'D'ye remember Buffalo?' I queried.

Then he knew me, and with laughter and ejaculation hailed me as a comrade; for at Buffalo his clothes had been striped while he did his bit of time in the Erie County Penitentiary. For that matter, my clothes had been likewise striped, for I had been doing my bit of time, too.

The game proceeded, and I learned the stake for which we played. Down the bank toward the river descended a steep and narrow path that led to a spring some twenty-five feet beneath. We played on the edge of the bank. The man who was 'stuck' had to take a small condensed-milk can, and with it carry water to the winners.

The first game was played and the coon was stuck. He took the small milk-tin and climbed down the bank, while we sat above and guyed him. We drank like fish. Four round trips he had to make for me alone, and the others were equally lavish with their thirst. The path was very steep, and sometimes the coon slipped when part way up, spilled the water, and had to go back for more. But he didn't get angry. He laughed as heartily as any of us; that was why he slipped so often. Also, he assured us of the prodigious quantities of water he would drink when some one else got stuck.

When our thirst was quenched, another game was started. Again the coon was stuck, and again we drank our fill. A third game and a fourth ended the same way, and each time that moon-faced darky nearly died with delight at appreciation of the fate that Chance was dealing out to him. And we nearly died with him, what of our delight. We laughed like careless children, or gods, there on the edge of the bank. I know that I laughed till it seemed the top of my head would come off, and I drank from the milk-tin till I was nigh waterlogged. Serious discussion arose as to whether we could successfully board the freight when it pulled up the grade, what of the weight of water secreted on our persons. This particular phase of the situation just about finished the coon. He had to break off from water-carrying for at least five minutes while he lay down and rolled with laughter.

The lengthening shadows stretched farther and farther across the river, and the soft, cool twilight came on, and ever we drank water, and ever our ebony cup-bearer brought more and more. Forgotten was the beaten woman of the hour before. That was a page read and turned over; I was busy now with this new page, and when the engine whistled on the grade, this page would be finished and another begun; and so the book of life goes on, page after page and pages without end—when one is young.

And then we played a game in which the coon failed to be stuck. The victim was a lean and dyspeptic-looking hobo, the one who had laughed least of all of us. We said we didn't want any water—which was the truth. Not the wealth of Ormuz and of Ind, nor the pressure of a pneumatic ram, could have forced another drop into my saturated carcass. The coon looked disappointed, then rose to the occasion and guessed he'd have some. He meant it, too. He had some, and then some, and then some. Ever the melancholy hobo climbed down and up the steep bank, and ever the coon called for more. He drank more water than all the rest of us put together. The twilight deepened into night, the stars came out, and he still drank on. I do believe that if the whistle of the freight hadn't sounded, he'd be there yet, swilling water and revenge while the melancholy hobo toiled down and up.

But the whistle sounded. The page was done. We sprang to our feet and strung out alongside the track. There she came, coughing and spluttering up the grade, the head-light turning night into day and silhouetting us in sharp relief. The engine passed us, and we were all running with the train, some boarding on the side-ladders, others 'springing' the side-doors of empty box-cars and climbing in. I caught a flat-car loaded with mixed lumber and crawled away into a comfortable nook. I lay on my back with a newspaper under my head for a pillow. Above me the stars were winking and wheeling in squadrons back and forth as the train rounded the curves, and watching them I fell asleep. The day was done—one day of all my days. Tomorrow would be another day, and I was young.

BULLS

IF THE tramp were suddenly to pass away from the United States, widespread misery for many families would follow. The tramp enables thousands of men to earn honest liv-ings, educate their children, and bring them up God-fearing and industrious. I know. At one time my father was a constable and hunted tramps for a living. The com-munity paid him so much per head for all the tramps he could catch, and also, I believe, he got mileage fees. Ways and means was always a pressing problem in our house-hold, and the amount of meat on the table, the new pair of shoes, the day's outing, or the text-book for school, were dependent upon my father's luck in the chase. Well I remember the suppressed eagerness and the suspense with which I waited to learn each morning what the results of his past night's toil had been—how many tramps he had gathered in and what the chances were for convicting them. And so it was, when later, as a tramp, I succeeded in eluding some predatory constable, I could not but feel sorry for the little boys and girls at home in that constable's house; it seemed to me in a way that I was defrauding those little boys and girls of some of the good things of life.

But it's all in the game. The hobo defies society, and society's watch-dogs make a living out of him. Some hoboes like to be caught by the watch-dogs—especially in winter-time. Of course, such hoboes select communities where the jails are 'good', wherein no work is performed, and the food is substantial. Also, there have been, and most probably still are, constables who divide their fees with the hoboes they arrest. Such a constable does not have to hunt. He whistles, and the game comes right up to his hand. It is surprising, the money that is made out of stone-broke tramps. All through the South—at least when I was hoboing—are convict camps and plantations, where the time of convicted hoboes is bought by the farmers, and where the hoboes simply have to work. Then there are places like the quarries at Rutland, Vermont, where the hobo is exploited, the unearned energy in his body, which he has accumulated by 'battering on the drag' or 'slamming gates', being extracted for the benefit of that particular community.

Now I don't know anything about the quarries at Rutland, Vermont. I'm very glad that I don't, when I remember how near I was to getting into them. Tramps pass the word along, and I first heard of those quarries when I was in Indiana. But when I got into New England, I heard of them continually, and always with danger-signals flying. 'They want men in the quarries,' the passing hoboes said; 'and they never give a "stiff" less than ninety days.' By the time I got into New Hampshire I was pretty well keyed up over those quarries, and I fought shy of rail-road cops, 'bulls', and constables as I never had before.

One evening I went down to the railroad yards at Con-

cord and found a freight train made up and ready to start.
I located an empty box-car, slid open the side-door, and
climbed in. It was my hope to win across to White River
by morning; that would bring me into Vermont and not
more than a thousand miles from Rutland. But after that,
as I worked north, the distance between me and the point
of danger would begin to increase. In the car I found a
'gay-cat', who displayed unusual trepidation at my
entrance. He took me for a 'shack' (brakeman), and when
he learned I was only a stiff, he began talking about the
quarries at Rutland as the cause of the fright I had given
him. He was a young country fellow, and had beaten his
way only over local stretches of road.

The freight got under way, and we lay down in one end
of the box-car and went to sleep. Two or three hours afterward, at a stop, I was awakened by the noise of the right-
hand door being softly slid open. The gay-cat slept on. I
made no movement, though I veiled my eyes with my
lashes to a little slit through which I could see out. A
lantern was thrust in through the doorway, followed by the
head of a shack. He discovered us, and looked at us for a
moment. I was prepared for a violent expression on his
part, or the customary 'Hit the grit, you son of a toad!'
Instead of this he cautiously withdrew the lantern and
very, very softly slid the door to. This struck me as
eminently unusual and suspicious. I listened, and softly
I heard the hasp drop into place. The door was latched on
the outside. We could not open it from the inside. One way
of sudden exit from that car was blocked. It would never
do. I waited a few seconds, then crept to the left-hand
door and tried it. It was not yet latched. I opened it,
dropped to the ground, and closed it behind me. Then I
passed across the bumpers to the other side of the train. I
opened the door the shack had latched, climbed in, and
closed it behind me. Both exits were available again. The
gay-cat was still asleep.

The train got under way. It came to the next stop. I
heard footsteps in the gravel. Then the left-hand door

was thrown open noisily. The gay-cat awoke, I made believe to awake; and we sat up and stared at the shack and his lantern. He didn't waste any time getting down to business.

'I want three dollars,' he said.

We got on our feet and came nearer to him to confer. We expressed an absolute and devoted willingness to give him three dollars, but explained our wretched luck that compelled our desire to remain unsatisfied. The shack was incredulous. He dickered with us. He would compromise for two dollars. We regretted our condition of poverty. He said uncomplimentary things, called us sons of toads, and damned us from hell to breakfast. Then he threatened. He explained that if we didn't dig up, he'd lock us in and carry us on to White River and turn us over to the authorities. He also explained all about the quarries at Rutland.

Now that shack thought he had us dead to rights. Was not he guarding the one door, and had he not himself latched the opposite door but a few minutes before? When he began talking about quarries, the frightened gay-cat started to sidle across to the other door. The shack laughed loud and long. 'Don't be in a hurry,' he said; 'I locked that door on the outside at the last stop.' So implicitly did he believe the door to be locked that his words carried conviction. The gay-cat believed and was in despair.

The shack delivered his ultimatum. Either we should dig up two dollars, or he would lock us in and turn us over to the constable at White River—and that meant ninety days and the quarries. Now, gentle reader, just suppose that the other door had been locked. Behold the precariousness of human life. For lack of a dollar, I'd have gone to the quarries and served three months as a convict slave. So would the gay-cat. Count me out, for I was hopeless; but consider the gay-cat. He might have come out, after those ninety days, pledged to a life of crime. And later he might have broken your skull, even your skull, with a blackjack in an endeavour to take possession of the money on your person—and if not your skull, then some other poor and unoffending creature's skull.

But the door was unlocked, and I alone knew it. The gay-cat and I begged for mercy. I joined in the pleading and wailing out of sheer cussedness, I suppose. But I did my best. I told a 'story' that would have melted the heart of any mug; but it didn't melt the heart of that sordid money-grasper of a shack. When he became convinced that we didn't have any money, he slid the door shut and latched it, then lingered a moment on the chance that we had fooled him and that we would now offer him the two dollars.

Then it was that I let out a few links. I called *him* a son of a toad. I called him all the other things he had called me. And then I called him a few additional things. I came from the West, where men knew how to swear, and I wasn't going to let any mangy shack on a measly New England 'jerk' put it over me in vividness and vigour of language. At first the shack tried to laugh it down. Then he made the mistake of attempting to reply. I let out a few more links, and I cut him to the raw and therein rubbed winged and flaming epithets. Nor was my fine frenzy all whim and literary; I was indignant at this vile creature, who, in default of a dollar, would consign me to three months of slavery. Furthermore, I had a sneaking idea that he got a 'drag' out of the constable fees.

But I fixed him. I lacerated his feelings and pride several dollars' worth. He tried to scare me by threatening to come in after me and kick the stuffing out of me. In return, I promised to kick him in the face while he was climbing in. The advantage of position was with me, and he saw it. So he kept the door shut and called for help from the rest of the train crew. I could hear them answering and crunching through the gravel to him. And all the time the other door was unlatched, and they didn't know it; and in the meantime the gay-cat was ready to die with fear.

Oh, I was a hero—with my line of retreat straight

behind me. I slanged the shack and his mates till they threw the door open and I could see their infuriated faces in the shine of the lanterns. It was all very simple to them. They had us cornered in the car, and they were going to come in and man-handle us. They started. I didn't kick anybody in the face. I jerked the opposite door open, and the gay-cat and I went out. The train-crew took after us.

We went over—if I can remember correctly—a stone fence. But I have no doubts of recollection about where we found ourselves. In the darkness I promptly fell over a grave-stone. The gay-cat sprawled over another. And then we got the chase of our lives through that graveyard. The ghosts must have thought we were going some. So did the train-crew, for when we emerged from the graveyard and plunged across a road into a dark wood, the shacks gave up the pursuit and went back to their train. A little later that night the gay-cat and I found ourselves at the well of a farmhouse. We were after a drink of water, but we noticed a small rope that ran down one side of the well. We hauled it up and found on the end of it a gallon-can of cream. And that is as near as I got to the quarries of Rutland, Vermont.

When the hoboes pass the word along, concerning a town, that 'the bulls is horstile', avoid that town, or, if you must, go through softly. There are some towns that one must always go through softly. Such a town was Cheyenne, on the Union Pacific. It had a national reputation for being 'horstile',—and it was all due to the efforts of one Jeff Carr (if I remember his name aright). Jeff Carr could size up the 'front' of a hobo on the instant. He never entered into discussion. In the one moment he sized up the hobo, and in the next he struck out with both fists, a club, or anything else he had handy. After he had man-handled the hobo, he started him out of town with a promise of worse if he ever saw him again. Jeff Carr knew the game. North, south, east, and west to the uttermost confines of the United States (Canada and Mexico included), the man-handled hoboes carried the word that Cheyenne was 'horstile'. Fortunately, I never encountered Jeff Carr. I passed through Cheyenne in a blizzard. There were eighty-four hoboes with me at the time. The strength of numbers made us pretty nonchalant on most things, but not on Jeff Carr. The connotation of 'Jeff Carr' stunned our imagination, numbed our virility, and the whole gang was mortally scared of meeting him.

It rarely pays to stop and enter into explanations with bulls when they look 'horstile'. A swift get-away is the thing to do. It took me some time to learn this; but the finishing touch was put upon me by a bull in New York City. Ever since that time it has been an automatic process with me to make a run for it when I see a bull reaching for me. This automatic process has become a mainspring of conduct in me, wound up and ready for instant release. I shall never get over it. Should I be eighty years old, hobbling along the street on crutches, and should a policeman suddenly reach out for me, I know I'd drop the crutches and run like a deer.

The finishing touch to my education in bulls was received on a hot summer afternoon in New York City. It was during a week of scorching weather. I had got into the habit of throwing my feet in the morning, and of spending the afternoon in the little park that is hard by Newspaper Row and the City Hall. It was near there that I could buy from push-cart men current books (that had been injured in the making or binding) for a few cents each. Then, right in the park itself, were little booths where one could buy glorious, ice-cold, sterilized milk and buttermilk at a penny a glass. Every afternoon I sat on a bench and read, and went on a milk debauch. I got away with from five to ten glasses each afternoon. It was dreadfully hot weather.

So here I was, a meek and studious milk-drinking hobo, and behold what I got for it. One afternoon I arrived at the park, a fresh book-purchase under my arm and a tremendous buttermilk thirst under my shirt. In the middle of the street, in front of the City Hall, I noticed, as I came along heading for the buttermilk booth, that a crowd had formed. It was right where I was crossing the street, so I stopped to see the cause of the collection of curious men. At first I could see nothing. Then, from the sounds I heard and from a glimpse I caught, I knew that it was a bunch of gamins playing pee-wee. Now pee-wee is not permitted in the streets of New York. I didn't know that, but I learned pretty lively. I had paused possibly thirty seconds, in which time I had learned the cause of the crowd, when I head a gamin yell 'Bull!' The gamins knew their business. They ran. I didn't.

The crowd broke up immediately and started for the sidewalk on both sides of the street. I started for the sidewalk on the park-side. There must have been fifty men, who had been in the original crowd, who were heading in the same direction. We were loosely strung out. I noticed the bull, a strapping policeman in a grey suit. He was coming along the middle of the street, without haste, merely sauntering. I noticed casually that he changed his course, and was heading obliquely for the same sidewalk that I was heading for directly. He sauntered along, threading the strung-out crowd, and I noticed that his course and mine would cross each other. I was so innocent of wrong-doing that, in spite of my education in bulls and their ways, I apprehended nothing. I never dreamed that bull was after me. Out of my respect for the law I was actually all ready to pause the next moment and let him cross in front of me. The pause came all right, but it was not of my volition; also it was a backward pause. Without warning, that bull had suddenly launched out at me on the chest with both hands. At the same moment, verbally, he cast the bar sinister on my genealogy.

All my free American blood boiled. All my liberty-loving ancestors clamoured in me. 'What do you mean?' I demanded. You see, I wanted an explanation. And I got it. Bang! His club came down on top of my head, and I was reeling backward like a drunken man, the curious faces of the onlookers billowing up and down like the waves of the sea, my precious book falling from under my arm into the dirt, the bull advancing with the club ready for another blow. And in that dizzy moment I had a vision. I saw that club descending many times upon my head; I saw myself, bloody and battered and hard-looking, in a police-court; I heard a charge of disorderly conduct, profane language, resisting an officer, and a few other things, read by a clerk; and I saw myself across in Blackwell's Island. Oh, I knew the game. I lost all interest in explanations. I didn't stop to pick up my precious, unread book. I turned and ran. I was pretty sick, but I ran. And run I shall, to my dying day, whenever a bull begins to explain with a club.

Why, years after my tramping days, when I was a student in the University of California, one night I went to the circus. After the show and the concert I lingered on to watch the working of the transportation machinery of a great circus. The circus was leaving that night. By a bonfire I came upon a bunch of small boys. There were about twenty of them, and as they talked with one another I learned that they were going to run away with the circus. Now the circus-men didn't want to be bothered with this mess of urchins, and a telephone to police headquarters had 'coppered' the play. A squad of ten policemen had been dispatched to the scene to arrest the small boys for violating the nine o'clock curfew ordinance. The policemen surrounded the bonfire, and crept up close to it in the darkness. At the signal, they made a rush, each policeman grabbing at the youngsters as he would grab into a basket of squirming eels.

Now I didn't know anything about the coming of the police; and when I saw the sudden eruption of brass-buttoned, helmeted bulls, each of them reaching with both hands, all the forces and stability of my being were overthrown. Remained only the automatic process to run. And I ran. I didn't know I was running. I didn't know anything. It was, as I have said, automatic. There was no reason for me to run. I was not a hobo. I was a citizen of that community. It was my home town. I was guilty of no wrong-doing. I was a college man. I had even got my name in the papers, and I wore good clothes that had never been slept in. And yet I ran—blindly, madly, like a startled deer, for over a block. And when I came to myself, I noted that I was still running. It required a positive effort of will to stop those legs of mine.

No, I'll never get over it. I can't help it. When a bull reaches, I run. Besides, I have an unhappy faculty for getting into jail. I have been in jail more times since I was a hobo than when I was one. I start out on a Sunday morning with a young lady on bicycle ride. Before we can get outside the city limits we are arrested for passing a pedestrian on the sidewalk. I resolve to be more careful. The next time I am on a bicycle it is night-time and my acetylene-gas-lamp is misbehaving. I cherish the sickly flame carefully, because of the ordinance. I am in a hurry, but I ride at a snail's pace so as not to jar out the flickering flame. I reach the city limits; I am beyond the jurisdiction of the ordinance; and I proceed to scorch to make up for lost time. And half a mile farther on I am 'pinched' by a bull, and the next morning I forfeit my bail in the police court. The city had treacherously extended its limits into a mile of the country, and I didn't know, that was all. I remember my inalienable right of free speech and peaceable assemblage, and I get up on a soap-box to trot out the particular economic bees that buzz in my bonnet, and a bull takes me off that box and leads me to the city prison, and after that I get out on bail. It's no use. In Korea I used to be arrested about every other day. It was the same thing in Manchuria. The last time I was in Japan I broke into jail under the pretext of being a Russian spy. It wasn't my pretext, but it got me into jail just the same. There is no hope for me. I am fated to do the Prisoner-of-Chillon stunt yet. This is prophecy.

I once hypnotized a bull on Boston Common. It was past midnight and he had me dead to rights; but before I got done with him he had ponied up a silver quarter and given me the address of an all-night restaurant. Then there was a bull in Bristol, New Jersey, who caught me and let me go, and heaven knows he had provocation enough to put me in jail. I hit him the hardest I'll wager he was ever hit in his life. It happened this way. About midnight I nailed a freight out of Philadelphia. The shacks ditched me. She was pulling out slowly through the maze of tracks and switches of the freight-yards. I nailed her again, and again I was ditched. You see, I had to nail her 'outside', for she was a through freight with every door locked and sealed.

The second time I was ditched the shack gave me a lecture. He told me I was risking my life, that it was a fast freight and that she went some. I told him I was used to going some myself, but it was no go. He said he wouldn't permit me to commit suicide, and I hit the grit. But I nailed her a third time, getting in between on the bumpers. They were the most meagre bumpers I had ever seen—I do not refer to the real bumpers, the iron bumpers that are connected by the coupling-link and that pound and grind on each other; what I refer to are the beams, like huge cleats, that cross the ends of freight cars just above the bumpers. When one rides the bumpers, he stands on these cleats, one foot on each, the bumpers between his feet and just beneath.

But the beams or cleats I found myself on were not the broad, generous ones that at that time were usually on box-cars. On the contrary, they were very narrow—not more than an inch and a half in breadth. I couldn't get half of the width of my sole on them. Then there was nothing to which to hold with my hands. True, there were the ends of the two box-cars; but those ends were flat, perpendicular surfaces. There were no grips. I could only press the flats of my palms against the car-ends for support. But that would have been all right if the cleats for my feet had been decently wide.

As the freight got out of Philadelphia she began to hit up speed. Then I understood what the shack had meant by suicide. The freight went faster and faster. She was a through freight, and there was nothing to stop her. On that section of the Pennsylvania four tracks run side by side, and my east-bound freight didn't need to worry about passing west-bound freights, nor about being overtaken by east-bound expresses. She had the track to herself, and she used it. I was in a precarious situation. I stood with the mere edges of my feet on the narrow projections, the palms of my hands pressing desperately against the flat, perpendicular ends of each car. And those cars moved, and moved individually, up and down and back and forth. Did you ever see a circus rider, standing on two running horses, with one foot on the back of each horse? Well, that was what I was doing, with several differences. The circus rider had the reins to hold on to, while I had nothing; he stood on the broad soles of his feet, while I stood on the edges of mine; he bent his legs and body, gaining the strength of the arch in his posture and achieving the stability of a low centre of gravity, while I was compelled to stand upright and keep my legs straight; he rode face forward, while I was riding sideways; and also, if he fell off, he'd get only a roll in the sawdust, while I'd have been ground to pieces beneath the wheels.

And that freight was certainly going some, roaring and shrieking, swinging madly around curves, thundering over trestles, one car-end bumping up when the other was jarring down, or jerking to the right at the same moment the other was lurching to the left, and with me all the while praying and hoping for the train to stop. But she didn't stop. She didn't have to. For the first, last, and only time on The Road, I got all I wanted. I abandoned the bumpers and managed to get out on a side-ladder; it was ticklish work, for I had never encountered car-ends that were so parsimonious of hand-holds and foot-holds as those car-ends were.

I heard the engine whistling, and I felt the speed easing down. I knew the train wasn't going to stop, but my mind was made up to chance it if she slowed down sufficiently. The right of way at this point took a curve, crossed a bridge over a canal, and cut through the town of Bristol. This combination compelled slow speed. I clung on to the side-ladder and waited. I didn't know it was the town of Bristol we were approaching. I did not know what necessitated slackening in speed. All I knew was that I wanted to get off. I strained my eyes in the darkness for a street-crossing on which to land. I was pretty well down the train, and before my car was in the town the engine was past the station and I could feel her making speed again.

Then came the street. It was too dark to see how wide it was or what was on the other side. I knew I needed all of that street if I was to remain on my feet after I struck. I dropped off on the near side. It sounds easy. By 'dropped off' I mean just this: I first of all, on the side-ladder, thrust my body forward as far as I could in the direction the train was going—this to give as much space as possible in which to gain backward momentum when I swung off. Then I swung, swung out and backward, backward with all my might, and let go—at the same time throwing myself backward as if I intended to strike the ground on the back of my head. The whole effort was to overcome as much as possible the primary forward momentum the train had imparted to my body. When my feet hit the grit, my body was lying backward on the air at an angle of forty-five degrees. I had reduced the forward momentum some, for when my feet struck, I did not immediately pitch forward on my face. Instead, my body rose to the perpendicular and began to incline forward. In point of fact, my body proper still retained such momentum, while my feet, through contact with the earth, had lost all their momentum. This momentum the feet had lost I had to supply anew by lifting them as rapidly as I could and running them forward in order to keep them under my forward-moving body. The result was that my feet beat a rapid and explosive tattoo clear across the street. I didn't dare stop them. If I had, I'd have pitched forward. It was up to me to keep on going.

I was an involuntary projectile, worrying about what was on the other side of the street and hoping that it wouldn't be a stone wall or a telegraph pole. And just then I hit something. Horrors! I saw it just the instant before the disaster—of all things, a bull, standing there in the darkness. We went down together, rolling over and over; and the automatic process was such in that miserable creature that in the moment of impact he reached out and clutched me and never let go. We were both knocked out, and he held on to a very lamb-like hobo while he recovered.

If that bull had any imagination, he must have thought me a traveller from other worlds, the man from Mars just arriving; for in the darkness he hadn't seen me swing from the train. In fact, his words were: 'Where did you come from?' His next words, and before I had time to answer, were: 'I've a good mind to run you in'. This latter, I am convinced, was likewise automatic. He was a really good bull at heart, for after I had told him a 'story' and helped brush off his clothes, he gave me until the next freight to get out of town. I stipulated two things: first, that the freight be east-bound, and second, that it should not be a through freight with all doors sealed and locked. To this he agreed, and thus, by the terms of the Treaty of Bristol, I escaped being pinched.

I remember another night, in that part of the country, when I just missed another bull. If I had hit him, I'd have telescoped him, for I was coming down from above, all holds free, with several other bulls one jump behind and reaching for me. This is how it happened. I had been lodging in a livery stable in Washington. I had a box-stall and unnumbered horse-blankets all to myself. In return for such sumptuous accommodation I took care of a string of horses each morning. I might have been there yet, if it hadn't been for the bulls.

One evening, about nine o'clock, I returned to the stable to go to bed, and found a crap game in full blast. It had been a market day, and all the negroes had money. It would be well to explain the lay of the land. The livery stable faced on two streets. I entered the front, passed through the office, and came to the alley between two rows of stalls that ran the length of the building and opened out on the other street. Midway along this alley, beneath a gas-jet and between the rows of horses, were about forty negroes. I joined them as an onlooker. I was broke and couldn't play. A coon was making passes and not dragging down. He was riding his luck, and with each pass the total stake doubled. All kinds of money lay on the floor. It was fascinating. With each pass, the chances increased tremendously against the coon making another pass. The excitement was intense. And just then there came a thundering smash on the big doors that opened on the back street.

A few of the negroes bolted in the opposite direction. I paused from my flight a moment to grab at the all kinds of money on the floor. This wasn't theft; it was merely custom. Every man who hadn't run was grabbing. The doors crashed open and swung in, and through them surged a squad of bulls. We surged the other way. It was dark in the office, and the narrow door would not permit all of us to pass out to the street at the same time. Things became congested. A coon took a dive through the window, taking the sash along with him and followed by other coons. At our rear, the bulls were nailing prisoners. A big coon and myself made a dash at the door at the same time. He was bigger than I, and he pivoted me and got through first. The next instant a club swatted him on the head and he went down like a steer. Another squad of bulls was waiting outside for us. They knew they couldn't stop the rush with their hands, and so they were swinging their clubs. I stumbled over the fallen coon who had pivoted me, ducked a swat from a club, dived between a bull's legs, and was free. And then how I ran! There was a lean mulatto just in front of me, and I took his pace. He knew the town better than I did, and I knew that in the way he ran lay safety. But he, on the other hand, took me for a pursuing bull. He never looked around. He just ran. My wind was good, and I hung on to his pace and nearly killed him. In the end he stumbled weakly, went down on his knees, and surrendered to me. And when he discovered I wasn't a bull, all that saved me was that he didn't have any wind left in him.

That was why I left Washington—not on account of the mulatto, but on account of the bulls. I went down to the depot and caught the first blind out on a Pennsylvania Railroad express. After the train got good and under way and I noted the speed she was making, misgiving smote me. This was a four-track railroad, and the engines took water on the fly. Hoboes had long since warned me never to ride the first blind on trains where the engines took water on the fly. And now let me explain. Between the tracks are shallow metal troughs. As the engine, at full speed, passes above, a sort of chute drops down into the trough. The result is that all the water in the trough rushes up the chute and fills the tender.

Somewhere along between Washington and Baltimore, as I sat on the platform of the blind, a fine spray began to fill the air. It did no harm. Ah, ha, thought I; it's all a bluff, this taking water on the fly being bad for the bo on the first blind. What does this little spray amount to? Then I began to marvel at the device. This *was* railroading! Talk about your primitive Western railroading—and just then the tender filled up, and it hadn't reached the end of the trough. A tidal wave of water poured over the back of the tender and down upon me. I was soaked to the skin, as wet as if I had fallen overboard.

The train pulled into Baltimore. As is the custom in the great Eastern cities, the railroad ran beneath the level of the streets on the bottom of a big 'cut'. As the train pulled into the lighted depot, I made myself as small as possible on the blind. But a railroad bull saw me, and gave chase. Two more joined him. I was past the depot, and I ran straight on down the track. I was in a sort of trap. On each side of me rose the steep walls of the cut, and if I ever essayed them and failed, I knew that I'd slide back into the clutches of the bulls. I ran on and on, studying the walls of the cut for a favourable place to climb up. At last I saw such a place. It came just after I had passed under a bridge that carried a level street across the cut. Up the steep slope I went, clawing hand and foot. The three railroad bulls were clawing right after me.

At the top, I found myself in a vacant lot. On one side was a low wall that separated it from the street. There was no time for minute investigation. They were at my heels. I headed for the wall and vaulted it. And right there was where I got the surprise of my life. One is used to thinking that one side of a wall is just as high as the other side. But that wall was different. You see, the vacant lot was much higher than the level of the street. On my side the wall was low, but on the other side—well, as I came soaring over the top, all holds free, it seemed to me that I was falling feet-first, plump into an abyss. There beneath me, on the sidewalk, under the light of a street-lamp was a bull. I guess it was nine or ten feet down to the sidewalk; but in the shock of surprise in mid-air it seemed twice that distance.

I straightened out in the air and came down. At first I thought I was going to land on the bull. My clothes did brush him as my feet struck the sidewalk with explosive impact. It was a wonder he didn't drop dead, for he hadn't heard me coming. It was the man-from-Mars stunt over again. The bull did jump. He shied away from me like a horse from an auto; and then he reached for me. I didn't stop to explain. I left that to my pursuers, who were dropping over the wall rather gingerly. But I got a chase all right. I ran up one street and down another, dodged around corners, and at last got away.

After spending some of the coin I'd got from the crap game and killing off an hour of time, I came back to the railroad cut, just outside the lights of the depot, and waited for a train. My blood had cooled down, and I shivered miserably, what of my wet clothes. At last a train pulled into the station. I lay low in the darkness, and successfully boarded her when she pulled out, taking good care this time to make the second blind. No more water on the fly in mine. The train ran forty miles to the first stop. I got off in a lighted depot that was strangely familiar. I was back in Washington. In some way, during the excitement of the get-away in Baltimore, running through strange streets, dodging and turning and retracing, I had got turned around. I had taken the train out the wrong way. I had lost a night's sleep, I had been soaked to the skin, I had been chased for my life; and for all my pains I was back where I had started. Oh, no, life on The Road is not all beer and skittles. But I didn't go back to the livery stable. I had done some pretty successful grabbing, and I didn't want to reckon up with the coons. So I caught the next train out, and ate my breakfast in Baltimore.

'PINCHED'

I RODE into Niagara Falls in a 'sidedoor Pullman', or, in common parlance, a box-car. A flat-car, by the way, is known amongst the fraternity as a 'gondola', with the second syllable emphasized and pronounced long. But to return. I arrived in the afternoon and headed straight from the freight train to the falls. Once my eyes were filled with that wonder-vision of down-rushing water, I was lost, I could not tear myself away long enough to 'batter' the 'privates' (domiciles) for my supper. Even a 'set-down' could not have lured me away. Night came on, a beautiful night of moonlight, and I lingered by the falls until after eleven. Then it was up to me to hunt for a place to 'kip'.

'Kip', 'doss', 'flop', 'pound your ear', all mean the same thing; namely, to sleep. Somehow, I had a 'hunch' that Niagara Falls was a 'bad' town for hoboes, and I headed out into the country. I climbed a fence and 'flopped' in a field. John Law would never find me there, I flattered myself. I lay on my back in the grass and slept like a babe. It was so balmy warm that I woke up not once all night. But with the first grey daylight my eyes opened, and I remembered the wonderful falls. I climbed the fence and started down the road to have another look at them. It was early—not more than five o'clock—and not until eight o'clock could I begin to batter for my breakfast. I could spend at least three hours by the river. Alas! I was fated never to see the river nor the falls again.

The town was asleep when I entered it. As I came along the quiet street, I saw three men coming toward me along the sidewalk. They were walking abreast. Hoboes, I decided, like myself, who had got up early. In this surmise I was not quite correct. I was only sixty-six and two-thirds per cent. correct. The men on each side were hoboes all right, but the man in the middle wasn't. I directed my steps to the edge of the sidewalk in order to let the trio go by. But it didn't go by. At some word from the man in the centre, all three halted, and he of the centre addressed me.

I piped the lay on the instant. He was a 'fly-cop' and the two hoboes were his prisoners. John Law was up and out after the early worm. I was a worm. Had I been richer by the experiences that were to befall me in the next several months, I should have turned and run like the very devil. He might have shot at me, but he'd have had to hit me to get me. He'd have never run after me, for two hoboes in the hand are worth more than one on the get-away. But like a dummy I stood still when he halted me. Our conversation was brief.

'What hotel are you stopping at?' he queried.

He had me. I wasn't stopping at any hotel, and, since I did not know the name of a hotel in the place, I could not claim residence in any of them. Also, I was up too early in the morning. Everything was against me.

'I just arrived,' I said.

'Well, you turn around and walk in front of me, and not too far in front. There's somebody wants to see you.'

I was 'pinched', I knew who wanted to see me. With that 'fly-cop' and the two hoboes at my heels, and under the direction of the former, I led the way to the city jail. There we were searched and our names registered. I have forgotten, now, under which name I was registered. I gave the name of Jack Drake, but when they searched me, they found letters addressed to Jack London. This caused trouble and required explanation, all of which has passed from my mind, and to this day I do not know whether I was pinched as Jack Drake or Jack London. But one or the other, it should be there today in the prison register of Niagara Falls. Reference can bring it to light. The time was somewhere in the latter part of June, 1894. It was only a few days after my arrest that the great railroad strike began.

From the office we were led to the 'Hobo' and locked in. The 'Hobo' is that part of a prison where the minor offenders are confined together in a large iron cage. Since hoboes constitute the principal division of the minor offenders, the aforesaid iron cage is called the Hobo. Here we met several hoboes who had already been pinched that morning, and every little while the door was unlocked and two or three more were thrust in on us. At last, when we totalled sixteen, we were led upstairs into the court-room. And now I shall faithfully describe what took place in that court-room, for know that my patriotic American citizenship there received a shock from which it has never fully recovered.

In the court-room were the sixteen prisoners, the judge, and two bailiffs. The judge seemed to act as his own clerk. There were no witnesses. There were no citizens of Niagara Falls present to look on and see how justice was administered in their community. The judge glanced at the list of cases before him and called out a name. A hobo stood up. The judge glanced at a bailiff. 'Vagrancy, your Honour,' said the bailiff. 'Thirty days,' said his Honour. The hobo sat down, and the judge was calling another name and another hobo was rising to his feet.

The trial of that hobo had taken just about fifteen seconds. The trial of the next came off with equal celerity. The bailiff said, 'Vagrancy, your Honour,' and his Honour said, 'Thirty days.' Thus it went like clockwork, fifteen seconds to a hobo—and thirty days.

They are poor dumb cattle, I thought to myself. But wait till my turn comes; I'll give his Honour a 'spiel'. Part way along in the performance, his Honour, moved by some whim, gave one of us an opportunity to speak. As chance would have it, this man was not a genuine hobo. He bore none of the ear-marks of the professional 'stiff'. Had he approached the rest of us, while waiting at a water-tank for a freight, we should have unhesitatingly classified him as a 'gay-cat'. Gay-cat is the synonym for tenderfoot in Hobo Land. This gay-cat was well along in years—somewhere around forty-five, I should judge. His shoulders were humped a trifle, and his face was seamed by weather-beat.

For many years, according to his story, he had driven team for some firm in (if I remember rightly) Lockport, New York. The firm had ceased to prosper, and finally, in the hard times of 1893, had gone out of business. He had been kept on to the last, though toward the last his work had been very irregular. He went on and explained at length his difficulties in getting work (when so many were out of work) during the succeeding months. In the end, deciding that he would find better opportunities for work on the Lakes, he had started for Buffalo. Of course he was 'broke', and there he was. That was all.

'Thirty days,' said his Honour, and called another hobo's name.

Said hobo got up. 'Vagrancy, your Honour,' said the bailiff, and his Honour said, 'Thirty days'.

And so it went, fifteen seconds and thirty days to each hobo. The machine of justice was grinding smoothly. Most likely, considering how early it was in the morning, his Honour had not yet had his breakfast and was in a hurry.

13*

But my American blood was up. Behind me were the many generations of my American ancestry. One of the kinds of liberty those ancestors of mine had fought and died for was the right of trial by jury. This was my heritage, stained sacred by their blood, and it devolved upon me to stand up for it. All right, I threatened to myself; just wait till he gets to me.

He got to me. My name, whatever it was, was called, and I stood up. The bailiff said, 'Vagrancy, your Honour,' and I began to talk. But the judge began talking at the same time, and he said, 'Thirty days'. I started to protest, but at that moment his Honour was calling the name of the next hobo on the list. His Honour paused long enough to say to me, 'Shut up!' The bailiff forced me to sit down. And the next moment that next hobo had received thirty days and the succeeding hobo was just in process of getting his.

When we had all been disposed of, thirty days to each stiff, his Honour, just as he was about to dismiss us, suddenly turned to the teamster from Lockport—the one man he had allowed to talk.

'Why did you quit your job?' his Honour asked.

Now the teamster had already explained how his job had quit him, and the question took him aback.

'Your Honour,' he began confusedly, 'isn't that a funny question to ask?'

'Thirty days more for quitting your job,' said his Honour, and the court was closed. That was the outcome. The teamster got sixty days all together, while the rest of us got thirty days.

We were taken down below, locked up, and given breakfast. It was a pretty good breakfast, as prison breakfasts go, and it was the best I was to get for a month to come.

As for me, I was dazed. Here was I, under sentence, after a farce of a trial wherein I was denied not only my right of trial by jury, but my right to plead guilty or not guilty. Another thing my fathers had fought for flashed through my brain—habeas corpus. I'd show them. But when I asked for a lawyer, I was laughed at. Habeas corpus was all right, but of what good was it to me when I could communicate with no one outside the jail? But I'd show them. They couldn't keep me in jail for ever. Just wait till I got out, that was all. I'd make them sit up. I knew something about the law and my own rights, and I'd expose their mal-administration of justice. Visions of damage suits and sensational newspaper headlines were dancing before my eyes when the jailers came in and began hustling us out into the main office.

A policeman snapped a handcuff on my right wrist. (Ah, ha, thought I, a new indignity. Just wait till I get out.) On the left wrist of a negro he snapped the other handcuff of that pair. He was a very tall negro, well past six feet—so tall was he that when we stood side by side his hand lifted mine up a trifle in the manacles. Also, he was the happiest and the raggedest negro I have ever seen.

We were all handcuffed similarly, in pairs. This accomplished, a bright nickel-steel chain was brought forth, run down through the links of all the handcuffs, and locked at front and rear of the double-line. We were now a chain-gang. The command to march was given, and out we went upon the street, guarded by two officers. The tall negro and I had the place of honour. We led the procession.

After the tomb-like gloom of the jail, the outside sunshine was dazzling. I had never known it to be so sweet as now, a prisoner with clanking chains, I knew that I was soon to see the last of it for thirty days. Down through the streets of Niagara Falls we marched to the railroad station, stared at by curious passers-by, and especially by a group of tourists on the veranda of a hotel that we marched past.

There was plenty of slack in the chain, and with much rattling and clanking we sat down, two and two, in the seats of the smoking-car. Afire with indignation as I was at the outrage that had been perpetrated on me and my forefathers, I was nevertheless too prosaically practical to lose my head over it. This was all new to me. Thirty days of mystery were before me, and I looked about me to find somebody who knew the ropes. For I had already learned that I was not bound for a petty jail with a hundred or so prisoners in it, but for a full-grown penitentiary with a couple of thousand prisoners in it, doing anywhere from ten days to ten years.

In the seat behind me, attached to the chain by his wrist, was a squat, heavily-built, powerfully-muscled man. He was somewhere between thirty-five and forty years of age. I sized him up. In the corners of his eyes I saw humour and laughter and kindliness. As for the rest of him, he was a brute-beast, wholly unmoral, and with all the passion and turgid violence of the brute-beast. What saved him, what made him possible for me, were those corners of his eyes—the humour and laughter and kindliness of the beast when unaroused.

He was my 'meat', I 'cottoned' to him. While my cuff-mate, the tall negro, mourned with chucklings and laughter over some laundry he was sure to lose through his arrest, and while the train rolled in toward Buffalo, I talked with the man in the seat behind me. He had an empty pipe. I filled it for him with my precious tobacco—enough in a single filling to make a dozen cigarettes. Nay, the more we talked the surer I was that he was my meat, and I divided all my tobacco with him.

Now it happens that I am a fluid sort of an organism, with sufficient kinship with life to fit myself in 'most anywhere. I laid myself out to fit in with that man, though little did I dream to what extraordinary good purpose I was succeeding. He had never been in the particular penitentiary to which we were going, but he had done 'one-', 'two-', and 'five-spots' in various other penitentiaries (a 'spot' is a year), and he was filled with wisdom. We became pretty chummy, and my heart bounded when he cautioned me to follow his lead. He called me 'Jack', and I called him 'Jack'.

The train stopped at a station about five miles from Buffalo, and we, the chain-gang, got off. I do not remember the name of this station, but I am confident that it is some one of the following: Rocklyn, Rockwood, Black Rock, Rockcastle, or Newcastle. But whatever the name of the place, we were walked a short distance and then put on a street car. It was an old-fashioned car, with a seat, running the full length, on each side. All the passengers who sat on one side were asked to move over to the other side, and we, with a great clanking of chain, took their places. We sat facing them, I remember, and I remember, too, the awed expression on the faces of the women, who took us, undoubtedly, for convicted murderers and bank-robbers. I tried to look my fiercest, but that cuff-mate of mine, the too happy negro, insisted on rolling his eyes, laughing, and reiterating, 'O Lawdy! Lawdy!'

We left the car, walked some more, and were led into the office of the Erie County Penitentiary. Here we were to register, and on that register one or the other of my names will be found. Also, we were informed that we must leave in the office all our valuables: money, tobacco, matches, pocket-knives, and so forth.

My new pal shook his head at me.

'If you do not leave your things here, they will be confiscated inside,' warned the official.

Still my pal shook his head. He was busy with his hands, hiding his movements behind the other fellows. (Our handcuffs had been removed.) I watched him, and followed suit, wrapping up in a bundle in my handkerchief all the things I wanted to take in. These bundles the two of us thrust into our shirts. I noticed that our fellow-prisoners, with the exception of one or two who had watches, did not turn over their belongings to the man in the office. They were determined to smuggle them in somehow, trusting to luck; but they were not so wise as my pal, for they did not wrap their things in bundles.

Our erstwhile guardians gathered up the handcuffs and chain and departed for Niagara Falls, while we, under new guardians, were led away into the prison. While we were in the office, our number had been added to by other squads of newly arrived prisoners, so that we were now a procession forty or fifty strong.

Know, ye unimprisoned, that traffic is as restricted inside a large prison as commerce was in the Middle Ages. Once inside a penitentiary, one cannot move about at will. Every few steps are encountered great steel doors or gates which are always kept locked. We were bound for the barber-shop, but we encountered delays in the unlocking of doors for us. We were thus delayed in the first 'hall' we entered. A 'hall' is not a corridor. Imagine an oblong cube, built out of bricks and rising six stories high, each story a row of cells, say fifty cells in a row—in short, imagine a cube of colossal honeycomb. Place this cube on the ground and enclose it in a building with a roof overhead and walls all around. Such a cube and encompassing building constitute a 'hall' in the Erie County Penitentiary. Also, to complete the picture, see a narrow gallery, with steel railing, running the full length of each tier of cells and at the ends of the oblong cube see all these galleries, from both sides, connected by a fire-escape system of narrow steel stairways.

We were halted in the first hall, waiting for some guard to unlock a door. Here and there, moving about, were convicts, with close-cropped heads and shaven faces, and garbed in prison stripes. One such convict I noticed above us on the gallery of the third tier of cells. He was standing on the gallery and leaning forward, his arms resting on the railing, himself apparently oblivious of our presence. He seemed staring into vacancy. My pal made a slight hissing noise. The convict glanced down. Motioned signals passed between them. Then through the air soared the handkerchief bundle of my pal. The convict caught it, and like a flash it was out of sight in his shirt and he was staring into vacancy. My pal had told me to follow his lead. I watched my chance when the guard's back was turned, and my bundle followed the other one into the shirt of the convict.

A minute later the door was unlocked, and we filed into the barber-shop. Here were more men in convict stripes. They were the prison barbers. Also, there were bath-tubs, hot water, soap, and scrubbing-brushes. We were ordered to strip and bathe, each man to scrub his neighbour's back —a needless precaution, this compulsory bath, for the prison swarmed with vermin. After the bath, we were each given a canvas clothes-bag.

'Put all your clothes in the bags,' said the guard. 'It's no use trying to smuggle anything in. You've got to line up naked for inspection. Men for thirty days or less keep their shoes and suspenders. Men for more than thirty days keep nothing.'

This announcement was received with consternation. How could naked men smuggle anything past an inspection? Only my pal and I were safe. But it was right here that the convict barbers got in their work. They passed among the poor newcomers, kindly volunteering to take charge of their precious little belongings, and promising to return them later in the day. Those barbers were philanthropists—to hear them talk. As in the case of Fra Lippo Lippi, never was there such prompt disemburdening. Matches, tobacco, rice-paper, pipes, knives, money, everything, flowed into the capacious shirts of the barbers. They fairly bulged with the spoil, and the guards made believe not to see. To cut the story short, nothing was ever returned. The barbers never had any intention of returning what they had taken. They considered it legitimately theirs. It was the barber-shop graft. There were many grafts in that prison, as I was to learn; and I, too, was destined to become a grafter—thanks to my new pal.

There were several chairs, and the barbers worked rapidly. The quickest shaves and hair-cuts I have ever seen were given in that shop. The men lathered themselves, and the barbers shaved them at the rate of a minute to a man. A hair-cut took a trifle longer. In three minutes the down of eighteen was scraped from my face, and my head was as smooth as a billiard-ball just sprouting a crop of bristles. Beards, moustaches, like our clothes and everything, came off. Take my word for it, we were a villainous-looking gang when they got through with us. I had not realized before how really altogether bad we were.

Then came the line-up, forty or fifty of us, naked as Kipling's heroes who stormed Lungtungpen. To search us was easy. There were only shoes and ourselves. Two or three rash spirits, who had doubted the barbers, had the goods found on them—which goods, namely, tobacco, pipes, matches, and small change, were quickly confiscated. This over, our new clothes were brought to us— stout prison shirts, and coats and trousers conspicuously striped. I had always lingered under the impression that the convict stripes were put on a man only after he had been convicted of a felony. I lingered no longer, but put on the insignia of shame and got my first taste of marching the lock-step.

In single file, close together, each man's hands on the shoulders of the man in front, we marched on into another large hall. Here we were ranged up against the wall in a long line and ordered to strip our left arms. A youth, a medical student who was getting in his practice on cattle such as we, came down the line. He vaccinated just about four times as rapidly as the barbers shaved. With a final caution to avoid rubbing our arms against anything, and to let the blood dry so as to form the scab, we were led away to our cells. Here my pal and I parted, but not before he had time to whisper to me, 'Suck it out.'

As soon as I was locked in, I sucked my arm clean. And afterwards I saw men who had not sucked and who had horrible holes in their arms into which I could have thrust my fist. It was their own fault. They could have sucked.

In my cell was another man. We were to be cell-mates. He was a young, manly fellow, not talkative, but very capable, indeed as splendid a fellow as one could meet with in a day's ride, and this in spite of the fact that he had just recently finished a two-year term in some Ohio penitentiary.

Hardly had we been in our cell half an hour, when a convict sauntered down the gallery and looked in. It was my pal. He had the freedom of the hall, he explained. He was unlocked at six in the morning and not locked up again till nine at night. He was in with the 'push' in that hall, and had been promptly appointed a trusty of the kind technically known as 'hall-man'. The man who had appointed him was also a prisoner and a trusty, and was known as 'First Hall-man'. There were thirteen hall-men in that hall. Ten of them had charge each of a gallery of cells, and over them were the First, Second, and Third Hall-men.

We newcomers were to stay in our cells for the rest of the day, my pal informed me, so that the vaccine would have a chance to take. Then next morning we would be put to hard labour in the prison-yard.

'But I'll get you out of the work as soon as I can,' he promised. 'I'll get one of the hall-men fired and have you put in his place.'

He put his hand into his shirt, drew out the handkerchief containing my precious belongings, passed it in to me through the bars, and went on down the gallery.

I opened the bundle. Everything was there. Not even a match was missing. I shared the makings of a cigarette with my cell-mate. When I started to strike a match for a light he stopped me. A flimsy, dirty comforter lay in each of our bunks for bedding. He tore off a narrow strip of the thin cloth and rolled it tightly and telescopically into a long and slender cylinder. This he lighted with a precious match. The cylinder of tight-rolled cotton cloth did not flame. On the end a coal of fire slowly smouldered. It would last for hours, and my cell-mate called it a 'punk'. And when it burned short, all that was necessary was to make a new punk, put the end of it against the old, blow on them, and so transfer the glowing coal. Why, we could have given Prometheus pointers on the conserving of fire.

At twelve o'clock dinner was served. At the bottom
of our cage door was a small opening like the entrance
of a runway in a chicken-yard. Through this were thrust
two hunks of dry bread and two pannikins of 'soup'. A
portion of soup consisted of about a quart of hot water
with floating on its surface a lonely drop of grease. Also,
there was some salt in that water.

We drank the soup, but we did not eat the bread. Not
that we were not hungry, and not that the bread was un-
eatable. It was fairly good bread. But we had reasons. My
cell-mate had discovered that our cell was alive with bed-
bugs. In all the cracks and interstices between the bricks
where the mortar had fallen out flourished great colonies.
The natives even ventured out in the broad daylight and
swarmed over the walls and ceiling by hundreds. My cell-
mate was wise in the ways of the beasts. Like Childe
Roland, dauntless the slug-horn to his lips he bore. Never
was there such a battle. It lasted for hours. It was shambles.
And when the last survivors fled to their brick-and-mortar
fastnesses, our work was only half done. We chewed
mouthfuls of our bread until it was reduced to the con-
sistency of putty. When a fleeing belligerent escaped into a
crevice between the bricks, we promptly walled him in
with a daub of the chewed bread. We toiled on until the
light grew dim and until every hole, nook, and cranny
was closed. I shudder to think of the tragedies of starvation
and cannibalism that must have ensued behind those
bread-plastered ramparts.

We threw ourselves on our bunks, tired out and hungry,
to wait for supper. It was a good day's work well done. In
the weeks to come we at least should not suffer from the
hosts of vermin. We had forgone our dinner, saved our
hides at the expense of our stomachs; but we were content.
Alas for the futility of human effort! Scarcely was our
long task completed when a guard unlocked our door. A
redistribution of prisoners was being made, and we were
taken to another cell and locked in two galleries higher up.

Early next morning our cells were unlocked, and down

in the hall the several hundred prisoners of us formed the lock-step and marched out into the prison-yard to go to work. The Erie Canal runs right by the back yard of the Erie County Penitentiary. Our task was to unload canal-boats, carrying huge stay-bolts on our shoulders, like railroad ties, into the prison. As I worked I sized up the situation and studied the chances for a get-away. There wasn't the ghost of a show. Along the tops of the walls marched guards armed with repeating rifles, and I was told, furthermore, that there was machine-guns in the sentry-towers.

I did not worry. Thirty days were not so long. I'd stay those thirty days, and add to the store of material I intended to use, when I got out, against the harpies of justice. I'd show what an American boy could do when his rights and privileges had been trampled on the way mine had. I had been denied my right of trial by jury; I had been denied my right to plead guilty or not guilty; I had been denied a trial even (for I couldn't consider that what I had received at Niagara Falls was a trial); I had not been allowed to communicate with a lawyer nor anyone, and hence had been denied my right of suing for a writ of habeas corpus; my face had been shaved, my hair cropped close, convict stripes had been put upon my body; I was forced to toil hard on a diet of bread and water and to march the shameful lock-step with armed guards over me —and all for what? What had I done? What crime had I committed against the good citizens of Niagara Falls that all this vengeance should be wreaked upon me? I had not even violated their 'sleeping-out' ordinance. I had slept outside their jurisdiction, in the country, that night. I had not even begged for a meal, or battered for a 'light piece' on their streets. All that I had done was to walk along their sidewalk and gaze at their picayune waterfall. And what crime was there in that? Technically I was guilty of no misdemeanour. All right, I'd show them when I got out.

The next day I talked with a guard. I wanted to send for a lawyer. The guard laughed at me. So did the other guards. I really was *incommunicado* so far as the outside world was concerned. I tried to write a letter out, but I learned that all letters were read, and censored or confiscated, by the prison authorities, and that 'short-timers' were not allowed to write letters anyway. A little later I tried smuggling letters out by men who were released, but I learned that they were searched and the letters found and destroyed. Never mind. It all helped to make it a blacker case when I did get out.

But as the prison days went by (which I shall describe in the next chapter), I 'learned a few'. I heard tales of the police, and police-courts, and lawyers, that were unbelievable and monstrous. Men, prisoners, told me of personal experiences with the police of great cities that were awful. And more awful were the hear-say tales they told me concerning men who had died at the hands of the police and who therefore could not testify for themselves. Years afterward, in the report of the Lexow Committee, I was to read tales true and more awful than those told to me. But in the meantime, during the first days of my imprisonment, I scoffed at what I heard.

As the days went by, however, I began to grow convinced. I saw with my own eyes, there in that prison, things unbelievable and monstrous. And the more convinced I became, the profounder grew the respect in me for the sleuth-hounds of the law and for the whole institution of criminal justice.

My indignation ebbed away, and into my being rushed the tides of fear. I saw at last, clear-eyed, what I was up against. I grew meek and lowly. Each day I resolved more emphatically to make no rumpus when I got out. All I asked, when I got out, was a chance to fade away from the landscape. And that was just what I did do when I was released. I kept my tongue between my teeth, walked softly, and sneaked for Pennsylvania, a wiser and humbler man.

THE PEN

FOR TWO DAYS I toiled in the prison-yard. It was heavy work, and, in spite of the fact that I malingered at every opportunity, I was played out. This was because of the food. No man could work hard on such food. Bread and water, that was all that was given us. Once a week we were supposed to get meat; but this meat did not always go around, and since all nutriment had first been boiled out of it in the making of soup, it didn't matter whether one got a taste of it once a week or not.

Furthermore, there was one vital defect in the bread-and-water diet. While we got plenty of water, we did not get enough of the bread. A ration of bread was about the size of one's two fists, and three rations a day was given to each prisoner. There was one good thing, I must say, about the water—it was hot. In the morning it was called 'coffee', at noon it was dignified as 'soup', and at night it masqueraded as 'tea'. But it was the same old water all the time. The prisoners called it 'water bewitched'. In the morning it was black water, the colour being due to boiling it with burnt bread-crusts. At noon it was served minus the colour, with salt and a drop of grease added. At night it was served with a purplish-auburn hue that defied all speculation; it was darn poor tea, but it was dandy hot water.

We were a hungry lot in the Erie County Pen. Only the 'long-timers' knew what it was to have enough to eat. The reason for this was that they would have died after a time on the fare we 'short-timers' received. I know that the long-timers got more substantial grub, because there was a whole row of them on the ground floor in our hall, and when I was a trusty, I used to steal from their grub while serving them. Man cannot live on bread alone and not enough of it.

My pal delivered the goods. After two days of work in the yard I was taken out of my cell and made a trusty, a 'hall-man'. At morning and night we served the bread to the prisoners in their cells; but at twelve o'clock a different method was used. The convicts marched in from work in a long line. As they entered the door of our hall, they broke the lock-step and took their hands down from the shoulders of their line-mates. Just inside the door were piled trays of bread, and here also stood the First Hall-man and two ordinary hall-men. I was one of the two. Our task was to hold the trays of bread as the line of convicts filed past. As soon as the tray, say, that I was holding was emptied, the other hall-man took my place with a full tray. And when his was emptied, I took his place with a full tray. Thus the line tramped steadily by, each man reaching with his right hand and taking one ration of bread from the extended tray.

The task of the First Hall-man was different. He used a club. He stood beside the tray and watched. The hungry wretches could never get over the delusion that sometime they could manage to get two rations of bread out of the tray. But in my experience that sometime never came. The club of the First Hall-man had a way of flashing out—quick as the stroke of a tiger's claw—to the hand that dared ambitiously. The First Hall-man was a good judge of distance, and he had smashed so many hands with that club that he had become infallible. He never missed, and he usually punished the offending convict by taking his one ration away from him and sending him to his cell to make his meal off of hot water.

And at times, while all these men lay hungry in their cells, I have seen a hundred or so extra rations of bread hidden away in the cells of the hall-men. It would seem absurd, our retaining this bread. But it was one of our grafts. We were economic masters inside our hall, turning the trick in ways quite similar to the economic masters of civilization. We controlled the food-supply of the population, and, just like our brother bandits outside, we made the people pay through the nose for it. We peddled the bread. Once a week, the men who worked in the yard received a five-cent plug of chewing tobacco. This chewing tobacco was the coin of the realm. Two or three rations of bread for a plug was the way we exchanged, and they traded, not because they loved tobacco less, but because they loved bread more. Oh, I know it was like taking candy from a baby, but what would you? We had to live. And certainly there should be some reward for initiative and enterprise. Besides, we but patterned ourselves after our betters outside the walls, who, on a larger scale, and under the respectable disguise of merchants, bankers, and captains of industry, did precisely what we were doing. What awful things would have happened to those poor wretches if it hadn't been for us, I can't imagine. Heaven knows we put bread into circulation in the Erie County Pen. Ay, and we encouraged frugality and thrift . . . in the poor devils who forwent their tobacco. And then there was our example. In the breast of every convict there we implanted the ambition to become even as we and run a graft. Saviours of society—I guess yes.

Here was a hungry man without any tobacco. Maybe he was a profligate and had used it all up on himself. Very good; he had a pair of suspenders. I exchanged half a dozen rations of bread for it—or a dozen rations if the suspenders were very good. Now I never wore suspenders, but that didn't matter. Around the corner lodged a long-timer, doing ten years for manslaughter. He wore suspenders, and he wanted a pair. I could trade them to him for some of his meat. Meat was what I wanted. Or perhaps he had a tattered, paper-covered novel. That was treasure-trove. I could read it and then trade it off to bakers for cake, or to the cooks for meat and the vegetables, or to the firemen for decent coffee, or to someone or other for the newspaper that occasionally filtered in, heaven alone knows how. The cooks, bakers, and firemen were prisoners like myself, and they lodged in our hall in the first row of cells over us.

In short, a full-grown system of barter obtained in the Erie County Pen. There was even money in circulation. This money was sometimes smuggled in by the short-timers, more frequently came from the barber-shop graft, where the newcomers were mulcted, but most of all flowed from the cells of the long-timers—though how they got it I don't know.

What of his pre-eminent position, the First Hall-man was reputed to be quite wealthy. In addition to his miscellaneous grafts, he grafted on us. We farmed the general wretchedness, and the First Hall-man was Farmer-General over all of us. We held our particular grafts by his permission, and we had to pay for that permission. As I say, he was reputed to be wealthy; but we never saw his money, and he lived in a cell all to himself in solitary grandeur.

But that money was made in the Pen I had direct evidence, for I was cell-mate quite a time with the Third Hall-man. He had over sixteen dollars. He used to count his money every night after nine o'clock, when we were locked in. Also, he used to tell me each night what he would do to me if I gave away on him to the other hall-men. You see, he was afraid of being robbed, and danger threatened him from three different directions. There were the guards. A couple of them might jump upon him, give him a good beating for alleged insubordination, and throw him into the 'solitaire' (the dungeon); and in the mix-up that sixteen dollars of his would take wings. Then again, the First Hall-man could have taken it all away from him by threatening to dismiss him and fire him back to hard labour in the prison-yard. And yet again, there were the ten of us who were ordinary hall-men. If we got an inkling of his wealth, there was a large liability, some quiet day, of the whole bunch of us getting him into a corner and dragging him down. Oh, we were wolves, believe me— just like the fellows who do business in Wall Street.

He had good reason to be afraid of us, and so had I to be afraid of him. He was a huge, illiterate brute, an ex-Chesapeake Bay oyster-pirate, an 'ex-con' who had done five

years in Sing Sing, and a general all-around stupidly car-
nivorous beast. He used to trap sparrows that flew into our
hall through the open bars. When he made a capture, he
hurried away with it into his cell, where I have seen him
crunching bones and spitting out feathers as he bolted it
raw. Oh, no, I never gave away on him to the other hall-
men. This is the first time I have mentioned his sixteen
dollars.

But I grafted on him just the same. He was in love with
a woman prisoner who was confined in the 'female
department'. He could neither read nor write, and I used
to read her letters to him and write his replies. And I
made him pay for it, too. But they were good letters. I laid
myself out on them, put in my best licks, and furthermore,
I won her for him; though I shrewdly guess that she was
in love, not with him, but with the humble scribe. I repeat,
those letters were great.

Another one of our grafts was 'passing the punk'. We
were the celestial messengers, the fire-bringers, in that
iron world of bolt and bar. When the men came in from
work at night and were locked in their cells, they wanted
to smoke. Then it was that we restored the divine spark,
running the galleries, from cell to cell, with our smoulder-
ing punks. Those who were wise, or with whom we did
business, had their punks all ready to light. Not every one
got divine sparks, however. The guy who refused to dig
up went sparkless and smokeless to bed. But what did we
care? We had the immortal cinch on him, and if he got
fresh, two or three of us would pitch on him and give
him 'what-for'.

You see, this was the working-theory of the hall-men.
There were thirteen of us. We had something like half a
thousand prisoners in our hall. We were supposed to do the
work, and to keep order. The latter was the function of the
guards, which they turned over to us. It was up to us to
keep order; if we didn't, we'd be fired back to hard labour,
most probably with a taste of the dungeon thrown in.

But so long as we maintained order, that long could we work our own particular grafts.

Bear with me a moment and look at the problem. Here were thirteen beasts of us over half a thousand other beasts. It was a living hell, that prison, and it was up to us thirteen there to rule. It was impossible, considering the nature of the beasts, for us to rule by kindness. We ruled by fear. Of course, behind us, backing us up, were the guards. In extremity we called upon them for help; but it would bother them if we called upon them too often, in which event we could depend upon it that they would get more efficient trusties to take our places. But we did not call upon them often, except in a quiet sort of way, when we wanted a cell unlocked in order to get at a refractory prisoner inside. In such cases all the guard did was to unlock the door and walk away so as not to be a witness of what happened when half a dozen hall-men went inside and did a bit of man-handling.

As regards the details of this man-handling I shall say nothing. And after all, man-handling was merely one of the very minor unprintable horrors of the Erie County Pen. I say 'unprintable'; and in justice I must also say 'unthinkable'. They were unthinkable to me until I saw them, and I was no spring chicken in the ways of the world and the awful abysses of human degradation. It would take a deep plummet to reach bottom in the Erie County Pen, and I do but skim lightly and facetiously the surface of things as I there saw them.

At times, say in the morning when the prisoners came down to wash, the thirteen of us would be practically alone in the midst of them, and every last one of them had it in for us. Thirteen against five hundred, and we ruled by fear. We could not permit the slightest infraction of rules, the slightest insolence. If we did, we were lost. Our own rule was to hit a man as soon as he opened his mouth —hit him hard, hit him with anything. A broom-handle, end-on, in the face, had a very sobering effect. But that was not all. Such a man must be made an example of; so the next rule was to wade right in and follow him up. Of course, one was sure that every hall-man in sight would come on the run to join in the chastisement; for this also was a rule. Whenever any hall-man was in trouble with a prisoner, the duty of any other hall-man who happened to be around was to lend a fist. Never mind the merits of the case—wade in and hit, and hit with anything; in short, lay the man out.

I remember a handsome young mulatto of about twenty who got the insane idea into his head that he should stand for his rights. And he did have the right of it, too; but that didn't help him any. He lived on the topmost gallery. Eight hall-men took the conceit out of him in just about a minute and a half—for that was the length of time required to travel along his gallery to the end and down five flights of steel stairs. He travelled the whole distance on every portion of his anatomy except his feet, and the eight hall-men were not idle. The mulatto struck the pavement where I was standing watching it all. He regained his feet and stood upright for a moment. In that moment he threw his arms wide apart and emitted an awful scream of terror and pain and heartbreak. At the same instant, as in a transformation scene, the shreds of his stout prison clothes fell from him, leaving him wholly naked and streaming blood from every portion of the surface of his body. Then he collapsed in a heap, unconscious. He had learned his lesson, and every convict within those walls who heard him scream had learned a lesson. So had I learned mine. It is not a nice thing to see a man's heart broken in a minute and a half.

The following will illustrate how we drummed up business in the graft of passing the punk. A row of newcomers is installed in your cells. You pass along before the bars with your punk. 'Hey, Bo, give us a light,' some one calls to you. Now this is an advertisement that that particular man has tobacco on him. You pass in the punk and go your way. A little later you come back and lean up casually against the bars. 'Say, Bo, can you let us have a little tobacco?' is what you say. If he is not wise to the game, the chances are that he solemnly avers that he hasn't any more tobacco. All very well. You condole with him and go your way. But you know that his punk will last him only the rest of that day. Next day you come by, and he says again, ' Hey, Bo, give us a light.' And you say, 'You haven't any tobacco and you don't need a light.' And you don't give him any, either. Half an hour after, or an hour or two or three hours, you will be passing by and the man will call out to you in mild tones, 'Come here, Bo.' And you come. You thrust your hand between the bars and have it filled with precious tobacco. Then you give him a light.

Sometimes, however, a newcomer arrives, upon whom no grafts are to be worked. The mysterious word is passed along that he is to be treated decently. Where this word originated I could never learn. The one thing patent is that the man has a 'pull'. It may be with one of the superior hall-men; it may be with one of the guards in some other part of the prison; it may be that good treatment has been purchased from grafters higher up; but be it as it may, we know that it is up to us to treat him decently if we want to avoid trouble.

We hall-men were middle-men and common carriers. We arranged trades between convicts confined in different parts of the prison, and we put through the exchange. Also, we took our commissions coming and going. Sometimes the objects traded had to go through the hands of half a dozen middle-men, each of whom took his whack, or in some way or another was paid for his service.

Sometimes one was in debt for services, and sometimes one had others in his debt. Thus, I entered the prison in debt to the convict who smuggled in my things for me. A week or so afterward, one of the firemen passed a letter into my hand. It had been given to him by a barber. The barber had received it from the convict who had smuggled in my things. Because of my debt to him I was to carry the letter on. But he had not written the letter. The original sender was a long-timer in his hall. The letter was for a woman prisoner in the female department. But whether it was intended for her, or whether she, in turn, was one of the chain of go-betweens, I did not know. All that I knew was her description, and that it was up to me to get it into her hands.

Two days passed, during which time I kept the letter in my possession; then the opportunity came. The women did the mending of all the clothes worn by the convicts. A number of our hall-men had to go to the female department to bring back huge bundles of clothes. I fixed it with the First Hall-man that I was to go along. Door after door was unlocked for us as we threaded our way across the prison to the women's quarters. We entered a large room where the women sat working at their mending. My eyes were peeled for that woman who had been described to me. I located her and worked near to her. Two eagle-eyed matrons were on watch. I held the letter in my palm, and I looked my intention at the woman. She knew I had something for her; she must have been expecting it, and had set herself to divining, at the moment we entered, which of us was the messenger. But one of the matrons stood within two feet of her. Already the hall-men were picking up the bundles they were to carry away. The moment was passing. I delayed with my bundle, making believe that it was not tied securely. Would that matron ever look away? Or was I to fail? And just then another woman cut up playfully with one of the hall-men—struck out her foot and tripped him, or pinched him, or did something or other. The matron looked that way and reprimanded the woman sharply. Now I do not know whether or not this was all planned to distract the matron's attention, but I did know that it was the opportunity. My particular woman's hand dropped from her lap down to her side. I stooped to pick up my bundle. From my stooping position I slipped the letter into her hand, and received another in exchange. The next moment the bundle was on my shoulder, the matron's gaze had returned to me because I was the last hall-man, and I was hastening to catch up with my companions. The letter I had received from the woman I turned over to the fireman, and thence it passed through the hands of the barber, of the convict who had smuggled in my things, and on to the long-timer at the other end.

Often we conveyed letters, the chain of communication of which was so complex that we knew neither sender nor sendee. We were but links in the chain. Somewhere, somehow, a convict would thrust a letter into my hand with the instruction to pass it on to the next link. All such acts were favours to be reciprocated later on, when I should be acting directly with a principal in transmitting letters, and from whom I should be receiving my pay. The whole prison was covered by a network of lines of communication. And we who were in control of the system of communication, naturally, since we were modelled after capitalistic society, exacted heavy tolls from our customers. It was service for profit with a vengeance, though we were at times not above giving service for love.

And all the time I was in the Pen I was making myself solid with my pal. He had done much for me, and in return he expected me to do as much for him. When we got out, we were to travel together, and, it goes without saying, pull off 'jobs' together. For my pal was a criminal—oh, not a jewel of the first water, merely a petty criminal who would steal and rob, commit burglary, and, if cornered, not stop short of murder. Many a quiet hour we sat and talked together. He had two or three jobs in view for the immediate future, in which my work was cut out for me, and in which I joined in planning the details. I had been with and seen much of criminals, and my pal never dreamed that I was only fooling him, giving him a string thirty days long. He thought I was the real goods, liked me because I was not stupid, and liked me a bit, too, I think, for myself. Of course I had not the slightest intention of joining him in a life of sordid, petty crime; but I'd have been an idiot to throw away all the good things his friendship made possible. When one is on the hot lava of hell, he cannot pick and choose his path, and so it was with me in the Erie County Pen. I had to stay in with the 'push', or do hard labour on bread and water; and to stay in with the push I had to make good with my pal.

Life was not monotonous in the Pen. Every day something was happening: men were having fits, going crazy, fighting, or the hall-men were getting drunk. Rover Jack, one of the ordinary hall-men, was our star 'oryide'. He was a true 'profesh', a 'blowed-in-the-glass' stiff, and as such received all kinds of latitude from the hall-men in authority. Pittsburg Joe, who was Second Hall-man, used to join Rover Jack in his jags; and it was a saying of the pair that the Erie County Pen was the only place where a man could get 'slopped' and not be arrested. I never knew, but I was told that bromide of potassium, gained in devious ways from the dispensary, was the dope they used. But I do know, whatever their dope was, that they got good and drunk on occasion.

Our hall was a common stews, filled with the ruck and the filth, the scum and dregs, of society—hereditary inefficients, degenerates, wrecks, lunatics, addled intelligences, epileptics, monsters, weaklings, in short, a very nightmare of humanity. Hence, fits flourished with us. These fits seemed contagious. When one man began throwing a fit, others followed his lead. I have seen seven men down with fits at the same time, making the air hideous with their cries, while as many more lunatics would be raging and gibbering up and down. Nothing was ever done for the men with fits except to throw cold water on them. It was useless to send for the medical student or the doctor. They were not to be bothered with such trivial and frequent occurrences.

There was a young Dutch boy, about eighteen years of age, who had fits most frequently of all. He usually threw one every day. It was for that reason that we kept him on the ground floor farther down in the row of cells in which we lodged. After he had had a few fits in the prison-yard, the guards refused to be bothered with him any more, and so he remained locked up in his cell all day with a Cockney cell-mate, to keep him company. Not that the Cockney was of any use. Whenever the Dutch boy had a fit, the Cockney became paralysed with terror.

The Dutch boy could not speak a word of English. He was a farmer's boy, serving ninety days as punishment for having got into a scrap with someone. He prefaced his fits with howling. He howled like a wolf. Also, he took his fits standing up, which was very inconvenient for him, for his fits always culminated in a headlong pitch to the floor. Whenever I heard the long wolf-howl rising, I used to grab a broom and run to his cell. Now the trusties were not allowed keys to the cells, so I could not get in to him. He would stand up in the middle of his narrow cell, shivering convulsively, his eyes rolled backward till only the whites were visible, and howling like a lost soul. Try as I would, I could never get the Cockney to lend him a hand. While he stood and howled, the Cockney crouched and trembled in the upper bunk, his terror-stricken gaze fixed on that awful figure, with eyes rolled back, that howled and howled. It was hard on him, too, the poor devil of a Cockney. His own reason was not any too firmly seated, and the wonder is that he did not go mad.

All that I could do was my best with the broom. I would thrust it through the bars, train it on Dutchy's chest, and wait. As the crisis approached he would begin swaying back and forth. I followed this swaying with the broom, for there was no telling when he would take that dreadful forward pitch. But when he did, I was there with the broom, catching him and easing him down. Contrive as I would, he never came down quite gently, and his face was usually bruised by the stone floor. Once down and writhing in convulsions, I'd throw a bucket of water over him. I don't know whether cold water was the right thing or not, but it was the custom in the Erie County Pen. Nothing more than that was ever done for him. He would lie there, wet, for an hour or so, and then crawl into his bunk. I knew better than to run to a guard for assistance. What was a man with a fit, anyway?

In the adjoining cell lived a strange character—a man who was doing sixty days for eating swill out of Barnum's swill-barrel, or at least that was the way he put it. He was a badly addled creature, and, at first, very mild and gentle. The facts of his case were as he had stated them. He had strayed out to the circus ground, and, being hungry, had made his way to the barrel that contained the refuse from the table of the circus people. 'And it *was* good bread,' he often assured me; 'and the meat was out of sight.' A policeman had seen him and arrested him, and there he was.

Once I passed his cell with a piece of stiff thin wire in my hand. He asked me for it so earnestly that I passed it through the bars to him. Promptly, and with no tool but his fingers, he broke it into short lengths and twisted them into half a dozen very creditable safety pins. He sharpened the points on the stone floor. Thereafter I did quite a trade in safety pins. I furnished the raw material and peddled the finished product, and he did the work. As wages, I paid him extra rations of bread, and once in a while a chunk of meat or a piece of soup-bone with some marrow inside.

But his imprisonment told on him, and he grew violent day by day. The hall-men took delight in teasing him. They filled his weak brain with stories of a great fortune that had been left him. It was in order to rob him of it that he had been arrested and sent to jail. Of course, as he himself knew, there was no law against eating out of a barrel. Therefore he was wrongfully imprisoned. It was a plot to deprive him of his fortune.

The first I knew of it, I heard the hall-men laughing about the string they had given him. Next he held a serious conference with me, in which he told me of his millions and the plot to deprive him of them, and in which he appointed me his detective. I did my best to let him down gently, speaking vaguely of a mistake, and that it was another man with a similar name who was the rightful heir. I left him quite cooled down; but I couldn't keep the hall-men away from him, and they continued to string him worse than ever. In the end, after a most violent scene, he threw me down, revoked my private detectiveship, and went on strike. My trade in safety pins ceased. He refused to make any more safety pins, and he peppered me with raw material through the bars of his cell when I passed by.

I could never make it up with him. The other hall-men told him that I was a detective in the employ of the conspirators. And in the meantime the hall-men drove him mad with their stringing. His fictitious wrongs preyed upon his mind, and at last he became a dangerous and homicidal lunatic. The guards refused to listen to his tale of stolen millions, and he accused them of being in the plot. One day he threw a pannikin of hot tea over one of them, and then his case was investigated. The warden talked with him a few minutes through the bars of his cell. Then he was taken away for examination before the doctors. He never came back, and I often wonder if he is dead, or if he still gibbers about his millions in some asylum for the insane.

At last came the day of days, my release. It was the day of release for the Third Hall-man as well, and the short-timer girl I had won for him was waiting for him outside the wall. They went away blissfully together. My pal and I went out together, and together we walked down into Buffalo. Were we not to be together always? We begged together on the 'main-dray' that day for pennies, and what we received was spent for 'shupers' of beer—I don't know how they are spelled, but they are pronounced the way I have spelled them, and they cost three cents. I was watching my chance all the time for a get-away. From some bo on the drag I managed to learn what time a certain freight pulled out. I calculated my time accordingly. When the moment came, my pal and I were in a saloon. Two foaming shupers were before us. I'd have liked to say good-bye. He had been good to me.

But I did not dare. I went out through the rear of the saloon and jumped the fence. It was a swift sneak, and a few minutes later I was on board a freight and heading south on the Western New York and Pennsylvania Railroad.

HOLDING HER DOWN

BARRING ACCIDENTS, a good hobo, with youth and agility, can hold a train down despite all the efforts of the train-crew to 'ditch' him—given, of course, night-time as an essential condition. When such a hobo, under such conditions, makes up his mind that he is going to hold her down, either he does hold her down, or chance trips him up. There is no legitimate way, short of murder, whereby the train-crew can ditch him. That train-crews have not stopped short of murder is a current belief in the tramp world. Not having had that particular experience in my tramp days I cannot vouch for it personally.

But this I have heard of the 'bad' roads. When a tramp has 'gone underneath,' on the rods, and the train is in motion, there is apparently no way of dislodging him until the train stops. The tramp, snugly ensconced inside the truck, with the four wheels and all the frame-work around him, has the 'cinch' on the crew—or so he thinks, until some day he rides the rods on a bad road. A bad road is usually one on which a short time previously one or several trainmen have been killed by tramps. Heaven pity the tramp who is caught 'underneath' on such a road— for caught he is, though the train be going sixty miles an hour.

The 'shack' (brakeman) takes a coupling-pin and a length of bell-cord to the platform in front of the truck in which the tramp is riding. The shack fastens the coupling pin to the bell-cord, drops the former down between the platforms, and pays out the latter. The coupling-pin strikes the ties between the rails, rebounds against the bottom of the car, and again strikes the ties. The shack plays it back and forth, now to this side, now to the other, lets it out a bit and hauls it in a bit, giving his weapon opportunity for every variety of impact and rebound. Every blow of that flying coupling-pin is freighted with death, and at sixty miles an hour it beats a veritable tattoo of death. The next day the remains of that tramp are gathered up along the right of way, and a line in the local paper mentions the unknown man, undoubtedly a tramp, assumably drunk, who had probably fallen asleep on the track.

As a characteristic illustration of how a capable hobo can hold her down, I am minded to give the following experience. I was in Ottawa, bound west over the Canadian Pacific. Three thousand miles of that road stretched before me; it was the fall of the year, and I had to cross Manitoba and the Rocky Mountains. I could expect 'crimpy' weather, and every moment of delay increased the frigid hardships of the journey. Furthermore, I was disgusted. The distance between Montreal and Ottawa is one hundred and twenty miles. I ought to know, for I had just come over it and it had taken me six days. By mistake I had missed the main line and come over a small 'jerk' with only two locals a day on it. And during these six days I had lived on dry crusts, and not enough of them, begged from the French peasants.

Furthermore, my disgust had been heightened by the one day I had spent in Ottawa trying to get an outfit of clothing for my long journey. Let me put it on record right here that Ottawa, with one exception, is the hardest town in the United States and Canada to beg clothes in; the one exception is Washington D.C. The latter fair city is the limit. I spent two weeks there trying to beg a pair of shoes, and then had to go on to Jersey City before I got them.

But to return to Ottawa. At eight sharp in the morning I started out after clothes. I worked energetically all day.

I swear I walked forty miles. I interviewed the housewives
of a thousand homes. I did not even knock off work for
dinner. And at six in the afternoon, aften ten hours of
unremitting and depressing toil, I was still shy one shirt,
while the pair of trousers I had managed to acquire was
tight and, moreover, was showing all the signs of an early
disintegration.

At six I quit work and headed for the railroad yards,
expecting to pick up something to eat on the way. But my
hard luck was still with me. I was refused food at house
after house. Then I got a 'hand-out'. My spirits soared, for
it was the largest hand-out I had ever seen in a long and
varied experience. It was a parcel wrapped in newspapers
and as big as a mature suit-case. I hurried to a vacant lot
and opened it. First, I saw cake, then more cake, all kinds
and makes of cake, and then some. It was all cake. No
bread and butter with thick firm slices of meat between—
nothing but cake; and I who of all things abhorred cake
most! In another age and clime they sat down by the
waters of Babylon and wept. And in a vacant lot in
Canada's proud capital, I, too, sat down and wept . . . over
a mountain of cake. As one looks upon the face of his dead
son, so looked I upon that multitudinous pastry. I suppose
I was an ungrateful tramp, for I refused to partake of the
bounteousness of the house that had had a party the night
before. Evidently the guests hadn't liked cake either.

That cake marked the crisis in my fortunes. Than it
nothing could be worse; therefore things must begin to
mend. And they did. At the very next house I was given
a 'set-down'. Now a 'set-down' is the height of bliss. One
is taken inside, very often is given a chance to wash, and
is then 'set-down' at a table. Tramps love to throw their
legs under a table. The house was large and comfortable,
in the midst of spacious grounds and fine trees, and sat
well back from the street. They had just finished eating,
and I was taken right into the dining-room—in itself a
most unusual happening, for the tramp who is lucky
enough to win a set-down usually receives it in the kitchen.

A grizzled and gracious Englishman, his matronly wife, and a beautiful young Frenchwoman talked with me while I ate.

I wonder if that beautiful young Frenchwoman would remember, at this late day, the laugh I gave her when I uttered the barbaric phrase, 'two-bits'. You see, I was trying delicately to hit them for a 'light piece'. That was how the sum of money came to be mentioned. 'What?' she said. 'Two-bits', said I. Her mouth was twitching as she again said 'What?' 'Two-bits', said I. Whereat she burst into laughter. 'Won't you repeat it?' she said, when she had regained control of herself. 'Two-bits', said I. And once more she rippled into uncontrollable silvery laughter. 'I beg your pardon,' said she; 'but what . . . what was it you said?' 'Two-bits', said I; 'is there anything wrong about it?' 'Not that I know of,' she gurgled between gasps; 'but what does it mean?' I explained, but I do not remember now whether or not I got that two-bits out of her; but I have often wondered since as to which of us was the provincial.

When I arrived at the depot, I found much to my disgust, a bunch of at least twenty tramps that were waiting to ride out the blind baggages of the overland. Now two or three tramps on the blind baggage are all right. They are inconspicuous. But a score! That meant trouble. No train-crew would ever let all of us ride.

I may as well explain here what a blind baggage is. Some mail-cars are built without doors in the ends; hence, such a car is 'blind'. The mail-cars that possess end doors, have those doors always locked. Suppose, after the train has started, that a tramp gets on to the platform of one of these blind cars. There is no door, or the door is locked. No conductor or brakeman can get to him to collect fare or throw him off. It is clear that the tramp is safe until the next time the train stops. Then he must get off, run ahead in the darkness, and when the train pulls by, jump on to the blind again. But there are ways and ways, as you shall see.

When the train pulled out, those twenty tramps swarmed upon the three blinds. Some climbed on before the train had run a car-length. They were awkward dubs, and I saw their speedy finish. Of course, the train-crew was 'on', and at the first stop the trouble began. I jumped off and ran forward along the track. I noticed that I was accompanied by a number of the tramps. They evidently knew their business. When one is beating an overland, he must always keep well ahead of the train at the stops. I ran ahead, and as I ran, one by one those that accompanied me dropped out. This dropping out was the measure of their skill and nerve in boarding a train.

For this is the way it works. When the train starts, the shack rides out the blind. There is no way for him to get back into the train proper except by jumping off the blind and catching a platform where the car-ends are not 'blind'. When the train is going as fast as the shack cares to risk, he therefore jumps off the blind, lets several cars go by, and gets on to the train. So it is up to the tramp to run so far ahead that before the blind is opposite him the shack will have already vacated it.

I dropped the last tramp by about fifty feet, and waited. The train started. I saw the lantern of the shack on the first blind. He was riding her out. And I saw the dubs stand forlornly by the track as the blind went by. They made no attempt to get on. They were beaten by their own inefficiency at the very start. After them, in the line-up, came the tramps that knew a little something about the game. They let the first blind, occupied by the shack, go by, and jumped on the second and third blinds. Of course, the shack jumped off the first and on the second as it went by, and scrambled around there, throwing off the men who had boarded it. But the point is that I was so far ahead that when the first blind came opposite me, the shack had already left it and was tangled up with the tramps on the second blind. A half dozen of the more skil-ful tramps, who had run far enough ahead, made the first blind, too.

At the next stop, as we ran forward along the track, I counted but fifteen of us. Five had been ditched. The weeding-out process had begun nobly, and it continued station by station. Now we were fourteen, now twelve, now eleven, now nine, now eight. It reminded me of the ten little niggers of the nursery rhyme. I was resolved that I should be the last little nigger of all. And why not? Was I not blessed with strength, agility, and youth? (I was eighteen, and in perfect condition.) And didn't I have my 'nerve' with me? And furthermore, was I not a tramp-royal? Were not these other tramps mere dubs and 'gay-cats' and amateurs alongside of me? If I weren't the last little nigger, I might as well quit the game and get a job on an alfalfa farm somewhere.

By the time our number had been reduced to four, the whole train-crew had become interested. From then on it was a contest of skill and wits, with the odds in favour of the crew. One by one the three other survivors turned up missing, until I alone remained. My, but I was proud of myself! No Crœsus was ever prouder of his first million. I was holding her down in spite of two brakemen, a conductor, a fireman, and an engineer.

And here are a few samples of the way I held her down. Out ahead, in the darkness,—so far ahead that the shack riding out the blind must perforce get off before it reaches me—I get on. Very well. I am good for another station. When that station is reached, I dart ahead again to repeat the manœuvre. The train pulls out. I watch her coming. There is no light of a lantern on the blind. Has the crew abandoned the fight? I do not know. One never knows, and one must be prepared every moment for anything. As the first blind comes opposite me, and I run to leap aboard, I strain my eyes to see if the shack is on the platform. For all I know he may be there, with his lantern doused, and even as I spring upon the steps that lantern may even smash down upon my head. I ought to know. I have been hit by lanterns two or three times.

But no, the first blind is empty. The train is gathering

speed. I am safe for another station. But am I? I feel the
train slacken speed. On the instant I am alert. A manœuvre
is being executed against me, and I do not know what it is.
I try to watch on both sides at once, not forgetting to keep
track of the tender in front of me. From any one, or all, of
these three directions, I may be assailed.

Ah, there it comes. The slack has ridden out the engine.
My first warning is when his feet strike the steps of the
right-hand side of the blind. Like a flash I am off the blind
to the left and running ahead past the engine. I lose myself in the darkness. The situation is where it has been
ever since the train left Ottawa. I am ahead, and the
train must come past me if it is to proceed on its journey.
I have as good a chance as ever for boarding her.

I watch carefully. I see a lantern come forward to the
engine, and I do not see it go back from the engine. It
must therefore be still on the engine, and it is a fair
assumption that attached to the handle of that lantern is a
shack. That shack was lazy, or else he would have put
out his lantern instead of trying to shield it as he came
forward. The train pulls out. The first blind is empty, and
I gain it. As before, the train slackens, the shack from the
engine boards the blind from one side, and I go off the
other side and run forward.

As I wait in the darkness I am conscious of a big thrill
of pride. The overland has stopped twice for me—for me,
a poor hobo on the bum. I alone have twice stopped the
overland with its many passengers and coaches, its govern-
ment mail, and its two thousand steam horses straining
in the engine. And I weigh only one hundred and sixty
pounds, and I haven't a five-cent piece in my pocket!

Again I see the lantern come forward to the engine.
But this time it comes conspicuously. A bit too conspicuously to suit me, and I wonder what is up. At any rate
I have something else to be afraid of than the shack on the
engine. The train pulls by. Just in time, before I make my
spring, I see the dark form of a shack, without a lantern,
on the first blind. I let it go by, and prepare to board the

second blind. But the shack on the first blind has jumped off and is at my heels. Also, I have a fleeting glimpse of the lantern of the shack who rode out the engine. He has jumped off, and now both shacks are on the ground on the same side with me. The next moment the second blind comes by and I am aboard it. But I do not linger. I have figured out my countermove. As I dash across the platform I hear the impact of the shack's feet against the steps as he boards. I jump off the other side and run forward with the train. My plan is to run forward and get on the first blind. It is nip and tuck, for the train is gathering speed. Also, the shack is behind me and running after me. I guess I am the better sprinter, for I make the first blind. I stand on the steps and watch my pursuer. He is only about ten feet back and running hard; but now the train has approximated his own speed, and, relative to me, he is standing still. I encourage him, hold out my hand to him; but he explodes in a mighty oath, gives up and makes the train several cars back.

The train is speeding along, and I am still chuckling to myself, when, without warning, a spray of water strikes me. The fireman is playing the hose on me from the engine. I step forward from the car-platform to the rear of the tender, where I am sheltered under the overhang. The water flies harmlessly over my head. My fingers itch to climb up on the tender and lam that fireman with a chunk of coal; but I know if I do that, I'll be massacred by him and the engineer, and I refrain.

At the next stop I am off and ahead in the darkness. This time, when the train pulls out, both shacks are on the first blind. I divine their game. They have blocked the repetition of my previous play. I cannot again take the second blind, cross over, and run forward to the first. As soon as the first blind passes and I do not get on, they swing off, one on each side of the train. I board the second blind, and as I do so I know that a moment later, simultaneously, those two shacks will arrive on both sides of me.

It is like a trap. Both ways are blocked. Yet there is another way out, and that way is up.

So I do not wait for my pursuers to arrive. I climb upon the upright ironwork of the platform and stand upon the wheel of the sand-brake. This has taken up the moment of grace and I hear the shacks strike the steps on either side. I don't stop to look. I raise my arms overhead until my hands rest against the down-curving ends of the roofs of the two cars. One hand, of course, is on the curved roof of one car, the other hand on the curved roof of the other car. By this time both shacks are coming up the steps. I know it, though I am too busy to see them. All this is happening in the space of only several seconds. I make a spring with my legs and 'muscle' myself up with my arms. As I draw up my legs, both shacks reach for me and clutch empty air. I know this, for I look down and see them. Also I hear them swear.

I am now in a precarious position, riding the ends of the down-curving roofs of two cars at the same time. With a quick, tense movement, I transfer both legs to the curve of one roof and both hands to the curve of the other roof. Then, gripping the edge of that curving roof, I climb over the curve to the level roof above, where I sit down to catch my breath, holding on the while to a ventilator that projects above the surface. I am on top of the train—on the 'decks', as the tramps call it, and this process I have described is by them called 'decking her.' And let me say right here that only a young and vigorous tramp is able to deck a passenger train, and also, that the young and vigorous tramp must have his nerve with him as well.

The train goes on gathering speed, and I know I am safe until the next stop—but only until the next stop. If I remain on the roof after the train stops, I know those shacks will fusillade me with rocks. A healthy shack can 'dewdrop' a pretty heavy chunk of stone on top of a car— say anywhere from five to twenty pounds. On the other hand, the chances are large that at the next stop the shacks will be waiting for me to descend at the place I climbed up. It is up to me to climb down at some other platform.

Registering a fervent hope that there are no tunnels in the next half mile, I rise to my feet and walk down the train half a dozen cars. And let me say that one must leave timidity behind him on such a *passear*. The roofs of passenger coaches are not made for midnight promenades, And if any one thinks they are, let me advise him to try it. Just let him walk along the roof of a jolting, lurching car, with nothing to hold on to but the black and empty air, and when he comes to the down-curving end of the roof, all wet and slippery with dew, let him accelerate his speed so as to step across to the next roof, down-curving and wet and slippery. Believe me, he will learn whether his heart is weak or his head is giddy.

As the train slows down for a stop, half a dozen platforms from where I had decked her I come down. No one is on the platform. When the train comes to a standstill, I slip off to the ground. Ahead, and between me and the engine, are two moving lanterns. The shacks are looking for me on the roofs of the cars. I note that the car beside which I am standing is a 'four-wheeler'—by which is meant that it has only four wheels to each truck. (When you go underneath on the rods, be sure to avoid the 'six-wheelers', —they lead to disasters.)

I duck under the train and make for the rods, and I can tell you I am mighty glad that the train is standing still. It is the first time I have ever gone underneath on the Canadian Pacific, and the internal arrangements are new to me. I try to crawl over the top of the truck, between the truck and the bottom of the car. But the space is not large enough for me to squeeze through. This is new to me. Down in the United States I am accustomed to going underneath on rapidly moving trains, seizing a gunnel and swinging my feet under the brake-beam, and from there crawling over the top of the truck and down inside the truck to a seat on the cross-rod.

Feeling with my hands in the darkness, I learn that

there is room between the brake-beam and the ground. It
is a tight squeeze. I have to lie flat and worm my way
through. Once inside the truck, I take my seat on the rod
and wonder what the shacks are thinking has become of
me. The train gets under way. They have given me up at
last.

But have they? At the very next stop, I see a lantern
thrust under the next truck to mine at the other end of the
car. They are searching the rods for me. I must make my
get-away pretty lively. I crawl on my stomach under the
brake-beam. They see me and run for me, but I crawl on
hands and knees across the rail on the opposite side and
gain my feet. Then away I go for the head of the train.
I run past the engine and hide in the sheltering darkness.
It is the same old situation. I am ahead of the train, and
the train must go past me.

The train pulls out. There is a lantern on the first blind.
I lie low, and see the peering shack go by. But there is also
a lantern on the second blind. That shack spots me and
calls to the shack who has gone past on the first blind.
Both jump off. Never mind, I'll take the third blind and
deck her. But heavens, there is a lantern on the third blind,
too. It is the conductor. I let it go by. At any rate I have
now the full train-crew in front of me. I turn and run back
in the opposite direction to what the train is going. I look
over my shoulder. All three lanterns are on the ground and
wobbling along in pursuit. I sprint. Half the train has
gone by, and it is going quite fast, when I spring aboard. I
know that the two shacks and the conductor will arrive
like ravening wolves in about two seconds. I spring upon
the wheel of the hand-brake, get my hands on the curved
ends of the roofs, and muscle myself up to the decks;
while my disappointed pursuers, clustering on the platform
beneath like dogs that have treed a cat, howl curses up at
me and say unsocial things about my ancestors.

But what does that matter? It is five to one, including
the engineer and fireman, and the majesty of the law and
the might of a great corporation are behind them, and I

am beating them out. I am too far down the train, and I
run ahead over the roofs of the coaches until I am over
the fifth or sixth platform from the engine. I peer down
cautiously. A shack is on the platform. That he has caught
sight of me, I know from the way he makes a swift sneak
inside the car; and I know, also, that he is waiting inside
the door, all ready to pounce out on me when I climb
down. But I make believe that I don't know, and I remain
there to encourage him in his error. I do not see him, yet
I know that he opens the door once and peeps up to assure
himself that I am still there.

The train slows down for a station. I dangle my legs
down in a tentative way. The train stops. My legs are still
dangling. I hear the door unlatch softly. He is all ready
for me. Suddenly I spring up and run forward over the
roof. This is right over his head, where he lurks inside the
door. The train is standing still; the night is quiet, and I
take care to make plenty of noise on the metal roof with
my feet. I don't know, but my assumption is that he is now
running forward to catch me as I descend at the next platform. But I don't descend there. Halfway along the roof
of the coach, I turn, retrace my way softly and quickly
to the platform both the shack and I have just abandoned.
The coast is clear. I descend to the ground on the off-side
of the train and hide in the darkness. Not a soul has seen
me.

I go over to the fence, at the edge of the right of way,
and watch. Ah, ha! What's that? I see a lantern on top of
the train, moving along from front to rear. They think I
haven't come down, and they are searching the roofs for
me. And better than that—on the ground on each side of
the train, moving abreast with the lantern on top, are two
other lanterns. It is a rabbit-drive, and I am the rabbit.
When the shack on top flushes me, the ones on each side
will nab me. I roll a cigarette and watch the procession go
by. Once past me, I am safe to proceed to the front of the
train. She pulls out, and I make the front blind without
opposition. But before she is fully under way and just

as I am lighting my cigarette, I am aware that the fireman has climbed over the coal to the back of the tender and is looking down on me. I am filled with apprehension. From his position he can mash me to a jelly with lumps of coal. Instead of which he addresses me, and I note with relief the admiration in his voice.

'You son-of-a-gun,' is what he says.

It is a high compliment, and I thrill as a school-boy thrills on receiving a reward of merit.

'Say', I call up to him, 'don't you play the hose on me any more'.

'All right,' he answers, and goes back to his work.

I have made friends with the engine, but the shacks are still looking for me. At the next stop, the shacks ride out all three blinds, and as before, I let them go by and deck in the middle of the train. The crew is on its mettle by now, and the train stops. The shacks are going to ditch me or know the reason why. Three times the mighty overland stops for me at that station, and each time I elude the shacks and make the decks. But it is hopeless, for they have finally come to an understanding of the situation. I have taught them that they cannot guard the train from me. They must do something else.

And they do it. When the train stops that last time, they take after me hot-footed. Ah, I see their game. They are trying to run me down. At first they herd me back toward the rear of the train. I know my peril. Once to the rear of the train, it will pull out with me left behind. I double, and twist, and turn, dodge through my pursuers, and gain the front of the train. One shack still hangs on after me. All right, I'll give him the run of his life, for my wind is good. I run straight ahead along the track. It doesn't matter. If he chases me ten miles, he'll nevertheless have to catch the train, and I can board her at any speed that he can.

So I run on, keeping just comfortably ahead of him and straining my eyes in the gloom for cattle-guards and

switches that may bring me to grief. Alas! I strain my eyes
too far ahead, and trip over something just under my feet,

I know not what, some little thing, and go down to earth
in a long, stumbling fall. The next moment I am on my
feet, but the shack has me by the collar. I do not struggle.
I am busy with breathing deeply and with sizing him up.
He is narrow-shouldered, and I have at least thirty pounds
the better of him in weight. Besides, he is just as tired as
I am, and if he tries to slug me, I'll teach him a few things.

But he doesn't try to slug me, and that problem is
settled. Instead, he starts to lead me back toward the train,
and another possible problem arises. I see the lanterns of
the conductor and the other shack. We are approaching
them. Not for nothing have I made the acquaintance of the
New York police. Not for nothing, in box-cars, by water-
tanks, and in prison-cells, have I listened to bloody tales of
man-handling. What if these three men are about to man-
handle me? Heaven knows I have given them provocation
enough. I think quickly. We are drawing nearer and nearer
to the other two trainmen. I line up the stomach and the
jaw of my captor and plan the right and left I'll give him
at the first sign of trouble.

Pshaw! I know another trick I'd like to work on him,
and almost regret that I did not do it at the moment I
was captured. I could make him sick, what of his clutch
on my collar. His fingers, tight-gripping, are buried inside
my collar. My coat is tightly buttoned. Did you ever see
a tourniquet? Well, this is one. All I have to do is to duck
my head under his arm and begin to twist. I must twist
rapidly—very rapidly. I know how to do it; twisting in a
violent, jerky way, ducking my head under his arm with
each revolution. Before he knows it, those detaining
fingers of his will be detained. He will be unable to withdraw them. It is a powerful leverage. Twenty seconds after
I have started revolving, the blood will be bursting out of
his finger ends, the delicate tendons will be rupturing, and
all the muscles and nerves will be mashing and crushing
together in a shrieking mass. Try it sometimes when

somebody has you by the collar. But be quick—quick as lightning. Also, be sure to hug yourself while you are revolving—hug your face with your left arm and your abdomen with your right. You see, the other fellow might try to stop you with a punch from his free arm. It would be a good idea, too, to revolve away from that free arm rather than toward it. A punch going is never so bad as a punch coming.

That shack will never know how near he was to being made very, very sick. All that saves him is that it is not in their plan to man-handle me. When we draw near enough, he calls out that he has me, and they signal the train to come on. The engine passes us, and the three blinds. After that, the conductor and the other shack swing aboard. But still my captor holds on to me. I see the plan. He is going to hold me until the rear of the train goes by. Then he will hop on, and I shall be left behind—ditched.

But the train has pulled out fast, the engineer trying to make up for lost time. Also, it is a long train. It is going very lively, and I know the shack is measuring its speed with apprehension.

'Think you can make it?' I query innocently.

He releases my collar, makes a quick run, and swings aboard. A number of coaches are yet to pass by. He knows it, and remains on the steps, his head poked out and watching me. In that moment my next move comes to me. I'll make the last platform. I know she's going fast and faster, but I'll only get a roll in the dirt if I fail, and the optimism of youth is mine. I do not give myself away. I stand with a dejected droop of shoulder, advertising that I have abandoned hope. But at the same time I am feeling with my feet the good gravel. It is perfect footing. Also I am watching the poked-out head of the shack. I see it withdrawn. He is confident that the train is going too fast for me ever to make it.

And the train *is* going fast—faster than any train I have ever tackled. As the last coach comes by I sprint in the same direction with it. It is a swift, short sprint. I cannot hope to equal the speed of the train, but I can reduce the difference of our speed to the minimum, and, hence, reduce the shock of impact, when I leap on board. In the fleeting instant of darkness I do not see the iron hand-rail of the last platform; nor is there time for me to locate it. I reach for where I think it ought to be, and at the same instant my feet leave the ground. It is all in the toss. The next moment I may be rolling in the gravel with broken ribs, or arms, or head. But my fingers grip the handhold, there is a jerk on my arms that slightly pivots my body, and my feet land on the steps with sharp violence.

I sit down, feeling very proud of myself. In all my hoboing it is the best bit of train-jumping I have done. I know that late at night one is always good for several stations on the last platform, but I do not care to trust myself at the rear of the train. At the first stop I run forward on the off-side of the train, pass the Pullmans, and duck under and take a rod under a day-coach. At the next stop I run forward again and take another rod.

I am now comparatively safe. The shacks think I am ditched. But the long day and the strenuous night are beginning to tell on me. Also, it is not so windy nor cold underneath, and I begin to doze. This will never do. Sleep on the rods spells death, so I crawl out at a station and forward to the second blind. Here I can lie down and sleep; and here I do sleep—how long I do not know—for I am awakened by a lantern thrust into my face. The two shacks are staring at me. I scramble up on the defensive, wondering as to which one is going to make the first 'pass' at me. But slugging is far from their minds.

'I thought you was ditched,' says the shack who had held me by the collar.

'If you hadn't let go of me when you did, you'd have been ditched along with me,' I answer.

'How's that?' he asks.

'I'd have gone into a clinch with you, that's all,' is my reply.

They hold a consultation, and their verdict is summed up in:

'Well, I guess you can ride, Bo. There's no use trying to keep you off.'

And they go away and leave me in peace to the end of their division.

I have given the foregoing as a sample of what 'holding her down' means. Of course, I have selected a fortunate night out of my experiences, and said nothing of the nights—and many of them—when I was tripped up by accident and ditched.

In conclusion, I want to tell of what happened when I reached the end of the division. On single-track, transcontinental lines, the freight trains wait at the divisions and follow out after the passenger trains. When the division was reached, I left my train, and looked for the freight that would pull out behind it. I found the freight made up on a side-track and waiting. I climbed into a box-car half full of coal and lay down. In no time I was asleep.

I was awakened by the sliding open of the door. Day was just dawning, cold and grey, and the freight had not yet started. A 'con' (conductor) was poking his head inside the door.

'Get out of that, you blankety-blank-blank!' he roared at me.

I got, and outside I watched him go down the line inspecting every car in the train. When he got out of sight I thought to myself that he would never think I'd have the nerve to climb back into the very car out of which he had fired me. So back I climbed and lay down again.

Now that con's mental processes must have been paralleling mine, for he reasoned that it was the very thing I would do. For back he came and fired me out.

Now, surely, I reasoned, he will never dream that I'd do it a third time. Back I went, into the very same car. But I decided to make sure. Only one sidedoor could be opened. The other side-door was nailed up. Beginning at the top of the coal, I dug a hole alongside of that door and lay down in it. I heard the other door open. The con climbed up and looked in over the top of the coal. He couldn't see me. He called to me to get out. I tried to fool him by remaining quiet. But when he began tossing chunks of coal into the hole on top of me, I gave up and for the third time was fired out. Also, he informed me in warm terms of what would happen to me if he caught me in there again.

I changed my tactics. When a man is paralleling your mental processes, ditch him. Abruptly break off your line or reasoning and go off on a new line. This I did. I hid between some cars on an adjacent side-track, and watched. Sure enough, that con came back again to the car. He opened the door, he climbed up, he called, he threw coal into the hole I had made. He even crawled over the coal and looked into the hole. That satisfied him. Five minutes later the freight was pulling out, and he was not in sight. I ran alongside the car, pulled the door open and climbed in. He never looked for me again, and I rode that coal-car precisely one thousand and twenty-two miles, sleeping most of the time and getting out at divisions (where the freights always stop for an hour or so) to beg my food. And at the end of the thousand and twenty-two miles I lost that car through a happy incident. I got a 'set-down', and the tramp doesn't live who won't miss a train for a set-down any time.

HOBOES THAT PASS IN THE NIGHT

IN THE course of my tramping I encountered hundreds of hoboes, whom I hailed or who hailed me, and with whom I waited at water-tanks, 'boiled-up', cooked 'mulligans', 'battered' the 'drag' or 'privates', and beat trains, and who passed and were seen never again. On the other hand, there were hoboes who passed and repassed with amazing frequency, and others, still, who passed like ghosts, close at hand, unseen, and never seen.

It was one of the latter that I chased clear across Canada over three thousand miles of railroad, and never once did I lay eyes on him. His 'monica' was Skysail Jack. I first ran into it at Montreal. Carved with a jack-knife was the skysail-yard of a ship. It was perfectly executed. Under it was 'Skysail Jack'. Above was 'B.W. 10—15—94'. This latter conveyed the information that he had passed through Montreal bound west, on October 15, 1894. He had one day start of me. 'Sailor Jack' was my monica at that particular time, and promptly I carved it alongside of his, along with the date and the information that I, too, was bound west.

I had misfortune in getting over the next hundred miles, and eight days later I picked up Skysail Jack's trail three hundred miles west of Ottawa. There it was, carved on a water-tank, and by the date I saw that he likewise had met with delay. He was only two days ahead of me. I was a 'comet' and 'tramp-royal', so was Skysail Jack; and it was up to my pride and reputation to catch up with him. I 'rail-roaded' day and night, and I passed him; then turn about he passed me. Sometimes he was a day or so ahead, and sometimes I was. From hoboes, bound east, I got word of him occasionally, when he happened to be ahead; and from them I learned that he had become interested in Sailor Jack and was making inquiries about me.

We'd have made a precious pair, I am sure, if we'd ever got together; but get together we couldn't. I kept ahead of him clear across Manitoba, but he led the way across Alberta, and early one bitter grey morning, at the end of a division just east of Kicking Horse Pass, I learned that he had been seen the night before between Kicking Horse Pass and Rogers' Pass. It was rather curious the way the information came to me. I had been riding all night in a 'side-door Pullman' (box-car), and nearly dead with cold had crawled out at the division to beg for food. A freezing fog was drifting past, and I 'hit' some firemen I found in the round-house. They fixed me up with the leavings from their lunch-pails, and in addition I got out of them nearly a quart of heavenly 'Java' (coffee). I heated the latter, and, as I sat down to eat, a freight pulled in from the west. I saw a sidedoor open and a road-kid climb out. Through the drifting fog he limped over to me. He was stiff with cold, his lips blue. I shared my Java and grub with him, learned about Skysail Jack, and then learned about him. Behold, he was from my own town, Oakland, California, and he was a member of the celebrated Boo Gang—a gang with which I had affiliated at rare intervals. We talked fast and bolted the grub in the half-hour that followed. Then my freight pulled out, and I was on it, bound west on the trail of Skysail Jack.

I was delayed between the passes, went two days without food, and walked eleven miles on the third day before I got any, and yet I succeeded in passing Skysail Jack along the Fraser River in British Columbia. I was riding 'passengers' then and making time; but he must have been riding passengers, too, and with more luck or skill than I, for he got into Mission ahead of me.

Now Mission was a junction, forty miles east of Vancouver. From the junction one could proceed south through Washington and Oregon over the Northern Pacific. I wondered which way Skysail Jack would go, for I thought I was ahead of him. As for myself I was still bound west to Vancouver. I proceeded to the water-tank to leave that information, and there, freshly carved, with that day's date upon it, was Skysail Jack's monica. I hurried on into Vancouver. But he was gone. He had taken ship immediately and was still flying west on his world-adventure. Truly, Skysail Jack, you were a tramp-royal, and your mate was the 'wind that tramps the world'. I take off my hat to you. You were 'blowed-in-the-glass' all right. A week later I, too, got my ship, and on board the steamship *Umatilla*, in the forecastle, was working my way down the coast to San Francisco. Skysail Jack and Sailor Jack—gee! if we'd ever got together.

Water-tanks are tramp directories. Not all in idle wantonness do tramps carve their monicas, dates, and courses. Often and often have I met hoboes earnestly inquiring if I had seen anywhere such and such a 'stiff' or his monica. And more than once I have been able to give the monica of recent date, the water-tank, and the direction in which he was then bound. And promptly the hobo to whom I gave the information lit out after his pal. I have met hoboes who, in trying to catch a pal, had pursued clear across the continent and back again, and were still going.

'Monicas' are the *nom-de-rails* that hoboes assume or accept when thrust upon them by their fellows. Leary Joe, for instance, was timid, and was so named by his fellows. No self-respecting hobo would select Stew Bum for himself. Very few tramps care to remember their pasts during which they ignobly worked, so monicas based upon trades are very rare, though I remember having met the following: Moulder Blackey, Painter Red, Chi Plumber, Boilermaker, Sailor Boy, and Printer Bo. 'Chi' (pronounced *shy*), by the way, is the argot for 'Chicago'.

A favourite device of hoboes is to base their monicas on the localities from which they hail, as: New York Tommy, Pacific Slim, Buffalo Smithy, Canton Tim, Pittsburg Jack, Syracuse Shine, Troy Mickey, K. L. Bill, and Connecticut Jimmy. Then there was 'Slim Jim from Vinegar Hill, who never worked and never will'. A 'shine' is always a negro, so called, possibly, from the high lights on his countenance. Texas Shine or Toledo Shine convey both race and nativity.

Among those that incorporated their race, I recollect the following: Frisco Sheeny, New York Irish, Michigan French, English Jack, Cockney Kid, and Milwaukee Dutch. Others seem to take their monicas in part from the colour-schemes stamped upon them at birth, such as: Chi Whitey, New Jersey Red, Boston Blackey, Seattle Browney, and Yellow Dick and Yellow Belly—the last a Creole from

Mississippi, who, I suspect, had his monica thrust upon him.

Texas Royal, Happy Joe, Bust Connors, Burley Bo, Tornado Blackey, and Touch McCall used more imagination in rechristening themselves. Others, with less fancy, carry the names of their physical peculiarities, such as: Vancouver Slim, Detroit Shorty, Ohio Fatty, Long Jack, Big Jim, Little Joe, New York Blink, Chi Nosey, and Broken-backed Ben.

By themselves come the road-kids, sporting an infinite variety of monicas. For example, the following, whom here and there I have encountered: Buck Kid, Blind Kid, Midget Kid, Holy Kid, Bat Kid, Swift Kid, Cookey Kid, Monkey Kid, Iowa Kid, Corduroy Kid, Orator Kid (who could tell how it happened), and Lippy Kid (who was insolent, depend upon it).

On the water-tank at San Marcial, New Mexico, a dozen years ago, was the following hobo bill of fare:

(1) Main-drag fair.
(2) Bulls not hostile.
(3) Round-house good for kipping.
(4) North-bound trains no good.
(5) Privates no good.
(6) Restaurants good for cooks only.
(7) Railroad House good for night-work only.

Number one conveys the information that begging for money on the main street is fair: number two, that the police will not bother hoboes; number three, that one can sleep in the round-house. Number four, however, is ambiguous. The north-bound trains may be no good to beat, and they may be no good to beg. Number five means that the residences are not good to beggars, and number six means that only hoboes that have been cooks can get grub from the restaurants. Number seven bothers me. I cannot make out whether the Railroad House is a good place for any hobo to beg at night, or whether it is good only for hobo-cooks to beg at night or whether any hobo, cook or non-cook, can lend a hand at night, helping the cooks of the Railroad House with their dirty work and getting something to eat in payment.

But to return to the hoboes that pass in the night. I remember one I met in California. He was a Swede, but he had lived so long in the United States that one couldn't guess his nationality. He had to tell it on himself. In fact, he had come to the United States when no more than a baby. I ran into him first at the mountain town of Truckee. 'Which way, Bo?' was our greeting, and 'Bound east' was the answer each of us gave. Quite a bunch of 'stiffs' tried to ride out the overland that night, and I lost the Swede in the shuffle. Also, I lost the overland.

I arrived in Reno, Nevada, in a box-car that was promptly side-tracked. It was Sunday morning, and after I threw my feet for breakfast, I wandered over to the Piute camp to watch the Indians gambling. And there stood the Swede, hugely interested. Of course we got together. He was the only acquaintance I had in that region, and I was his only acquaintance. We rushed together like a couple of dissatisfied hermits, and together we spent the day, threw our feet for dinner, and late in the afternoon tried to 'nail' the same freight. But he was ditched, and I rode her out alone, to be ditched myself in the desert twenty miles beyond.

Of all desolate places, the one at which I was ditched was the limit. It was called a flag-station, and it consisted of a shanty dumped inconsequentially into the sand and sage-bush. A chill wind was blowing, night was coming on, and the solitary telegraph operator who lived in the shanty was afraid of me. I knew that neither grub nor bed could I get out of him. It was because of his manifest fear of me that I did not believe him when he told me that east-bound trains never stopped there. Besides, hadn't I been thrown off of an east-bound train right at that very spot not five minutes before? He assured me that it had stopped under orders, and that a year might go by before another was stopped under orders. He advised me that it was only a dozen or fifteen miles on to Wadsworth and that I'd better hike. I elected to wait, however, and I had the pleasure of seeing two west-bound freights go by without stopping, and one east-bound freight. I wondered if the Swede was on the latter. It was up to me to hit the ties to Wadsworth, and hit them I did, much to the telegraph operator's relief, for I neglected to burn his shanty and murder him. Telegraph operators have much to be thankful for. At the end of half a dozen miles, I had to get off the ties and let the east-bound overland go by. She was going fast, but I caught sight of a dim form on the first 'blind' that looked like the Swede.

That was the last I saw of him for weary days. I hit the high places across those hundreds of miles of Nevada desert, riding the overlands at night, for speed, and in the day-time riding in box-cars and getting my sleep. It was early in the year, and it was cold in those upland pastures. Snow lay here and there on the level, all the mountains were shrouded in white, and at night the most miserable wind imaginable blew off from them. It was not a land in which to linger. And remember, gentle reader, the hobo goes through such a land, without shelter, without money, begging his way and sleeping at night without blankets. This last is something that can be realized only by experience.

In the early evening I came down to the depot at Ogden. The overland of the Union Pacific was pulling east, and I was bent on making connections. Out in the tangle of tracks ahead of the engine I encountered a figure slouching through the gloom. It was the Swede. We shook hands like long-lost brothers, and discovered that our hands were gloved. 'Where'd ye glahm 'em?' I asked. 'Out of an engine-cab,' he answered; 'and where did you?' 'They belonged to a fireman,' said I; 'he was careless.'

We caught the blind as the overland pulled out, and mighty cold we found it. The way led up a narrow gorge between snow-covered mountains, and we shivered and shook and exchanged confidences about how we had covered the ground between Reno and Ogden. I had closed my eyes for only an hour or so the previous night, and the blind was not comfortable enough to suit me for a snooze. At a stop, I went forward to the engine. We had on a 'double-header' (two engines) to take us over the grade.

The pilot of the head engine, because it 'punched the wind', I knew would be too cold; so I selected the pilot of the second engine, which was sheltered by the first engine. I stepped on the cowcatcher and found the pilot occupied. In the darkness I felt out the form of a young boy. He was sound asleep. By squeezing, there was room for two on the pilot, and I made the boy budge over and crawled up beside him. It was a 'good' night; the 'shacks' (brakemen) didn't bother us, and in no time we were asleep. Once in a while hot cinders or heavy jolts aroused me, when I snuggled closer to the boy and dozed off to the coughing of the engines and the screeching of the wheels.

The overland made Evanston, Wyoming, and went no farther. A wreck ahead blocked the line. The dead engineer had been brought in, and his body attested the peril of the way. A tramp, also, had been killed, but his body had not been brought in. I talked with the boy. He was thirteen years old. He had run away from his folks in some place in Oregon, and was heading east to his grandmother. He had a tale of cruel treatment in the home he had left that rang true; besides, there was no need for him to lie to me, a nameless hobo on the track.

And that boy was going some, too. He couldn't cover the ground fast enough. When the division superintendents decided to send the overland back over the way it had come, then up on a cross 'jerk' to the Oregon Short Line, and back along that road to tap the Union Pacific the other side of the wreck, that boy climbed upon the pilot and said he was going to stay with it. This was too much for the Swede and me. It meant travelling the rest of that frigid night in order to gain no more than a dozen miles or so. We said we'd wait till the wreck was cleared away, and in the meantime get a good sleep.

Now it is no snap to strike a strange town, broke, at midnight, in cold weather, and find a place to sleep. The Swede hadn't a penny. My total assets consisted of two dimes and a nickel. From some of the town boys we learned that beer was five cents, and that the saloons kept open all night. There was our meat. Two glasses of beer would cost ten cents, there would be a stove and chairs, and we could sleep it out till morning. We headed for the lights of a saloon, walking briskly, the snow crunching under our feet, a chill little wind blowing through us.

Alas, I had misunderstood the town boys. Beer was five cents in one saloon only in the whole burg, and we didn't strike that saloon. But the one we entered was all right. A blessed stove was roaring white-hot; there were cosy, cane-bottomed arm-chairs, and a none-too-pleasant-looking barkeeper who glared suspiciously at us as we came in. A man cannot spend continuous days and nights in his clothes, beating trains, fighting soot and cinders, and sleeping anywhere, and maintain a good 'front'. Our fronts were decidedly against us; but what did we care? I had the price in my jeans.

'Two beers,' said I nonchalantly to the barkeeper, and while he drew them, the Swede and I leaned against the bar and yearned secretly for the arm-chairs by the stove.

The barkeeper set the two foaming glasses before us, and with pride I deposited the ten cents. Now I was dead game. As soon as I learned my error in the price I'd have dug up another ten cents. Never mind if it did leave me only a nickel to my name, a stranger in a strange land. I'd have paid it all right. But the barkeeper never gave me a chance. As soon as his eyes spotted the dime I had laid down, he seized the two glasses, one in each hand, and dumped the beer into the sink behind the bar. At the same time, glaring at us malevolently, he said:

'You've got scabs on your nose. You've got scabs on your nose. You've got scabs on your nose. See!'

I hadn't either, and neither had the Swede. Our noses were all right. The direct bearing of his words was beyond our comprehension, but the indirect bearing was clear as print: he didn't like our looks, and beer was evidently ten cents a glass.

I dug down and laid another dime on the bar, remarking carelessly, 'Oh, I thought this was a five-cent joint.'

'Your money's no good here,' he answered, shoving the two dimes across the bar to me.

Sadly I dropped them back into my pocket, sadly we yearned toward the blessed stove and the arm-chairs, and sadly we went out the door into the frosty night.

But as we went out the door, the barkeeper, still glaring, called after us, 'You've got scabs on your nose, see!'

I have seen much of the world since then, journeyed among strange lands and peoples, opened many books, sat in many lecture-halls; but to this day, though I have pondered long and deep, I have been unable to divine the meaning in the cryptic utterance of that barkeeper in Evanston, Wyoming. Our noses *were* all right.

We slept that night over the boilers in an electric-lighting plant. How we discovered that 'kipping' place I can't remember. We must have just headed for it, instinctively, as horses head for water or carrier-pigeons head for the home-cote. But it was a night not pleasant to remember. A dozen hoboes were ahead of us on top the boilers, and it was too hot for all of us. To complete our misery, the engineer would not let us stand around down below. He gave us our choice of the boilers or the outside snow.

'You said you wanted to sleep, and so, damn you, sleep,' said he to me, when, frantic and beaten out by the heat, I came down into the fire-room.

'Water', I gasped, wiping the sweat from my eyes, 'water'.

He pointed out of doors and assured me that down there somewhere in the blackness I'd find the river. I started for the river, got lost in the dark, fell into two or three drifts, gave it up, and returned half-frozen to the top of the boilers. When I had thawed out, I was thirstier than ever. Around me the hoboes were moaning, groaning, sobbing, sighing, gasping, panting, rolling and tossing and floundering heavily in their torment. We were so many lost souls toasting on a griddle in hell, and the engineer, Satan Incarnate, gave us the sole alternative of freezing in the outer cold. The Swede sat up and anathematized passionately the wanderlust in man that sent him tramping and suffering hardships such as that.

'When I get back to Chicago,' he perorated, 'I'm going to get a job and stick to it till hell freezes over. Then I'll go tramping again.'

And, such is the irony of fate, next day, when the wreck ahead was cleared, the Swede and I pulled out of Evanston in the ice-boxes of an 'orange special', a fast freight laden with fruit from sunny California. Of course, the ice-boxes were empty on account of the cold weather, but that didn't make them any warmer for us. We entered them through hatchways in the top of the car; the boxes were constructed of galvanized iron, and in that biting weather were not pleasant to the touch. We lay there, shivered and shook, and with chattering teeth held a council wherein we decided that we'd stay by the ices-boxes day and night till we got out of the inhospitable plateau region and down into the Mississippi Valley.

But we must eat, and we decided that at the next division we would throw our feet for grub and make a rush back to our ice-boxes. We arrived in the town of Green River late in the afternoon, but too early for supper. Before meal-time is the worst time for 'battering' back-doors; but we put on our nerve, swung off the side-ladders as the freight pulled into the yards, and made a run for the houses. We were quickly separated; but we had agreed to meet in the ice-boxes. I had bad luck at first; but in the end, with a couple of 'hand-outs' poked into my shirt, I chased for the train. It was pulling out and going fast. The particular refrigerator-car in which we were to meet had already gone by, and half a dozen cars down the train from it I swung on to the side-ladders, went up on top hurriedly, and dropped down into an ice-box.

But a shack had seen me from the caboose, and at the next stop a few miles farther on, Rock Springs, the shack stuck his head into my box and said: 'Hit the grit, you son of a toad! Hit the grit!' Also he grabbed me by the heels and dragged me out. I hit the grit all right, and the orange special and the Swede rolled on without me.

Snow was beginning to fall. A cold night was coming on. After dark I hunted around in the railroad yards until I found an empty refrigerator car. In I climbed—not into the ice-boxes, but into the car itself. I swung the heavy doors shut, and their edges, covered with strips of rubber, sealed the car air-tight. The walls were thick. There was no way for the outside cold to get in. But the inside was just as cold as the outside. How to raise the temperature was the problem. But trust a 'profesh' for that. Out of my pockets I dug up three or four newspapers. These I burned, one at a time, on the floor of the car. The smoke rose to the top. Not a bit of the heat could escape, and, comfortable and warm, I passed a beautiful night. I didn't wake up once.

In the morning it was still snowing. While throwing my feet for breakfast, I missed an east-bound freight. Later in the day I nailed two other freights and was ditched from both of them. All afternoon no east-bound trains went by. The snow was falling thicker than ever, but at twilight I rode out on the first blind of the overland. As I swung aboard the blind from one side, somebody swung aboard from the other. It was the boy who had run away from Oregon.

Now the first blind of a fast train in a driving snowstorm is no summer picnic. The wind goes right through one, strikes the front of the car, and comes back again. At the first stop, darkness having come on, I went forward and interviewed the fireman. I offered to 'shove' coal to the end of his run, which was Rawlins, and my offer was accepted. My work was out on the tender, in the snow, breaking the lumps of coal with a sledge and shovelling it forward to him in the cab. But as I did not have to work all the time, I could come into the cab and warm up now and again.

'Say', I said to the fireman, at my first breathing spell, 'there's a little kid back there on the first blind. He's pretty cold.'

The cabs on the Union Pacific engines are quite spacious, and we fitted the kid into a warm nook in front of the high seat of the fireman, where the kid promptly fell asleep. We arrived at Rawlins at midnight. The snow was thicker than ever. Here the engine was to go into the round-house, being replaced by a fresh engine. As the train came to a stop, I dropped off the engine steps plump into the arms of a large man in a large overcoat. He began asking me questions, and I promptly demanded who he was. Just as promptly he informed me that he was the sheriff. I drew in my horns and listened and answered.

He began describing the kid who was still asleep in the cab. I did some quick thinking. Evidently the family was on the trail of the kid, and the sheriff had received telegraphed instructions from Oregon. Yes, I had seen the kid. I had met him first in Ogden. The date tallied with the sheriff's information. But the kid was still behind somewhere, I explained, for he had been ditched from that very overland that night when it pulled out of Rock Springs. And all the time I was praying that the kid wouldn't wake up, come down out of the cab, and put the 'kibosh' on me.

The sheriff left me in order to interview the shacks, but before he left he said:

'Bo, this town is no place for you. Understand? You ride this train out, and make no mistake about it. If I catch you after it's gone. . . .'

I assured him that it was not through desire that I was in his town; that the only reason I was there was that the train had stopped there; and that he wouldn't see me for smoke the way I'd get out of his darn town.

While he went to interview the shacks, I jumped back into the cab. The kid was awake and rubbing his eyes. I told him the news and advised him to ride the engine into the round-house. To cut the story short, the kid made the same overland out, riding the pilot, with instructions to make an appeal to the fireman at the first stop for per-mission to ride in the engine. As for myself, I got ditched. The new fireman was young and not yet lax enough to break the rules of the Company against having tramps in the engine; so he turned down my offer to shove coal. I hope the kid succeeded with him, for all night on the pilot in that blizzard would have meant death.

Strange to say, I do not at this late day remember a detail of how I was ditched at Rawlins. I remember watch-ing the train as it was immediately swallowed up in the snow-storm, and of heading for a saloon to warm up. Here was light and warmth. Everything was in full blast and wide open. Faro, roulette, craps, and poker tables were running, and some mad cowpunchers were making the night merry. I had just succeeded in fraternizing with them and was downing my first drink at their expense, when a heavy hand descended on my shoulder. I looked around and sighed. It was the sheriff.

Without a word he led me out into the snow.

'There's an orange special down there in the yards,' said he.

'It's a damn cold night,' said I.

'It pulls out in ten minutes,' said he.

That was all. There was no discussion. And when that orange special pulled out, I was in the ice-boxes. I thought my feet would freeze before morning, and the last twenty miles into Laramie I stood upright in the hatchway and danced up and down. The snow was too thick for the shacks to see me, and I didn't care if they did.

My quarter of a dollar bought me a hot breakfast at Laramie, and immediately afterwards I was on board the blind baggage of an overland that was climbing to the pass through the backbone of the Rockies. One does not ride blind baggages in the daytime; but in this blizzard at the top of the Rocky Mountains I doubted if the shacks would have the heart to put me off. And they didn't. They made a practice of coming forward at every stop to see if I was frozen yet.

At Ames' Monument, at the summit of the Rockies,—I forget the altitude,—the shack came forward for the last time.

'Say, Bo,' he said, 'you see that freight side-tracked over there to let us go by?'

I saw. It was the next track, six feet away. A few feet more in that storm and I could not have seen it.

'Well, the "after-push" of Kelly's Army is in one of them cars. They've got two feet of straw under them, and there's so many of them that they keep the car warm.'

His advice was good, and I followed it, prepared, however, if it was a 'con game' the shack had given me, to take the blind as the overland pulled out. But it was straight goods. I found the car—a big refrigerator car with the leeward door wide open for ventilation. Up I climbed and in. I stepped on a man's leg, next on some other man's arm. The light was dim, and all I could make out was arms and legs and bodies inextricably confused. Never was there such a tangle of humanity. They were all lying in the straw, and over, and under, and around one another. Eighty-four husky hoboes take up a lot of room when they are stretched out. The men I stepped on were resentful. Their bodies heaved under me like the waves of the sea, and imparted an involuntary forward movement to me. I could not find any straw to step upon, so I stepped upon more men. The resentment increased, so did my forward movement. I lost my footing and sat down with sharp abruptness. Unfortunately, it was on a man's head. The next moment he had risen on his hands and knees in wrath, and I was flying through the air. What goes up must come down, and I came down on another man's head.

What happened after this is very vague in my memory. It was like going through a threshing-machine. I was bandied about from one end of the car to the other. Those eighty-four hoboes winnowed me out till what little was left of me, by some miracle, found a bit of straw to rest upon. I was initiated, and into a jolly crowd. All the rest of that day we rode through the blizzard, and to while the time away it was decided that each man was to tell a story. It was stipulated that each story must be a good one, and, furthermore, that it must be a story no one had ever heard before. The penalty for failure was the threshing-machine. Nobody failed. And I want to say right here that never in my life have I sat at so marvellous a story-telling debauch. Here were eighty-four men from all the world—I made eighty-five; and each man told a masterpiece. It had to be, for it was either masterpiece or threshing-machine.

Late in the afternoon we arrived in Cheyenne. The blizzard was at its height, and though the last meal of all of us had been breakfast, no man cared to throw his feet for supper. All night we rolled on through the storm, and next day found us down on the sweet plains of Nebraska and still rolling. We were out of the storm and the mountains. The blessed sun was shining over a smiling land, and we had eaten nothing for twenty-four hours. We found out that the freight would arrive about noon at a town, if I remember right, that was called Grand Island.

We took up a collection and sent a telegram to the authorities of that town. The text of the message was that eighty-five healthy, hungry hoboes would arrive about noon and that it would be a good idea to have dinner ready for them. The authorities of Grand Island had two courses open to them. They could feed us, or they could throw us in jail. In the latter event they'd have to feed us anyway, and they decided wisely that one meal would be the cheaper way.

When the freight rolled into Grand Island at noon, we were sitting on the tops of the cars and dangling our legs in the sunshine. All the police in the burg were on the reception committee. They marched us in squads to the various hotels and restaurants, where dinners were spread for us. We had been thirty-six hours without food, and we didn't have to be taught what to do. After that we were marched back to the railroad station. The police had thoughtfully compelled the freight to wait for us. She pulled out slowly, and the eighty-five of us, strung out along the track, swarmed up the side-ladders. We 'captured' the train.

We had no supper that evening—at least the 'push' didn't, but I did. Just at supper time, as the freight was pulling out of a small town, a man climbed into the car where I was playing pedro with three other stiffs. The man's shirt was bulging suspiciously. In his hand he carried a battered quart-measure from which arose steam. I smelled 'Java'. I turned my cards over to one of the stiffs who was looking on, and excused myself. Then, in the other end of the car, pursued by envious glances, I sat down with the man who had climbed aboard and shared his 'Java' and the hand-outs that had bulged his shirt. It was the Swede.

At about ten o'clock in the evening, we arrived at Omaha.

'Let's shake the push,' said the Swede to me.

'Sure', said I.

As the freight pulled into Omaha, we made ready to do so. But the people of Omaha were also ready. The Swede and I hung upon the side-ladders, ready to drop off. But the freight did not stop. Furthermore, long rows of policemen, their brass buttons and stars glittering in the electric lights, were lined up on each side of the track. The Swede and I knew what would happen to us if we ever dropped off into their arms. We stuck by the side-ladders, and the train rolled on across the Missouri River to Council Bluffs.

'General' Kelly, with an army of two thousand hoboes lay in camp at Chautauqua Park, several miles away. The after-push we were with was General Kelly's rearguard, and, detraining at Council Bluffs, it started to march to camp. The night had turned cold, and heavy wind-squalls, accompanied by rain, were chilling and wetting us. Many police were guarding us and herding us to the camp. The Swede and I watched our chance and made a successful get-away.

The rain began coming down in torrents, and in the darkness, unable to see our hands in front of our faces, like a pair of blind men we fumbled about for shelter. Our instinct served us, for in no time we stumbled upon a saloon—not a saloon that was open and doing business, not merely a saloon that was closed for the night, and not even a saloon with a permanent address, but a saloon propped up on big timbers, with rollers underneath, that was being moved from somewhere to somewhere. The doors were locked. A squall of wind and rain drove down upon us. We did not hesitate. Smash went the door, and in we went.

I have made some tough camps in my time, 'carried the banner' in infernal metropolises, bedded in pools of water, slept in the snow under two blankets when the spirit thermometer registered seventy-four degrees below zero (which is a mere trifle of one hundred and six degrees of frost); but I want to say right here that never did I make a tougher camp, pass a more miserable night, than that night I passed with the Swede in the itinerant saloon at Council Bluffs. In the first place, the building, perched up as it was in the air, had exposed a multitude of openings in the floor through which the wind whistled. In the second place, the bar was empty; there was no bottled firewater with which we could warm ourselves and forget our misery. We had no blankets, and in our wet clothes, wet to the skin, we tried to sleep. I rolled under the bar, and the Swede rolled under the table. The holes and crevices in the floor made it impossible, and at the end of half an hour I crawled up on top of the bar. A little later the Swede crawled up on top his table.

And there we shivered and prayed for daylight. I know, for one, that I shivered until I could shiver no more, till the shivering muscles exhausted themselves and merely ached horribly. The Swede moaned and groaned, and every little while, through chattering teeth, he muttered. 'Never again, never again.' He muttered this phrase repeatedly, ceaselessly, a thousand times; and when he dozed, he went on muttering it in his sleep.

At the first grey of dawn we left our house of pain, and outside, found ourselves in a mist, dense and chill. We stumbled on till we came to the railroad track. I was going back to Omaha to throw my feet for breakfast; my companion was going on to Chicago. The moment for parting had come. Our palsied hands went out to each other. We were both shivering. When we tried to speak, our teeth chattered us back into silence. We stood alone, shut off from the world; all that we could see was a short length of railroad track, both ends of which were lost in the driving mist. We stared dumbly at each other, our clasped hands shaking sympathetically. The Swede's face was blue with the cold, and I know mine must have been.

'Never again what?' I managed to articulate.

Speech strove for utterance in the Swede's throat; then, faint and distant, in a thin whisper from the very bottom of his frozen soul, came the words:

'Never again a hobo.'

He paused, and, as he went on again, his voice gathered strength and huskiness as it affirmed his will.

'Never again a hobo. I'm going to get a job. You'd better do the same. Nights like this make rheumatism.'

He wrung my hand.

'Good-bye, Bo,' said he.

'Good-bye, Bo,' said I.

The next we were swallowed up from each other by the mist. It was our final passing. But here's to you. Mr Swede, wherever you are. I hope you got that job.